Arthur Miller Plays 2

Arthur Miller Plays 2

The Misfits
After the Fall
Incident at Vichy
The Price
The Creation of the World
Playing for Time

ARTHUR MILLER

methuen | drama
LONDON · NEW YORK · OXFORD · NEW DELHI · SYDNEY

METHUEN DRAMA
Bloomsbury Publishing Plc
50 Bedford Square, London, WC1B 3DP, UK
1385 Broadway, New York, NY 10018, USA
29 Earlsfort Terrace, Dublin 2, Ireland

BLOOMSBURY, METHUEN DRAMA and the Methuen Drama logo
are trademarks of Bloomsbury Publishing Plc

Originally published in Great Britain in 1981 by Martin Secker and
WarburgLimited, London, as *Arthur Miller's Collected Plays Volume II*
Reissued with a new cover design 1994, 2009
Reissued with a new cover design in 2022

Series design: Ben Anslow
Cover image: Arthur Miller returns to London,
Sep. 05, 1956 © Keystone Press / Alamy Stock Photo;
Decorative seamless pattern © AnastasiiaM / Shutterstock

A catalogue record for this book is available from the British Library.

ISBN: PB: 978-1-3503-3396-3
ePDF: 978-1-3503-3398-7
eBook: 978-1-3503-3397-0

Printed and bound in Great Britain

To find out more about our authors and books visit
www.bloomsbury.com and sign up for our newsletters.

Contents

Arthur Miller: Chronology of Professionally Produced Plays

	First US production	First UK production
The Man Who Had All the Luck	23.1.44	28.4.60
All My Sons	29.1.47	11.5.48
Death of a Salesman	10.2.49	28.7.49
An Enemy of the People		
(adapted from Ibsen)	28.12.50	
The Crucible	22.1.53	9.11.54
A Memory of Two Mondays	29.9.55	29.9.58
A View from the Bridge		
(one-act version)	29.9.55	
(two-act version)	28.1.65	11.10.56
After the Fall	23.1.64	31.10.67
Incident at Vichy	3.12.64	10.1.66
The Price	7.2.68	4.3.69
The Creation of the World and		
Other Business	30.11.72	17.8.74
Up from Paradise (musical)	23.4.74	
The Archbishop's Ceiling	30.4.77	1.4.85
The American Clock	24.5.80	18.4.83
Two-Way Mirror	26.10.82	1.89
Playing for Time		
(adapted from his screenplay)	22.9.85	10.11.05
Danger: Memory!	8.2.87	6.4.88
The Golden Years	(world première)	6.11.87
The Ride Down Mount Morgan	17.7.97	11.10.91
The Last Yankee	5.1.91	21.1.93
Broken Glass	9.3.94	4.8.94
Mr. Peters' Connections	17.5.98	20.7.00
Resurrection Blues	3.8.02	14.2.06
Finishing the Picture	21.9.04	

INTRODUCTION

Glancing through the plays collected here, one cannot help wondering about the meaning of "realism." I have from the beginning been dubbed a realistic playwright, for both good and specious reasons. My first play to draw any attention, *All My Sons,* was indeed in the tradition of Ibsen's social plays. And at the time, 1947, I myself made something of this descent in order to regenerate interest and respect for a then neglected master. But critics and commentators, like most of the rest of us, are lazy people, and once I had been labeled it seemed no longer necessary for them to look twice at the plays that followed. *Death of a Salesman* was not, of course, in the realist tradition, having broken out into a quite new synthesis of psychological and social dimensions, and *The Crucible* was a work of another tradition altogether, and so on.

The metaphorical preoccupations of the present collection may be even more evident, but probably disguised for some by a design that asks for a realistic recognition of events and characters on the surface of a highly condensed interior life. To be sure, I have "wanted life to seem like this," but I may have succeeded too well. After seeing *Death of a Salesman,* Thomas Mann said to me, "They are like aborigines" (the characters), and he was sure that in the hands of a European playwright the play would have contained one or more speeches announcing in some overt way its philosophical intention. But for me it was a victory that such speeches were not needed, even if the cost was that the play might seem so inevitable and natural that an author was hardly even required. But that was precisely what I had been after.

It also strikes me, now that these plays stand in a row, that without having planned it three of them deal in some degree or another with what has come to be called the Holocaust. One, *After the Fall*, may seem surprising under that category, but it may be time to assert that that watershed of our history was at the center of the play's theme. Another, *Incident at Vichy*, was overtly about the Jews' destruction, but from the point of view of peacetime, postwar society, where the same questions haunt us—the anomie and paralysis before the knowledge of mass destruction. And *Playing for Time*, over a decade later, completes that theme here. But perhaps I ought to draw attention, in the likely event no one else does, to an echo of the theme in *The Creation of the World and Other Business*, where the dilemma for God Himself is his inability to determine his own responsibility for the indifference to murder in the minds of his most gratifyingly successful creatures.

The truth is that I have never been able to settle upon a single useful style. Indeed, a great part of the energy that goes into a play is involved in working out its form and style. Form in the theater is particularly important, for obvious reasons, and the style of a play alerts an audience as to how to receive it, and at which level of emotion the evening is purporting to function. I suspect, in fact, that because of shifts in style from one play to the next, several of them have had to appear a second time in order to be accepted at all, or even sensibly judged. It has been said often enough to bear repeating—an author is better off writing the same thing in the same way, otherwise he risks losing what audience he may have gained. But fitting means to matter is the name of the game for me, and a far more rewarding pleasure.

THE MISFITS

AUTHOR'S NOTE

A glance at *The Misfits* will show that it is written in an unfamiliar form, neither novel, play, nor screenplay. A word of explanation is perhaps in order.

It is a story conceived as a film, and every word is there for the purpose of telling the camera what to see and the actors what they are to say. However, it is the kind of tale which the telegraphic, diagrammatic manner of screenplay writing cannot alone convey because its sense depends as much on the nuances of character and place as on the plot. It therefore became necessary to do more than merely indicate what happens and to create through words the emotions which the finished film should possess. It was as though a picture were already in being, and the writer were recreating its full effects through language, so that as a result of a purely functional attempt to make a vision of a film clear to others, a film which existed as yet only in the writer's mind, there was gradually suggested a form of fiction itself, a mixed form if you will, but one which it seems to me has vigorous possibilities for reflecting contemporary existence. Movies, the most widespread form of art on earth, have willy-nilly created a particular way of seeing life, and their swift transitions, their sudden bringing together of disparate images, their effect of documentation inevitable in photography, their economy of storytelling, and their concentration on mute action have infiltrated the novel and play writing—especially the latter—without being confessed to or, at times, being consciously realized at all. *The Misfits* avowedly uses the perspectives of the film in order to create a fiction which might have the peculiar immediacy of image and the reflective possibilities of the written word.

THE MISFITS

ONE

There is a permanent steel arch across Main Street bearing a neon sign which reads, WELCOME TO RENO THE BIGGEST LITTLE CITY IN THE WORLD.

It is a quiet little town. We can see through our windshield almost to the end of Main Street, a dozen blocks away. Everything is sharp to the eye at this altitude, the sky is immaculate, and the morning jazz coming from the dashboard is perky. It is a clean town. The great gambling palaces are modernistic, battleship gray, and all their neon signs are lit in the sunshine. The traffic light changes and our vehicle moves cautiously ahead. But a block on we are halted by a policeman who steps off the sidewalk, stops a truck coming the other way, and escorts an old lady slowly across the street. She goes into the sedate bank and trust company next to which is an elegant women's clothing store and next to that a store with "Craps" in gold letters on its windows. Some stores feature "Horse Betting," others "Casino," and others "Wedding Rings." In this momentary halt a loud buzzing draws our attention. A gambling emporium on the left, glistening inside, is broadcasting the buzzing noise into the street and flashing a sign over the sidewalk which says "Jackpot," indicating that somewhere within a customer has struck the full count.

The policeman, who wears gold-framed eyeglasses, waves us on, but a woman steps up to the side window of our vehicle. She is carrying a three-month-old baby on her arm, and a suitcase.

The woman: "Am I headed right for the courthouse, mister?"

Driver's voice: "Straight on one block and then two left."

The woman: "Thank you kindly. It's awfully confusin' here."

Driver's voice: "It sure is, ma'am."

She steps back to the sidewalk. There is a rural pathos in her eyes, an uprooted quality in the intense mistrust with which she walks. She is thin, and her polka-dot dress is too large. She is clutching the baby and the suitcase as though she were continuously counting them.

Our vehicle moves again, keeping pace with her for a moment. The morning jazz from the dashboard remains bright and untroubled. The neon signs flash in the sunlight. The few people on the sidewalks are almost all women, and women who are alone. Many of them are strolling with the preoccupied air of the disconnected, the tourist, the divorcée who has not yet memorized the town. The jazz number ends and a hillbilly disc jockey greets his listeners. As he drawls we continue on down Main Street. Through the window of a supermarket we see a woman holding a large bag of groceries on one arm while with the other she is pulling down the arm of a slot machine; not even looking at the revolving drums, she walks away and out the door, hoping to be stopped by the crash of money which does not come. Farther on, a couple-in-love stares at bridal gowns in a store window. There is a door next to the store and a sign on it, reading "Divorce Actions One Flight Up." It is a prospering town with one brand-new hotel facing the Truckee River, a gray facade covered with cantilevered balconies. Beyond it rise the dry brown mountains capped with snow. One can see immense distances here, even boulders sticking out of the mountains' face. The disc jockey, in a baritone drawl, says, "Weel, folks . . ." and for a moment there is only the sound of rustling paper coming through the radio as he evidently searches for the commercial. Two Indian young men in dungarees stand on a corner watching us pass by; their faces are like the faces of the blind, which one cannot look at too long.

The commentator chuckles. "Folks? Here's somethin' to think about while you're a-waitin' for your vacuum-packed Rizdale Coffee to come to a boil. For the third month a-runnin', we've beat out Las Vegas. Four hundred and eleven divorces have been granted as of yesterday compared to three hundred and ninety-one for Vegas. No doubt about it, pardners, we are the Divorce Capital of the World. And speakin' of divorce, would you like to cut loose of a bad habit? How about rootin' yourself out of that chair and gettin' over to Haber's Drug Store and treat yourself to a good night's sleep with good old Dream-E-Z?"

We are going down a tree-lined street, almost suburban, the houses very small, some of them frayed and nearly poor. Here is a peaceful, almost somnolent quality of a hot Nevada day. As we turn . . .

"Now naturally we don't claim to provide you with any special type of dream, friends. Dream-E-Z's only one of them names they made up back East in New York. But it does work. I can rightly swear your sleepless nights are over; you get the dream ready, and we'll give you the sleep. Dream-E-Z's a real little bottle of rest, folks, and relaxation, and peace. Put that burden down, Mother. Daddy? Let yourself go. Dream-E-Z. Come on, folks, let's get together here. . . . Say it with me now like we always do . . . all together. . . ." A school of violins soars into a music of wafting sleep. "Dream-Eeeeee-Zeeeeee."

The vehicle comes to a halt at the curb and the engine is shut off and the radio with it.

Guido hops out of what we now see is a tow truck and comes around and lifts a battery out of the back. He walks up the driveway with it. The legend on the back of his jumper reads, "Jack's Reno Garage."

He goes behind the house, where a new Cadillac convertible stands with its hood open. The car is banged up all around, its fenders dented. He is resting the battery on the fender to get a new grip on it before lowering it into place when he hears a plane overhead. He looks up.

A great jet liner roars over, flying quite low. Guido watches it until it disappears toward the mountains, a certain longing and expert appraisal in his eyes. Then he lowers the battery into its rack and works at connecting it. He is about forty—it is hard to tell precisely because he is tanned and healthy, with close-cropped hair, strong arms, and a wrestler's way of moving his neck; from the rear he seems the athlete, even to the pigeon-toed walk and the voice that is a little too high. But face to face, talking with him, he seems to have a university-bred sophistication. Perhaps he is a football-playing poet. Then, quite suddenly, his black eyes seem to thicken into stupidity and he is a local, a naive spender of time underneath broken cars, a man in the usual industrial daze munching his sandwich at lunchtime and watching the girls go by.

Now, as he works at the battery, which is a simple job requiring only automatic fingers, his gaze spreads, and he seems to see or be longing to see something soft or something vast. The skin around his eyes and over the bridge of his nose is whiter than the rest—the mark of aviator's goggles—so that when he blinks a parrotlike look appears, the look of some heavily blinking tropical bird.

The voice of a woman turns him around.

"Young man? You have the time?"

Holding the screen door open, Isabelle shades her eyes against the morning sun. Her left arm is in a sling but she holds an alarm clock in her hand. She is a sixty-year-old tomboy with hair bobbed high in the manner of the twenties, a Buster Brown cut which somehow marks her as a woman who is impatient of details, for it rarely needs combing. She is in an old wrapper, which she holds together with her elbows. Her nose and cheeks are faintly purpled, her voice cracks and pipes, and she looks on the world with an amused untidiness that approaches an air of wreckage and a misspent intelligence. But with her first words—which cause her to cough and clear her throat—a suggestion of great kindness emerges from her. There is a cut to her speech which banishes the sentimental. She seems never to expect anything in return; she would be kind even to her executioner, perhaps apologizing for getting him up so early in the morning. For people in general she has little but despair, yet she has never met an individual she couldn't forgive. A flavor of the South sweetens her words. Seeing her, Guido feels like smiling, as most people do. She is standing there shading her eyes like an Indian as she waits to hear the time of day. He looks at his watch. As though arraigning the entire clock industry, she adds: "I've got six or eight clocks in this house, and none of them work."

"It's twenty after nine."

"*After!*" Isabelle comes farther out on the porch and calls up to a second-floor window: "Dear girl? It's twenty after!" No answer comes from the window. "Darling?"

Roslyn appears behind the screen; we can barely make out her features. Her voice is excited as she calls down: "Five minutes! What about you?"

"I'm all set. I just ironed my sling. The lawyer said nine-thirty sharp, darling."

"Okay!"

Isabelle turns on hearing the car's engine start. Guido emerges from behind the wheel and stands over the engine, listening. Isabelle comes over to him, still carrying the clock which she has forgotten to set or wind.

"I hope you're not the kind to be miserly. It's brand new, you know. She ought to get a good price."

"Is that the right mileage? Twenty-three miles?"

"We only took two rides in it. It's the damn men in this town—they kept runnin' into her just to start a conversation." With a proud smile: "She's a stunner, y'know."

Roslyn's voice: "Will you come up here, Iz?"

"Coming, dear girl!" Then back to Guido, who is facing the upstairs window for a glimpse: "Now you be your most generous self. You mustn't go by appearances—it's brand new, a divorce present from her husband, don't y'know."

"They giving presents for divorces now?"

"Why not? On the anniversary of *our* divorce my husband has never failed to send me a potted yellow rose. And it'll be nineteen years July." She is already his friend, and laughs, squeezing his arm and leaning in toward his face. "Of course he never paid me the alimony, but I wouldn't want to put a man out anyway—if his heart's not in it, y'know." She starts toward the porch.

"You break your arm in the car?"

"Oh, no. My last roomer before this girl—we celebrated her divorce and I . . . misbehaved. I'm just so sick and tired of myself!"

She is suddenly almost in tears and vanishes into the house. His interest piqued, Guido glances up at the window, then, taking out a pad and pencil, starts circling the car, noting down the damage.

Isabelle hurries through the house and up the stairs and goes into a room. Chaos: bureau drawers hang open; the bed is covered with letters, toilet articles, magazines, hair curlers.

From the closet, Roslyn calls: "Could we do my answers again, Iz?"

"Oh, sure, dear." Isabelle goes to a mirror and takes a slip of paper which is stuck in the frame. She sits on the bed, holding a pair of bent glasses to her nose. "Let's see. 'Did your husband, Mr. Raymond Taber, act toward you with cruelty?' " There is no answer from the closet. "Darling?"

After a moment: "Well . . . yes."

Isabelle: "Just say yes, dear."

A golden girl comes bursting out of the closet, zipping up her dress, and goes to the bureau, where with her free hand she searches for something in the disorder of jars, papers, and odds and ends, while glancing at her hair in the mirror. Each detail of her appearance is in perfectly good order but the total effect is windy; she can be obsessed with how she looks now, and entirely oblivious as she turns her head too quickly for her hairdo to stay in place and in a freshly pressed dress gets on her hands and knees to look under the bed for something. But, quick as she is, a certain stilled inwardness lies coiled in her gaze. She glances at Isabelle.

"Yes."

She adjusts her dress in the mirror, absorbed at the same time in the effort of answering. As with so many things she does, so many objects she examines, so many events she passes through, a part of her is totally alone, like a little child in a new school, mystified as to how it got here and passionately looking for a friendly face.

Isabelle reads on: " 'In what ways did his cruelty manifest itself?' "

"He . . . How's it go again?"

" 'He persistently and cruelly ignored my personal rights and wishes, and resorted on several occasions to physical violence against me.' " The older woman looks up from the slip of paper.

"He persistently . . ." She breaks off, troubled. "Must I say that? Why can't I just say he wasn't *there*? I mean, you could touch him but he wasn't there."

"Darling child, if that was grounds for divorce there'd be about eleven marriages left in the United States. Now just repeat—"

A car horn blows. Isabelle hurries to the window. Below, Guido, putting his notepad away, speaks up to her: "They'll call in their estimate from the office."

Roslyn comes beside Isabelle and calls down: "Those dents weren't my fault, you know!"

Guido now sees Roslyn for the first time, still behind the window screen, but more or less clearly. He is strangely embarrassed and ashamed of his own shyness.

"I'll recommend the best price I can, miss. You can drive her now. I put a battery in."

"Oh, I'll never drive *that* car again. We'll call a cab."

"I'll give you a lift in my truck if you're leavin' right away."

"Swell! Two minutes! Get dressed, Iz! You got to be my witness!"

Isabelle grasps Roslyn's hand with a quick surge of feeling. "This'll be my seventy-seventh time I've witnessed for a divorce. Two sevens is lucky, darlin'."

"Oh, Iz, I hope!"

Roslyn smiles, but fear and a puzzled consternation remain in her eyes. The old lady hurries out of the room, opening the sash of her wrapper with her good hand.

TWO

There is a small park across the street from the Reno court-house. The crosswalks are lined with benches and there is a greenish statue of a man, wife, and child facing the direction of the court—a pioneer family group to remind the litigants of the great treks that passed through here on the way West. It is a pleasant place to sit on a hot day, the shade of the tree being a rare luxury in this territory. Derelicts and old men lounge here to watch the strangers go by—sometimes young people examining proofs of their wedding pictures from the photo shops across the avenue, sometimes land claimants spreading out their maps. Anything that happens sooner or later ends up in court, and this park is where the parties can sit and stare at the issues while the traffic flows past on four sides.

Guido's tow truck pulls up. Quickly he jumps out, comes around to open the door on the other side, and helps Isabelle down.

"Easy does it, now."

"Aren't you a dear!" Isabelle pats his shoulder.

Roslyn is almost out of the truck already, but he reaches and takes her hand, anyway. She is still clutching the slip of paper, and starts past him.

Roslyn: "Thanks a lot. We got to run now."

Guido gently blocks her way. "If you're not going back East right away I'd be glad to take you out and show you the country. Some beautiful country around here, you know."

Roslyn, distracted by her mission, thanks him with her eyes. "I'd love to see it, but I don't know what I'm going to do yet. All I could think about here was when my six weeks would be up."

Guido: "Can I call you?"

"I don't know where I'll be, but okay." Rosyln starts to move, waving back. "Thanks again!"

Isabelle taps his arm. "*My* name is Isabelle Steers."

Guido laughs at her jibe. "Okay, Isabelle. You could come along if you like."

"That's a sweet afterthought! Oh, you Reno men!" She laughs and trots after Roslyn.

Guido, somehow moved, quickened, remains staring as they walk across the paved paths that section the grass in front of the courthouse. Men on park benches look up at Roslyn as she passes; newspapers lower as she goes by.

The young polka-dot woman carrying her baby is shaking hands with a lawyer on the courthouse steps. They part. Gaunt-eyed, the woman passes Roslyn. Roslyn and Isabelle approach the steps of the court; Roslyn is rapidly going over her lines from her prompting paper. Her anxiety is hardened now.

"I can't memorize this; it's not the way it was."

Isabelle laughs. "You take everything so seriously, dear! Just say it; it doesn't have to be true. It's not a quiz show, it's only a court."

They start up the courthouse steps, and as Roslyn looks up after putting her paper away she is stopped by what she sees. A man is descending the steps toward her. He is well built, tall, about thirty-eight, wearing a soft straw hat and a tie with a big design. His mind is constantly trying to tune in on the world, but the message is never clear. He feels self-conscious now, having to plead; he was successful early in life and this pleading threatens his dignity. He expects that the simple fact of his having come here will somehow convince his wife how guilty she is. But he will forgive her and she will idolize him again. He is Raymond Taber, her husband. He manages a hurt, embarrassed grin, as though confessing to a minor error he made.

"Just got off the plane. I'm not too late, am I?"

Roslyn looks at him; a rising fear for herself holds her silent. He comes down the steps to her.

"Don't, Raymond. Please, I don't want to hear anything."

His resentment floods his face. "Give me five minutes, will you? After two years, five minutes isn't—"

"You can't have me, so now you want me, that's all. Please . . . I'm not blaming you. I never saw it any different. I just don't believe in the whole thing any more." She starts around him and he takes her arm.

"Kid, I understand what—"

"You don't understand it, because nobody understands it!" With her finger she presses his chest. "You aren't *there*, Raymond!" She steps back. "If I'm going to be alone, I want to be alone by myself. Go back, Raymond—you're not going to make me sorry for you any more."

She leaves him standing there in an impotent fury and beckons to Isabelle, who puts her arm around her. Roslyn is inwardly quaking with sobs, but she will not cry as they hurry up the steps together and into the courthouse.

Guido watches from his truck window until the two women disappear. He has seen the argument but could not hear it. Now he drives down Main Street, bemused. A train is parked across Main Street. At the crossing gate he stops, switches off the engine, and settles back in his seat to wait. His eyes show a certain fixed daze of introspection. He happens to turn and comes alert and calls out: "Gay!"

Gay Langland is standing at the foot of the train steps with a woman. His dog is at his heels. He turns toward the truck and waves, calling: "Wait up! I was just going over to see you!"

A conductor stands with a watch in hand a few yards off. The woman, about forty-two, is expensively dressed. She is afraid she has been a fool and is trying to find out by searching Gay's eyes; she wears a joyless smile that is full of fear and unhappiness.

Gay is just turning back from his look at Guido. "Good luck now, Susan. I won't forget you, you can be sure of that."

She glances down at his proffered handclasp, and she clearly feels the formality and rejection in the gesture; she starts to shake his hand, trying to maintain composure, but suddenly she throws her arms around him and tears flood her eyes.

Gay: "Now, now, honey, you be a good sport."

Conductor: "Board!"

Woman: "I don't even know where to write you!"

Gay, reassuring her as he moves her toward the steps: "General Delivery. I'll get it." He gets her onto the step and she turns to him.

"Will you think about it, Gay? It's the second largest laundry in St. Louis."

"I wouldn't want to kid you, Susan. I ain't cut out for business."

The train starts to move. The conductor hops aboard and grasps her arm to help her up. Gay walks along with the train. She has lost all her composure and is weeping.

"Will you think of me? Gay!"

"You know I will, honey! 'Bye!"

She manages a masculine, brave salute as she moves away. Even after the woman is out of sight Gay stands with his arm raised, a compassionate farewell that is full of his relief. Now he walks along the platform, the dog at his heels. Guido has pulled the truck over to the curb; Gay comes and rests his arms on the sill of the window, and he seems weary into his voice.

"How you doin', boy? You ready to cut out of this town? 'Cause I sure am."

"I been thinkin' about it." Guido gestures toward the departed train; there is a certain onlooker's excitement around his eyes, a suggestive yet shy thirst for detail. "Which one was that?"

Gay smiles at his friend's heavy curiosity, but there is a refusal to join Guido in cynicism toward her. "Susan. Damn good sport, that woman."

He opens the door and lets himself down on the edge of the seat. The traffic goes by quietly. Gay is forty-nine years old, a big-knuckled cowboy, a wondrous listener. He takes off his hat and wipes his sweat band. His mind is elsewhere but not in any particular place—simply not here and not now. It is the middle of a weekday morning with a stateful of sand and mountains around him. Now he seems either contented or exhausted; it is not clear which. Toward Guido he has a business friendliness, but there is no business. Maybe he has many such friends. One senses that he does not expect very much, but that he sets the rhythm for whoever he walks with because he cannot follow. And he has no desire to lead. It is always a question of arranging for the next few days, maybe two weeks; beyond that there is only the state, and he knows people all over it. Homeless, he is always home inside his shoes and jeans and shirt, and interested. When he listens, he seems to feel that life is a pageant that is sometimes loud, sometimes soft, sometimes a head-shaking absurdity, and sometimes dangerous. It is a pageant with no head and no tail. He listens, he is interested, and like a wood-chuck he can go suddenly into the ground and come up later in an-other place. He needs no guile because he has never required himself to promise anything, so his betrayals are minor and do not cling. "If you have to you will," he seems to believe. The moral world is full of women and he has, with their gratitude, eased many of them out of it, modestly. His refusal to mock the departed woman encourages Guido to confess his own feeling now.

Guido: "I just met a girl sweet enough to eat, Gay. Hell of a lookin' woman."

Gay, looking at him with pleased surprise: "She sure must be, for you to get worked up. Look, whyn't we take out to the moun-tains?"

"I wanted to pile up about five hundred this time. I ought to get a new engine."

"Hell, that engine'll fly you anywhere. You been more than two months on this job, fella—that's enough wages for one year. You gonna get the habit. I tell you, I'm just dyin' for some fresh air and no damned people, male or female. Maybe we can even do a little mustangin' up there."

Guido looks off, indecisively. "I'll meet you over the bar later. Let's talk about it."

"That's the way!" Getting out, Gay slams the door shut. "Hope I get a look at that girl!"

"Only trouble is, when I think of all the useless talkin' you gotta do I get discouraged."

"Hell, there's nothin' more useful than talkin' to a good-look-ing woman. You been moody lately—might perk you up. See you later, now!"

Gay steps back, they wave to each other, and the truck takes off. Gay starts walking, a mildly revived spirit showing in his eyes.

At a certain point Main Street becomes a bridge crossing the narrow Truckee River, which flows between buildings. Roslyn and Isabelle are walking along, but Isabelle stops her at the railing. The heat of noon seems to have wilted them.

Isabelle: "If you throw your ring in you'll never have a divorce again."

Puzzled, Roslyn touches her ring protectively.

Isabelle: "Go ahead, honey, everybody does it. There's more gold in that river than the Klondike."

Roslyn, with a certain revulsion: "Did you do it?"

Isabelle: "Me? Oh, I lost my ring on my honeymoon!"

Roslyn: "Let's get a drink."

Isabelle: "That's my girl!"

A few doors down is a casino. Open to the street, a seeming half-acre of big-chested slot machines reflect rose and blue neon light. Most of the aisles are empty now, but a few early risers are pulling at the levers, blinking in this sea of chrome, staring at glints like fish in a dim underworld. Sound is hushed here. The two women sit at a table near the bar and watch the scattered players.

A waiter comes and Roslyn orders: "Scotch, I guess. On ice."

Isabelle: "Rye and water."

The sound of well-oiled levers is peaceful in the neon gloom. The two women sit in silence for a moment, looking around. An old man nearby makes the sign of the cross over a machine and pulls the lever.

Isabelle touches her friend's arm: "Cheer up, dear!"

"I will, I just hate to fight with anybody. Even if I win I lose. In my heart, you know?"

"Darling, you're free! Maybe the trouble is you're not used to it yet."

"No, the trouble is I'm always back where I started. I never had anybody much, and here I—"

"Well, you had your mother, though, didn't you?"

Roslyn quells a strange feeling of shame. "How do you have somebody who disappears all the time? Both of them weren't . . .

there. She'd go off with a patient for three months. You know how long three months is to a kid? And he came around when his ship happened to need repairs...."

The waiter comes and sets down their drinks and goes. Isabelle raises her glass. "Well, here's to the whole damned thing, darling!"

Roslyn, suddenly grasping Isabelle's arm: "You're a fine woman, Iz. You're practically the only woman who was ever my friend."

"Listen! Don't leave; settle down here. There's a school here; you could teach dancing.... 'Cause there's one thing about this town—it's always full of interesting strangers." Tears show in Roslyn's eyes and Isabelle is surprised. "Oh, my dear girl, I'm sorry; what'd I—"

"I suddenly miss my mother. Isn't that the stupidest thing?" She determinedly raises her drink, smiling. "To ... to life! Whatever that is."

They laugh and drink. Roslyn sees Gay's dog sitting patiently at the foot of the bar.

Roslyn: "Oh, look at that dear dog! How sweet it sits there!"

Isabelle: "Yeah, dogs are nice."

She and Isabelle see Gay placing a glass of water before the dog, Margaret. Margaret drinks. Gay glances at the two women, nods just for hello, and as he straightens up to turn back to the bar Guido enters, dressed in a clean shirt and dress trousers. Guido sees Roslyn and comes over as Gay starts to greet him.

Guido: "Oh, hello! How'd you make out?"

Roslyn, shyly: "Okay. It's all over."

He nods, uncertain how to proceed, and beckons Gay over, partly as a relief for his tension.

"Like you to meet a friend of mine. This is Gay Langland. Mrs. Taber ..."

Gay, realizing she is the one: "Oh! How-de-do."

Guido, of Isabelle: "And this is ..."

"Isabelle Steers." To Roslyn: "One thing about Reno men, they do remember the name."

They laugh. Isabelle is blooming. She loves new people. "Why don't you boys sit down?"

Gay: "Well, thank you. Sit down, Guido. Waiter? What're you girls drinkin'?"

Isabelle: "Whiskey. We're celebrating the jail burned down."

The waitress comes to the table.

Gay: "Get four doubles." To Roslyn: "You sure made a big impression on my friend here, and"—to Guido—"I can see why."

Roslyn glances at Guido, but his intensity turns her to Gay and she speaks to him: "You a mechanic too?"

Isabelle: "Him? He's a cowboy."

Gay, grinning: "How'd you know?"

Isabelle: "I can smell, can't I?"

Gay: "You can't smell cows on me."

Isabelle: "I can smell the look in your face, cowboy." She reaches across and laughs. "But I love every miserable one of you! I had a cowboy friend. . . ." She quickly sips. "He had one arm gone, but he was more with one arm than any man with two. I mean like cooking—" They all laugh. "I'm serious! He could throw a whole frying pan full of chops in the air and they'd all come down on the other side. Of course, you're all good-for-nothin', as you know."

Gay: "That may be, but it's better than wages."

The waitress arrives with the drinks.

Guido: "I suppose you're headin' back East now, huh?"

Roslyn: "I can't make up my mind; I don't know what to do."

Gay: "You mean you don't have a business to run, or school to teach, or—"

"Me? I didn't even finish high school."

"Well, that's real *good* news."

"Why? Don't you like educated women?"

"Oh, they're all right. Always wantin' to know what you're *thinkin'*, that's all. There sure must be a load of thinkin' goin' around back East."

"Well, maybe they're trying to get to know you better." Roslyn smiles wryly. "You don't mind that, do you?"

"I don't at all. But did you ever get to know a man by askin' him questions?"

"You mean, he's going to lie."

"Well, he might not—but then again, he just might!"

Isabelle guffaws and the question-and-answer period gives way.

Gay: "Let's get another drink!"

Roslyn: "Sure, let's have some more!" His openness relaxes her; he is avowedly engaging her and it awakens her pleasurably.

Gay, calling to the waiter: "Fella? See if you can get us four more, will ya?" He turns to Guido, relaxed and happy, trying to open the way. "How about it, Pilot? We takin' out of this town today?"

Spurred, awkward, Guido falters into his campaign: "You been out of Reno at all, Mrs. Taber?"

Roslyn: "I walked to the edge of town once, but—it looks like nothing's out there."

Guido: "Oh."

Gay: "That might just be where everything is."

Roslyn: "Like what?"

"The country."

"What do you do there?"

"Just live."

Drawn in, Roslyn searches Gay's eyes, asking: "How can you . . . just live?"

"Well . . . you start by going to sleep. Then, you get up when you feel like it. Then you scratch yourself"—they chuckle—"fry yourself some eggs, see what kind of day it is, throw a stone, ride a horse, visit, whistle. . . ."

Roslyn's eyes meet his. "I know what you mean."

Isabelle: "Might be nice, dear, whyn't you go out for a ride?"

Guido: "If it hit you right, I've got an empty house out in the country just beyond Hawleyville. It's yours if you want a little peace and quiet before you go back."

Roslyn, grinning: "Oh, is the last woman gone now?"

"No! No kidding." With a sudden self-exposure that is difficult for Guido: "I never offered it before."

"Well, thanks. I wouldn't stay there, but I *was* thinking of renting a car and seeing what the country—"

"Gay's got a truck, or I could get my car."

"No. Then you'll have to drive me back."

"Oh, I don't mind!"

"It's all right—I always . . ." She is a little flustered at having to stand against him; she touches his hand. ". . . like to feel I'm on my own, y'know? I'll rent a car. Where can I?"

Gay: "Right now?"

Roslyn: "Why not?"

Gay stands up. "Okay! You sure don't waste your time, do you?"

Guido: "I just got to stop over at the garage and tell the boss I quit."

Gay: "Now, that's the boy!"

They go down an aisle of slot machines toward the street. All at once there is a goal, a path through the shapeless day.

THREE

Roslyn's rented station wagon is speeding along a straight, endless highway a quarter of a mile behind Gay's ten-year-old pickup truck. Except for the two vehicles the highway is deserted. On both sides the bare Nevada hills are spread out, range beyond range. An occasional dirt trail winding into them raises the surprising thought that one could follow it and arrive at a human place in the interior. No house shows; only an occasional line of fence indicates that cattle range here sometimes. The hills front the highway like great giants' chests; to the eye speeding past, their undulating crests rise and fall as though the earth were silently breathing. The noon sun is lighting up red woundlike stains on their surfaces, a sudden blush of purple on one, the next faintly pink, another buff. Despite the hum of the engines the land seems undisturbed in its silence, a silence that grows in the mind until it becomes a wordless voice.

Roslyn, driving with Isabelle beside her, constantly turns from the road to stare at the great round hills. Her look is inward, her eyes widened by an air of respect.

Roslyn: "What's behind them?"

Isabelle: "More hills."

"What's that beautiful smell? It's like some kind of green perfume."

"Sage, darling."

"Oh, sure! I never smelled it except in a bottle!" Laughing: "Oh, Isabelle, it's beautiful here, isn't it?"

Isabelle, sensing Roslyn's excitement: "I better tell you something about cowboys, dear."

Roslyn laughs warmly: "You really worry about me, don't you!"

"You're too believing, dear. Cowboys are the last real men in the world, but they're as reliable as jackrabbits."

"But what if that's all there is? Really and truly, I mean."

"I guess a person just doesn't want to believe that."

"You think I'm reliable?"

"I guess you would be if you had somebody to be reliable *to.*"

"I don't know any more. Maybe you're not supposed to believe anything people say. Maybe it's not even fair to them."

"Well ... don't ask me, dear. This world and I have always been strangers—down deep, I mean."

They fall silent. The hills and their colors float across Roslyn's eyes.

Up ahead, Guido is at the wheel of the truck. Beside him, Gay dozes with his hat over his eyes.

Guido: "I couldn't hear what he said to her but"—he glances at Gay for corroboration—"it looked like *she* left *him.* The husband." He waits, but Gay is silent. "She's kind of hard to figure out, y'know? One minute she looks dumb and brand new. Like a kid. But maybe he caught her knockin' around, huh?" Gay is silent. "She sure *moves,* doesn't she?"

Gay: "Yeah. She's real prime."

Guido starts to speak again, but, glancing at Gay, decides to let him sleep. They ride in silence. They pass two Indians on brown-and-white paints riding slowly behind a small herd of cattle off to the right. Now Guido slows down and, sticking his head out the window, waves back at Roslyn. He turns off the highway onto a dirt trail, glancing into his mirror.

Roslyn follows in his dust across the sage flat toward the hills. In a moment they are climbing the belly of a hill. Now they are winding around behind it, rising all the time, the road becoming stony and the curves abrupt. Smashed and splintered outcroppings of rock force the trail to meander. They drive down a gap and then up a steep gorge whose flanks almost blot out the sky. Quite suddenly a house appears at the head of the gorge; Roslyn pulls up behind the truck and the motors are shut off.

She and Isabelle emerge, looking at the house. The men join

them. A small cloud of buff dust slowly floats away. For a moment the sudden appearance of this vacant building enforces its silence on them.

An odd, almost otherworldly air emerges from the rather modern, ranch-style house. Its windows look out on the swiftly falling land toward the unseen highway far below and the next swell of hills rising beyond. In this vastness it seems as terribly alone as a stranded boat.

It has never been completed. Black composition sheathing panels show where the clapboards were never put on, and the boards lie in a graying, weathered pile on the ground nearby, morning glories winding through them. The gabled roof is partly shingled, but a large area is still bare to the black tarpaper underneath. Sawhorses stand in weeds and sage. An unfinished wing of bare studs and joists sticks out of one side, little sage bushes starting up through the foundation. There is an abortive look to the place, a sense of its having been immobilized by sudden catastrophe or whimsically left incomplete by people who suddenly ran away to another idea. It is not a farm or a ranch; its only visible reason for being here is that it stands at the focal point of a vast view. Yet someone rich enough to build for that reason would hardly have thought of so conventional and small a house. Its very pointlessness is somehow poetic to Roslyn, like an unrealized longing nailed together.

Roslyn: "Why isn't it finished?"

Guido, cryptically: "It's weather-tight. Come on in."

Guido leads them in through the side door. He stops before they are well inside the doorway and turns to Roslyn, patting the black insulation batting between the open studs of a partition. "Insulated." She nods, not quite sure what he is referring to, and he leads on into the living room. With a wide sweep of his arm he says: "Living room," and she nods, looking around at the complete assortment of furniture, from the Morris chair to the studio couch, the drapeless dirty windows, the sections of wall lined with knotty-pine boards and the sections which still show bare studs, the dusty Indian blankets on the Grand Rapids couch. The place is not damp but it seems so. Light is grayed by the dust on the windows.

Guido opens a door and presses himself against the jamb, inviting her to look out. "This was going to be a new bedroom."

Roslyn sticks her head into the stud skeleton of a wing built onto the house. The sun is bright in her face, and lights the ground underneath the uncovered floor joists. "It's even nice now!"

Encouraged, Guido rushes to a series of three windows at the front of the room. "Picture windows."

"Oh!"

But when he arrives at the windows and looks out, the view is gray glass, and he hurries to open the front door. "Look at that."

With Gay and Isabelle behind her she stands in the threshold, looking out and down at the oceanic roll of mountains falling away below. "God, it goes forever."

"See the bathroom." Guido touches her elbow and she follows him across the living room. Passing the fireplace, he touches it, glancing up to where it goes through the ceiling. "Fireplace."

She nods. "Brick."

"Kitchen."

She follows into the kitchen area, noting the spider in the sink and the damp-wrinkled box of soap flakes on the stove.

"Gas refrigerator." He opens the freezer door and she looks in. His pride is riding him and she is drawn toward him. He closes the door and hurries through a doorway—quickly, as though he might lose her interest.

"Ceramic tile."

In the bathroom she inspects the tile. He crosses the bathroom and opens another door and she comes up to his side.

"And here's our—" He breaks off at the sight of an ornately framed wedding photograph hanging over the bed. Two rosaries are suspended from the frame. "My wife. She died here."

"Oh. I'm sorry." Roslyn glances at the barren room. A double bed, a dresser, a window, an unpainted composition-board wall. His face, and his wife's in the photograph, are curiously unmarked, new. A sadness presses in on Roslyn, and she looks at Guido's face beside her, seeing for the first time the twisting private agony behind his eyes.

Guido: "She was due to have a baby. I was setting the capstone on the chimney, and ... she screamed, and that was that."

Roslyn: "Couldn't you call the doctor?"

"She didn't seem to be that sick. Then I got a flat and didn't have a spare. Everything just happened wrong. It'll do that sometimes."

"Oh, I know. Couldn't you live here any more?"

Guido is surprised by her flow of sympathy, and he is swept into cultivating it now. Yet one senses a fear in him of mockery, and his manner with her is tentative and delicate. "We knew each other since we were seven years old, see."

"You should find another girl."

Guido, with a certain trace of vague condescension toward the idea: "I don't know. Being with anybody else, it just seems ... impossible, you know? She wasn't *like* other women. Stood behind me hundred per cent, uncomplaining as a tree."

Roslyn senses an invidious comparison; she laughs lightly. "But maybe that's what killed her." Quickly, as she sees he feels a slur: "I mean, a little complaining helps sometimes." But he does not understand, and, striving for gaiety—and pardon—she takes his arm, starting him out of the room. "Come! Show me the rest of it! It's beautiful!"

They emerge into the living-room area. Gay is sprawled on the couch; Isabelle is holding up an Indian blanket to examine it.

Roslyn: "Isn't it beautiful here, Iz?"

Isabelle: "It'd be perfect if somebody'd go out in the car and get the bottle of whiskey I bought with my own money."

Guido: "Hey, that's right!" Glad for the reprieve, he jumps to the ground from the front-door threshold—there being no step.

Roslyn wanders about the room, touching things.

Gay: "Glasses are in the kitchen, Isabelle. I'm real tired."

Isabelle: "No, darling, you're just a cowboy. You fellas won't get up unless it's rainin' down your neck."

Gay laughs as the old woman goes into the kitchen area. He turns and watches Roslyn, who has halted at a dirty window to look out. He runs his eyes over her back, her legs.

"Too rough for you, Roslyn?"

A certain abstracted suspense emanates from her. "Oh, I don't mind that."

"Should've seen his wife. She helped pour the cement, knocked in nails. She was a real good sport."

She looks around at the room as though trying to summon the walls' memories. "And now she's dead. . . . Because he didn't have a spare tire."

"Well, that's the way it goes."

Their eyes meet; hers resent his contradiction of her mood's truth.

"Goes the other way too, though; don't forget that." His immovable resolution keeps her staring at him for a moment, and despite herself a vague gratitude softens her face.

Guido jumps up into the room with a small bag of groceries and a bottle. He looks at them and at Isabelle drying glasses on her sling and calls out: "Boy, it's nice to see people in here! Come on, folks, let's get a drink." Going to Isabelle in the kitchen area: "I'll start the refrigerator. It makes ice quick."

"Ice!" Isabelle calls through the open studs to Roslyn: "We stayin' that long?"

"I don't know. . . ."

She unwittingly looks to Gay for the decision, and he speaks to her uncertainty.

"Sure! come on, there's no better place to be! And you couldn't find better company, either!"

"All right!" Roslyn laughs.

"That's it, sport!" Gay calls to the kitchen: "Turn on that ice, Guido boy!"

Isabelle comes in, balancing a tray and glasses, which Gay leaps up to take—along with the bottle from her sling. Gay pours.

Gay: "Let's get this stuff a-flowin' and make the desert bloom."

Isabelle: "Flow it slow. We only got the one bottle."

Gay grasps Roslyn's wrist and puts the glass into her hand. "There you are, now! Put that in your thoughts and see how you come out."

She smiles at him, warmed by his persistence.

Guido enters and takes a glass. "Come on, sit down, everybody! Let's get comfortable."

Roslyn sits on the couch, Isabelle beside her. The two men take chairs.

Guido addresses Roslyn, his hope flying: "Say, I'm really glad you like this place."

Isabelle: "Well, here's to Nevada, the leave-it state."

Roslyn: "The what state?"

They are already starting to chuckle.

"The leave-it state. You want to gamble your money, leave it here. A wife to get rid of? Get rid of her here. Extra atom bomb you don't need? Just blow it up here and nobody will mind in the slightest. The slogan of Nevada is, 'Anything goes, but don't complain if it went!' "

Gay: "God, that's no lie!"

Guido: "How come you never went back home, Isabelle? You came out here for your divorce, didn't you? Originally?"

Isabelle drinks, glances diffidently at Roslyn. "Tell you the truth, I wasn't beautiful enough to go home."

Roslyn: "Oh, Isabelle!"

"It's true, darling. Beauty helps anywhere, but in Virginia it's a necessity. You practically need it for a driver's license. I love Nevada. Why, they don't even have mealtimes here. I never met so many people didn't own a watch. Might have two wives at the same time, but no watch. Bless 'em all!"

Roslyn, relaxing, is leaning her head back on the couch as they drink. Their rhythm has slowed. Their laughter slides away now.

Roslyn: "How quiet it is here!"

Sprawled out, Gay speaks with avowed seriousness. "Sweetest sound there is."

They sip their drinks. There is a skylike silence in the room.

Guido: "There's an Indian store about five miles"—Roslyn looks at him quizzically—"if you wanted to shop. Groceries, everything. If you decided to stay a while."

Gay, plainly, without any insinuation: "Be glad to come by and do your chores. If you liked."

Roslyn drinks again and gets up. They watch as, in a closed world of her own, she wanders to a half-empty bookcase. Unable to bear the silence she turns to the men. "Could we have a fire?"

Guido: "Sure! It's a good fireplace." He springs up and piles wood into the fireplace. He looks up at her, dares to smile, thankful for her command.

She smiles back abstractedly and, turning from Guido, sees that Gay has been watching the silent exchange. She smiles at Gay and he replies with a frankly intensified gaze at her. She says to Isabelle: "Maybe they know your friend." To the men: "You ever know a fellow named Andy?"

Gay: "Andy who?"

Isabelle: "Stop it, darling! You can't go lookin' for a man."

Gay: "What'd he, take off?"

"Not exactly. He just didn't come back." Isabelle laughs at herself. "Andy Powell? You ever—"

"Sure! Fella with one arm. Call him Andy Gump sometimes?"

Isabelle, a little excited in spite of herself, laughing: "That's him!"

Roslyn, hopefully for Isabelle, asks Gay: "Where is he?"

"Saw him at the rodeo only last month."

Roslyn: "Could you find him if you—"

Isabelle: "Dear girl, you got to stop thinkin' you can change things."

A mystifying flood of protest reddens Roslyn's face. "But if there's something you could do . . . *I* don't know what to *do,* but if I knew, I'd do it!"

She suddenly finds the three of them looking at her in silence, looking at her as though she had challenged them in some secret way. Gay's interest is heightened; Isabelle feels a little ashamed and ineffectual; Guido is vaguely frightened by this burst of feeling and drawn to her. Because there is no one here to receive her meaning as she intends it, she says, almost laughing: "Is there a phonograph or a radio? Let's get some music."

Guido: "There's no electricity."

Roslyn: "How about the car radio?"

Gay: "Now who'd've thought of that? Turn it on, Guido!"

Guido: "You always got an idea, don't you." Excitedly he rushes out, hopping down to the ground.

Gay: "How about another drink, Roslyn? It'll keep the first one warm."

Roslyn: "I'd love it."

The car engine is heard starting outside. With strangely youthful energy Isabelle gets up and heads for the kitchen. "Think I'll make a sandwich. How about you people?"

Roslyn: "Okay."

Isabelle goes into the kitchen area. Gay, close to Roslyn, pours a drink into her glass and says in a private tone: "I hope you're going to stay on here. Any chance?"

Her face fills with a sadness that approaches a strange self-abandonment. "Why? What difference would it make?"

"Might make all the difference in the world as time goes by."

She looks at him with the unconcealed intensity of a searcher, and he does not evade it. Jazz is heard from the car radio outside. The engine is shut off. Gay touches her arm. "Like to dance?"

"Okay."

He draws her to him. He is a fair dancer. Guido enters, and is rather caught in midair by this progress.

Roslyn calls over Gay's shoulder to Guido: "Thanks! Iz, give him another drink. It's a very nice house, Guido."

Isabelle comes out of the kitchen area. Guido goes around them and forces an interest in stoking up the fire. In his face, seen in the firelight, there is rapid, planning thought.

Isabelle, making sandwiches with one hand: "That's pretty good dancing, cowboy!"

Gay: "Hey, what're you makin' my feet do?"

Roslyn is getting quite high; her body is moving more freely. "Relax. Join your partner, don't fight her."

"*I* ain't fightin' her."

She breaks and tries to move him into a lindy. He does it awkwardly, but amazed at himself.

Guido: "What *are* you doin'?"

Guido and Isabelle are watching with intrigued smiles. Guido drinks deeply now, a competitive tension rising in him. Isabelle speaks with quiet pride to Guido: "She taught dancing, y'know, before she was married."

"No kiddin'! In a dance hall?"

"Something like that, I guess."

The information tends to place Roslyn for Guido. Suddenly he breaks in between her and Gay. "How about the landlord?" Lightly, to Gay: "Move over, boy, huh?"

"Just watch out for those pretty little feet there!"

Guido looks directly at Roslyn, his eyes firing, an almost ludicrous familiarity in his grin. "Oh, she knows how to get out of the way. Let's go!"

With a clap of his hands, he astounds them all by breaking into a boogie lindy. Roslyn immediately, and happily, accepts the challenge. They come together, part, dance back to back, and he puts her to her mettle.

Gay: "Where in hell you learn that, Pilot?" To Isabelle: "I never knew him to dance at all!" Calling: "Look at Pilot comin' out from under the bushel!"

The number ends, and on the last beat Guido has her pressed close, and in the silence she deftly, but definitely—smiling, however—breaks his grip on her body, her expression striving to deny the easy victory in his eyes.

Gay: "You two oughta put on a show! That's some goin', Roslyn!"

Roslyn: "Whew!" Panting, getting high, she staggers to the door. Another number starts from the radio. Guido goes to her, clasps her waist, and turns her around to him familiarly. "Come on, honey, this is a good one. I haven't danced in years." They dance with quicker knowledge of each other now. After a moment she asks: "Didn't your wife dance?"

"Not like you. She had no . . . gracefulness."

Roslyn stays close to him and looks up into his face: "Why'n't you *teach* her to be graceful?"

"You can't learn that."

"How do you know? I mean, how do you *know*?"

Guido is stumped by her veering thought. Resentment mars his face.

Roslyn: "You see? She died, and she never knew how you could dance! It's nobody's fault, but to a certain extent"—she holds thumb and index finger a half inch apart—"I mean just to a certain extent maybe you were strangers."

Guido, injured, his tone on the verge of contempt: "I don't feel like discussing my wife." He stops dancing.

Roslyn takes his arm. The jazz is going, she is high now, and a depth of sadness comes over her face. "Oh, don't be mad! I just meant that if you loved her you could have taught her anything. Because we have to die, we're really dying right now, aren't we? All the husbands and all the wives are dying every minute, and they are not teaching one another what they really know." She sees he is at a loss and genuinely tries to plead with him. "You're such a nice man, Guido." She wipes her hair out of her eyes to blot out the sight of his resentful face, and suddenly: "I want air!"

Turning quickly to the front door she starts to step out. Gay rushes from the couch and catches her before she goes down where the step is missing. Isabelle rushes right behind him.

Gay: "You better lie down, girl."

Isabelle: "Come on, let's get back home. Heist her down, cowboy."

Roslyn: "No, I'm all right, I'm all—"

She starts once again to walk out the door. Guido leaps down to the ground and she falls into his arms, standing up. She is looking into his face, laughing in surprise at her sudden drop, when he thrusts his lips against hers, squeezing her body to him. She pushes him away.

Above them on the threshold Isabelle calls with fear in her voice: "Help me down! Get in the car, Roslyn!"

Roslyn sends Guido falling a step back and staggers away. Momentarily alone, she looks around her. The radio jazz is still playing. She flies into a warm, longing solo dance among the weeds, and coming to a great tree she halts and then embraces it, pressing her face against its trunk.

Guido, Isabelle, and Gay are watching now in a group at the doorway of the house, mystification on their faces. Guido, still resentful, takes a step toward her, but Gay touches him and he stops. Gay goes through the weeds to the tree and gently tries to turn Roslyn's shoulder, for her face is hidden under her arm. As soon as he touches her she turns and faces him and, astonishingly, her face is bright and laughing. Gay starts to smile, but he is bewildered.

Roslyn: "You were worried about me! That's so sweet!"

Gay: "Just want to keep you in one pretty piece."

He puts his arm around her and she lets herself be led to her station wagon, which is parked beside Gay's beat-up pickup truck.

At the car's open door, Gay turns to Guido and begins to speak, but Guido cuts him off: "Go ahead, you drive her, I'll take your truck."

Gay moves Roslyn into the car, and she says: "No, don't leave Guido all alone. Go ahead, Iz. . . . Ride with poor Guido." In apology she reaches toward Guido: "It's a beautiful house, Guido!"

Gay gets in beside her.

Both vehicles descend the rocky trail to the highway below, the truck ahead. Inside the station wagon, Roslyn is sitting beside Gay, one leg tucked under, her foot almost touching Gay's hip. She is in the momentary calm after a quick storm, blurred eyes staring out at the passing hills that rise from the roadside. She turns to look at Gay's profile; a calm seems to exude from him, an absence of uncertainty which has the quality of kindness, a serious concern for which she is grateful. She speaks: "I didn't mean to hurt his feelings. Did I hurt his feelings?"

Gay, grinning: "You sure brought out the little devil in him—surprised me." He laughs. "He did look comical doin' that dance!" He guffaws.

They have arrived at the foot of the trail. The truck has entered the highway, turned, and moved off. Now Gay stops the car, he looks left and right for traffic, and his eyes fall on Roslyn; she is looking at him searchingly, a residual smile lingering on her face.

"You're a real beautiful woman. It's . . . almost kind of an honor sittin' next to you. You just shine in my eyes." She laughs softly, surprised. "That's my true feeling, Roslyn." He pulls up the brake, shifts around to face her. "What makes you so sad? I think you're the saddest girl I ever met."

"You're the first man ever said that. I'm usually told how happy I am."

"You make a man *feel* happy, that's why."

He tries to embrace her; she gently stops him. "I don't feel that way about you, Gay."

Gay, pleased, somehow, holds up her chin. "Well, don't get discouraged, girl—you might! Look, whyn't you try it out here a while? You know, sometimes if a person don't know what to do, the best thing is to just stand still . . . and I guarantee you'd have something out here you wouldn't find on every corner."

She asks him with her eyes.

"I may not amount to much some ways, but I am a good friend."

Roslyn, touching his hand: "Thanks."

Gay, encouraged, quickly puts the car in gear: "Let me take you back, and you get your things. . . ." He drives onto the highway with heightened urgency. "Try it for a week, see what happens." They drive for a moment. "You ever hear the story of the city man out in the country? And he sees this farmer sittin' on his porch, and he says, 'Mister, do you know how I can get back to town?' And the fella says, 'Nope.' And the city man says, 'Well can you tell me how to get to the post office?' And the fella says, 'Nope.' 'Well, do you know how to get to the railroad station?' 'Nope.' 'Mister,' he says, 'you sure don't know much, do you?' And the farmer on the porch says, 'Nope. But I ain't lost.' "

They laugh together. A certain reserve dissolves in her, as she senses a delicacy in his feeling, an unwavering attention on her. Even when he turns away she feels herself in the center of his gaze.

She asks: "Don't you have a home?"

"Sure. Never was a better one, either."

"Where is it?"

"Right here."

With a gesture of his head he indicates the open country. She looks out the window for a house on the moonlit land, but seeing only the deserted hills she again faces his profile, drawn by his self-containment. She turns back to the night outside, trying to touch a point of rest in the vastness there.

FOUR

The end of night. Stars recede and go out, the sun's rim appears above the sea of hills, and the sky swiftly catches fire, sucking the vision of the eye toward the circular horizon and an earth in peace. Bird songs as clear as the air whistle the sun back into the sky. The eye tires of distances and seeks detail, and rapacity emerges; a rabbit hops from under a sage bush and a shadow passes over it. A hawk, serene, floats in narrowing circles above. The bird songs become jagged and strident. Swallows from nowhere dive at the soaring hunter to drive him off. A butterfly lights on a stone and a chameleon's tongue flicks out and takes it.

The sunlight moves into the bedroom of Guido's house, where Roslyn is asleep. The screaming of the birds seems to be penetrating her dreams; her face tenses and one fist begins to close. The empty pillow beside her head is dented.

The door to the living room opens and Gay stands there looking down at her, his gaze fingering the outlines of her body under the sheet. The picture of Guido and his wife is gone from over the bed, only the hook remaining. There is desire in Gay's face and the scent of her body still clings to his, but his eyes are searching as though through a mist emanating from her. Some wonder has taken place and is still unfolding itself within him, an unforetold consequence of pleasure. Unconsciously he smooths his hair back and in the gesture is a worry that he is not quite young any more.

She stirs under his stare and now opens her eyes, and he comes and knee-bends beside the bed. As her eyes open he leans in and kisses her. She seems for a moment not to know where she is. Then she smiles, and her eyes look around the room and she stretches. "Boy, I'm hungry!"

"Come on out, I got a surprise."

He walks out of the room. She sits up, her face showing a pleasurable anticipation, and she starts out of bed.

Gay goes to the stove and turns over some eggs in a pan. Near him is a kitchen table set for two. He turns and sees Roslyn in a terry-cloth robe emerging from the bedroom doorway.

She looks about in surprise. "You been *cleaning*?"

She moves, sees the table set, the breakfast sizzling on the stove, and in a vase a few wild flowers. Something outside the door catches her eyes. She looks and sees a mop standing in an empty pail among the weeds. Now she turns to him. She is moved by this effort. She hurries toward him at the stove. "Here, let me cook."

"Just sit down, it's all done."

He dishes out eggs for both of them and sits opposite her. She stares at him. He starts eating.

"You always do this?"

"Uh-uh. First time for me."

"Really and truly?"

Gay nods; his having gone out of himself is enough.

She starts eating. "Oooo! It's delicious!"

She eats ravenously. He watches with enjoyment. "You really go all out, don't you? Even the way you eat. I like that. Women generally pick."

In reply she smiles and returns to eating, and it joins them for a moment. Now she looks up at him and says with a full mouth: "The air makes you hungry, doesn't it?"

He laughs softly. Now he is sipping his coffee. He lights a cigarette, always trying to sound her.

She eats like one who has starved. Now she stops for a breath. "I love to eat!" Happily she looks around the room. "I'd never know it was the same house. It even smells different."

Suddenly she goes around the table and kisses his cheek. "You like me, huh?"

He draws her down to his lap, kisses her on the mouth, holds her with his head buried in her. She pats his neck, an uneasiness rising into her face mixed with her happiness. He relaxes his hold. She gets up, walks to the doorway, looks out at the endless hills, the horizon, the empty sky.

"Birds must be brave to live out here. Especially at night." She turns to him, explaining. "Whereas they're so small, you know?"

"M-m."

Roslyn, almost laughing: "You think I'm crazy?"

"Uh-uh. I just look that way 'cause I can't make you out."

"Why?"

"I don't know. . . . You got children?"

She shakes her head. Some embarrassment seems to have risen in her at the question; she turns out again, and seeing a butterfly lighting on the threshold, does a knee-bend and holds out her finger toward it but it flies off. She spreads out on her stomach with her head in the doorway. Now she glances back at him and decides to answer him.

"I didn't want children. Not with him."

"He did, though, huh?"

"Children supposedly bring you together. But what if they don't, you know? Because I've known couples, so-called happily married, and one time"—she turns to him, rolling onto her side— "the wife was actually in the hospital to have the baby and he was calling me up. I mean *calling me up.* And they're still supposed to be happily married."

"I guess you believe in true love, don't you?"

"I don't know, but somebody ought to invent where you can't have kids unless you love each other. Because kids know the difference. I always knew." Suddenly, even cheerfully: "If you want to go anywhere I don't mind being alone."

Gay comes over to her and knee-bends beside her, runs his fingers through her hair. "I look like I want to leave?"

"I just want you to do what you feel like."

"I never saw anything like it."

"What?"

"You ain't kiddin'. Even when you're kiddin', you ain't kiddin'."

She laughs. "Most people don't like it."

"Makes me feel peaceful." He sits on the floor. For a moment they are silent. "You know, they come out here from New York, Chicago, St. Louis—and find them a cowboy. Cowboy's supposed to be dumb, y'know, so they'll tell him everything. And they'll do everything, everything they couldn't do back home. And it's pitiful."

"Why is it pitiful?"

"Cowboy's laughin' at them and they don't know it. Sure is nice to meet somebody who's got respect for a man."

"You ever think of getting married again?"

"Oh, I've thought of it lots of times, but never in daylight."

She laughs easily, recognizing his nature, and he grins in admission of it.

He comes to a complete stillness, and whatever strategic quality structured their questions and answers falls away. His direct, unwavering gaze awakens a wisp of fear in her. "I'll tell you this, though. I wouldn't know how to say good-bye to you, Roslyn. It surprises me."

The silence suddenly seems like an onrushing wave that will smother her. She reaches thankfully for his hand, but her eyes are growing distant, protecting her.

He looks around at the room. "There'd be a lot to do around this place if you were going to stay awhile."

She is on her feet, drawing him up by the hand. "Let's go in the sun!"

They drop down to the ground from the threshold and walk through the weeds reflectively, hand in hand.

"You got respect for a man. I can't stand these women all the time sayin' what they would do and what they wouldn't do."

She laughs.

"And they go and do it anyway."

They sit on the lumber pile. She looks up at the blue, cloudless sky. "I really make you peaceful?"

He nods. "I sure wish I knew whether you were stayin' or goin'."

She bends to a pebble and cleans the dirt off it. "When I know myself I'll tell you. Okay? Let's just live—like you said in the bar?" Apologetically, with almost a laugh: "I don't know where I am yet—you know?"

She gets off the lumber and her eye happens to fall on a cement block in the weeds. Grateful for even this small escape, she almost dances over to it. "Look! Couldn't we use this for a step?"

He walks over and picks up the block. "Just might at that." He goes the few yards to the front door and sets the block under it. "There now!"

"Let me try it." She hurries and runs up the step into the house, then turns and hops down again. "It's perfect! I can come in and I can go out." Again she jumps up into the house and out again, and her pure enthusiasm moves him, and he laughs with the surprise of a youth. She senses his naive, genuine feeling, and with sudden gratitude and hope cries out: "Oh, you're a dear man, Gay!" He kisses her speaking mouth as she once more comes dancing out of the doorway.

FIVE

There were weeds around the house, hunks of dried cement, and scabs of bare ground. Now Gay is hoeing in a new vegetable garden nearby and flowers have been planted around the rocks, a fallen fence has been repaired, and a hose is spouting water over new grass. Sweat is dripping from his chin as he works the hoe around young vegetable plants. A deep hum in the sky raises his head. The sound grows. He turns in a circle.

Roslyn appears in the doorway, then comes down toward him, carrying a pitcher of lemonade and a glass. The roar is descending on them, and as she reaches him a small biplane zooms over the ridge of the house, waggling its wings. Gay yells: "Guido!" and waves. The plane swings around in a curve over the falling valley and she waves with him. It disappears.

Roslyn: "Where's he going?"

Gay: "Sssh!" He listens. She is puzzled. "He might be gonna land back there. There's a place." They listen. Silence. "I guess not. Probably just sayin' hello."

"Here, have some lemonade."

"Thanks." He takes it and drinks and she sits on a stone.

"What does he do, just fly around?"

He hands back the glass and picks a splinter out of his palm. "He might be goin' for eagles. Now and again the ranchers hire Guido to shoot eagles."

"Why?"

"They kill a lot of lambs. He gets fifty bucks a bird. It's nice work."

"Why doesn't he ever come around? I hope he's not mad at me."

"Oh, no. Women don't mean too much to Guido. He's probably been layin' around readin' his comic books, that's all."

He works the ground again. Squatting on the stone, she seems to join the sun and the earth in staring at him, watching his hoe awakening the soil around the plants. He senses an importance for her in his expertness, and he winks down at her.

She smiles and breaks her stare. "I like you, Gay."

"That's good news."

"You like me?"

"Well, it's close to ninety degrees out here, and I'm hoein' a garden for the first time since I was ten years old, so I guess I must like you pretty good."

She reaches out and touches a plant. "I never really saw anything grow before. How tiny those seeds were—and still they know they're supposed to be lettuces!"

"You say the damnedest things, you know that?"

They laugh quietly. He works the ground. She looks off now at the distant hills. She is almost content; she knows she might well be content but something gnaws at her, and she listens to it.

"In Chicago everybody's busy."

He glances at her; he doesn't quite understand what she means, but the feeling is a welcoming one, so he lets it go.

"You ever get lonesome for your children?"

For a moment he works in silence; it might be reticence or a bad recollection. She starts to change the subject but he speaks.

"I see them couple of times a year. They come whenever I'm in a rodeo. I'm a roper." He works for a moment, bends, and tosses a rock out of the garden. "I do get lonesome. Sure."

"They must like you."

"I guess they do. My daughter's almost your size now. You size twelve?"

"Uh-huh."

"So's she. I bought her a dress for Christmas. Size twelve."

Effortlessly she jumps up and goes to him; her movement is imperative and surprises him. She embraces him and kisses him passionately. Her face is very serious, nearly in pain. He lets the hoe drop from his hand. Roslyn sees he is puzzled. "Go ahead. Work." She returns to the stone and sits. He resumes hoeing. "What happened; you just stop loving your wife?"

He speaks out of vivid memory and it is discomfiting to go into. "Well . . . I come home one night and find her wrapped up in a car with a fella. Turned out to be one of my real old friends, too. Cousin of mine, matter of fact."

"Huh! And you didn't have any idea, before?"

The intensity of a blush tightens his eyes.

"God, no! In those days I thought you got married, and that was it. But nothin's it. Not forever."

"That's what I could never get used to—everything's always changing, isn't it?"

Gay rests on the hoe, looking down at her. "You been fooled an awful lot, haven't you?"

With a certain shame that is without self-pity, she whispers: "Yes."

"Well, let's just see if it turns out different this time. You're not going anywhere?"

"I'm here."

"Well, let's leave it that way for now. Okay?"

"How dear you are! You didn't get mad at me."

She kisses him again quickly, then, filled with an unspeakable relief, a sense of somehow having been pardoned and accepted, she clasps her hands together with her face toward the sky, her whole body on tiptoe. "I love this whole state!"

She laughs at herself and he grins in surprise. She picks up his hoe and hands it to him as though to keep the present image of him from vanishing. "Here. I love to see a man working around his house."

But his eye has caught something on the ground. He bends to a plant. "Now what have we here?"

He unfolds the leaves of a nibbled lettuce. Now he turns about and sees several more damaged plants farther up the row. He scans the brushy borders of the garden.

"It's plain old rabbit, and I'm gonna get him!" He drops his hoe and starts toward his truck beside the house, calling, "Margaret! Come here now!"

The dog appears around a corner, alert and eager. Gay goes to his truck and takes a shotgun out from behind the seat, then a handful of shells. He is loading the gun when Roslyn comes to him, still carrying the lemonade pitcher. She is trying to appear smiling, but her anxiety is clear.

"Maybe they won't eat any more."

Gay, busy with his gun, eager for the kill, speaks rapidly of what he knows: "No, ma'am. Once they zeroed in on that garden it's them or us. There won't be a thing left by the end of the week."

He starts past her with his gun. She touches his arm. She is trying to suppress her anxiety and it thins her voice. "Couldn't we wait another day and see? I can't stand to kill anything, Gay."

"Honey, it's only a rabbit."

"But it's alive, and . . . it doesn't know any better, does it?"

"Now you just go in the house and let me—"

She grasps his arm and her adamance astounds him. "Please, Gay! I know how hard you worked—"

"Damn right I worked hard!" He points angrily at the garden and tries to laugh. "I never done that in my life for anybody! And I didn't do it for some bug-eyed rabbit!"

He takes off toward the garden, the eager dog at his heel. She tries to turn back to the house, but is driven to follow him. A little breathless now, with the ice-filled lemonade pitcher still clinking in her hand: "Gay, please listen."

Gay turns on her now, smiling, but his eyes full of anger. "You go in the house now and stop bein' silly!"

"I am not silly!"

He starts off again, she calls: "You have no respect for me!"

Gay turns, suddenly furious, red-faced.

She pleads now: "Gay, I don't care about the lettuce!"

"Well, *I* care about it! How about some respect for me?"

A sound from behind the house turns them both. Gay walks a few steps toward one corner when, from a trail that climbs the hill behind the house, Guido appears, helping Isabelle along. She is no longer wearing a sling, but her arm is still bandaged.

Roslyn runs toward her with high relief and joy. "Isabelle, Guido, how are you?"

Isabelle: "Dear girl!"

The women embrace. Gay comes and shakes Guido's hands, happy at this visit. "How you been, fella? We never heard you land."

Isabelle holds Roslyn before her. "My, you look thrivin'!"

Guido has been glancing at the place, and now walks to get a better vantage. "Am I in the right place?" His voice cracks into a giggle.

Roslyn is extraordinarily sympathetic toward him, and Guido, despite the conventionality of his remarks, is moved by what he sees.

"Did you see the vegetable garden?" Roslyn turns to draw in Gay and even to give him preeminence. "Gay did it. Took him a whole week just to get the soil turned over."

Gay walks up beside her, and now that her feeling for him has returned he puts an arm around her waist. With wry pride: "Mowed the grass and put in them flowers, too. Even got your windows unstuck, and your fireplace don't smoke any more."

Guido turns from Gay to Roslyn. There is a subtle resentment toward both of them, but at the same time his eyes seem charged with a vision beyond them. "Roslyn, you must be a magician. The only thing this boy ever did for a woman was to get out the ice cubes."

They all laugh, trying to obliterate his evident uneasiness.

Roslyn, pointing to the outdoor furniture and taking Guido's arm: "We got chairs! Come, sit down!"

Gay intercepts them. "Let's show him the inside. Wait'll you see this, Guido! I've moved the furniture around so many times I'm gettin' long ears."

He and Guido move together toward the doorway. Roslyn and Isabelle follow behind. The men go into the house.

Isabelle: "Darling, you look so lovely! You found yourself, haven't you?"

Roslyn tries to dispel her own hesitation and ends by hugging Isabelle. "I'm so glad you came! Look, we have a step now."

She helps Isabelle into the house, Isabelle giving a marveling look at the flower bed beside the step as she mounts up.

"Watch your arm—how is it?"

"It's still weak as a bird's wing, but—" Entering the living room, she breaks off. "Well, I never in my life . . ."

Guido and Isabelle look at each detail in the room. Indian blankets cover the formerly bare studs; wild flowers brighten the tables and window sills; the furniture is rearranged, cleaned; the newly curtained windows are no longer smeared with dust and cobwebs; and the fireplace is all white. There is a feeling here of a shelter.

Tears flow into Isabelle's eyes. "Well! Huh! My—it's magical!" She looks at Roslyn, then she addresses Gay, almost rebuking him. "I just hope you know that you have finally come in contact with a real woman." She suddenly throws her arms around Roslyn. "Oh, my darling girl!"

"Come, see the bedroom. Come, Guido." Roslyn pulls them both to the bedroom. "I hope you don't mind we changed things around. . . ."

Gay, with an excitement previously unknown to him, opens the refrigerator and takes out cubes. Roslyn, Guido, and Isabelle enter the bedroom; it too is transformed, repainted, brightly curtained, with a carpet on the floor, a few botanical pictures on the walls, a dressing table, a bright spread on the bed. Guido looks about and his eyes fall on the place above the bed where the picture of himself and his dead wife had been. A print of a Western landscape hangs there now.

Roslyn sees the direction of his gaze. "Oh! I put your picture in the living room!"

"Uh-huh. Put a closet in?"

"Gay did it."

She swings the door of the closet open to show him. Inside the door half a dozen photos of her are tacked up. They are girlie photos for the doorway of a second-class nightclub, herself in net tights, on her back, in bizarre costumes. She realizes only now, partly by the flush on his face as he sees the photos, that she has shown them to him.

"Oh, they're stupid, don't look at them!" She closes the door. He looks embarrassed for her, perplexed. "Gay put them up for a joke. Come. Let's have a lot of drinks!"

She shepherds them into the living room and goes on to the kitchen to spread crackers around a piece of cheese on a platter. Gay is coming to them with drinks.

Guido's face is flushed as he strives against his envy. "Man, you sure got it made this time."

Roslyn calls from the kitchen area with high joy: "Sit down, everybody. I got wonderful cheese. It's so nice to have company!" They are dispersing to the couch and chairs, but she rushes to Guido, who is about to sit on the couch. "No! Sit in the big chair." Leading him—he is embarrassed—to the most imposing chair in the room: "This must have been your chair, wasn't it?"

"Matter of fact it was. I did all my studying in this chair. When I was still ambitious." He sits stiffly, like one who feels vaguely threatened at being served.

She rushes back to the kitchen area. "Maybe you'll get ambitious again, you can't tell. I'll get you some cheese." She gets the cheese tray from the kitchen counter and, returning to Guido, points with it toward his wedding photograph on a table. "I put your picture there—is that all right?"

"Oh, you don't have to keep it out, Roslyn."

"Why? It's part of the house, Guido. Y'know?" She sets the tray down and sits beside Gay on the couch, taking a drink from the table where he set it for her. Now they are settled. "I mean, it's still your house. Here, Isabelle, rest your arm on this." She leaps up with a cushion from the couch and sets it under Isabelle's bandaged arm.

"Oh, don't bother with me, dear."

"Why? Might as well be comfortable."

Roslyn goes back to the couch and sits beside Gay, as Guido speaks. His voice is suddenly portentous. "I'm going to tell you something, Roslyn." With a strained, self-deprecating grin that lowers a driving pressure onto his words: "I hope you don't mind, Gay, because I love this girl, and you might as well know it."

Putting a proprietary arm loosely around Roslyn's shoulders, Gay grins. "Well, you'd be out of your head if you didn't."

Guido faces Roslyn. A formality sets in that is faintly self-pitiful and oddly dangerous. "I spent four years in the war: two tours. Fifty missions. And every time I came back to base I started to design this house. But somehow I could never get it to look like my idea of it. And now it almost does. You just walk in, a stranger out of nowhere, and for the first time it all lights up. And I'm sure you know why, too."

Roslyn, her voice faint in the face of his curiously intense feeling: "Why?"

"Because you have the gift of life, Roslyn. You really want to live, don't you?"

His remorseless sincerity silences the room.

Roslyn: "Doesn't everybody?"

Guido glances at the picture. "No, I think most of us ... are just looking for a place to hide and watch it all go by."

Isabelle: "Amen!"

Guido, raising his glass, persisting in his formality: "Here's to your life, Roslyn—I hope it goes on forever."

She quickly reaches over and clicks her glass with his. "And yours. And yours, Isabelle." And with the faintest air of an afterthought: "And yours, Gay."

We notice the slightest flicker in Gay, an awareness that he has been placed slightly to one side. They drink.

Roslyn moves closer to Gay. "Gay did all the work, you know."

"Yeah, and the rabbits are really enjoyin' it, too." He grins, and only now puts his arm around her.

Guido sees the reconciliation of a conflict in them and he feigns ignorance, but there is condescension in his question: "You think you could break away from paradise long enough to do some mustangin'?"

"Mustangin'!" Gay's look sharpens. "Now you're sayin' something. You been up to the mountains?"

"I took a quick look up there this morning. Spotted fifteen horses."

"That's not bad. I'd sure like to lay my hand on a rope again. What do you say?"

Isabelle turns to Roslyn, shaking her head. "I will never understand cowboys. All crazy about animals, but the minute they got nothin' to do they go runnin' up the mountains to bother those poor wild horses." Passionlessly, to the men: "Shame on you!"

Roslyn: "Horses?"

Gay: "Sure, honey. Nevada mustang. Used to ship them all over the United States once upon a time. Mostly gone now, though." He turns back to Guido: "We'll have to pick up another man."

"Dayton Rodeo's on today. We could probably find a fella down there."

"Hey, that's an idea! Roslyn, you never saw a rodeo."

Isabelle: "Oh, you gotta see a rodeo."

Roslyn: "I'd love to. If you come with us, Iz."

"I'm all set."

Roslyn springs up. "I'll get dressed up!" She quickly looks at Gay. "Let's have some fun today!"

Gay: "Now that's a girl! Get goin' right now." He gets up and shoos her toward the bedroom, and as she starts away he grabs her hand and she turns back to him, her face warmed by the return of his connection with her. "Honey, when you smile it's like the sun comin' up."

He lets her go and she flies toward the bedroom.

SIX

The four are silent in the station wagon as they drive into the sun on the empty highway. Gay drives with one hand resting on Roslyn's bright silken dress where it flows off her thigh.

Behind them Guido blinks at time passing by. "I'd like to have stopped home and got cleaned up a little." He feels his stubble, glancing ahead at Roslyn's brushed hair.

She turns back to him. "Why? You look nice, Guido. Doesn't he, Iz?"

"Better than a lot I've known."

Guido smiles moodily. "You're just one mass of compliments, Isabelle. Hey! Hold it!" He grabs Gay's shoulder, at the same time spinning around in his seat to look at something they have passed. "Stop!"

Gay brakes the car, and Guido points back toward a bar and gas station. "The guy next to that phone booth. I think it's that kid from California. Back up!"

Gay turns and cranes out the window. "What kid?"

"That what's-his-name—the rodeo rider was working the Stinson Rodeo with you last year."

"Perce Howland?" Gay shouts and backs the car along the highway, fast.

Perce Howland is sitting on his saddle, his back against a glass-enclosed phone booth beside the highway. He is resting his chin on his hands, his eyes staring at the bare ground. Noticing the reversing car, he looks toward it with sleepy eyes. He is in his late twenties, a bucking-horse rider—which is to say a resident of nowhere, who sleeps most often in his clothes, rich and broke in the same afternoon, celebrated in the lobbies of small hotels where a month earlier he might have been thrown out for loitering. He does not yet have the cauliflower ear, the missing front teeth, or the dazed eye of his tribe, but his face has been sewn and his bones broken.

Glancing up at the approaching car on the deserted highway, his eyes already show their expectant, seeking quality. There is a naiveté in his strangely soft, gentle movements, a boyishness which is itself a force.

A great glad smile opens on his face as he sees through the side window of the car coming to a halt before him. He gets up and goes to the car. "Gay Langland! Why, you old buzzard, you!"

Gay grabs his arm. "What are you sittin' out here for?"

"I hitched a ride to the Dayton Rodeo but the fella changed his mind and left me here. Hey, Pilot, how you doin'? Boy, it's sure good to see you two scoundrels!"

Gay draws Roslyn closer to his window. "Like you to meet this fella, Roslyn. This is Perce Howland."

She nods.

Perce removes his hat. "Well, old Gay is sure comin' up in the world. How do, ma'am." He shakes her hand; there is a certain embarrassed shyness on him. He regards her as one of Gay's passing divorcées.

Guido starts to introduce him to Isabelle when the bell rings inside the phone booth. Hurrying toward it, he carefully puts his hat on as though he were to face someone in there. " 'Scuse me, I been tryin' to call home but they keep puttin' me into Wyoming!"

He steps into the booth and closes the door. "Hello, Ma? Perce, Ma."

The four in the car sit in silence, listening to his muffled voice. Perce's emotion quickly reaches them, holding them still.

"Hello? You there? It's Perce, Ma. I'm okay. No, I'm in Nevada now. I *was* in Colorado. Won another bull-ridin', Ma. Hundred dollars. Yeah, real good rodeo. I was goin' to buy you a birthday present with it but I was comin' out of my boots. . . . No, Ma, I haven't been in a hospital since I told you. I just bought some boots, that's all, Ma." Astounded: "What in the world would I want to get married for? *I only bought some—*" He breaks off. "Whyn't you try believin' me once in a while, make everybody feel better, huh?" She is obviously berating him. "Okay, okay, I'm sorry." Trying to bring brightness back: "They give me a silver buckle on top of the prize money!" Holding the buckle of his belt toward the phone: "Got a buckin' horse on it and my entire name wrote out underneath. Ain't you proud?" His smile goes; he touches his cheeks. "No, no, my face is all healed up, good as new. You will too recognize me! Okay, operator! Ma? say hello to Frieda and Victoria, will ya?" A silence. He is being severely instructed and his patience is waning. He opens the door for air. Sweat is burning his eyes. "Okay, say hello to him, too. No, Ma, it just slipped my mind, that's all. . . . *Okay,* I'm sayin' it now." Near an outburst: "Well, you married him, I didn't! Tell him hello for me. Maybe I'll call you Christmas. . . . Hello? Hello!" He is cut off, but with a deeply troubled mumble he adds: "God bless you, too."

His somber look is disappearing as he comes out on the sidewalk. He is a little embarrassed at having shown so much emotion before these others, and he tries to laugh, shaking his head and mopping his face. "You wouldn't be goin' down to the Dayton Rodeo, would you?"

Guido: "Why? You entered?"

Perce: "I aim to if I can get a ride out there. . . . And if I can raise ten bucks for the entrance fee. . . . And if I can get a loan of a buckin' horse when I get down there." He laughs. "I'm real equipped!"

Gay: "How'd you like to do some mustangin' with us? We need a third man."

Perce: "Boy, you still flyin' that five-dollar airplane?"

Guido: "Lot safer than a buckin' horse."

Perce: "Lot higher, too, comin' down."

Roslyn: "Your plane that bad?"

Gay: "Now don't start worryin' about him, honey."

Roslyn, laughing: "Well, I just asked."

Gay, to Perce and Guido: " 'Cause if she starts worrying, she can *worry.*"

Perce is surprised and drawn toward her intensity. "You got a right to if you ever seen that DC-six-and-seven-eighths he flies. I didn't know they still had mustangs around here."

Guido: "I spotted fifteen this morning."

Gay, quickly: "Well, there might be more, though."

Perce: "What're you gonna get outa fifteen?" He laughs, not knowing why. "Like if there was a thousand or somethin' it'd make some sense. But just to go up there and take fifteen horses ... I mean the *idea* of it, y'know? Just kinda hits me sideways."

His sensitivity seems to move over into Roslyn's face. She seems grateful he is there.

Gay: "It's better than wages, ain't it?"

Perce: "Hell, anything's better than wages."

Gay: "Tell you what. We'll drive you down to the rodeo, put up ten for the entrance fee, and I'll get a loan of some good stock for you down there. You come along with us tomorrow morning and help us run some mustang."

Perce thinks for a moment, then says: "And you buy a bottle of good whiskey right in there so I'm primed up for the rodeo."

Gay: "Just wait right there." He starts into the bar, putting his hand in his pocket.

Perce turns to Roslyn, intense curiosity and excitement in his face. He cannot place her. "You an ... old friend of Gay's?"

"Pretty old."

He nods slightly, and awkwardly turns, as though escaping the insoluble, and goes to get his saddle to put it into the car.

SEVEN

They are driving through a new kind of territory. There is not even sage here, but only a sterile white alkali waste. It is midday.

Gay is at the wheel, Roslyn beside him, Guido and Perce in the rear seat. Guido has a whiskey bottle tilted to his lips. They are all a little high. Guido passes the bottle to Roslyn over her shoulder; she silently drinks, then hands it over to Gay, who takes a short one and hands it back. Guido never takes his brooding eyes from Roslyn. She makes a half-turn in her seat and gives the bottle to Perce, who drinks and then holds the bottle on his knee, staring out at the white waste going by.

Their eyes are narrowed against the harsh light. They have been driving a long time. Now Gay overtakes a horse-van trailer hitched to a new car, and as they pass it Perce leans out his window and waves at the Stetson-hatted cowboy driver. Then he speaks to Roslyn, resuming a conversation that had died out.

Perce: "I've broke this arm twice in the same place. You don't do that fakin' a fall, y'know. I don't fake anything. Some of these riders'll drop off and lay there like they're stone dead. Just putting on a show, y'know. I don't fake it, do I, Gay?"

Gay: "That's right. You're just a natural-born damn fool."

Roslyn: "Why! That's wonderful . . . to be that way?" To Perce: "I know what you mean. I used to dance in places . . . and everybody said I was crazy. I mean I really tried, you know? Whereas people don't know the difference."

Guido, who has been looking at her feverishly, as though his several concepts of her were constantly falling to pieces: "What kind of dancing you do?"

Roslyn, with embarrassment: "Oh . . . just what they call interpretive dancing. Nightclubs. You know."

Perce sticks his head in between her and Gay. "I went to a nightclub once—in Kansas City. Name of it was 'The Naked Truth.' And they wasn't kiddin', either!"

He laughs, but an uneasiness on her face dampens him.

Gay calls out, "Here we come!"

Their attention is drawn to the first glimpse of the town. A long, gradual curve of highway lies directly ahead, an arc of concrete raised above the valley bottom of white gypsum. At the distant end of the road is a row of wooden buildings and beyond them the mountains piled up like dumps of slag the color of soot. From this distance the desolation is almost supernatural, the mind struggling with the question of why men would ever have settled here. There is no tree, no bush, no pool of water. To right and left the blank white flatland stretches away, dampened here and there by acid stains of moisture left from the spring rains. Gradually a perverse beauty grows out of the place. It is so absolute, its ugliness is so direct and blatant as to take on honesty and the force of something perfectly defined, itself without remorse or excuse, a town set up beside a railroad track for the purpose of loading gypsum board from the nearby plant.

Gay and Guido have been here many times for the yearly rodeo, Perce and Roslyn never. As the road straightens and they can see into the town's interior, the silence which has held them is broken by Gay explaining, with a grin, that this is the last wide-open town in the West. There is no police force and practically no law. Except for this one day there are never strangers here, and most of the natives are related closely enough to settle disputes among themselves. He is grinning but he is not making light of his instruction to her to stay close to him. There is no help here; there will not necessarily be trouble, but there has been, and they still carry sidearms in this place, and use them. "Like in the movies," Roslyn says, her eyes wide with incipient laughter, but they do not laugh—not entirely because of fear but from a sense of absurdity,

the kind of absurdity so senseless as to rise to a logic, a law, a principle of destruction, as when one is knocked down by a bicycle and
killed on the way to a wedding. Without warning, they realize that
the town is packed with people, perhaps two thousand, a mob boiling around on the highway between the row of buildings and the
railroad tracks. Its uproar strikes at them through the car windows,
a clash and rumble of humanity enslaved by its own will a hundred
miles out in this sun-stricken powderland.

Gay slows the car to avoid the first humans, men standing in
the middle of the highway, talking, looking into the windows as
they pass. Now there are cars parked along the roadside, jalopies
mostly, and some recent models caked with talc. The door of one of
them swings open; a girl of twelve runs out with a little boy, and
they dash toward the dense mob as though they knew where they
were going. An old man stands peeing in the sun and chewing a
wad of tobacco as he turns with the car passing him by. Gay can
barely move ahead now as the car is engorged by the crowd.

Perce suddenly sticks his head out of the window. "There's old
Rube! Hey, Rube! Whatcha say!" Rube waves back. "Hey, there's
old Bernie! Whatcha say, Bernie!" Bernie waves back. Perce draws
his head into the car and leans in between Gay and Roslyn. "Hey,
they got some real riders here today! Hope I draw me a good horse!"

Gay: "Just come out in one piece, now, 'cause you gotta go
mustangin' tomorrow."

Roslyn is looking at Perce's face, a few inches from her eyes;
she sees the pure lust for glory in him. A new emotion flows from
her toward him—a kind of pity, a personal involvement in his coming trial.

He jerks away to call out the window again: "There's Franklin!
Hey, Franklin boy!"

The car moves into the heart of the crowd.

There are cowboys in working clothes, and many in the tight
shirts and jeans they saw in movies. There are many kids, dressed
like their elders. There are farmers in overalls, women in Sunday
best. A cowboy is trying to back a horse out of a little trailer van
right into the stream of traffic; three girls not yet sixteen walk in
front of a gang of cowboys who are trying to make them; a mother

holds onto her teenage daughter's wrist as she pushes through the crowd. Two overweight deputies, with .45s hanging from their hips, bounce a Cadillac up and down to unhook its bumper from a battered pickup truck behind it. In the pickup is a gang of kids with a farmer driving. In the Cadillac, its convertible top down, are three betting types and a show girl, all bouncing up and down and striving to retain their dignity and their sunglasses.

Above the people and the cars, mixed with their roar, is a cacophony of jazz; each bar's jukebox is pouring its music into the street, one number changing to another as the car passes the screen doorways. An enormously loud voice from a nearby public-address system announces something indistinguishable; then there is the sound of a crowd roaring as in a stadium—the rodeo arena is in action at the far end of the street.

Roslyn suddenly turns to watch an Indian standing perfectly still while the crowd pours around him. He is staring off at something—or at nothing—with a bundle of clothes under his arm.

Gay nudges his car to the left, even letting the fenders press people out of the way, and pulls up facing one of the bars. He takes Roslyn's hand and draws her out of the car past the steering wheel; the four, with their arms raised against the crush of people, squeeze into the saloon. The dog sits up in the front seat, looking around calmly, seeing everything, turning her head from one familiar face to another. An old man comes out the screen door, sees the dog, and goes to the window to look in at her. She looks at him. He is bleary. His shirtfront is streaked with tobacco juice. Deep blackheads swarm around his nose. He reaches into his pocket and takes out coins from which powdery talc sifts down. He tosses a quarter to the dog and she sniffs it on the seat and looks back at him in puzzlement. He winks at her and disappears into the crowd with his secret.

The sound of money clinking turns people around; a sweet little old lady is hurrying through the crowd, violently shaking a well-filled collection can. She wears a toque hat askew on her gray head and a brocade dress down to her shins. Something like "Oyez, oyez," is coming out of her voice box, and she is smiling wittily under incensed, climactic eyes. She pulls the screen door open and pushes into the saloon.

This bar is fifty feet long. The customers are ranked back to the opposite wall and order drinks from a distance the width of a hand-ball court. There is a spidery atmosphere of a hundred hands raised to pass drinks back and empties returning to the bar. Two juke-boxes are playing different records and a television set on high is speaking, its eye rolling in its head. Five bartenders face the mob, serving and collecting, grimly glancing right and left along the ma-hogany to ward off any attack upon the vertical platoon of bottles behind them. Overhead, reflected in the yardage of the mirror on the wall, a morose elkhead stares through the smoke. A printed sign hanging from a piece of twine around its neck reads, "Don't shoot this elk again," and the careful eye can see the bullet holes that drew sawdust instead of blood.

The old lady pushes up to a cowboy and his girl at the bar and shakes the can under their surprised faces.

Old lady: "Church Ladies' Auxiliary, Tom."

"Sure." He drops a coin in the collection can.

The old lady turns to his girl. "How about you, sinner?"

"Oh, Ma! I got no money yet!"

The old lady shakes the can at another prospect nearby. "Come on, Frank. Church Ladies' Auxiliary."

"You just got me in the bar next door."

"That'll larn you to stay put. Come on!"

He groans and puts in money.

Roslyn, Gay, Perce, Isabelle, and Guido, with drinks in hand which they can barely raise to their lips, are pressed together at the bar, standing in the paralyzing noise like people in a subway. A grizzled old man with startling silver hair forces his way through and hoists a seven-year-old boy onto the bar. Holding the boy's knees, he explains to Gay, "I gotta hold onto him tight or first thing y'know he run off to school."

Gay nods understandingly, and the old man smiles through his haze, "Hya, Coz, not many of us left."

"Well, things are tough all over, Pop."

The old man yells at the bartender: "Draft of pop for my grandson Lester!" He is full of holiday cheer and, taking a paddle-ball from the boy, he says to Gay: "Ever try one of these? Damned-est thing I ever saw. Stand clear, now!"

With which he swats away at the elusive ball, while people

around him shield their faces from his unpredictable blows. The bartenders come alert.

Roslyn has found room to get her glass to her lips and drinks fast, calling: "Hey, I can do that! Can I try?"

The old man, sensing action, offers her the paddle at once. "Betcha two dollars you can't do ten!"

Perce: "I'll take that! Go ahead, Roz!"

Roslyn, untwisting the rubber band: "Oh, I can do more than ten! I *think*!"

Pushing his back against the crowd, the old man spreads his arms. "Clear away, clear away, we got a bet goin'!"

News of a bet miraculously squeezes the crowd back, and a space opens around Roslyn. She starts to hit the ball and does it obviously well. She has a drink still in one hand. Perce counts each stroke, two dollars in his hand. By the time she gets to six, a cowboy yells at Perce: "Five bucks she don't do fifteen!"

Perce, nodding and still counting: "Nine, ten, eleven . . ."

Perce reaches toward the surprised old man, who hands him the two dollars.

Second cowboy: "Ten she don't make twenty!"

Perce: "Thirteen, fourteen, fifteen, sixteen, seventeen, eighteen, nineteen, twenty, twenty-one, two, three, four, five, six . . ." Perce collects from both cowboys, counting on. From all over the saloon voices call new bets and money passes in all directions.

"Ten here too!"

"Five here!"

"I'll take five!"

"Fifteen here!"

Roslyn is now working the ball with great earnestness, sipping her drink at the same time, an alcoholic distance spreading in her eyes. Isabelle, counting aloud with Perce, picks up her drink and takes a gulp and looks at it with disgust. She sees a bottle of whiskey and pours some into her glass, drinks, and sets it down. The little boy sitting on the bar beside her, his eyes fascinated at Roslyn's attack on the ball, lifts his pop glass—which Isabelle has just inadvertently spiked—drinks, and studies the new effect upon him, and tastes some more.

The crowd is roaring out Roslyn's count now. The little old lady, trying to push through the circle of men who have formed around Roslyn and Perce, manages to peep through the bodies, and her eyes fasten on the growing wad of money in Perce's upraised hand. With a new spurt of greedy determination she pushes through to Perce, who calls: "Thirty-six, thirty-seven, thirty-eight, thirty-nine, forty! Forty-one, forty-two . . ."

Suddenly she starts hitting the ball at the floor and receiving it back on the bounce. A roar of excited appreciation goes up at this new risk she is taking. Even the bartenders are on tiptoe, stretching to see over the crowd.

"Ten bucks she don't do seventy!"

Perce nods, takes the money without losing his count: "Fifty-four, fifty-five . . ."

A second cowboy suddenly steps out and pats Roslyn low on the back. Guido, standing beside Gay, looks and sees Gay's mild irritation. Gay now scans the faces in the crowd. The eyes around him are coursing Roslyn's body. Guido bursts out laughing: "She'll do anything!" and Gay sees in Guido's expression the same near-lewdness of some of the crowd. A new shout goes up.

Now she is hitting the ball on the bounce, and backhand, taking a drink at the same time. Perce is continuing his count at her side, absorbed, young, somehow at one with Roslyn as he urges her on with his counting. The old lady steps up close to Roslyn, calling into her ear as she shakes the collection can. "Play for the Lord! Steady, sinner!"

Roslyn, unnerved: "Please!"

Old lady to Perce, demanding the money in his hand: "Help the good work, boy, do it while the spirit's in ya."

Perce: "Seventy-one, seventy-two, *shut up,* four, *seventy-five* . . ."

A shout goes up at this new victory. Roslyn is now a foot from the second cowboy with her back to him, and he grabs her from behind and starts to kiss her. Gay is on him and is about to hit him when he is pulled away by others. Two bartenders leap the bar. Guido appears next to Gay and draws on his arm, grabbing Roslyn with his other hand; he pulls both of them toward the door.

The old man turns to his grandson on the bar, and is about to take the boy down when he notices the bemused look in his face. He takes the half-full glass out of his little hand, sniffs it, then tastes it. First surprise penetrates his fog, and then with a genuinely avaricious wheedling tone, "Lester!" he asks, bending down into the boy's somnolent face, "where'd you get the money?"

On the street outside, Gay draws Roslyn out of the mob into a space between two parked cars. Just behind them, Perce, Guido, and Isabelle are counting the money in Perce's hat. Moved by his protective passion, Roslyn clasps his face. "I'm sorry, Gay, I didn't mean to do it that long! But thanks for helping me! I embarrass you?"

The threat of losing her in the moments earlier, the lust of others for her, has wiped out his reserve. "I'd marry you."

Roslyn, with a sad and joyous mixture: "Oh, no, Gay, you don't have to! But thanks for saying that."

Perce bursts in, Guido behind him. "Hundred and forty-five dollars! Ain't she great, Gay? She is the greatest yet!"

With which Perce throws an arm around her as he puts the money in her hand. Instantly the old lady appears under Perce's arm, shaking the can.

Isabelle: "Don't shake that at me! I'm still payin' off this broken arm!" Suddenly Isabelle, seeing someone in the crowd, shouts, "Charles!" and runs into the passing mob.

The old lady, shaking the can under Roslyn's face, fixes her with her missionary stare. "Sinner! I can tell you want to make a big donation. You got it in the middle of your pretty eyes. You're lookin' for the light, sinner, I know you and I love you for your life of pain and sin. Give it to the one that understands, the only one that loves you in your lonely desert!"

At first amused, then drawn and repelled, then half-frightened, and yet somehow reached by this woman's mad desire to bless her, she starts to hand the old lady the whole wad of money.

But Gay intercepts. "She ain't sinned that much." He hands the old lady one bill. "Here's ten . . ." He gives her another. "And here's ten more to settle for the twenty."

Old lady: "Lord be praised! We're gonna buy a fence around the graveyard, keep these cowboys from pasturing their horses on the graves. Sweetheart, you've gone and helped our dead to rest in peace! Go reborn!"

Isabelle rushes up to Roslyn out of the crowd. "Guess who's here! Dear girl, guess who is here!"

"Who?"

"My husband! I couldn't believe it. They're on vacation."

"Oh. His wife too?"

"Sure! Clara. You remember my talkin' about Clara, she was my best friend? And she's sweeter than ever!"

Gay: "Sure must be, to make you so glad to see her."

"Oh, Charles could never've stayed married to me. I even lost the vacuum cleaner once." The men burst out laughing, and she joins them, and waves her arm toward her former husband, who is evidently somewhere deep in the crowd. "They still haven't found it! Come, you'll meet them."

Gay stops them. "Let's meet you later, Isabelle. We still got to get this boy a horse to ride."

"Okay, we'll be around someplace. But I won't be mustangin' with you—they're gonna stay at my house for a week." She reaches for Perce's hand and squeezes it. "Good luck, young fella!" Patting Roslyn's hand, she backs into the moving crowd, waving happily. "See you, dear girl!"

Pressed together by the surrounding crowd, the four move toward the end of the street and the rodeo arena. Perce puts his head between Gay and Roslyn. "Can I kiss her for luck?"

"Once."

Perce kisses her as they move.

Gay draws him away from her. "You don't need all that luck. Come on, let's get you registered." He starts off ahead with Perce, laughing over his shoulder to Roslyn. She waves to him as he vanishes into the crowd.

The rodeo arena is a homemade corral surrounded by a collapsing post-and-rail fence, with splintered bleachers three tiers high along one side. A chute of planks is at one end and near it a low tower for the judge. A sea of parked cars surrounds the area.

From the stands the only visible building is a small church leaning in the direction of the distant mountains, its cross of boards twisting under the weight of weather into the form of an X.

The stands are packed and the mob has surrounded the fence. There is always a certain threading movement of people looking for one another—fathers for their daughters, wives for husbands, fellows for girls, and loners from the hills who want only to move through the only crowd of strangers they will touch until the same time next year.

A rider on a bucking horse charges out of the chute. The timing judge in the tower, his stopwatch in his hand at the end of a heavy gold chain, drinks from a pint bottle, his eyes flicking from watch to rider. The contestant is staying on the black horse. It charges directly toward the fence and the crowd there clambers backward, and for a moment the Indian is left in the clear, watching impassively. The horse swerves away, the crowd surges back, and the Indian is lost among the people again.

Roslyn and Guido are in the stands. Guido looks on, half-interested. She is watching avidly. He turns and stares at her beside him, his eyes absorbing the molding of her face, her neck, her body.

The crowd roars suddenly, and people around them half-stand in their seats. Alarm shows in her face as she stands. The rider scoots from the horse's flying hooves.

"Gee, I didn't know it was so dangerous!"

Guido, deliberatively, as though declaring his determination toward her: "Same as everything else worth doing."

She looks at him with surprise. Whiskey and sun have dissolved his strategy, and he simply stares longingly into her eyes. She turns to see the outrider coming alongside the bucking horse and undoing its bucking strap.

"What'd he just take off?"

"Oh, that's the bucking strap. Grabs them where they don't like it. Makes them buck."

"Well, that's not fair!"

He starts to laugh, but her intensity stops him. "You couldn't have a rodeo otherwise."

"Well, then you shouldn't have a rodeo!"

The crowd suddenly roars and stands, and she and Guido rise, but he is staring at her with deep puzzlement as she turns toward the arena where the bucking horse has chased the rider over the fence. A few yards away Gay and Perce sit straddling the closed chute, their legs slung over the top. Now Gay looks at the people in the stands.

"I hope you're sober."

Perce, following Gay's eyes: "Hell, I've won prizes where I couldn't remember the name of the town." He sees Roslyn in the stands and waves. "There she is!"

Gay waves to her now and she stands up, waving her furred sweater. Guido raises his arm.

Perce, seeing her passionate encouragement, turns to Gay. "I wouldn't try to move in on you, Gay—unless you wouldn't mind."

Gay nearly blushes. "Boy—I'd mind."

They both laugh at this unwitting avowal of their conflict and Gay slaps Perce on the back with warmth as a horse is led into the chute at their feet.

"Well, here I go!"

Perce descends from the fence onto the restive horse with Gay lending a hand, and he looks up at Gay.

"My address is Black River—"

He is cut off by the public-address system.

Public-address system: "On a bucking horse, Perce Howland out of Black River, Wyoming!"

"California, not Wyoming!" he yells over his shoulder.

A cowboy pulls the bucking belt tight. The horse kicks the chute planks.

Gay: "You ready, boy?"

Perce: "Go! Go!"

Gay: "Open up!"

An attendant opens the gate; the horse charges out. The crowd roars. Perce is holding on. The horse bucks under him, high and wild.

In the stands Guido has come alive. "Go it, boy!"

Roslyn is looking on, torn between hope of Perce's victory and terror; she holds her hands to her ears as she watches.

The timing judge drinks, his stopwatch in his hand.

From the chute fence, Gay glances at Roslyn in the stands. She is watching with tears in her eyes. The horse leaps in close to where she is sitting, and for an instant she can see Perce's teeth bared with the tension of his fight as he is flung up and down, the sky over his head.

The horse is twisting Perce, wracking his body as it comes down on the packed earth. Now she shouts as though to rescue Perce, calling his name. She turns to Guido for help. He strikes the air with his fist, a look of near-rage on his face, a flow of animal joy that disconcerts her, and, more alone now than before with her terror, she turns back to the field.

A sudden roar goes up from the crowd, and Gay rises up on the fence with a look of what almost seems like joy on his face, but his rising movement is to help. Perce is being thrown. He lands on his face and lies still.

Gay jumps down from the fence and runs toward Perce. Guido is pushing his way down the bleacher rows to the field; Roslyn remains standing on her bench behind him, stretching to see over the crowd, staring and weeping, her face as blank as if she had been struck. Now she starts down the bleachers toward the field.

Gay reaches Perce and starts to lift him to his feet. Guido arrives and they half-carry Perce toward a gate in the fence, Guido clapping his hat onto his head.

Roslyn catches up with them as they emerge into an area of parked cars. An ambulance is standing in front of the church.

Roslyn: "Where's the doctor?"

Perce: "Where's my hat, Pa?"

Gay: "You got it on, Perce."

Perce suddenly pulls away and yells at Roslyn, who has grasped his arm.

Perce: "Lemme go, Frieda!"

Gay comes up to him, holding out his hand to calm him, "Take it easy, boy, she ain't your sister." Perce is staring, perplexed, at Roslyn. She is cold with fright. But they move him along again. They arrive at the ambulance. An attendant is waiting, an affable grin on his face. "Well now, you've been messin' around with the wrong end of a horse, haven't you?" He holds Perce's face, pressing his cheekbones in his hair-covered hands.

Roslyn: "Let him sit down."

She sits him on the edge of the ambulance floor. The attendant's movements do not quicken. She looks distrustfully at him.

Roslyn: "Are you a doctor?"

Perce starts to rise. "I don't want a doctor."

Attendant: "Hold it, boy. I'm no doctor. I'll just clean you up a little." He presses Perce down, wipes his hands on his trousers, and reaches into the ambulance for something.

Roslyn, with a growing feeling of helplessness: "Well, isn't there a doctor?"

The attendant reappears with a bottle of alcohol and a swab.

Gay: "Not for sixty miles."

Gay bends and looks closely at Perce's face as the attendant swabs it; then he straightens up. "He ain't bad hurt."

"How do you know? Let's take him!" She reaches down to lift Perce. "Come with me, I'll take you in my car."

Gay, forcefully, not too covertly taking her from Perce: "Now don't start runnin' things, Roslyn."

"He's your friend, isn't he? I don't understand anything!"

A loud yelp of pain from Perce turns her about; the attendant is pressing adhesive tape across the bridge of his nose. Perce delicately touches his nose as Gay bends down to him where he sits on the edge of the ambulance floor. "You all right, ain't you, Perce?" Perce exhales a breath of pain, then feels his nose.

"Perce, you all right?"

Perce blinks, looks up at Gay, still dazed. "Did I make the whistle?"

"Almost, boy. You done good, though."

"That was a rank horse. Wasn't it?"

"Oh, that was a killer. You done good."

Perce tries to stand, but falls forward onto his hands and knees. Roslyn quickly bends to lift him up.

Gay: "Leave him alone, Roz, he'll get up." He separates her from Perce, who remains for a moment on all fours, catching his breath.

In horror, in a sea of helpless nonunderstanding, she looks down at him. Now he raises himself with great difficulty to his feet. Guido hands him his hat, which has again fallen off. The public-address system erupts, incomprehensibly.

Perce: "Oh! That me?"

Gay: "Not yet. You still got a coupla minutes."

Roslyn: "What for?"

"He's got a bull to ride. Come on, Perce, walk yourself around a little bit."

Gay, putting Perce's arm over his shoulder, walks down an aisle of parked cars with him. Perce is not surefooted yet, but is getting steadier. They walk slowly, in the sea of steel.

Roslyn: "Guido, he's not going in there again!"

Guido, with an uncertain celebration of life's facts: "I guess he wants to ride that bull."

"But . . ." Frustrated, she runs to Gay and Perce and moves with them.

"Just let him walk it off, Roz, come on now." Gay presses her aside.

She has to squeeze in beside them, sometimes forced behind them by an obstructing fender. "What are you doing it for, Perce? Here, why don't you take what we won in the bar." Struggling with her purse to get money out, she tries to keep up with them. "You helped me win it, Perce, come on, take it. Look, it's over a hundred dollars. You don't have to go back in there!" He halts. She presses up to him. He is staring at her. She feels encouraged now. She gently touches his cheek, smiling pleadingly.

Perce: "I like ya to watch me now. I'm pretty good ridin' bulls."

"But why're you doing it?"

"Why, I put in for it, Roslyn. I'm entered."

The public-address system again erupts incomprehensibly.

Perce: "Get me up there, Gay, I'm just warmin' up!"

They start for the arena. She hurries along with them. Guido is following, still smiling at her concern. He is progressively drunker.

Roslyn: "Gay, please!"

But Perce and Gay continue moving toward the chutes.

Perce turns to her over his shoulder. "I like ya to watch me, Roslyn! Don't you be scared, now!"

Roslyn turns to Guido, who is standing beside her, as though for help. Beneath his troubled look she sees he is blandly accepting the situation. Reasonably, he says, "They don't mind getting busted up!" She turns quickly, scanning the world for help. No human being is in sight—only row after row of cars, mute, iron. The roar of the crowd mixes with the babble of the public-address system.

The bloody-eyed face of an immense white Brahma bull appears under Perce and Gay where they sit on the chute wall. Its handlers are respectfully hogging it into position. Now a handler loops the bucking belt around the bull's hind quarters, letting it hang loose for the moment. Perce is wide-eyed with fear and calculation. He is blinking hard to clear his head and softly working a wad of tobacco in his cheek. Gay turns to him from the bull, which is now directly under them. In Gay's eyes is a look of brutal pride in Perce. "You okay, boy? You want it?"

Perce hesitates, looking down at the bull; he has the excitement of one already injured. Then: "Hell, yes." He leans out over the bull to straddle it.

"Perce!"

He looks up and Gay does. Gay smiles pridefully, almost tauntingly, toward Roslyn, who has climbed the bottom rung of the fence a few yards away and is calling: "Gay, don't let him! Perce, here's your prize! Why . . ." She holds out the money toward him. Guido, no longer smiling, is beside her.

She is cut off by the public-address system: "Now folks, who do you think is back with us? We still got some real men in the West! On a Brahma bull, again, out of Black Hills, Colorado, *Perce Howland*!" The crowd roars.

Roslyn is struck dumb by the inexorable march of it all. She looks down, calling defeatedly: "Gay!"

Gay helps as Perce descends and straddles the bull. Mounted, he turns up to Roslyn. "You watch me now, sport!"

A handler yanks the bucking belt up tight. The bull shoots its head up, the gate opens, and Perce goes charging out into the arena.

Standing so close to the chute, Roslyn can feel the earth shake as the bull pounds out across the arena, and once having felt the thunder of its weight she nearly goes blind, seeing only tattered impressions that filter through her fear: the bull's corded neck, its oddly deadened eyes fixed on some motionless vision of vengeance, the pounding on the earth that seems to call up resounding answers from deep below the ground. The beast humps into the air and shifts direction, coming down, and Perce's body twists and doubles over, straightening only to be wracked again, flung and compressed as though he were tied to the end of a whip. A grimace of teeth-clenching anguish spreads over his face, and when he comes down from a leap his head is thrown back against the darkening sky like that of a supplicant. The crowd is roaring, but she does not hear it; customers are fighting the air with their fists and tearing with bared teeth at a hundred imagined demons, dogs are barking, pop bottles smash, strangers are squeezing one another's arms, a portable radio in the stands is loudly advertising an airline's cuisine, and the sun itself is setting behind the blind mountains; she is in a void, a silence of incomprehension, glimpsing only the bull's steady, remorseless stare and Perce's head snapping back like a doll's, the manly determination of his mouth belied by the helpless desolation in his eyes.

Guido has stopped cheering. Out of his half-drunken lethargy a new inner attention has straightened him, and he turns to her as though to comfort her, but she runs into the crowd behind her. A coarse call, a roar, an "Ohhh" from the crowd turns her around to the arena.

Perce is lying in the dirt, his shoulder twisted over half his face. The silence of the mountains spreads over the arena and the stands. The barebacked bull is lunging and blindly kicking near Perce's body, and the outrider is trying to maneuver it toward the chute, his expression drained of sport, his body pivoting his horse with every threatened feint of the white bull.

Gay is running across the bull's path. He doubles back and around the turning bull; the outrider's horse shields him for a moment and he drags Perce along the soft sand to the fence. Guido helps him lift Perce over it.

The crowd is standing, watching in silence. The grunted, growling breathing of the bull can be heard now. A cloud of gray dust hangs over the arena, but is already being carried away by the rising night breeze.

EIGHT

Darkness brightens the neon glare from the bars, and bluish vestigial light still glows along the mountain ridges. Cars are parked tightly against the bar fronts, one of which has been pushed in, its stucco face hanging agape. The crowd is thinner now and moving at promenade pace. The families are leaving in their cars and trucks. There are many small squads of cowboys moving in and out of the bars, with one girl to a squad. Unknowable conversations are going on in parked cars, between the freights, around unlit corners, between man and man and man and woman, some erupting in a shout and strange condemnations, or laughter and a reentry into the bars.

Roslyn is cradling her head in her arm in the front seat of the car. Her face is tired from weeping and she is still breathing shakily in the aftermath of a sobbing spell.

Gay calls her name from the window opposite. He has a wryness in his look, knowing she is displeased with him. "Come on, honey, we're gonna have some drinks." The hurt in her face makes him open the door and he sits beside her.

Roslyn: "Is he still unconscious?"

Gay: "Probably, but it ain't noticeable." He turns his head and she follows his gaze through the rear window.

Perce, his head enormously wrapped in white bandage, is heatedly arguing with the rodeo judge behind the car. Guido is standing between them, blinking sleepily.

"He's arguing with the judge about who won the bull ride. You still mad at me?"

Her resentment gives way to relief at seeing Perce alive. Now she turns to Gay. "Why did you hit me?"

"I didn't hit you. You were gettin' in the way and I couldn't carry him, that's all."

"Your face looked different." She stares at him now, a question in her eyes. "You looked like you . . . could've killed me. I . . . know that look."

"Oh, come on, honey. I got a little mad 'cause you were gettin' me all tangled up. Let's have some drinks, come on now."

Roslyn, glancing back at Perce: "He still hasn't seen a doctor?" Gay turns his back to her impatiently. "He might have a concussion! I don't understand anything; a person could be dying and everybody just stands around. Don't you care?"

Gay returns to the seat beside her. With anger in his voice: "I just went in for that boy with a wild bull runnin' loose—what're you talkin' about? I'm damn lucky I'm sittin' here myself, don't you know that?"

"Yes. You did." She suddenly takes his hand, kisses it, and holds it to her cheek. "You did!" She kisses his face. "You're a dear, good man. . . ."

Gay, holding her, wanting her to understand him: "Roslyn, honey . . ."

"It's like you scream and there's nothing coming out of your mouth, and everybody's going around, 'Hello, how are you, what a nice day,' and it's all great—and you're dying!" She struggles to control herself and smiles. "You really felt for him, didn't you?"

Gay shrugs. "I just thought I could get him out. So I did, that's all."

Roslyn, her face showing the striving to locate him and herself: "But if he'd died . . . you'd feel terrible, wouldn't you? I mean, for no reason like that?"

"Honey . . . we all got to go sometime, reason or no reason. Dyin's as natural as livin'; man who's too afraid to die is too afraid to live, far as I've ever seen. So there's nothin' to do but forget it, that's all. Seems to me."

Perce sticks his head into the car. The tape is still on his nose, the bandage like a turban on his head. He is slightly high from the shock. Guido sticks his head in on the other side of the car.

Perce: "Hey, Roslyn! Did you see me?"

"Oh, you were wonderful, Perce! Get in and we'll take you back to—"

"Oh, no, we got to have some fun now!"

Gay: "Sure, come on!"

Roslyn hesitates, then: "Okay. How do you feel?"

"Like a bull kicked me."

Guido opens the door for her. Gay gets out on Perce's side of the car. As she emerges from the car she quietly asks Guido: "Is he really all right?"

"In two weeks he won't remember this—or you either. Why don't you give your sympathy where it's appreciated?"

Roslyn, pointedly but with a warm laugh: "Where's that?"

She walks past him; he follows. They meet Gay and Perce in front of the saloon.

Perce: "In we go!"

Gay has her arm as her escort; Perce is on her other side, his open hand wavering over her back but not touching her: he is recognizing Gay's proprietary rights. Guido walks behind them. They enter the crowded saloon and take seats around a table.

There is a feverish intensity in Perce's speech and in his eyes. As they sit, he calls over to the bartender: "Hey, whiskey! For eight people."

He gets into his chair. He is strangely happy, as though he had accomplished something necessary, some duty that has given him certain rights. He laughs, and talks without diffidence to Roslyn now. "Boy, I feel funny! That man give me some kind of injection? Whoo! I see the prettiest stars, Roslyn." He reaches for her hand and holds it. Gay, whose arm is over the back of Roslyn's chair, grins uncomfortably. Roslyn pats Perce's hand and then removes her own. Perce does not notice this, and again takes her hand. "I never seen stars before. You ever see stars, Gay? Damn bull had the whole milky way in that hoof!" Gay laughs. Guido smiles with a private satisfaction. Roslyn is torn between concern for his condition and a desire to celebrate her relief that he is alive. "Say, was that you cryin' in the ambulance? Was that her, Gay?"

"Sure was."

Perce rises from his chair, fervently shaking her hand: "Well, I want to thank you, Roslyn."

A waiter puts two glasses of whiskey before each of them, and Perce raises his high.

Perce: "Now! Here's to my buddy, old elderly Gay!"

Roslyn: "Gay's not old!"

Perce: "And here's to old, elderly Pilot. And his five-dollar elderly airplane." They all have glasses raised. "And my friend, Roslyn! We're all buddies, ain't we, Gay?"

Gay grins to dilute the growing seriousness of Perce's meaning. "That's right."

The jukebox explodes with "Charley, My Boy."

Perce: "Then what're you gettin' mad at me for, buddy? Can I dance with her?"

Gay: "Sure! Roslyn, whyn't you dance with Perce?"

Roslyn: "Okay." She gets up and goes onto the dance area with Perce.

Guido: "Nothin' like being young, is there, Gay?"

"That's right. But you know what they say—there's some keeps gettin' younger all the time." He grins at Guido, who turns back to watch the dancers with a faintly skeptical smile. Perce is doing a flat-footed hicky step, and she is trying to fall into it with him. Half-kidding, he nevertheless seems to be caught by an old memory, as he moves with straight-backed dignity.

"My father used to dance like this." Now he twirls her around, and himself starts to circle her; a dizziness comes over him.

"What's the matter!"

"Whoo!"

She catches him as he stumbles. "C'mon, let's see the world." Taking her hand, he goes out a door in the rear of the saloon. She glances back to see Gay turning drunkenly in his chair, and she waves to him as she is pulled out through the back door.

They emerge behind the saloon. Trash, a mound of empty liquor bottles and beer cans, broken cartons, are littered about, but a few yards off the desert stretches away in the moonlight. He looks up at the sky and then turns to her. Wordless, he starts to sit on the ground, taking her hand and drawing her down, too, and they sit side by side on the sprung seat of an abandoned, wheelless car. Now he smiles weakly at her.

"Nobody ever cried for me. Not for a long time, anyway ..." Full of wordless speech, longing to make love to her and be loved by her, he takes her hand. "Gay's a great fella, ain't he?"

"Yes."

"I want to lie down. Okay?"

"Sure."

He lies in her lap, and suddenly covers his eyes. "Damn that bull!"

She smoothes his forehead. Now he opens his eyes. "Just rest. You don't have to talk."

"I can't place you, floatin' around like this. You belong to Gay?"

"I don't know where I belong."

"Boy, that's me, too. How come you got so much trust in your eyes?"

"Do I?"

"Like you were just born."

"Oh, no!"

"I don't like to see the way they grind women up out here. Although a lot of them don't mind, do they?"

"Some do."

"Did you really cry for me before?"

"Well, you were hurt and I—" She breaks off, seeing the wondrous shake of his head. "Didn't anybody ever cry for you?"

"No stranger. Last April the twelfth, I got kicked so bad I was out all day and all night. I had a girl with me and two good buddies. I haven't seen her or them since."

"They left you alone?"

"Listen ... let me ask you something ... I can't talk to anybody, you know?" She waits for him to speak. "I ... I don't understand how you're supposed to do."

"What do you mean?"

"Well, see, I never floated around till this last year. I ain't like Gay and Pilot, I got a good home. I did have, anyway. And one day my old man ... we were out back and suddenly, *bam!* Down he went. Some damn fool hunters."

"They killed him?"

"Uh-huh. And ... she changed."

"Who?"

"My mother. She was always so dignified ... walked next to him like a saint. And pretty soon this man started comin' around, and she ... she changed. Three months, they were married. Well, okay, but I told her, I says, 'Mama, you better get a paper from Mr. Brackett because I'm the oldest and Papa wanted me to have the ranch.' And sure enough, the wedding night he turns around and offers me wages. On my own father's place."

"What does *she* say?"

Shaking his head in an unrelieved agony, and with a mystical reaching in his tone: "I don't know; she don't *hear* me. She's all *changed around*. You know what I mean? It's like she don't remember me any more."

She nods, staring.

"What the hell you depend on? Do you know?"

"I don't know. Maybe ..." She is facing the distant horizon, staring at her life. "Maybe all there really is is what happens next, just the next thing, and you're not supposed to remember anybody's promises."

"You could count on mine, Roslyn. I think I love you."

"You don't even know me."

"I don't care."

He raises his face to hers, but his eyes are suddenly pain-wracked, and he grips his head. "That damn bull!"

The back door suddenly swings open, throwing the light of the saloon on them. Gay comes out, walking unsteadily, blinking in the sudden darkness. He calls: "Roslyn?"

"Here we are!" She gets up with Perce.

Gay comes over, shepherding them toward the door. "Come on, now, I want you to meet my kids."

"Your kids here?"

"They come for the rodeo. I ain't seen them in a year. You oughta see the welcome they give me, Roslyn! Nearly knocked me over." They go through the door and up a short corridor. "She's gonna be nineteen! She got so pretty! Just happen to be here for the rodeo, the both of them! That great?"

"Oh, I'm so glad for you, Gay!" They go into the saloon.

Gay, now drawing Roslyn by the hand, and she holding onto Perce's hand, come up to the crowded bar, where Guido is standing in a drunken swirl of his own. The air is muddy with smoke and jazz. Perce is blinking hard, trying to see. Roslyn watches him even as she attends to Gay.

Gay reaches Guido first. "Where are they?"

"Where are who?" Guido turns to him slowly.

"My kids! I told them I'd be back in a minute. You heard me tell them."

"Went out there." Guido points toward the door to the street, then looks appraisingly at Roslyn and Perce.

Gay looks hurt and angered, then pushes through the door and goes out. He looks about at the parked cars and the moving groups of people and the armed deputies, and he yells: "Gaylord! Gaylord?"

Now Roslyn comes out of the bar, helping Perce. Guido is with them, carrying a bottle. Their attention is instantly on Gay, except for Perce, who immediately lays his cheek on the car fender, embracing it.

"Rose-May! Gaylord! Gaylorrrrd?"

Guido comes up beside Gay, a muddled, advice-giving look on his face. Roslyn remains holding onto Perce.

Guido bays: "Gaylord! Here's your father!" He sways, pointing at Gay.

People are beginning to congest around them, some seriously curious, some giggling, some drunk. Roslyn remains with Perce just behind Gay and Guido, watching Gay, tears threatening her eyes.

"Gaylord, where you gone to? I told you I was comin' right back. You come here now!"

A woman, middle-aged, dressed like a farmer's wife, comes up to Gay. "Don't you worry, mister, you'll probably find them home."

Gay looks at her, at the security emanating from her sympathetic smile. He turns and climbs up onto the hood of the car; he is very drunk, and shaken. He looks over the crowded street from this new elevation. Just below him Roslyn and Guido are looking up into his face, and he seems twice his normal size. Drunks mill around below, the bar lights blink crazily behind him, the armed deputies look on blankly from the doorways, and the jazz cacophony is flying around his ears like lightning. His hat askew, his eyes perplexed, and his need blazing on his face, he roars out: "Gaylord! *I know you hear me!*"

There is now a large crowd around the car, the faces of alien strangers. Gay bangs his fist on the roof of the car. "I know you hear me! Rose-May—you come out now!" He suddenly slips on the hood and rolls off onto the ground, flat on his back. Roslyn screams and runs to him, as the crowd roars with laughter; she quickly lifts up his head and kisses him.

"I'm sure they're looking for you, Gay. They must've thought you'd left." He stares dumbly at her. "Oh, poor Gay, poor Gay!" She hugs his head and rocks him, crouched beside him in the gutter.

NINE

The car is speeding on the dark highway. Guido is driving, the dog asleep beside him. In the back seat Roslyn has one arm around the unconscious Perce, whose legs hang out a window, the other arm around Gay, asleep against her breast. Her eyes are closed.

Suddenly the car bumps up and down, and Guido is trying to bring it back on the highway. For an instant the headlights catch a figure scurrying off the road shoulder. The car swerves back onto the highway. Now a man rises from the roadside, brushes himself off, picks up his bundle, and walks impassively on. It is the Indian.

The ride is smooth again, and Roslyn has opened her eyes. She is drunk and exhausted, a feeling of powerlessness is on her. Guido has a vague look of joy on his face as he drives. She speaks in a helpless monotone, as in a dream: "Aren't you going too fast? Please, huh?"

"Don't worry, kid, I never kill anybody I know."

The speedometer is climbing toward eighty.

"A fellow smashed up my best girl friend. All they found were her gloves. Please, Guido. She was beautiful, with black hair. . . ."

"Say hello to me, Roslyn."

"Hello, Guido. Please, huh?"

His eyes are glazed and oddly relaxed, as though he were happy in some corner of his mind. "We're all blind bombardiers, Roslyn—we kill people we never even saw. I bombed nine cities. I sure must've broken a lot of dishes but I never saw them. Think of all the puppy dogs must've gone up, and mail carriers, eyeglasses

... Boy! Y'know, droppin' a bomb is like tellin' a lie—makes everything so quiet afterwards. Pretty soon you don't hear anything, don't see anything. Not even your wife. The difference is that I *see* you. You're the first one I ever really *saw*."

"Please, Guido, don't kill us. . . ."

"How do you get to know somebody, kid? I can't make a landing. And I can't get up to God, either. Help me. I never said help me in my life. I don't *know* anybody. Will you give me a little time? Say yes. At least say hello Guido."

She can hear the murderous beating of wind against the car. "Yes. Hello, Guido."

From over ninety the speedometer begins to descend.

"Hello, Roslyn."

Headlights hit the dark, unfinished house, illuminating the unfinished outside wall and the lumber and building materials lying around on the ground. Now the motor is shut off, but the lights remain on.

No one is moving inside the car. Guido, exhausted, stares at his house. The dog is asleep beside him. Now he opens the door and lumbers out of the car. He opens the rear door and blearily looks in.

Roslyn is sleeping, sitting upright. Perce is still asleep on her lap, his feet out the window; Gay is on the floor. Guido stares at her, full of longing and sorrow for himself. He looks down at Perce, then at Gay, and as though they were unbearably interfering he steps back from the car and walks into the darkness.

Loud hammer blows open Roslyn's eyes; Gay sits up. "Okay, I'll drive, I'll drive."

"We're here, Gay."

"Where?"

She sees something in the headlights through the windshield; carefully she slides from under Perce's head and out the door, and walks unsteadily from the car toward the house, mystified. She walks in the headlight beams; the hammer blows are a few feet away. Awe shows on her face.

Guido is drunkenly hammering a sheathing board to the unfinished wall of the house. It is on crooked, but he gives it a final pat of satisfaction, then goes to the lumber pile and takes off another board, nearly falling with that, and lays it up against the wall, trying to butt it up against the previously nailed board. He hammers, as in a dream, the kind of pleasure and pain that comes of being freed of early logic, yet being driven toward some always receding center.

Roslyn comes up to him, not daring to touch him. "Oh, I'm sorry, Guido. Guido? I'm so sorry." He continues dumbly hammering. "Won't you hit your hand, it's so dark? It's dark, Guido, look how dark it is." He hammers on. She almost turns, spreading her arms and looking skyward. "Look, it's all dark!" A sob breaks from her. "Please! Please stop!"

From nearby Gay calls angrily: "What the hell you stompin' the flowers for?"

Roslyn turns to Gay, who comes up to Guido and swings him around by the shoulder and bends to the ground. "You busted all the damn heliotropes!"

Gay is on his hands and knees now, trying to stand up the fallen flowers. Guido is looking down dumbly, the hammer in his hand.

Gay: "Look at that! Look at that, now!" He holds up a torn stem. "What in hell good is that, now?"

Roslyn: "He was trying to fix the house."

Rising unsteadily to his feet, Gay asks menacingly: "What call *he* got to fix the house?"

Roslyn: "Don't! Don't! Please, Gay! He . . . he's just trying to say hello. It's no crime to say hello."

From behind them they hear Perce crying out: "Who's doin' that?"

They turn to see Perce staggering into the headlight beams, trying to free his head and arms from yards of unraveling bandage flowing off his head. He is fighting it off like a clinging spider web, turning around and around to find its source.

"Who's doin' that?"

Roslyn hurries toward him. "Don't! Don't take it off!" She reaches him and tries to unwind his arms.

"Get it off. What's on me?"

"Stop tangling it. It's your bandage."

He stops struggling and looks at the bandage as though for the first time. "What for a bandage?"

Roslyn is starting to laugh despite her concern. A few yards away, Guido is quietly but deeply laughing, glassy-eyed. Gay is beginning to feel the laughter's infectiousness. Feeling a hysteria of laughter coming on, Roslyn tries to wind the bandage on again. "It's for your head."

Perce: "My—" He breaks off as he raises his hands and feels the bandage wrapped around his head. "I have this on all night?" He looks angrily at Guido and Gay, who are roaring now, and to them he says: "Who tied this on me?" He is trying to pull it off his head.

She tries to stop his hands. "The ambulance did it. Don't take it off."

Perce, unwinding and unwinding the bandage: "You leave me at a disadvantage all night? Who put it on? Gay, you . . ." He lunges toward Gay and trips on a board, and the whole pile of lumber topples on him with a great crash. Guido and Gay fall about, dying with hysteria.

Roslyn, between laughter and tears, tries to extricate Perce from the lumber. "Get him up. Gay, come here. Guido! Carry him. Please. He can't help himself." The men come to help her, and still laughing crazily they lift Perce and almost carry him to the door of the house. She goes inside ahead of them.

Looped in their arms, Perce demands: "Who put it on? Leave me at a disadvantage all night?" She and Guido get him through the door of the house. "Where's this? Let me alone. Where is this place?" He lies on a couch as Guido sprawls on his favorite chair, catching his breath.

Roslyn: "This is my house . . . or Guido's." She laughs. "Well, it's a house, anyway."

Perce closes his eyes. Suddenly the house is quiet. She covers Perce with an Indian blanket, and the touch stirs him to resistance. "No, Ma, don't, don't!" He turns his face away.

Now she stands and sees Gay sitting outside the door on the step. She goes down to him, starting to wipe the hair out of his eyes, and he takes her hand. A curious inwardness, a naked supplication has come into his face.

"Wish you'd met Gaylord, Rose-May. If I had a new kid now, I'd know just how to be with him, just how to do. I wasted these kids. I didn't know nothin'."

"Oh, no, I'm sure they love you, Gay. Go to sleep now."

He grasps her hand, preventing her from leaving. "Would you ever want a kid? With me?"

She pats his hand, starting to turn away. "Let me just turn the lights off in the car."

He raises up, struggling to get on his feet.

"Whyn't you sleep now . . ."

"I don't wanna sleep now!" He staggers to his feet, swaying before her. "I asked you a question! Did I ask you to turn the lights off in the car? What are you runnin' away from all the time?" With a wide gesture toward windows and walls that nearly tumbles him: "I never washed the windows for my wife even. Paint a fireplace! Plant all them damn heliotropes!"

He suddenly goes to the doorway and yells into the house: "What're they all doin' here? What're you bringin' them around for?"

"I didn't bring them, they just—"

"Where are you at? I don't know where you're at."

Trying not to offend him and still speak her truth, she embraces him. "I'm here, Gay. I'm with you. But . . . what if some day you turn around and suddenly you don't like me any more? Like before, when Perce got hurt, you started to give me a look. . . . I know that look and it scares me, Gay. 'Cause I couldn't ever stay with a stranger."

"Honey, I got a little mad. That don't mean I didn't like you. Didn't your papa ever spank you, and then take you up and give you a big kiss?" She is silent. "He did, didn't he?"

"He was never there long enough. And strangers spank for keeps." She suddenly presses herself against him and he embraces her. "Oh, love me, Gay! Love me!"

He raises her face and kisses her. She smiles brightly.

Roslyn: "Now we made up, okay?"

Gay: "Yes, okay, okay!" Laughing softly, he hugs her.

"You sleep now . . . you're tired. Sleep, darling."

"And tomorrow I'll show you what I can do. You'll see what living is."

She nods in agreement, gently pressing him to the doorway. He goes into the dark house, talking. "We'd make out. I could farm. Or run cattle, maybe. I'm a damn good man, Roslyn—best man you'll ever see. Show you tomorrow when we hit those mountains. Ain't many around can keep up with old Gay. You wait and see."

She hears the bed groaning, then silence. She walks unsteadily to the car, reaches in, and pushes the switch. The lights go off. Now she stands erect and looks up at the oblivious moon, a vast sadness stretching her body, a being lost, a woman whose life has forbidden her to forsake her loneliness. She cries out, but soft, to the sky: "Help!"

For a long time she stands there, given to the dreadful clouds crossing the stars, racing to nowhere.

TEN

A plume of dust is moving across the desert, following Gay's old but still serviceable truck. On the open bed, lashed to the back of the cab, is a drum of gasoline with a hand-cranking pump protruding from its top. It is bumping along over the sage, here and there crunching a whitened skeleton of winter-killed cattle.

Gay is driving; Roslyn beside him has the dog in her lap, its muzzle on her shoulder. Perce spits out the window. His nose is still taped. The sun narrows their eyes. They bump along, facing the desert before them.

Roslyn can feel the dog shivering. She looks at it, then turns to Gay. "Why is the dog shivering?"

"She'll do that up here."

Suddenly Guido's plane zooms down over the roof of the cab and they see it flying straight ahead of them a few feet off the ground toward the mountains, its wings waggling a greeting. They shout in surprise. Gay waves out the window and speeds up the truck. His face and Perce's gain excitement, the knitting together of action.

True night is covering the mountains; it is the end of twilight, when the purple light is turning blue. Splashes of stars are tumbling onto the sky. The mountains, secretive and massive, wait. At their foot, the campfire shimmers—the only moving thing in the world.

The four are sitting around the fire. Nearby stands the truck, and a little farther away the lashed plane, both flickered by moon and firelight like intruding monsters resting before an onslaught.

A hiatus in the talk. Guido is telling a story, unable to keep his eyes from Roslyn across the fire from him. She is putting away the last of the dried dishes into the tote box. Now she listens raptly. Gay is idly going through the dog's fur for fleas, and Perce waits for Guido's next word, full of respect for him.

Guido looks skyward. "That star is so far away that by the time its light hits the earth, it might not even be up there any more." He looks at Roslyn. "In other words, we can only see what something was, never what it is now."

Roslyn: "You sure know a lot, don't you, Pilot?" Perce shakes his head.

Guido: "Oh, astronomy's all in the library books. Nothin' to it but reading."

Roslyn looks up at the sky. "Still, it's wonderful to know things."

"You got something a lot more important."

"What?"

Guido, glancing up at the sky: "That big connection. You're really hooked in; whatever happens to anybody, it happens to you. That's a blessing."

Roslyn, laughing: "People say I'm just nervous."

"If there hadn't been some nervous people in the world, we'd still be eating each other."

Gay, suddenly clapping his hands as though to clean them: "Well, I don't know about you educated people, but us ignorant folks got to hit the sack."

He gets up; a certain tension between him and Guido has sharpened his movements.

Roslyn: "Why is the dog shivering?"

Gay looks at the dog, then glances toward the mountains. "Got a whiff of those horses, I guess. They must be close by, Guido."

Roslyn has stretched over to stroke the dog. Suddenly it bares its teeth and nearly snaps her hand. She leaps away, terrified.

Gay is instantly furious. "Hey, you damn fool! Come here!" The dog crawls to him on her belly and he slaps her.

Roslyn: "Oh, don't hit her, she didn't mean anything! The horses ever kick her or something?"

Guido: "It's not the horses she's afraid of." They all look at him. He has the compact look of one who is taking a stand. "It's us."

Gay: "What're you talkin' about now, Guido? I never mistreated this dog." His anger is sharpening now.

Guido, holding his position, pitched high: "Just common sense, Gay. She's been up here enough times to know what's going to happen. There's wild animals up there that'll be dead tomorrow night."

There is a flare of astonishment in Roslyn's face. But the men all assume she knows this and Guido goes right on. "How's she know she's not next? They're not as stupid as people, you know."

Gay unrolls Roslyn's bedroll beside the fire. "Here now, honey, you can keep yourself nice and warm by the fire."

Guido has busied himself with his bedroll. Perce, however, is caught by the look in her face.

And now Gay, looking up from her bedroll, finds that she has not moved, and a strange look of fright is on her face.

At last she turns to him. "You kill them?"

"No, no, we sell them to the dealer."

Roslyn, her voice small, incredulous, even as somewhere in her this news does not come as a surprise: "He kills them?"

Gay, with complete neutrality, as a fact: "They're what they call chicken-feed horses—turn them into dog food. You know— what you buy in the store for the dog or the cat?"

She has begun to quiver. He goes to her and starts to take her hand kindly. "I thought you knew that. Everybody . . ."

She gently removes her hand from his, staring incomprehensibly into his face, turns, and walks into the darkness.

". . . knows that." He hesitates for a moment, then, as much to cover his embarrassment before Guido and Perce as anything else, he picks up her bedroll and starts after her. "Maybe you better sleep on the truck. In case something comes crawling around. . . ." He walks after her into the darkness.

He comes on her beside the truck, tosses the bedroll aboard, and smooths it out. She is staring wide-eyed, shaking slightly. He turns her to him. Slowly she raises her eyes to him. In her face we see the astonishment and the agony she feels as two contrasting ideas of him clash in her mind.

Gay: "Get some sleep now. Come on."

He starts to lift her aboard, but she gently stops him—gently enough to tell him how afraid of him she is. She is looking at him as though she had never seen him before.

"Honey, I just round them up. I sell them to the dealer. Always have."

But her stare is unbroken.

"No need to look at me that way, honey. Now you're looking at *me* like a stranger."

The imminent threat of her estrangement breaks his heart and he sweeps her into his arms with a muffled cry: "Honey!"

He holds her away so he can see her.

Roslyn: "I . . . I thought . . ."

"What?"

"They were for riding, or . . ."

"Sure, they used to be—especially Christmas presents for kids. 'Cause they're small horses, you see, the kids loved them for Christmas. But"—he almost smiles—"kids ride motor scooters now. Used to breed them a lot, too; mustang puts a lot of stamina into a breed."

She is beginning to listen, to perceive a dilemma in which he too is caught.

"When I started, they used a lot of them I caught. There was mustang blood pullin' all the plows in the West; they couldn't have settled here without somebody caught mustangs for them. It . . . it just got changed around, see? I'm doin' the same thing I ever did. It's just that they . . . they changed it around. There was no such thing as a can of dog food in those days. It . . . it was a good thing to do, honey, it was a man's work, and I know how to do it. And I wanted you to see what I can do." He smiles. "Aside from sittin' around the house and movin' furniture."

"But they kill them now."

He is silent, struggling for an answer.

"You . . . you know it's not right, don't you? You're just saying this, but you know."

Gay's own guilt has been touched, and he cannot carry it

alone. "Honey, if I didn't do it, somebody would. They're up here hunting all the time."

"I don't care about others!"

"You ate that steak tonight, didn't you? And you—"

Roslyn claps her hands to her ears. "I don't care!"

"You've bought food for my dog, haven't you? What'd you think was in those cans?"

"I don't want to hear it!"

"Honey, nothin' can live unless something dies."

"Stop it!"

She clambers aboard the truck, climbs into the bedroll, turns on her side, and covers her eyes with her hands. He hesitates, then hoists onto the truck bed and sits next to her. He knows he has all but lost her; only her evident agony tells him that parting will not be easy for her. At last, talking to her hidden face: "Roslyn, we never kidded, you and I. I'm tellin' you I don't want to lose you. You got to help me a little bit, though. Because I can't put on that this is all as bad as you make it. All I know is—everything else is wages; up here I'm my own man. And that's why you liked me, isn't it?"

A silence grows.

"I liked you because you were kind."

"I haven't changed."

"Yes. You have. This changes it."

"Honey, a kind man can kill."

"No he can't!"

"Well, if it's bad, maybe you gotta take a little bad with the good or you'll go on the rest of your life runnin'."

She suddenly faces him, her eyes full of tears. "What's there to stop for? You're the same as everybody!"

She bursts into disappointed weeping, covering her face. In a moment he lays a hand on her. "Yes. Maybe we're all the same. Including you." She uncovers her face, starting to raise on her elbows indignantly. His voice is calm again. "We start out doin' something, meaning no harm, something that's naturally in us to do. And somewhere down the line it gets changed around into something bad. Like dancin' in a nightclub. You started out just wanting to dance, didn't you? And little by little it turns out that people ain't interested in how good you dance, they're gawkin' at you with something altogether different in their minds. And they turn it sour, don't they?" Memory dissolves her anger, and she lies back. "I could've looked down my nose at you, too—just a kid showin' herself off in nightclubs for so much a night. But I took my hat off to you. Because I know the difference."

Her eyes search his. He looks off at the dark mountains.

"This ... this is how I dance, Roslyn. And if they made somethin' else out of it, well ... I can't run the world any more than you could. I hunt these horses to keep myself free. That's all."

Roslyn: "You ... take your hat off ... to me?" He bends and kisses her on the lips. "You mean it, don't you! Oh, Gay!"

They hold each other in the silence. He comes down off the truck bed. With troubled eyes he leans down and holds his mouth on hers and she presses his shoulders down upon her.

He stands erect, touches her eyelids. He goes from her to the diminishing fire, sits on his bedroll, and takes off his shoes. Perce and Guido are in their bedrolls nearby. The dog comes and lies down, and Gay mutters: "Shame on you, you fool." He climbs into his bedroll.

Guido turns in his bedroll. "I could fly her back in the morning, if you want me to."

Gay simply looks at Guido with an instinctive, as yet unformed, suspicion.

Guido: "I was wondering how she agreed to come up here."

Perce flicks a cigarette into the fire. "She's got a lot of right. If you come to think of it, it don't make too much sense for fifteen horses."

Gay sighs. "Don't worry yourselves about her now. She's comin' along fine."

He turns on his side. Beside him the dog lies with head on paws, the firelight flickering on its eyes. Its breathing is still short and rapid. Gay, to the dog, very softly: "You quiet down now. Everybody's showin' off."

No one moves. Beyond the circle of light the land is empty. The night is filled with the firelit eyes of the dog, which blink toward the mountains and the still unseen animals that are to die.

ELEVEN

The first rays of dawn are brightening the sky. Perce is on the truck bed, cranking gas from the drum into the plane. Guido is on top of the wing, holding the hose and peering into the tank.

Gay walks over to a mound partially covered with drift sand. He reaches down, grasps something, and pulls; a tarpaulin is peeled off, revealing a dozen truck tires. On the wing Guido raises his hand, peering into the tank, and calls: "Okay, hold it!"

Gay calls to them from the pile of tires: "Let's go, Perce, gimme a hand here!"

Perce hops off the truck, gets in behind the wheel, and backs to the tires. Guido clambers down off the wing, reaches into the open-sided cockpit, and draws out a shotgun pistol, which he proceeds to load from a box of shells.

Roslyn, who is rolling up the bedrolls and tying them, happens to look and sees the pistol in Guido's hand, hesitates, then returns to her job. The dog comes up to her. She smiles down at the animal, then with some initial fear reaches down and pats it. Happily she calls: "She's not snapping any more, Gay!"

Gay is just heaving a truck tire onto the bed of the truck with Perce's help. He turns to her, smiling. "Things generally look a little different in the morning."

Guido calls from the plane: "I guess I'm ready, Gay!"

He is drawing out of the plane a shredded Air Force jacket whose lamb's-wool lining is visible through slits in the outside leather. He and Gay go to each wingtip and unlash the plane. Perce goes to the tail and unlashes it. Roslyn comes near and watches now. Perce now comes alongside her and stands. Gay walks back to the cockpit with Guido.

Gay: "How you want her?"

Guido looks up at the sky, holding a palm up to feel the breeze. He points: "That way."

Gay goes to the tail, lifts it, and swings the plane to face the direction of take-off. Then he walks along the plane to the propeller and waits. Guido is about to get into the cockpit.

Roslyn, as though to relieve the weirdly charged atmosphere, calls rather gaily to Guido: "Boy, that's some jacket! Little breezy, isn't it?"

Guido: "Went on a lot of missions in this thing. Wouldn't take a hundred dollars for it . . . bulletproof." They chuckle as he climbs in and sits. To Roslyn: "Glad you decided to stay with us. Probably never see this again in history, y'know."

Roslyn: "Take care, now."

Guido mutely thanks her for her solicitude. "Okay, boy, turn your partner and do-si-do! Switch off!"

Gay glances behind him to see if there is any obstruction to his back step, reaches up, turns the propeller several times. Guido slips his goggles on.

Guido: "Switch on! With feeling now!" They laugh. Gay turns the propeller until it is horizontal and pulls down hard, but the engine does not start. "And again! And let us pray." Gay with special care grasps the propeller, pulls down. The engine huffs and dies. "That's that damn car gas for ya. Okay, let's try her again."

Again Gay yanks down on the propeller. The engine smokes, huffs, and with a sudden resolution clatters up to a roar. Guido straps himself in, lays the pistol in his lap, and with a wave to them guns the engine. The plane moves away from them, gains speed, and takes the air. Now it wheels in air and comes back, roaring over their heads and away toward the mountains. They turn with it.

The three squint against the prop blast. Gay is the first to move; he looks for an instant at Perce and Roslyn. They feel his glance. Without reason, they feel separated from him, and he smiles.

Gay: "Here we go." He turns toward the truck and starts to walk, Perce and Roslyn following him.

Guido lifts his goggles and looks up at the clear blue sky. His lips move as though in prayer. He lowers his goggles and looks down. The barrier face of the mountains suddenly passes under the plane. Now the sharp interior walls and steep valleys show, manless, half in shadow, with patches of grass here and there. A hidden secret world is opened. The plane flies just within the crests of the mountains, turning with the valleys, which Guido scans through the open-sided cockpit. Suddenly his head moves sharply.

Instantly he pulls the stick back; the plane abruptly climbs. Now he banks and turns, the plane shuddering on uneven steps of air. Now he checks his instruments and grasps the pistol in his right hand. With a glance over the side to aim himself, he presses the stick forward and dives.

The herd is coming up to him fast. Now the animals start to gallop along the wall of the valley. Guido flattens his dive and zooms in over the horses, his wingtips only yards from the valley walls. He pulls the stick back and the plane noses upward; he points the pistol down as he passes over the herd, and fires. With the shot the horses surge ahead even faster. He is conscious of having held his breath, of having felt a strange tremor in his engine at the moment of acceleration. With a sigh he flies toward the sky, turns tightly, lines himself up with the herd, and once more starts his dive.

The truck bumps along on the sage desert, but now it crosses a border where the sage and soil end and a prehistoric lake bed begins. It is a floor of clay, entirely bare, white, and flat as a table. Now the truck halts close to a little hummock bordering the lake bed.

Perce emerges as the engine is turned off. He looks around as Roslyn comes down out of the cab. Gay comes from the other side of the truck and walks around to them where they stand scanning the lake bed. The silence is absolute. There is no wind.

Roslyn: "It's . . . like a dream!"

Set between mountain ranges the lake bed stretches about twenty-five miles wide and as long as the eye can see. Not a blade of grass or stone mars its absolutely flat surface, from which heat waves rise. In the distance it glistens like ice.

Perce: "I seen a picture of the moon once. Looked just like this."

Gay: "He'll be drivin' the horses out of that pass."

She and Perce look toward an opening in the mountain face perhaps a mile away. "Does anybody own this land?"

"Government, probably. Just call it God's country. Perce? Let's get that drum off."

Gay goes to the truck, hops onto the bed, and proceeds to unlash the gasoline drum. Perce stands on the ground and helps jimmy the drum to the edge of the truck. Now Gay hops down and both men let it down to the ground and roll it off to one side. Roslyn watches for a moment, then goes to the cab and leans in. The dog is quivering on the floor of the cab. She reaches toward it tentatively.

Gay goes to one of the tires; he draws a rope from inside it and experimentally circles it over his head and throws it.

Perce, seeing him occupied, walks over to the cab and looks in from the side opposite to that of Roslyn. She is pressing her face against the dog's. Then she reaches up to the rearview mirror, turns it to look at herself, sees Perce, and smiles.

He speaks as though voicing a premonition: "I'd be a little careful what I said to Gay. For a while out here."

Gay's face appears beside his. "Got to get the glasses."

Perce steps aside. Gay moves into the truck doorway, hardly looking at Roslyn, who now shakes dust out of her hair in the rearview mirror. He reaches behind the seat and draws out a large binocular case. Looking at her now, grinning, an uncertainty still in his eyes, he takes the binoculars out of the case and puts the glasses to his eyes. Perce is watching him. He holds the glasses up to his eyes for a long moment, looking toward the pass.

She steps over to Gay, forcing a bright tone: "See anything?"

Gay, putting the glasses on a tire on the truck bed: "Climb up, make yourself comfortable. He'll be awhile yet."

He gives her a boost. She mounts the truck bed. He climbs up and sits inside a pile of two tires, his legs hanging over the edge at the knees, his armpits supporting his trunk.

Gay: "Go ahead. It's comfortable."

She does as he did; Perce mounts onto the truck.

Roslyn: "It is comfortable! Try it, Perce."

Perce does the same. The three sit in silence as Gay again raises the glasses and looks through them.

Gay turns to her. "You lookin' real good today, honey. Maybe tonight we go down to Reno and dance, okay?"

"Okay."

"I'd of brought your umbrella for you but I didn't think of it."

"I'm all right. It's not too hot."

She reaches over and touches his knee reassuringly, for she sees his anxiety about her. Now she withdraws her hand, and scans the lake bed.

Gay, for a moment, continues looking at her profile. He has sensed the dampened quality of her feeling. He turns and glances at Perce, who is on his other side. Perce is staring toward the pass, clearly preoccupied.

For a moment Gay sits staring straight ahead; then he turns to her. "I forgot to tell you something last night."

She looks at him with quick interest.

"Lots of cow outfits use the pastures up in those mountains, and when they find the mustangs there they just shoot 'em and leave 'em for the buzzards. 'Cause they eat up all the good grass, see."

She nods that she understands, but he sees he has not pierced her dampened air, and he turns to Perce.

"You know that, don't you, Perce?"

"Huh? Oh sure, I know that."

"Whyn't you say so?"

"I just said so."

Gay raises the glasses. "Nothin' but misfit horses, that's all they are, honey."

He studies the pass through the glasses. Putting the glasses down, he turns to her with a warm memory in his eyes. "Wished you'd been here in the old days." Stretching an arm toward the pass: "They'd come pourin' out of those passes, three, four, five hundred at a time. And we'd build us a big corral out here and funnel them right in. Some of them were real beautiful animals, too. Made sweet riding horses."

For a moment she feels the breadth of his memories. "It must have been wonderful."

"Best life any man could've had."

"I wished I'd been here . . . then."

Perce: "I hear something."

Gay: "What?"

Perce: "Tick, tick, tick, tick, tick."

Gay: "It's my watch."

Roslyn: "Boy, it's quiet here! You can hear your skin against your clothes." She tries to laugh.

Gay, exhaling, relaxing in the tire: "Ayah!" He leans back, closing his eyes. Perce and Roslyn, in effect, are becoming joined by a viewpoint toward Gay, who at every moment seems to be gathered up by a quickening forward rhythm. They look at each other, forced, as it were, to an awareness of looking on him with the same eyes.

Perce: "I hear something!"

Gay listens. He raises the glasses, sees nothing, puts them down.

Gay: "What?"

Perce: "Engine, sounds like."

They listen.

Gay: "Where?"

Perce, indicating with an open hand the general direction of the pass: "Out that way."

Gay, after listening for a moment: "Too soon. He wouldn't be in pass yet."

Roslyn: "Wait." She listens. "I hear it."

Gay strains to hear. Now a certain pique is noticeable in him because he can't hear it. "No—just your blood pumpin' in your head, is all."

Roslyn: "Ssh."

Gay watches her. Perse is also tensed to listen.

Gay: "I always had the best ears of anybody, so don't tell me you—"

Perce, suddenly pointing, and screwing up out of the tire to sit on its rim: "Isn't that him?"

The three look into the distant sky, Roslyn and Gay trying to locate the plane, at the same time wriggling out of the tires, to sit on the rims.

She suddenly cries out and points. "I see it! There! Look, Gay!"

Almost insulted, he scans the sky, then unwillingly raises the glasses and sees the mountain pass up close; flying out of it is the plane, tiny even in the glasses. He puts down the glasses, blinks his eyes hard. "He never worked this fast before. I'd've seen him but I didn't expect him so soon."

Perce: "I could see him glinting in the sun. It was the glint. That's why."

Gay seems to accept the apology. Now, very distantly, an explosion is heard.

Roslyn: "What's that?"

Gay: "He fired a shot."

She watches the pass with growing apprehension and fascination. Perce glances at her in concern, then back to the pass. They are all perspiring now in the warming sun.

Gay: "I've sat here waitin' two-three hours before he come out. That's why I didn't see him." Now, however, he glances at Perce and nods. "You got good eyes, though, boy." He raises the glasses again. Silence. They watch the pass. The sun is higher; heat waves rise around them like a transparent sea. Suddenly Gay straightens.

"There they come. One ... two ... three ... four ... five ... six. I guess he'll go back for the others now."

Perce: "Give me a look, heh?"

Gay hands Perce the binoculars. "See the others yet?"

"No. There's ... six. And a little colt."

Roslyn's flesh moves; she shifts the position of one hand to relax her tension.

Gay notices her shock without facing her, and he asks Perce: "You sure?"

"Ya. It's a spring foal."

Gay, watching the pass, can feel Roslyn's deepening stillness beside him.

Perce keeps the glasses up. "It's a colt, all right." He lowers the glasses and faces Gay. He speaks with finality, not quite accusing, but nevertheless with an implication of question as to what will be done with it: "It's a colt, Gay."

Gay, concerned, but with barely a look at Perce, takes the glasses. Perce turns to watch the pass again. Roslyn is staring at Gay's profile as though it were constantly changing in her mind. Now Gay lowers the glasses, faces her fully. He will not be condemned. "Want a look?"

He gives her the glasses. She hesitates, but then raises them to her eyes. The lenses find the herd, galloping in file, the colt bringing up the rear with its nose nearly touching its mare's tail. Now the plane dives down on them and they lift their heads and gallop faster. The image shakes, as her hands lose their steadiness, then flows out crazily as the strength goes out of her hands. She sits there, blind.

Gay stands, and raises the glasses again. She wipes her fingers over her eyes. Another shot is heard. She opens her eyes to look. Perce and Gay are fixed on the distant spectacle. She gets to her feet and hops down off the truck. Perce looks to her.

She is barely audible: "Maybe it's cooler in the truck." She walks to the cab and climbs in.

Gay and Perce remain on the truck bed, sitting on the tires again. Gay, with a glance, notes Perce's new uneasiness.

"It's all right. She's goin' to make it fine."

Perce makes no attempt to reply. A challenge has somehow grown up before him. Their posture and movements relax now.

Perce: "I thought you said there was fifteen. There's only six."

"Probably lost a few. That'll happen."

"Don't make much sense for six, does it?"

"Six is six. Better'n wages, ain't it?" Perce doesn't answer. "I said it's better than wages, ain't it?"

Perce, with damaged conviction, looking at his shoe soles: "I guess anything's better'n wages."

They sit in silence. Then Gay crosses his legs.

"Perce? We've just about cleaned 'em out up here, but if you're interested in some real money, there's a place about a hundred miles northeast—Thighbone Mountain. I never bothered up there 'cause it's awful tough to get 'em out. You gotta horseback up in there. But I believe there must be five hundred on Thighbone. Maybe more." Perce is silent, staring at the pass. "There'd be *real* money. You could buy yourself some good stock, maybe even a little van—hit those rodeos in style."

Perce cannot look at him. His voice oddly quiet, he says: "I don't know, Gay. Tell you the truth, I don't even know about rodeos any more."

"I'm beginnin' to smell wages all over you, boy."

"I sure wish my old man hadn't of died. You never saw a prettier ranch."

"Fella, when you get through wishin', all there is is doin' a man's work. And there ain't much of that left in this country."

They are brought bolt upright by a ferocious snarling of the dog and Roslyn's screaming. Both of them leap off the truck bed as Roslyn jumps out of the cab, going backward. Gay rushes to the cab and sees the dog on the seat, its teeth bared, snarling.

Roslyn: "She was shaking so I—"

Gay reaches in and throws the dog out of the truck. With tail between its legs, it crawls back to him. He reaches in behind the seat, takes out a length of cord, ties it to the dog's collar, and lashes the dog to the bumper. The dog crawls under the truck in the shade and lies down. Gay now goes to Roslyn, who is quivering; he starts to put his arm around her.

Roslyn halts and looks up into his face as though he must do something to calm the animal immediately. "She's scared to death, Gay!"

"Well, even a dog can't have it just right *all* the time."

The ring of his voice meets the sharp sound of a shot close by. It turns him toward the sky, and he immediately starts toward the truck, walking sideways as he talks to her behind him. Perce, a few paces away, turns to look for the plane.

Gay: "Just roll with it, honey, and see how you make out just this once."

He gets to the truck and immediately reaches behind the seat and draws out two iron spikes and a short-handled sledgehammer.

Now he glances for an instant toward the plane, which is just completing a dive. It is much closer now, its wing dents visible. The horses are galloping straight toward the bare white lake bed, but they are still on the sage-dotted desert.

All business now, Gay walks past Perce, who is staring at Roslyn. She is looking toward the horses. "Give us a hand here, Perce."

Perce, his eyes grown dreamy and strangely inward, follows Gay, who hands him a spike. He props it up as Gay drives it into the ground, ties a rope to it, and then, after pacing off several yards, does the same with the second spike and ties a rope to that.

Now Gay leaves Perce, walks to the truck, and tosses the hammer in behind the cab. For an instant he glances at Roslyn. She is wide-eyed, staring off at the horses. Gay passes her again, unties the dog, leads it to one of the spikes and ties it there. The three stand in silence, watching the plane and the horses, which have reached the border of the white lake bed and have broken file, scattering right and left in order to remain on the familiar sage desert, frightened of crossing over into the strange, superheated air coming off the clay. Two of them have turned back toward the mountains and a flare of hope brightens Roslyn's face.

The plane lays over on one wing in a long climb and dives down, down on the horses within a yard of their heads. Guido has turned them, and now they break out onto the lake bed, re-forming their herded grouping. The plane now flies above the lake bed itself and is not climbing for another dive.

Gay takes Roslyn's arm and walks her quickly to the truck cab, but she resists entering. They stop.

"Up you go, honey."

Before she can speak he hoists her into the cab, slams the door, quickly puts his head in, turns her face to him, and kisses her lips. "Now you watch some real ropin'!" With great joy he steps away and leaps up onto the truck bed. Perce is still on the ground, indecisively standing there. "Git up there, Perce, let's see what you can do now!"

Perce feels the force of Gay's command, and also sees what is evidently Gay's victory—for Roslyn is sitting motionless in the cab. He leaps aboard the truck bed.

The plane is just touching down on the lake bed and taxiing toward the truck. The horses are now trotting only, but so far away they seem like specks of illusion.

As the plane comes in fast, Gay hands Perce the end of a webbing strap whose other end is buckled to the post at Gay's corner. Perce passes the strap across his back and buckles the end to the post at his corner, so that both men are held, if rather precariously, to the cab and cannot fall backward. Gay now turns to the pile of tires behind him and takes out a coil of rope from the top tire. This Perce does too, from the pile behind him. Both men heft their ropes, grasping them a foot behind the nooses, turning them until the twist is out of them and they hang limber.

The plane taxis up, and the motor stops as it comes between the two spikes driven into the ground. Guido jumps out of the cockpit and runs to one spike, then the other, lashing the ropes to the plane struts. The dog, leashed to one of the spikes, snarls at him but he brushes it off and ties the rope. With his goggles on his forehead, his face puffed with preoccupation, he trots over to the cab and jumps in behind the wheel. Without a glance at Roslyn he turns the key, starts the engine, puts the truck in gear, and roars off at top speed across the lake bed, peering ahead through the windshield.

"Grab hold now, we're gonna do a lot of fast turning."

She grasps the dashboard, excitement pumping into her face. The faded Air Force insignia on his shoulder is next to her face.

Through the windshield the open lake bed spreads before them. A mile off, two black dots are rapidly enlarging. Now their forms become clear: two horses standing, watching the oncoming truck, their ears stiffly raised in curiosity.

She turns to Guido. His goggles are still on his forehead; a look of zealous calculation is coming into his face. She is feeling that first heat of real terror, and turns to look forward, her hands grasping the dashboard tighter. The two horses, a hundred yards off now, their rib cages expanding and contracting, their nostrils spread, turn and gallop, keeping close together. Guido steers right up to the flying rear hooves of the horses. Now they wheel, and Guido turns sharply with them—the truck leaning dangerously—and works brake and gas pedal simultaneously. Now the horses run straight, and in doing so they separate from each other by a foot or two;

Guido presses the truck into this space, which quickly widens, and he speeds even faster. Now there is one horse on each side of the truck, running abreast of the cab windows.

Roslyn looks at the horse running only a yard to one side of her. She could reach out and touch its eyes. It is a medium-size brown stallion, glistening with sweat. She hears the high screaming wheeze of its breathing, and the strangely gentle tacking of its un-shod hooves on the hard lake bed. It is stretching out now, and its stricken eyes seem blind and agonized. Suddenly, from behind, a noose falls over its ears and hangs there askew.

On the truck bed, Perce is whipping his rope to make its noose fall over the stallion's ears.

Guido, unable to see him, yells to him past Roslyn's face, and he is calling with such urgency that he seems furious. "Go on, get him! Throw again, Perce!"

At this instant Roslyn sees the other horse beyond Guido's head as a noose falls cleanly down over its neck. Guido calls out the window on his side: "Attaboy, Gay!"

Up behind the cab, Gay and Perce squint against the wind tearing at their hatbrims and their shirts. Gay, having just lassoed his horse, is now letting go of the rope, his horse swerving off to the left, away from the truck. The rope stretches to its limit, then suddenly yanks the heavy truck tire off the top of the pile behind him. The horse feels the pull of the dragging tire and the suffocating squeeze of the noose, rears in air, and comes to a halt.

The truck has never slowed. Perce, who has coiled up his rope, circles it over his head and throws it. The noose falls over the stallion's head. Veering away to the right, it pulls a tire off from behind Perce.

Gay shouts with joy: "That's the way!"

Perce returns a grateful look and Gay stretches and claps him on the shoulder, laughing. They are suddenly joined.

Guido steers sharply to reverse the truck's direction; Roslyn is looking out the window at the stallion being forced to a halt by the dragging tire. Now it turns with lowered head to face the tire; now it raises up in the air, its forefeet flailing. Suddenly the truck speeds up again, changing direction.

Roslyn turns to Guido and yells: "Won't they choke?"

Guido: "We're comin' back in a minute."

They are speeding toward three rapidly enlarging specks; forms emerge; the three horses turn and run. Now a fourth, that of the colt, appears from behind the screening body of the mare. The colt runs with its nose in the mare's long, full tail.

Both men are twirling their lassos over their heads, leaning outward over the truck's sides. The sound of clattering hooves grows louder and louder in their ears. Gay's body absorbs the motion of the truck, his hands gently guide the rope, giving it form and life, and a startling pleasure shines in his eyes.

Perce is now above and a length behind the big mare and her colt. He is readying his noose, getting set. Suddenly Roslyn's head sticks out of the window of the cab, looking up at him pleadingly. She is almost within arm's length of the colt, which is galloping beside her. The fright and pain in her face surprise him. And Gay yells against the wind: "Get that horse!" Now Gay throws his noose at the horse on his side, and Perce throws his rope. It lands over the mare's head and she veers to the right, the colt changing course with her. He turns and watches the mare being halted by the dragging tire, the colt running almost rib to rib with her.

The one remaining horse is trotting away toward the brushy edge of the lake bed and the safety of the nearby hills. Guido sees it and speeds across the distance, and Gay lassos this horse a few yards before the sage border; once it is caught Guido circles back, leaving it bucking and flinging its heavily maned neck against the remorseless noose. Straight ahead in the far distance all of them see the stallion. While the other horses stand still, some of them with drooping heads, the stallion is flailing at the rope with his forefeet, charging toward the tire and snapping at it with his teeth.

Guido speeds toward him, glancing at Roslyn. "Now we tie them up so they don't choke. We'll pick them up tomorrow morning in the dealer's van."

She is staring at the approaching stallion, and when he has stopped the truck beside it he merely gets out with a rope in his hand without turning back to her.

Gay and Perce have hopped off and Guido joins them. They

are thirty feet from the animal, sizing him up. His sweat has blackened him, and he shines in the sun. Gay and Guido move toward him, spreading out. Their steps are quiet and all their movements small. The horse, seeing men for the first time, suddenly stamps down on the clay and, twisting his head, flies to one side. He is yanked off balance by the tire rope, and stumbles onto his shoulder and springs up again. His wind is screeching in his throttle now and blood is trickling from one nostril, and he is lowering his head to cough. The men advance, hefting their ropes.

Roslyn: "The others are his mares?"

Perce, who is still near the truck, turns quickly and sees Roslyn looking at him from the window. He nods. "That was his colt."

Gay: "Get on that tire, Perce!"

The command sends Perce running away to the tire, which is sliding behind the stallion; in air now, the animal comes down awkwardly on his hind feet and runs a length, and Perce jumps onto the tire, digging his heels into the clay and holding onto the rope.

The stallion faces them again, groaning for air. The men stand still. Now Gay twirls his noose over his head and the stallion makes an abortive charge at Perce, who scampers off the tire. As the stallion's profile for an instant presents itself to Gay, he flings his noose onto the ground; its right forefoot comes down as it runs past, and Gay jerks his rope and the fetlock is caught. Gay runs around the rear of the horse, flipping the rope over its back; on the other side he pulls in fast, and the right knee bends and the hoof is tight up against the stallion's ribs. Guido quickly throws and his noose sails over its face and behind its ears; with Perce holding the tire rope taut from the neck, Guido half knee-bends with his rope over his thighs and pulls, and the two nooses squeeze now from opposite directions. They are choking the stallion down. On the other side of the animal Gay wraps his rope around his arm and with all his power leans back. The stallion's trussed right hoof is drawing up tighter and tighter into its ribs, and slowly it leans down until its knee hits the ground. Without for an instant releasing the tautness of his rope, Gay comes toward the stallion, hand over hand on the nylon, and when he is two feet away—Guido and Perce are still leaning with all their weight on their throttle nooses—he raises up one boot and, setting his heel on the stallion's shoulder, pushes so that the stallion rolls onto its right side. But as it falls its right hoof flies out, and the rope is yanked through Gay's glove. The men scatter as the stallion bursts up from the ground, running at them, springing high and twisting its body like a great fish springing out of water. Perce runs to the sliding tire and digs in; the animal is jerked about by the neck and stands there, hawking air.

For a moment they are still. Now Guido walks softly and picks up his rope and Gay gets his, which is still noosed to the fetlock. After a moment when nothing moves but the horse's expanding and contracting rib cage, Gay suddenly flips his rope into the air over the horse's back, running around its rear at the same time, and once again he pulls and bends up the right leg. Faster this time, he comes in hand over hand to the stallion while Guido and Perce choke him down, and when he is close he jerks his rope suddenly and the horse goes down onto one knee. Now, to their surprise, its nose slowly lowers and rests on the ground as though it were doing an obeisance, blood running out of its nostrils onto the clay, its wind blowing up little puffs of talc. Gay pushes it over with his boot, and before it hits the ground he flips his rope around the left front fetlock. He knots both forefeet together and cuts the excess rope, stands away from the free hind feet, then delicately approaches, and with one movement wraps them together and draws them to the forefeet.

They have not heard her talking; Roslyn has come out of the truck and she is talking quietly. Only now in the quiet Perce senses her there and turns. She is smiling and her eyes are larger than life. "Why are you killing them? Gay?" She begins to move toward the three men when a drumming in the ground turns them. The stallion has broken out of the truss and his hind feet are flailing free, his head beating the ground. Gay rushes to the tire and pulls his head flat against the earth. "Grab this, Perce!"

Perce takes the rope from him. Now he runs to Guido and grabs his rope, and circling behind the horse he twirls the noose over his head. The hind hooves are cracking against the forehooves and Gay knows the rope around the forefeet may tear. He throws and nooses both hind hooves together, comes around toward the head, and is drawing the hind legs up tight when he sees her hands.

She is pulling his rope, trying to get it away from him, and she is strangely smiling, calling into his face: "Okay, you won—you won, Gay!"

"Get away, that horse is wild!"

"Oh, Gay, darling—Gay!"

Gay yanks his rope and swings his arm at the same time—for she is coming at him with her smile, and her fists are hitting his arm—and she goes flying backward and falls.

Perce is in front of Gay. "Hey!"

For an instant they face each other.

Gay: "Get on that tire."

"No need to hit her."

"Get on that tire, Perce. Don't say anything to me. Just get on that tire and hold this horse!"

On the lake bed's silence they hear her sobs. They see her, all three turning now as she walks toward the truck, weeping into her hands.

Perce goes to the tire and holds the neck rope taut. Gay trusses the stallion tight, four hooves together. Now Perce stands. None of them looks toward the truck. Gay lights a cigarette. They wipe the sweat off their faces. Her sobs come to them softly through the air. The three men and the stallion on the ground suck air. The horse coughs. Guido looks down at it, noting the old scars on its shoulders and quarters. One ear is bitten off at the tip. "Boy, this son of a bitch must've kicked the shit out of every stud in Nevada."

Perce sees now that Roslyn's muffled weeping has entered Gay, who stares down at the trussed stallion. "I guess comin' up here the first time like her, there might not seem much sense to it at that, for only six horses. Not knowin' how it used to be." An ironic, nearly bitter flicker of a grin passes over Gay's lips. "I never thought of it, but I guess the fewer you kill the worse it looks."

He raises his eyes toward the distance, and the two other men know his vision, the picture in his mind of the hundreds that once poured out of these passes. Gay glances down at the stallion once more. An embarrassment, almost a shyness, has crept over him as he turns to them. Even his stance seems suddenly awkward and not quite his own.

"What you say we give her this herd?"

Guido laughs; he does not believe it. But Perce reaches thankfully to grasp Gay's arm, when he sees Roslyn coming up behind them.

Gay faces her and his offer is dying in his throat at the sight of her eyes, the unbelievable distance in them, a coldness that seems to reach into her soul.

Roslyn: "How much do you want for them? I'll pay you."

The tendons stiffen in Gay's neck. With his eyes narrowed, he seems like a man being drenched.

"I'll give you two hundred dollars. Is that enough?"

"Let's get on the truck." Gay is walking past her.

Perce almost leaps after him. "But Gay! You were just sayin' you'd give them to her."

Gay slows to a halt and thinks. The hurt is in his eyes like burning smoke. "I did think of that. But I sell to dealers only. All they're lookin' to buy is the horse."

Without moving toward him, her indignation still in her voice, Roslyn states as a fact: "I didn't mean to insult you, Gay."

"No insult. I was just wondering who you think you been talkin' to since we met, that's all."

He walks to the truck and hops aboard. In silence the others take their places, Guido behind the wheel with her beside him, and Perce on the back with Gay.

Guido starts the engine and drives slowly toward the next horse they must tie up. He feels the waves of anger emanating from her. The silence between them gnaws at him. "Brother, what a day."

She does not speak or look at him.

"I nearly hit the side of that mountain before. Cylinder cut out just at the bottom of a dive. That's the closest I ever come, I tell you."

She does not move. For a moment he can only glance at her in alarm, for she is evidently close to a state of shock.

"I . . . I know how you feel. I really do. . . ."

She is beginning to rock from side to side. Her alarm seems to require him to speak. "Took me a while to get used to it myself. Tell

you the truth, the only part of it I ever liked is the flying. Truthfully
. . . you don't know me. I used to be afraid of too many things. I had
to force myself. Because you can't run away from life, and life is
cruel sometimes. . . ."

She claps her hands to her ears, a groan coming through her
clenched teeth. It frightens him.

"Maybe you ought to wait in the plane. You want to? Look, I
know how you feel but I can't stop it now. I know him. There'd be
hell to pay!"

She looks at him directly, with a challenging contempt.

He suddenly senses a path for himself, a realization shows on
his face, an excitement of a new kind.

"Listen, you want me to stop this?"

Her eyes open wide in surprise.

"You're through with Gay now, right?" She seems perplexed
and he presses on against his own faltering. "Well, tell me. He
doesn't know what you're all about, Roslyn, he'll never know.
Come back with me; give me a week, two weeks. I'll teach you
things you never knew. Let me show you what I am. You don't
know me. What do you say? Give me a reason and I'll stop it.
There'll be hell to pay, but you give me a reason and I'll do it!"

A power of contemptuous indignation has been rising in her,
but he has seen nothing but what seemed to be her excitement at his
offer. And when her voice strikes at him now, he almost leaps in
surprise.

"A *reason*! You! Sensitive fella? So full of feelings? So sad
about your wife, and crying to me about the bombs you dropped
and the people you killed. *You* have to get something to be human?
You were never sad for anybody in your life, Guido! You only
know the sad words! You could blow up the whole world, and all
you'd ever feel is sorry for *yourself!*"

A scream has entered her voice and it chills him. He stops the
truck near the mare and colt and gets out. Guido seems transfixed
as he walks around the truck to join Gay and Perce, who are hopping off the back. He moves up close to Gay, looks at the mare, and
says in a peculiarly intimate, comradely way: "Let's get the old
lady, come on."

"She's fifteen if she's a day." Gay uncoils his rope, hefting it loose. The mare stands with her head stretched toward them, getting their scent. "Probably wouldn't last the winter."

Perce sees Roslyn turning away from the sight of the mare with a crazed look in her eyes. As Gay and Guido move toward the animal, the colt makes a bleating cry and runs a few yards and tumbles, rolling over and over, then springs up and runs back and collides with the mare, which does not budge.

Gay calls back over his shoulder, "Perce!"

Perce walks slowly to the tire and sits on it, grasping the rope.

The mare circles to keep Guido and Gay in front of her. They are easier in their movements with her than with the stallion; she moves more weightily because she is heavier and her foal is constantly in her way. They approach her with small movements to position themselves for the throw, and she observes them through her terrified eyes, but there is a waiting quality about her, an absence of fury. The foal makes a pass toward her teats, and then, as though remembering, jerks up its head to watch the approaching men.

Now Gay halts. He is on one side of the mare, Guido in front of her. He tosses a noose behind her forefeet. Guido shouts and rushes at her face, and she backs into the noose which Gay pulls tight and, running behind her, yanks to trip her to her knees. Guido walks up beside her and pushes her and she falls to earth. Gay lashes her four feet together and drops his rope. Perce lets go his rope, draws up his knees, and rests his arms on them, looking into the distance. The foal walks to him and sniffs the ground a yard from his hand.

Gay takes out his cigarettes. Guido blows his nose. They are standing with their backs to the truck. The three sense Roslyn's eyes on them, and this knowledge is like a raging sea on which they ride, falling and rising within themselves, yet outwardly even more relaxed than if all were calm under them.

Gay inhales, and Perce knows now that he is gathering himself to turn about and go back to the truck to resume the roping of the remaining horses. The hurt is deepening in Gay's face and this somber look of loss, this groping for his pride, is dangerous. "We can rope the others on the way back. What you reckon this mare weighs?"

In Guido's eyes the emptiness is like a lake as he surveys the mare's body.

Now Perce slowly turns. Roslyn is looking skyward through the windshield and he knows she can hear this. "There's hardly beer money in it for six, Gay."

Gay's eyes remain defiantly fixed on Guido's profile as he waits for the figures and Perce says no more.

Now Guido looks at him. "She might be six hundred pounds."

Gay: "The two browns be about four hundred, I'd say."

Guido: "Just about, ya."

"Must be five hundred on the stallion, anyway."

"A little lighter, I'd say. Call it nineteen hundred—two thousand pounds altogether."

"How's that come out, now?"

Guido looks up in the air, figuring. "Well, six cents a pound, that's—" He figures with silent, moving lips.

In the momentary silence they hear Roslyn's sobs fully pouring out of her. Gay and Guido keep their eyes on each other.

"Be about hundred and ten, hundred and twenty dollars, Gay."

"Okay, how you want to cut it?"

"Any way you like. . . . I'll take fifty for myself and the plane."

"Okay. I guess I oughta have about forty for the truck and me. That'd give you twenty-five, Perce—that all right?"

Perce, staring at the mare, seems not to have heard.

"Perce?"

"You fellas take it. I just went along for the ride, anyway."

Perce turns so sharply that the other two start. They see Roslyn walking. She is heading across the open lake bed.

"Roslyn!" Gay takes a step, and halts himself.

She has swerved about. Her shadow sketches toward them. Forty yards away, she screams, her body writhing, bending over as though to catapult her hatred.

"You liars! All of you!" Clenching her fists, she screams toward their faces: *"Liars!"*

Unnerved, Gay flinches.

"Man! Big man! You're only living when you can watch something die! Kill everything, that's all you want! Why don't you just kill yourselves and be happy?"

She runs toward them, but stops as though afraid, and says directly toward Gay: "You. With your God's country. Freedom!" She screams into his face: *"I hate you!"*

Unable to bear it, Gay mutters: "We've had it now, Roslyn."

"You sure did—more than *you'll* ever know. But you didn't want it. Nobody does. I pity you all." Looking from one to another and beyond them to imagined others: "You know everything except what it feels like to be alive. You're three dear, sweet dead men."

"She's crazy!"

The weird resonance of Guido's cry turns them all to him. His eyes seem peeled back, fanatical, as though he had been seized from within by a pair of jaws which were devouring him as he stands there. His head and hands are shaking, he seems about to fly off the ground at her, and he goes onto his toes and down and up again. "They're all crazy!" Now he moves away from Gay and back again, flinging his words toward Roslyn and beyond her toward the sky. "You try not to believe it. Because you need them. You need them but they're crazy!" Tears spurt out of his eyes onto his cheeks, but his ferocity is undiminished. "You struggle, you build, you try, you turn yourself inside out for them, but nothing's ever enough! It's never a deal, something's always missing. It's gotta be perfect or they put the spurs to you! We ask them too much—and we tell them too little. I know—I got the marks!" He hits his chest with his fist, heaving for breath; the veins are standing out on his neck. Suddenly he looks down at the ground dizzily. He walks away and after a few yards he stops, throwing his head back, trying to catch his breath. She, exhausted, looking at nothing, bends over and seems to crumple, sitting on the ground, weeping quietly. Perce is looking at her through the corner of his eye. Gay walks around the prostrate mare, goes to the truck, and climbs onto the back. Perce goes over to her as though to help her up, but she gets to her feet, the talc caked on her jeans, and walks weakly toward the truck and gets in. Perce comes around and gets behind the wheel beside her. Now Guido returns, staring at the ground as though he had puzzled himself. He hops aboard. The truck starts away.

A blasted look is on Gay's face, as though he had been beaten in a fistfight in a cause he only half-believed. Squinting against the wind, his eyes hover on the high mountains, full of wish, almost expecting the sight of the hundreds, the full herds clambering into the open, the big horses and the sweet mares that gentled so quickly, the natural singlefooters, the smooth gallopers that just swept the ground under them, hardly touching it. . . .

TWELVE

The clinking of Guido's wrench is the only sound; all else is silence. He finishes screwing in his number-four spark plug, unclips a wire, lays his wrench on number five, and screws it out. His flashlight tucked under his arm illuminates his hands. He is whistling under his breath, strangely energized, glancing quickly now and then at the others and brimming over with some private hope of his own.

A few yards from him Gay stands staring out at the sky's starry arch, seeing nothing. A sense of mourning flows from his very stance; he has his hands on his hips as though he must support his back. He seems exhausted.

Squatting on his heels, Perce is motionless, smoking. He is ten yards from Gay, and yet he can feel his mood. Off to his left, in the cab of the truck, Roslyn is resting her head against the doorframe, staring out over Perce's head toward a trussed horse lying on its side. As night deepens, only its darker mass is visible, and it never moves. Roslyn closes her eyes and seems to sleep.

Gay calls over to Guido: "How long you gonna be with that?"

"No time at all now." Guido's voice is high and crisp. He scrapes carbon from the plug's electrode and blows out the chips.

Roslyn sees Perce standing up. He walks over to her and stands. In the moonlight his face seems bonier and hard. His voice is close to a whisper, yet loud enough to avoid any air of conspiracy. "I'd turn them loose. If you wanted."

"No, don't fight."

"He got himself up so high he can't get down now." He looks over toward Gay, who is standing with his back to them. She feels in Perce his impatient love for the older man, and she knows his uncertainty about what to do.

"It doesn't matter, anyway." She looks toward the trussed horse. "It's all a joke—how easy they agree to die! It's like a dream, look, it doesn't even move. Is it sleeping?"

"Might be, sure."

"Couldn't they leave the colt here?"

"Wouldn't stay. Follow the truck right into town. Probably drop on the way in."

He turns and leans against the door, looking with her toward the dark shape of the trussed horse. "I wish I'd met you a long time ago. Save me a lot of broken bones."

She turns to him, then reaches out and touches his arm.

He faces her. "I'd just about gave up—expectin' anything." He comes in closer to her, taking a breath. "I'd cut them loose for you."

They hear Guido's voice and turn quickly, seeing Gay going to him at the engine. Guido hands him the flashlight, which he shines on a spark plug in Guido's hand. Holding it up close to his eyes, Guido passes a feeler gauge between the electrode and the ground pin, then knocks the ground pin to lessen the gap and measures it again. They can hear his voice and his quiet laugh.

Guido: "Buck up, boy. Before you know it you'll be up to your neck in girls again."

Gay is annoyed, wanting to be off as quickly as possible.

But Guido goes on: "I just been thinking ... I don't know how we got so stupid. The world's full of mountains ... Colorado, Montana, Canada, even Mexico; and where there's mountains there's *got* to be horses. Probably we couldn't clean them all out till we're too stiff to walk. Now if we worked awhile, and I'd even sell my house—I don't know what I was keepin' it for anyway—and put everything into a good plane ... we could get this thing on a business basis."

Gay shifts onto one hip, a deepening disgust and anger rising into his face.

Guido: "Why, we never even watered the horses before we

weighed them in! We could put fifty pounds on just these five if we let them drink. We just been foolin' around with it."

Impatiently indicating for him to resume working on the spark plug, Gay hardly moves his lips. "I want to get out of here, come on."

As he screws the spark plug into the engine, Guido's confidence seems to flow. "With a good plane we could fly into Reno from anywhere—check in at the Mapes, have us a time, and off we go again! Boy, we wouldn't need anybody in this world!" He has taken the flashlight, and waits for Gay's reply.

Gay's face is flushed as though he were exerting himself to lift something. At last he bursts out in a pained voice: "Why don't you shut up, Guido?" Guido straightens in shock at the rumble of disgust he hears. "Just shut up, will you?"

But Guido smiles directly into Gay's threatening gaze. "Meet you at the dealer's in the morning; get his winch truck if we're early. Six o'clock, okay?"

Gay's non-reply is his agreement, and Guido moves away along the wing, goes to the cockpit, and climbs in. Gay stands before the propeller. "Okay, give her a twist—switch off!"

For a moment Gay seems not to have heard. His eyes are sightless, inward-looking. Roslyn and Perce can see him standing there.

"Turn her over, boy, huh?"

Gay faces the plane, reaches up, turns the propeller. The engine clicks like a clock being wound. Gay seems to be moving in slow motion, pulling the blade down, then gradually raising his arms and pulling it down again, priming the cylinders.

Perce walks along the length of the truck and Roslyn turns to watch him. He disappears around the back of it. She looks at the plane again.

Guido: "Okay! Switch on!"

Gay positions himself more carefully. The propeller is horizontal. He lays both hands on the blade, swings his right leg across his left, and quickly pulls and hops away as the engine clatters up to a puffing roar. He walks backward along the wing until he clears it. Guido motions from the cockpit for him to watch out for the dog, which is still tied to a stake under the wing. Gay motions for Guido to take off.

The engine's roar increases and the propeller becomes a wheel in the moonlight. The plane bucks forward and back against the grip of the wheel brakes as Guido warms the engine. In the cockpit Guido is focusing the flashlight on his gauges. Now the engine roars up to its peak.

Roslyn turns quickly, seeing Perce getting in behind the wheel beside her. He starts the truck engine. She looks through the windshield toward Gay, who is now holding the dog's body down as the wing of the plane passes over it. The truck is suddenly in motion as the plane taxis away in the direction of the moon. She involuntarily grabs Perce's arm to stop him, but he now switches on the headlights and swerves the truck toward the trussed horse. Roslyn leans out the window and sees the plane taxiing off into the darkness, and Gay turning from it and finding the truck gone. He swings about, looks toward her, and starts to run. The truck's brakes squeal and it skids to a halt beside the trussed horse; Perce leaps out and runs to it, with an open clasp knife in his hand. He leans over the horse's belly and cuts the rope around its hooves, and it starts scrambling to stand up. He rushes to the tire and cuts the rope; the horse, on its feet, trots away for a few yards and stands stiffly. Perce starts to run after it and shoo it off but he sees Gay bearing down on him and hears his roaring voice. He jumps into the truck, grinds it into gear, and jams the gas pedal to the floor. The wheels spin for an instant and it jerks and roars away.

A wordless command bellows from Gay's furious face. He rushes toward the horse, which now trots, not very fast. The rope is trailing from its neck and he reaches down for it, but the animal's sense of him speeds it into a canter. Gay lunges for the rope and falls, and the horse clatters off into the darkness. He gets to his feet, turns in a circle. The headlights of the truck are impossibly distant now. He runs toward them. Tears are on his cheeks and angry calls come from his throat, but more than anger is his clear frustration, as though above all his hand had been forced from his grip on his life and he had been made smaller.

The truck halts beside another horse. Perce leaps out, cuts it loose, and rushes back into the truck and speeds it away. A wave of guilt passes over Roslyn's face now. She scans the lake bed for a sign of Gay. In her uncertainty she turns to Perce. His mildness has vanished and he seems inspired, a wild, rebellious joy on his face.

Guido has taxied close to the edge of the lake bed. For a moment he sits slumped on the torn cushions, staring out at nothing, wanting the engine's roar to enter and overwhelm his mind. He cuts the throttle; the plane slows, and he turns it about to face the wind. Far across the lake bed the mountain face gleams in the moonlight as though covered with snow; the white clay stretching away before him is luminescent with a greenish-silvery light that does not brighten the air but clings to the ground like a heavy gas. He has nowhere to go and no reason to move; the threat of total emptiness angers him. He guns the engine and the plane hurries. As he starts to press the stick forward to raise the tail and climb, his eye catches the truck's moving headlights; but he realizes that, oddly, it is not moving toward the sage desert and the homeward direction. Airborne, he flattens the trajectory of the plane, banks sharply, leans out the side of the cockpit a man's height above the earth. A horse is just crossing the headlight beams below—a horse running free. He pushes the stick forward, settling himself to watch the ground coming up beneath him, striving to remember where each horse was tethered, envisioning the crash should he hit one as he comes in to land.

A mile away the headlight beams pick up the stallion's form. Roslyn looks out and as it nears she cries out: "Oh, Perce! I don't know!" He glances at her surprised, perplexed, and brakes the truck.

The trussed stallion, ears cocked to the truck's sound, arches up his head. Perce runs to the tire. The stallion yanks it as he saws the rope. Roslyn runs out of the cab, glancing about guiltily for a sign of Gay. Suddenly the rope parts. The stallion, free, kicks up his rear legs, rushes past them, and turns about. Perce pulls her out of the way and yells wordlessly to scare off the beast. Before the reality of the freed stallion, Roslyn feels an ecstatic, terrified conviction. Almost unaware of her own voice, she cries out: "Go! Go home! Go home!"

Perce runs toward the stallion, which turns and gallops away, his neck rope trailing. Breathless, they watch him for a moment, then run to the truck. Roslyn gets into the cab. Perce halts, scanning the glowing lake bed, calculates the location of the two remaining horses, and hurries into the truck.

From the open cockpit of the taxiing plane Guido methodically keeps turning his eyes across the breadth of the lake bed, swinging the plane in wide arcs. Now two specks of light move very far away. He guns the plane toward them.

The headlights are larger in Gay's eyes. He has changed direction with their every movement, and now, impossibly distant, he still runs mechanically, anesthetized by his impotence. A tacking sound stops him instantly.

Trying to control his wheezing breath, wiping sweat from his eyes, he turns about slowly, listening. The moon is glowing and the lake bed seems bright, but night begins a few inches off the ground. His heart is surging in his chest, a pulse beating in his eyes. Again a shadow moves. He widens his eyes to be sure. He slowly sits down on his heels and makes himself small. A shadow moves again. He senses its direction now; surprisingly, it is not headed for the mountains. He turns toward the center of the lake bed. Gradually his eyes perceive the black forms of the mare and colt far off under the moon. Now he turns back toward the moving form. The tacking sound is closer now.

Silently he rises and moves toward the trussed mare, keeping his mouth wide open to let his breath escape without sound. He sees the colt getting to its feet now and lengthens his steps, keeping his head down. He halts at the sudden jagged sound of the mare's snickering. Off to his left, the stallion's form moves closer to her, and it stands over her trussed form. Gay sees its neck stretching down to her. He is moving again, crouching low, and now he runs. The stallion's head shoots up and it backs and stands, listening. The moon makes a yellow disk of one eye as Gay comes in from the side and grasps its neck rope in both gloved hands. The horse bares its teeth and gouges for his shoulder, and he slips his hands farther down along the rope, murmuring to it, but it suddenly swerves and gallops. Gay wraps the rope around his arm and runs behind, trying to dig in his heels. A quick burst of force yanks him about and he falls. He is being dragged on his side, the talc blinding him. The rope suddenly slackens; he scrambles to his feet and the shoulder of the horse hits the side of his head as it gallops past, and he is pulled to the ground again. He sits up, swinging his boots around in front of him, seeking the clay with his heels. The stallion coughs and wheels, and for a moment stands facing him where he sits. The noose, he knows, is not tight enough to make it wheeze as it does, and he again wraps the rope around his arm, digging his heels in and preparing in his mind to roll away if it should charge him there. The stallion backs, experimentally it seems, testing his weight on the rope.

Gay starts sidling toward the mare. She is a length away. He reaches her without taking his eyes from the stallion, and feels with his elbow for the shape of her, trying to sense how far he must move to reach her neck rope and the tire. At his touch she shudders; he feels her quarter, and sidles so that she is between him and the stallion, which is restive on its hooves but not pulling hard any more. Gay gets his heels under him and creeps sideways toward the mare's neck. Now he has her neck rope under his arm. He becomes still. He will have to unwrap the rope to tie it to the mare's noose.

The stallion eyes him, gasping. Gay murmurs to him across the mare's neck: "Whoa now, whoa now, whoa now . . ." He begins to unwrap his arm, always keeping both hands around the rope. The stallion's head rises, and Gay stops moving. He knows the movement of the rope is vibrating into the stallion's body and can set him going again. After a moment, he again moves his arm to uncoil the rope. The mare suddenly blows out a high snicker, and the stallion flings its head into the air; Gay is yanked toward him over the mare's body. He goes with the force and lets it carry him to his feet; he leaps for the stallion's neck to pull the noose tight with both hands and the animal gallops, kicking out its hind legs, but Gay can feel it trembling and its power weakening. He hangs from the noose, pulling it down with all his force, the backs of his thighs being pounded by the horse's knees.

The stallion halts. Gay hangs his full weight from the tightening noose. The stallion's neck lowers and his shaking knees start to buckle. Gay yanks again, a short scream escaping his throat as a broken, thin cry vibrates in the stallion's head. Gay hears an engine. He yanks again, raising his feet off the ground, pulling the stallion's head lower. The headlight beams hit his face and burn his eyes. He hears the brakes squealing and the doors opening.

On both Roslyn's and Perce's faces is a look of near awe. The stallion is motionless, groaning against the asphyxiating noose. And yet between it and Gay hanging from its neck there is a strange relation, an aura of understanding; it is as though the vanquished beast belonged to Gay now, however this came to be, and that it knew this even as it would not come to earth.

Perce picks up the rope end and lashes it to the truck bumper. "Okay, let him go!"

Gay springs away from the horse, which tucks in its head and walks slowly and halts.

Swaying on his feet, Gay moves to the truck and lies over the hood, his arms outstretched.

He slowly opens his cramped hands. Roslyn does not approach him. She watches him from her distance, as Perce does, and she seems to soften under the power of his struggle. A wonder is rising in her eyes. She takes a step toward him, but Perce reaches out quickly and stops her. She sees fear in Perce's face, and she becomes afraid not so much of Gay's violence as of having done a thing which now she cannot comprehend.

The plane engine is heard, and in a moment it comes to a halt nearby. The engine is cut; Guido leaps out and runs toward Gay. Seeing him heaving for breath and the stallion tied, he laughs toward Perce and bends over Gay to give him a quick hug.

"You held him! Good boy! We'll get them all back tomorrow! Get your wind now, just get your wind now...." He warmly pats Gay's back.

Gay is still sucking air, his trunk bent over the truck hood, his eyes staring at the stallion. Guido grips his shoulder. "Don't you worry, boy—we ain't through here. Not by a long shot! We're only starting! I'll go up to Thighbone Mountain with you—hear? There's five thousand dollars up there, but we gotta work at it. We'll *horse-*

back in up there! And there's more, there's more—but we gotta work at it! 'Cause we don't need nobody in this world, Gay—and I guess you know it now, don't you?" Toward Roslyn: "To hell with them all!"

Gay, oblivious of Guido, is staring at the mustang, his cheek pressed against the truck hood. His eyes seem to be peering toward a far point, and about him is a stillness, as though he were alone here. He straightens, slipping a hand into his pocket.

Guido reaches to him: "Come on, I'll fly you back. They can take the—" He breaks off, seeing a clasp knife opening in Gay's hand. When he looks again into his face he sees tears in his eyes, and he is bewildered and, for the moment, silent.

Gay walks straight at him as though he did not see him, and Guido, stepping out of his path, asks: "What are—?" But Gay has bent to the rope at the bumper and is cutting it, his hand shaking. Guido grabs at his hand and holds it, and understands enough to raise a panic in his eyes as he stands pressed close to his friend. Gay's caked lips move; in a cracked whisper, looking into Guido's face but blind to him: "It's all finished."

"What the hell'd you catch him for?"

"Just . . . done it. Don't like nobody makin' up my mind for me, that's all."

A tremor seems to go through his body, and his brows tense together as though he would weep in anger. He weakly presses Guido to move aside, but Guido holds his wrist.

"I'll go with you to Thighbone!"

Gay shakes his head. He looks beyond Guido to the darkened hills, and anger hardens his face and straightens him. "God damn them all! They changed it. Changed it all around. They smeared it all over with blood, turned it into shit and money just like everything else. You know that. I know that. It's just ropin' a dream now." He slips his wrist out of Guido's grasp. "Find some other way to know you're alive . . . if they got another way, any more." He turns to the rope and leans his weight on the knife; the rope, cut, falls to the ground.

For a moment, the stallion does not move. With the pressure off the noose it stretches its neck and, taking a step to the side, almost stumbles to the ground, rights itself, and walks. Then it halts, stands unsteadily, and goes away. Gay walks over to the mare and cuts her hoof ropes and then the rope to the tire; she weightily clambers up and trots away, the foal following with its nose in her flying tail.

The four stand listening to the fading sound of the hooves. Gay, closing his knife and slipping it into his pocket, walks from Guido, looking at no one, absorbed in himself.

There eyes follow him as he goes by and gets into the truck behind the wheel, exhausted, silent. For a moment he stares ahead through the windshield. Roslyn is on the opposite side of the truck now, looking across the empty seat at him. In this moment it is unknown what he will do, and she does not move. He turns to her, his loneliness in his eyes. "Drive you back . . . if you want."

Hesitant and afraid of him still, she gets into the seat, but not close to him. Her open stare is full of his pain and his loss.

Perce has come up to her window. "I'm pleased to have met you, Roslyn."

Roslyn: "Don't hurt yourself any more, will you?"

He thanks her with his eyes. "If you ever feel like droppin' a card, my address is just Black River . . . California."

Gay starts the engine and turns to Guido, who is on his side of the truck. "See you around. Give you a call in a couple days."

Guido, his eyes sharpened with resentment, laughs. "Where'll you be? Some gas station, polishing windshields?"

"You got me there, Pilot." Gay turns forward and starts the truck rolling.

Guido jumps onto the running board, laughing and yelling at him: "Or making change in the supermarket!"

Guido jumps off, and makes a megaphone of his hands, furiously calling: "Try the laundromat—they might need a fella to load the machines!"

But the truck is moving away, and his need is wide; he cries out, his fist in the air: "Gay! Where you goin'?"

He has come to a halt, angry and lost. Perce stands there, tears flowing into his eyes.

Gay drives in silence, exhausted. Roslyn is still a distance from him on the seat. Now she turns to him, not knowing his feeling.

They seem like strangers for a moment.

"I'll leave tomorrow." She is asking, but he remains silent. "Okay?" He drives on. "You'll never believe it, but I didn't mean to harm you. . . . I honor you. You're a brave man."

He is silent.

"You don't like me any more. Do you?"

Now she turns forward. Her voice wavers. Everything seems to be moving away from her.

"But you know something? For a minute, when those horses galloped away, it was almost like I gave them back their life. And all of a sudden I got a feeling—it's crazy!—I suddenly thought, 'He must love me, or how would I dare do this?' Because I always just ran away when I couldn't stand it. Gay—for a minute you made me not afraid. And it was like my life flew into my body. For the first time."

He sees the dog in the headlight beams, tied to one of the stakes, and halts the truck.

She opens her door, but turns back to him as though she cannot leave. And suddenly she cries out, desperately: "Oh, Gay, what is there? Do you know? What is there that stays?"

He turns to her for the first time. There are tears in his eyes. He draws her to him and kisses her. She is weeping with joy, trying to see through his eyes into him.

Gay: "God knows. Everything I ever see was comin' or goin' away. Same as you. Maybe the only thing is . . . the knowin'. 'Cause I know you now, Roslyn, I do know you. Maybe that's all the peace there is or can be. I never bothered to battle a woman before. And it was peaceful, but a lot like huggin' the air. This time, I thought I'd lay my hand on the air again—but it feels like I touched the whole world. I bless you, girl."

She flies to his face, kissing him passionately. The dog barks outside. She runs out of the cab to it, and it greets her joyfully. She unties it and claps her hands to make it follow. The dog leaps onto the truck bed and she reenters the cab, her face infused with an overflowing love. He starts the truck and they drive. Suddenly, with the quick rapture of her vision: "If . . . if we weren't afraid! Gay? And there could be a child. And we could make it brave. One person in the world who would be brave from the beginning! I was scared to last night. But I'm not so much now. Are you?"

He clasps her close to his hip. He drives. The love between them is viable, holding them a little above the earth. The headlights pick up clumps of sage now, and the ride is bumpy.

Roslyn: "How do you find your way back in the dark?"

Gay nods, indicating the sky before them: "Just head for that big star straight on. The highway's under it; take us right home."

She raises her eyes to the star through the streaks and dust of the windshield. The sound of Guido's plane roars in and away, invisible overhead. The truck's headlights gradually disappear, and with them all sound. Now there is only the sky full of stars, and absolute silence.

AFTER THE FALL

The Characters:

QUENTIN	CHAIRMAN
FELICE	HOLGA
DAN	FATHER
MOTHER	MAGGIE
ELSIE	LOU
LOUISE	MICKEY
CARRIE	LUCAS
	HARLEY BARNES

Nurses, porter, secretary, hospital attendant,
a group of boys, and passers-by

Copyright © 1964 by Arthur Miller
New York premiere January 23, 1964

AFTER THE FALL

ACT ONE

The action takes place in the mind, thought, and memory of Quentin.

Except for one chair there is no furniture in the conventional sense; there are no walls or substantial boundaries.

The setting consists of three levels rising to the highest at the back, crossing in a curve from one side of the stage to the other. A stairway, center, connects them. Rising above all, and dominating the stage, is the blasted stone tower of a German concentration camp. Its wide lookout windows are like eyes which at the moment seem blind and dark; bent reinforcing rods stick out of it like broken tentacles.

On the two lower levels are sculpted areas; indeed, the whole effect is neolithic, a lavalike, supple geography in which, like pits and hollows found in lava, the scenes take place. The mind has no color but its memories are brilliant against the grayness of its landscape. When people sit they do so on any of the abutments, ledges, or crevices. A scene may start in a confined area, but spread or burst out onto the entire stage, overrunning any other area.

People appear and disappear instantaneously, as in the mind; but it is not necessary that they walk off the stage. The dialogue will make clear who is "alive" at any moment and who is in abeyance.

The effect, therefore, will be the surging, flitting, instantaneousness of a mind questing over its own surfaces and into its depths.

The stage is dark. Now there is a sense that some figure has moved in the farthest distance; a footstep is heard, then others. As light dimly rises the persons in the play move in a random way up from be-

*neath the high back platform. Whispering emanates from them. Some
sit at once, others come farther downstage, seem to recognize one another; still others move alone and in total separateness; in short, there
is a totally random congeries of movements in a slow but not dream-
like rhythm. One of them, Quentin, a man in his forties, moves out of
this mass and down the depth of the stage to the chair. This chair faces
front, toward the audience. A sharp light now isolates it. All movement
ceases. Quentin reaches forward over the chairback to shake the hand
of the Listener, who, if he could be seen, would be sitting just beyond
the edge of the stage itself.*

QUENTIN: Hello! God, it's good to see you again! I'm very well. I
hope it wasn't too inconvenient on such short notice. Fine, I just
wanted to say hello, really. Thanks. *He sits on invitation.* How've
you been? You look sunburned. . . . Oh! I've never been to South
America, you enjoy it? That's nice. . . . Do I? I guess I am, I'm quite
healthy—I do a lot of walking now. *Slight pause.* I started to call
you a couple of times this year. Last year too. . . . Well, I lost the
impulse; I wasn't sure what I wanted to say, and at my age it's dis-
couraging to still have to go wandering around in one's mind. Actually, I called you on the spur of the moment this morning; I have a
bit of a decision to make. You know—you mull around about
something for months and all of a sudden there it is and you're at a
loss for what to do. Were you able to give me two hours? It might
not take that long, but I think it involves a great deal and I'd rather
not rush. Fine.
   He sets himself to begin, looks off.
Ah . . .
   Interrupted, he turns back to Listener, surprised.
I've quit the firm, didn't I write you about that? Really! I was sure
I'd written. . . . Oh, about fourteen months ago; a few weeks after
Maggie died. . . . No, no. I've withdrawn completely. I still hold my
interest, such as it is, but I'm out of it. . . . Well, it just got to where I
couldn't concentrate on a case any more; not the way I used to. It's
hard to describe; it all lost its necessity; I was going on because I'd
started out to become a successful attorney, and I'd become one—I
felt I was merely in the service of my own success. There has to be

some semblance of a point, and I couldn't find it any more. Although I do wonder sometimes if I am simply trying to destroy myself. . . . Well, I have walked away from what passes for an important career. . . . Not very much, I'm afraid; I still live in the hotel, see a few people, read a good deal—*Smiles*—stare out the window. I don't know why I'm smiling; maybe I feel that's all over now, and I'll harness myself to something again. Although I've had that feeling before and done nothing about it, I—

Again, interrupted, he looks surprised.

God, I wrote you about *that,* didn't I? Maybe I dream these letters. . . . Mother died. Oh, it's four, five months ago, now. Yes, quite suddenly; I was in Germany at the time and . . . it's one of the things I wanted to talk to you about. I . . . met a woman there. *He grins.* I never thought it could happen again, but we became quite close. In fact, she's arriving tonight for some conference at Columbia. She's an archaeologist. . . . I'm not sure, you see, if I want to lose her, and yet it's outrageous to think of committing myself again. . . . Well, yes, but look at my life. A life, after all, is evidence, and I have two divorces in my safe-deposit box.

He stands, moves, thinks.

I tell you frankly I'm a little afraid. . . . Of who and what I'd be bringing to her. And I thought if I could say aloud what I see when I'm alone . . . Well, for example, this:

He sits again, leans forward.

You know . . . more and more I see that for many years I looked at life like a case at law. It was a series of proofs. When you're young you prove how brave you are, or smart; then, what a good lover; then, a good father; finally, how wise, or powerful or what-the-hell-ever. But underlying it all, I see now, there was a presumption. That one moved not in a dry circle but on an upward path toward some elevation, where . . . God knows what . . . I would be justified, or even condemned. A verdict, anyway. I think now that my disaster really began when I looked up one day . . . and the bench was empty. No judge in sight. And all that remained was the endless argument with oneself, this pointless litigation of existence before an empty bench. . . . Which, of course, is another way of saying—despair, and no great news. Some of the best, most energetic lawyers I

know believe in nothing, and even find a joy in proving again and
again that men are worthless, including their own clients. Despair
can be a way of life, providing you believe in it. And I say to myself,
pick it up, take it to heart, and move on again. Instead, I seem to be
hung up, waiting for some . . . believable sign. And the days and the
months . . . and now the years . . . are draining away. *Slight pause.* A
couple of weeks ago I became aware of a strange fact. With all this
darkness, the truth is that every morning when I awake, I'm full of
hope! With everything I know . . . I open up my eyes . . . I'm like a
boy! For an instant there's some . . . unformed promise in the air. I
jump out of bed, I shave, I can't wait to finish breakfast—and then
. . . it seeps in my room, the world, my life, and its pointlessness.
And I thought . . . if I could corner that hope, find what it consists
of, and either kill it for a lie, or really make it mine . . .

Felice enters in sweater and skirt, sits on the floor.

FELICE: I just saw you walking by, that's all, and I thought, why
don't I talk to you? You do remember me, don't you?

QUENTIN, *with a glance at Felice:* For instance, I ran into a girl on
the street last month; I'd settled her divorce a few years ago and she
recognized me. And I hadn't had a woman in so long and she obviously wanted to . . .

FELICE: No! I just wanted to be near you. I love your face. You
have a kind face. . . . You remember in your office, when my husband was refusing to sign the papers?

QUENTIN, *to Listener:* It's this: somehow, whatever I look at, I seem
to see its death.

He turns to her.

FELICE: Well, see, he was always so childish alone with me; like a
little stubborn boy. And when you talked to him—I could see it, he
felt like a man. Like he had dignity. And me too. I felt like a
grown-up woman. And I swear . . . when we walked out of your office, I . . . I almost loved him! And he asked me something when we
got down in the street. Should I tell you? Or do you know already?

QUENTIN, *in frustration:* I'm afraid it's pointless, I don't know
why I—

Breaks off, still to Listener.

Well, just that he asked her to go to bed with him, one last time . . .

FELICE: How did you know that!

QUENTIN—*he is caught by her suddenly; his tone is answering her:* Because it's very hard to see the death of love, and simply walk away. *He is now turning to face her.*

FELICE: You think I should have?

QUENTIN: Well, what harm would it have done?

FELICE: That's what *I* wondered! Except, it would be funny, wouldn't it? The same day we got a divorce? See, I wanted it to mean something, the divorce!

QUENTIN: Honey ... you never stop loving whoever you loved. Hatred doesn't wipe it out.

Louise appears, brushing her hair. Maggie sits up from the upper platform, her breathing beginning to be heard. And Quentin becomes active and agitated, and speaks to the Listener.

Why do I make such stupid statements? I don't believe that! These goddamned women have injured me; have I learned nothing?

Holga appears beneath the tower, her arms full of flowers.

HOLGA: Would you like to see Salzburg? I think they play *The Magic Flute* tonight.

Quentin is facing up to her. A pause. He turns back to Listener.

QUENTIN: It's that ... I don't know what I'd be bringing to that girl.

Holga is gone, and Maggie and Louise.

I don't know what I believe about my own life! What? *He turns to Felice.* Well, death in the sense that she was trying so damned hard to be hopeful, and I ...

FELICE: I don't deny he loved me, but ... everything came down to how much mileage you got on a Volkswagen! I just wished we could get lost in some goddamn wilderness or something, and scream and bite each other and ... and start going *toward* something!

QUENTIN: Well, you're in the wilderness now, aren't you? You live alone, leave the bed unmade, get a hamburger at three in the morning, sleep with who you like. You feel you're going toward something?

FELICE: I think so. I feel I'm good now, as a dancer ... or almost. I almost feel free, when I dance. Not quite, but ... sometimes I only have to think high and I go high; I have a long thought and I fly across the floor; sometimes, sometimes I'm almost exactly what I imagine, and when that happens ...

She has danced out of sight.

QUENTIN: Death in this sense: I'm sure her hope is real to her, but I sit there and see the day her legs will lose their spring, and her body will no longer follow those high leaping thoughts.... Yes, but there's always time to die, why reach for it? In fact, she came back again the other night, almost flew into my room! And it struck me with great force—how little I really believe in life.

Felice appears, standing, with a coat on; she is straight, nearly ecstatic.

FELICE: I had my nose fixed! Are you very busy? The doctor took the bandage off but I put it back on. I wanted you to be the first. Do you mind?

QUENTIN: No. But why me?

FELICE: Because ... remember that night when I came up here? I was trying to make up my mind ... I mean there's something sort of insincere about changing your nose. I mean there could be. If that's all that makes or breaks you, the shape of a piece of cartilage? I mean if you're going to go through life building everything on *that* ... You don't absolutely have to answer, but ... I think you wanted to make love to me that night. Didn't you?

QUENTIN: I did, yes.

FELICE: I knew it! And it just clicked something for me. Because you really listened to me and didn't just try to roll me over. I felt it didn't matter what kind of nose I had, so I—I might as well have a short one! Can I show it to you?

QUENTIN: I'd like very much to see it.

FELICE: Close your eyes.

He does. She lifts the invisible bandage.

Okay.

He looks. She raises her arm in blessing.

I'll always bless you. Always!

He turns away, slowly returns to the chair as she walks into darkness.

QUENTIN, *to the Listener:* Maybe it's this; she meant nothing to me, it was a glancing blow, and yet it's not impossible that I stand in her mind like some corner she turned in her life. I feel like a mirror in which she somehow saw herself as . . . glorious. The truth is, I even liked her first nose better!

Two pallbearers in the distance carry an invisible coffin.

It's like my mother's funeral; I still hear her voice in the street sometimes, loud and real, calling my name. She's under the ground but she's not impressively dead to me. That whole cemetery . . . I saw it like a field of buried mirrors in which people saw themselves. I don't seem to know how to grieve. Or is it just some hardness in it bothers me?

Holga appears above, flowers in her arms.

God, maybe I ought to live alone; or maybe I don't believe that grief is grief unless it kills you.

Holga is gone. Dan appears. A nurse is whispering in his ear.

Like when I flew back and met my brother in the hospital.

The nurse hurries out, and Dan speaks to the empty air.

DAN: I'm so glad you got here, kid; I wouldn't have wired you but I don't know what to do. You have a good flight?

Now Father appears in a "bed." The same nurse is puffing up his pillow.

FATHER: Is that my sons in the hall? Where's my wife?

QUENTIN, *to Dan:* But what's the alternative? She's dead, he has to know.

FATHER: Why don't they come in? Where's my daughter?

DAN: But he was only operated on this morning. How can we walk in and say, "Your wife is dead"? It's like sawing off his arm. Suppose we tell him she's on her way, then give him a sedative?

QUENTIN: But Dan, I think it belongs to him, doesn't it? After fifty years you . . . owe one another a death?

DAN, *in agony:* Kid, the woman was his right hand. Without her he was never very much, you know. He'll fall apart.

QUENTIN: I can't agree; I think he can take it, he's got a lot of stuff.

Without halt, to the Listener:

Which is hilarious! . . . Well, because! He was always the one who idolized the old man, and I saw through him from the beginning; suddenly we're changing places, like children in a game! I don't know what I am to anybody!

DAN, *as though he had come to a decision:* All right; let's go in, then.

QUENTIN: You want me to tell him?

DAN, *unwillingly, afraid but challenged:* I'll do it.

QUENTIN: I could do it, Dan.

DAN, *relieved:* All right; if you don't mind.

They turn together toward Father in the "bed." He does not see them yet. They move with the weight of their news.

QUENTIN: It belongs to him, Dan, as much as his wedding.

He turns to the Listener as he walks.

Or is it simply that . . .

They have come to a halt near Father's "bed."

. . . I am crueler than he?

The nurse glances up at them and goes upstage, but waits there, apparently squinting into an upheld hypodermic needle. Now Father sees them and raises up his arm.

FATHER: For cryin' out loud! Look who's here! I thought you were in Europe!

QUENTIN: Just got back. How are you?

DAN: You look wonderful, Dad.

FATHER: What do you mean, "look"? I *am* wonderful! I tell you, I'm ready to go through it again!

They laugh proudly with him.

I mean it—the way that doctor worries, I finally told him, "Look, if it makes you feel so bad you lay down and I'll operate!" Very fine man. I thought you'd be away couple months more.

QUENTIN, *hesitantly:* I decided to come back and—

DAN, *breaking in, his voice turning strange:* Sylvia'll be right in. She's downstairs buying you something.

FATHER: Oh, that's nice! I tell you something, fellas—that kid is more and more like Mother. Been here every day . . . Where is Mother? I been calling the house.

The slightest empty, empty pause.

DAN: One second, Dad, I just want to—

Crazily, without evident point, he starts calling, and moving upstage toward the nurse. Quentin is staring at his father.

Nurse! Ah . . . could you call down to the gift shop and see if my sister . . .

FATHER: Dan! Tell her to get some ice. When Mother comes you'll all have a drink! I got a bottle of rye in the closet.

To Quentin, as Dan comes in closer:

I tell you, kid, I'm going to be young. I've been thinking all day since I woke up—Mother's right; just because I got old I don't have to act old. I mean we could go to Florida, we could—

QUENTIN: Dad.

FATHER: What? Is that a new suit?

QUENTIN: No, I've had it.

FATHER, *remembering—to Dan, of the nurse:* Oh, tell her glasses, we'll need more glasses.

Dan feels forced to turn and start out.

QUENTIN: Listen, Dad.

Dan halts, and turns back.

FATHER, *totally unaware:* Yeah?

QUENTIN—*he takes Father's hand:* Mother died.

Father's hand grips his abdomen as though he were stabbed; his right arm rises like a policeman ordering a stop. A gasp flies out of him.

She had a heart attack last night on her way home.

FATHER: Oh, no, no, no, no.

QUENTIN, *grasping his hand again:* We didn't want to tell you but—

FATHER: Ahhh! Ahhh, no, no, no.

DAN: There's nothing anybody could have done, Dad.

FATHER—*he claps his hands together:* Oh! Oh! Oh!

QUENTIN, *grasping his hand again:* Now look, Dad, you're going to be all right, you'll—

FATHER—*it is all turning into a deep gasping for breath; he struggles on his "bed," half trying to get off, his head constantly turning as though he were looking for his wife:* Oh boy. Oh boy! No, no.

DAN: Now look, Dad, you're a hell of a fella. Dad, listen—

FATHER: Goddamn it! I couldn't take care of myself, I knew she was working too hard!

QUENTIN: Dad, it's not your fault, that can happen to anyone.

FATHER: But she was sitting right here. She was . . . she was right here!

Now he weeps uncontrollably into his hands. Quentin puts an awkward arm around him.

QUENTIN: Pa . . . Pa . . .

Now Quentin grips him with both arms. Dan moves in close as though to share him. He lays a hand on Father's shoulder.

FATHER: Oh, boys—she was my right hand!

He raises his fist and seems about to lose his control again.

DAN: We'll take care of you, Dad. I don't want you to worry about—

FATHER: No-no. It's ... I'll be all right. I'll ... God! ... Now I'm better! Now, *now* I'm better!

They are silent; he keeps shaking his head.

So where is she?

QUENTIN: In the funeral parlor.

FATHER, *shaking his head—an explosive blow of air:* Paaaaaah!

QUENTIN: We didn't want to tell you but we figured you'd rather know.

FATHER: Ya. *Pats Quentin's hand.* Thanks. Thanks. I'll ... *He looks up at Quentin.* I'll just have to be stronger.

QUENTIN: That's right, Dad.

FATHER, *to no one:* This ... will make me stronger. *But the weeping threatens; he clenches his jaws, shakes his head, and indicates a point.* She was right here!

Lights go out on him and Dan. Quentin comes slowly to the Listener.

QUENTIN: Yes, I'm proud I didn't kid him, it bothers me. I don't know, maybe that he took it so for granted I was also devastated. . . . This? I hadn't thought of this as grief. I hope it is.

The tower gradually begins to light.

Still, a couple months later he bothered to register and vote. . . . Well, I mean ... it didn't kill him either, with all his tears. I don't know what the hell I'm driving at! I—*He is caught by the bright tower.* I don't get the connection at the moment but ... I visited a concentration camp in Germany. . . .

He has started toward the tower when Felice appears, raising her arm in blessing.

FELICE: Close your eyes, okay?

QUENTIN, *turned by her force:* I don't understand why that girl sticks in my mind. . . . Yes!

He moves toward her now.

She did; she offered me some . . . love, I guess. And if I don't return it . . . or if it doesn't change me somehow, it . . . it's like owing for a gift you didn't ask for.

FELICE: I'll always bless you!

Her arm raised, she walks into darkness.

QUENTIN: When she left, I did a stupid thing. I don't understand it. There are two light fixtures on the wall of my hotel room. *Against his own disgust.* I noticed for the first time that they're . . . a curious distance apart. And I suddenly saw that if you stood between them—*He spreads out his arms*—you could reach out and rest your . . .

Just before he completely spreads his arms Maggie sits up; her breathing sounds. He drops his arms, aborting the image. Maggie goes dark.

Maybe I can get to it later. I can't now. . . .

Now Holga appears and is bending to read the legend fixed to the wall of a torture chamber.

Yes, with this woman . . . Holga. She took me there.

HOLGA, *turning to "him":* It's a general description. No, I don't mind, I'll translate it.

She returns to the legend; he slowly approaches behind her.

"In this camp a minimum of two hundred thousand Dutch, Belgian, Russian, Polish, French, and Danish prisoners of war were killed. Also, four thousand two hundred and seven refugees from the Spanish Republican Army. The door to the left leads into the chamber where their teeth were extracted for gold; the drain in the floor carried off the blood. At times instead of shooting, they were individually strangled to death. The barracks on the right were the bordello where women prisoners were forced to—"

QUENTIN, *touching her shoulder:* I think you've had enough, Holga.

HOLGA: No, if you want to see the rest . . . *She bursts into tears, but in silence, and quickly turns away.* Come, I don't mind.

QUENTIN, *taking her arm:* Let's walk, dear. Country looks lovely out there.

They walk. The light changes to day.

Here, this grass looks dry; let's sit down.

They sit. Pause.

I always thought the Danube was blue.

HOLGA: Only the waltz. Although it does change near Vienna. Out of some lingering respect for Strauss, I suppose.

QUENTIN: I don't know why this hit me so; I suddenly got a cracking headache in there.

HOLGA: I'm sorry. It's just that you seemed so interested in the Nazi period, and we were passing so close . . .

QUENTIN: No, I'm glad I saw it.

HOLGA, *starting to rise; she senses an estrangement:* I have some aspirin in the car.

QUENTIN, *lightly touching her:* We'll go soon. I just want to . . . sit for a minute.

HOLGA, *to raise his spirits:* You still want to see Salzburg?

QUENTIN: Oh, sure.

HOLGA: I'd love to show you Mozart's house. And the cafés are excellent there.

QUENTIN, *turning to her now:* Was there somebody you knew died here?

HOLGA: Oh, no. I feel people ought to see it, that's all. No one comes here any more. I've brought foreign colleagues once or twice.

QUENTIN: But why do you come back? It seems to tear you apart.

HOLGA: I suppose . . . one doesn't want to lose the past, even if it's dreadful. You're the first person I've met in a very long time who wants to talk about it.

QUENTIN: Yes, but I'm an American.

HOLGA: Oh, Americans too. In fact, when I first visited America after the war I was three days under questioning before they let me in. It was impossible to explain to them. How could one be in forced labor for two years if one were not a Communist? And of course, not being Jewish either, it was very suspicious. I was ready to turn back, I was so frightened. In fact, it was only when I told them I had blood relatives in several Nazi ministries that they were reassured. You see? Here it's not talked about, and outside it's not understood. It's as though fifteen years of one's life had simply vanished in some insane confusion. So I was very glad you were so interested.

QUENTIN, *glancing up at the tower:* I guess I thought I'd be indignant, or angry. But it's like swallowing a lump of earth. It's strange.

He starts to cover his eyes and she presses him to lie down, and speaks cheerfully . . .

HOLGA: Come, lie down here for a while and perhaps—

QUENTIN: No, I'm—*He has fended off her hand.* I'm sorry, dear, I didn't mean to push you away.

HOLGA, *rebuffed and embarrassed:* I see wildflowers on that hill; I'll pick some for the car!

She gets up quickly.

QUENTIN: Holga?

She continues off. He jumps up and hurries to her, turning her. Holga.

He does not know what to say.

HOLGA, *holding back tears:* Perhaps we've been together too much. I could rent another car at Linz; perhaps we could meet in Vienna sometime.

QUENTIN: I don't want to lose you, Holga.

HOLGA: I understand that you're leaving soon. I never expected any . . .

QUENTIN: But you do expect something, everybody does. You're not a woman to go to bed just for the ride.

HOLGA: No, I'm not. But I have settled since several years to live for my work. I am not helpless alone. It's simply that from the moment you spoke to me I felt somehow familiar, and it was never so before. . . . It isn't a question of getting married; I am not ashamed this way. But I must have *something.*

QUENTIN: I don't give you anything? Tell me; because I've been told that before, but never so calmly.

HOLGA: You give me very much. . . . It's difficult for me to speak like this—I am not a woman who must be reassured every minute, those women are stupid to me.

QUENTIN: We're good friends, Holga; say it to me.

HOLGA: You have nothing; but perhaps that's all you want. I can understand that after what you've lived.

QUENTIN: That's not it, Holga; there's nothing as dull as adventure. I've had all I can use.

HOLGA: But perhaps that's all there is for you.

QUENTIN—*he turns her face to him:* Holga. Are you weeping ...
for *me*?

HOLGA: Yes.

QUENTIN, *struck:* Don't go away; not yet. Will you?

HOLGA: I hear your wings opening, Quentin.

QUENTIN: I don't want to abuse your feeling for me, you understand? The truth is—and I couldn't say this if I didn't trust you—I
swear I don't know if I have lived in good faith. And the doubt ties
my tongue when I think of promising anything again.

HOLGA: But how can one ever be sure of one's good faith?

QUENTIN, *surprised:* God, it's wonderful to hear you say that. All
my women have been so goddamned sure!

HOLGA: But how can one ever be?

QUENTIN—*he kisses her gratefully:* Why do you keep coming back
to this place?

   Pause. Holga is disturbed, uncertain.

HOLGA: I ... don't know. Perhaps ... because I didn't die here.

QUENTIN—*turns quickly to Listener:* What?

HOLGA: Although that would make no sense! I don't really know!

QUENTIN—*goes to the chair:* That people ... what? "Wish to die for
the dead"? No, no, I can understand it; survival can be hard to bear.
But I ... I don't think I feel that way ...

   *Maggie again appears in bed on the upper level; she begins to
heave for breath. Her face is still indistinguishable. Instantly Quentin
turns away as from an opposite side of the stage a piano is heard and a
woman, Mother, is in midsong with a romantic ballad from a musical
of the twenties.*

Although I do think of my mother now, and she's dead. Yes!

   He turns to Holga.

Maybe the dead do bother her.

HOLGA: It was the middle of the war. I had just come out of a class
and there were leaflets on the sidewalk. A photograph of a concentration camp. And emaciated people. It was dropped there by British Intelligence; one tended to believe the British. I had had no idea.
Truly. Any more, perhaps, than Americans know how a Negro
lives. I was seventeen; I lived in my studies; I planned how to cut my
hair differently. It is much more complicated than it seems later.

There were many officers in my family. It was our country. It isn't easy to turn against your country; not in a war. There are always reasons—do Americans turn against America because of Hiroshima? No, there are reasons always.

~~Pause.~~ *Pause.*

And I took the leaflet to my godfather—he was still commanding our Intelligence. And I asked if it were true. "Of course," he said, "why does it excite you"? And I said, "You are a swine. You are all swine." I threw my briefcase at him. And he opened it and put some papers in and asked me to deliver it to a certain address. And I became a courier for the officers who were planning to assassinate Hitler. . . . They were all hanged.

QUENTIN: Why not you?

HOLGA: They didn't betray me.

QUENTIN: Then why do you say good faith is never sure?

HOLGA, *after a pause:* It was my country . . . longer perhaps than it should have been. But I didn't know. And now I don't know how I could not have known. I can't imagine not knowing, now.

QUENTIN: Holga . . . I bless your uncertainty. Maybe that's why you're so wonderful to be with. You don't seem to be looking for some goddamned . . . moral *victory.* Forgive me, I didn't mean to be distant with you. I—*Looks up at the tower*—think this place frightens me! And how is that possible? All empty!

HOLGA: I'll get the flowers. And maybe we can buy some cheese and apples and eat while we drive!

She starts away.

QUENTIN: And you forgive me?

HOLGA—*turns, and with great love:* Yes! I'll be right back! And we'll go right away!

She hurries away.

Quentin stands in stillness a moment; the presence of the tower bores in on him; its color changes; he now looks up at it and addresses the Listener.

QUENTIN: But it's empty now! In fact, the view from here is rather pastoral; and the stone walls are warm in the sun, and quiet. I think . . . I may have imagined it more monstrous. Or bizarre. I helped a mason years ago before I went to college—I see the problem building such high walls in sandy soil... how dare one think of that? I think of the footings—they must go ten feet down. At least ten! I know footings! But I never thought the stones would look so ordinary.

Now he turns out.

Why do I *know* something here? Even hollow now and empty, it has a face; and asks a sort of question: "What do you believe ... as true as this?" Yes! Believers built this, maybe that's the fright—and I, without belief, stand here disarmed. I can see the convoys grinding up this hill; and I inside; no one knows my name and yet they'll smash my head on a concrete floor! And no appeal.

He turns quickly to the Listener.

Yes! It's that I no longer see some last appeal, and here there was none either! Socialism once, then love; some final hope is gone that always saved before the end!

Mother appears; at the same time her coffin appears above.

MOTHER: Not too much cake, darling, there'll be a lot of food at this wedding. *Calling upstage.* Fanny? Cut him a small piece ... well, not *that* small!

QUENTIN: Mother! That's strange. And murder. Or is it her comfort brings her to me in this place?

MOTHER: Fanny? Not too hot ironing my husband's dress shirt! *Turns suddenly to an invisible boy.* You are going to wear garters tonight, Quentin, and don't argue with me.... Because it's my brother's wedding and your stockings are not to hang over your shoes!

QUENTIN—*he has started to laugh but it turns into:* Why can't I mourn her? And Holga wept in there ... why can't I weep? Why do I feel an understanding with this slaughterhouse?

Now Felice appears, raising her arm.

I don't understand what I'm supposed to be to anyone!

Felice is gone. Mother laughs. He turns to her, addressing the Listener.

I don't know, some wedding in the family. I don't get it.

MOTHER—*her laughter turning bitter:* God! Why must every wedding in this family be a catastrophe! ... Because the girl is pregnant, darling, and she's got no money, she's stupid, and I tell you this one is going to end up with a mustache! Five beautiful men like that and one after the other ... I don't know where they *find* such women!

QUENTIN, *watching her, seated:* But what the hell has this to do with a concentration camp?

MOTHER: And wants a tight gown! As though she's fooling some-body! That's why, darling, when you grow up, I hope you learn how to disappoint people. Especially women. Never forget it, dear, you're a man, and a man has all the choices. Will you stop playing with matches? *Slaps an invisible boy's hand.* You'll pee in bed! Why don't you practice your penmanship instead? You write like a mon-key, darling.

QUENTIN, *shaking his head, glancing up at the tower:* I don't get it.

Father suddenly appears, holding an invisible phone to his ear. Quentin instantly stands.

MOTHER: And where is your father? If he went to sleep in a Turkish bath again, I'll ...

Quentin is moving toward Father as though wanting to hear what he is saying in phone; he is making a shushing gesture to Mother.

What are you talking about, I didn't end up calling all the Turkish baths the night my brother Herbert got married? Forgot all about it ... and nothing bothers him!

She laughs warmly. Quentin has arrived at Father, peers at his profile.

FATHER: Herman? Cable Hamburg.

MOTHER: Like the night of the Dempsey-Tunney fight.

QUENTIN: Ssh!

He turns back, eager to hear what Father is saying.

MOTHER: ... The men's-room door gets stuck so by the time he gets out there's a new champion. Cost him a hundred dollars to go to the men's room!

FATHER: No, sixty thousand tons; sixty; Vera Cruz, the *Bismarck*'s due.

MOTHER: But you mustn't laugh at him, he's a wonderful man, it's just that sometimes he can drive you out of your mind.

FATHER: Then cable Southampton, turn him back to Finland Monday. A.T.O.

MOTHER: My wedding? Oh, no dear, my wedding ... there was happiness.

Quentin turns to her.

Well, look at your father; to this day he walks into a room you want to bow! Not like my sisters, one after the other running into the house, "Mama, I'm in love!" And with what? With who? I wasn't allowed to *see* your father till his father and Grandpa had agreed! . . . *Because,* I decided for once somebody was not going to break my mother's heart. . . . What are you talking about, of course I loved him! *Warmly.* He'd take me to a restaurant—one look at him and the waiters started moving tables around; if he saw a thick water glass he'd walk out; there could be a line around the block to a Broadway show, he'd go right up to the box office and they'd find two tickets. *Because,* dear—people know that this is a *man.* Even Doctor Strauss, at my wedding he came over to me says, "Rose, I can see it looking at him, you've got a wonderful man," and he was always in love with me, Strauss. . . . Oh, sure, but he was only a medical student then, didn't have a penny, my father wouldn't let him in the house. Who knew he'd end up so big in gallstones? That poor boy—used to bring me novels to read, poetry, philosophy, God knows what! One time we even sneaked off to hear Rachmaninoff together. . . .

She laughs sadly; with wonder more than bitterness:

That's why, you see, two weeks after we were married; sit down to dinner and Papa hands me a menu, and asks me to read it to him. . . . Couldn't *read*! I got so frightened I nearly ran away! . . . "Why"? Because your grandmother is such a fine, unselfish woman; two months in school and they put him into the shop! That's what some women are, my dear . . . and now he goes and buys her a new Packard every year and two more for his brothers! Damned fool, I could kill him! And what are we paying a chauffeur for, I can't find him half the time anyway! . . . Because if they're going to have chauffeurs I'm going to have a chauffeur—it's all our money anyway!

With a strange and deep fear:

Please, darling, I want you to *draw* the letters, that scribbling is ugly, dear; and your posture, your speech, it can all be beautiful! Ask Miss Fisher, for years they kept my handwriting pinned up on the bulletin board; they made up a special new prize to give me on graduating day. God, I'll never forget it, valedictorian of the class with a scholarship to Hunter in my hand—*A blackness flows into her soul*—and I come home, and Grandpa says, "You're getting married!" It had never come into my mind! I was like . . . like with small wings, just getting ready to fly; I slept all year with the catalogue under my pillow. To learn, to learn everything! Oh, darling, the whole thing is such a mystery!

Father enters the area, talking to the young, invisible Quentin.
FATHER: Quentin, would you get me the office on the phone? *To Mother as he kisses her lightly on the cheek:* Why would you call the Turkish bath?

MOTHER: I thought you forgot about the wedding.

FATHER: I wish I could but I'm paying for it.

MOTHER: He'll pay you back!

FATHER: I believe it, I just wouldn't want to hang by my hair that long.

He turns, goes to an invisible phone, stands.
Herman? Hold the wire. *To Mother:* Why don't you both go up and get dressed?

MOTHER, *moving up the stairs:* I don't want to be late, now.

FATHER: There's time; she won't give birth if we're a half-hour late.

MOTHER: Don't be so smart! He fell in love, what's so terrible about that?

FATHER: They all fall in love on my money. Only I can't fall in love unless I pay for it. I married into a love nest! *He turns to the invisible Quentin, warmly smiling.* Did they pass a law that kid can't get a haircut? *Reaching into his pocket, tossing a coin.* Here, at least get a shine. *To Mother:* I'll be right up, dear, go ahead, get dressed. *In "phone":* Herman? The accountant still there? Put him on.

QUENTIN, *suddenly, recalling:* Oh, yes!

MOTHER: I'll put in your studs. God, he's so beautiful in a tuxedo!

She goes a distance out of the area but halts on the stair, turns, eavesdrops.
FATHER: Billy? You finished? Well what's the story, where am I?

Quentin now turns up toward Mother on the stairs.
QUENTIN: . . . Yes!

FATHER: Don't you read the papers? What'll I do with Irving Trust, I can't give it away. What bank?

Mother descends a step, alarmed.

I been to every bank in New York, I can't get a bill paid, how the hell they going to lend me money? No-no, there's no money in London, there's no money in Hamburg, there ain't a cargo moving in the world, the ocean's empty, Billy. . . . Now tell me the truth, where am I?

Pause. Mother descends another step. Quentin is below, watching her. Now Mother descends into the area. Father stands almost stiffly, as though to take a storm.

MOTHER: What's that about? What are you "winding up"?

Father stands staring; he speaks unheard, but she seems to have heard an additional shocking fact, then another, and another.

What are you talking about? When did this start? . . . Well, how much are you taking out of it? . . . You lost your mind? You've got over four hundred thousand dollars' worth of stocks, you can sell the . . . You sold those wonderful stocks! When? . . . Eight months! I just bought a new grand piano, why didn't you say something? And a silver service for my brother, and you don't say anything? . . .

More subdued, walks a few steps in thought.

Well then, you'd better cash your insurance; you've got at least seventy-five thousand cash value. . . .

Halts, turning in shock.

When?

Father is gradually losing his stance, his grandeur; he pulls his tie loose.

All right, then—we'll get rid of my bonds. Do it tomorrow. . . . What do you mean? Well you get them back, I've got ninety-one thousand dollars in bonds you gave me. Those are my bonds. I've got bonds. . . .

Breaks off; open horror on her face and now a growing contempt.

You mean you saw everything going down and you throw good money after bad? Are you some kind of a moron?

FATHER: You don't walk away from a business; I came to this country with a tag around my neck like a package in the bottom of the boat!

MOTHER: I should have run the day I met you!

FATHER, *as though stabbed:* Rose!

He sits, closing his eyes, his neck bent.

MOTHER: I should have done what my sisters did, tell my parents to go to hell and thought of myself for once! I should have run for my life!

FATHER: Sssh, I hear the kids.

A sharp shaft of light opens a few yards away and he glances toward it.

MOTHER: I ought to get a divorce!

FATHER: Rose, the college men are jumping out of windows!

MOTHER: But your last dollar? *Bending over, into his face:* You are an idiot!

Her nearness forces him to stand; they look at each other, strangers.

QUENTIN—*he looks up at the tower:* Yes! For no reason—they don't even ask your name!

FATHER—*he looks toward the column of light:* Somebody crying? Quentin's in there. You better talk to him.

Quentin walks upstage, away from the light. She goes in some trepidation toward it. A foot or so from it she halts.

MOTHER: Darling? You better get dressed. Don't cry, dear, it'll be all right. He'll come back bigger than ever!

She is stopped short by something "Quentin" has said.

What *I* said? Why, what did I say? . . . Are you crazy? I'd never say a thing like that, I thought you were upstairs. Well I was a little angry, that's all, but I never said *that*. I think he's a wonderful man! *Laughs.* How could I say a thing like that? Quentin!

The light rapidly fades, and as though he is disappearing she extends her arms toward the fading light.

But I didn't say anything!

With a cry toward someone lost.

Darling, I didn't say anything!

Instantly Holga appears beneath the tower, with flowers in her arms. She looks about for him.

HOLGA: Quentin? Quentin?

He is still staring at Mother, from whom he turns toward Holga. Now Holga sees him and comes down to him.

Look! The car will be all sweet inside!

QUENTIN—*he absently sniffs the flowers, staring at her:* You love me, don't you?

HOLGA: Yes.

QUENTIN, *glancing up at the tower:* Do you ever feel when you come here some vague . . . complicity?

HOLGA: Quentin . . . no one they didn't kill can be innocent again.

QUENTIN—*slight pause:* Then how do you get so purposeful, Holga? You work so hard, you seem so full of joy and hope.

HOLGA: While I was getting the flowers just now I thought I ought to tell you something. In a bombing once I lost my memory, and wandered everywhere with crowds across the countryside looking for a safe place. Every day, one turned away from people dying on the roads. Until one night I tried to jump from the railing of a bridge. An old soldier pulled me back and slapped my face and made me follow him; he'd lost a leg at Stalingrad, was furious that I would kill myself; I walked behind his crutches over Germany looking for some sign of who I'd been. And suddenly there was a door with a tremendous lion's-head brass knocker; I ran; I knocked; my mother opened it. My life came back! And I turned to ask the soldier in; to thank him; to feed him; to give him everything I had! But he was gone. I've been told that I imagined him, but even now at times I turn a corner and expect to find him. If we could even . . . nod to one another! I know how terrible it is to owe what one can never pay. And for a long time after I had the same dream each night—that I had a child; and even in the dream I saw that the child was my life; and it was an idiot. And I wept, and a hundred times I ran away, but each time I came back it had the same dreadful face. Until I thought, if I could kiss it, whatever in it was my own, perhaps I could rest. And I bent to its broken face, and it was horrible . . . but I kissed it.

QUENTIN: Does it still come back?

HOLGA: At times. But it somehow has the virtue now . . . of being mine. I think one must finally take one's life in one's arms, Quentin.

She takes his hand.

Come, I think they play *The Magic Flute* tomorrow. You like *The Magic Flute*?

QUENTIN—*he kisses her:* One thing about you, you tell the goddamned funniest stories!

HOLGA—*hits him and mock-pouts:* You're making fun of me!

QUENTIN: Let's get out of this dump, and . . . where we going?

HOLGA, *laughing:* Salzburg!

QUENTIN: I'll race you to the car, last one there's a rotten egg. Or do you say a rancid wurst?

HOLGA, *laughing:* Okay, I'm racing!

She gets set.

QUENTIN: Go!

They start running, but while she goes off into darkness Quentin comes down to the chair.

QUENTIN: I miss her badly. And yet, I can't sign my letters to her "With love." I put "Sincerely" or "As ever," some such brilliant evasion. I've lost the sense of some absolute necessity, I think. Living alone does that; I walk down the street, I see the millions of apartment windows lighting up—I swear I don't understand how each man knows which door to go to. Can they all be in love? Is that what sorts them out? I don't think so; it's some kind of innocence, a deep belief that all their destinations are ordained. With me, whether I open a book or think of marrying again, it's so damned clear I've chosen what I do—it cuts the strings between my hands and heaven. It sounds foolish, but I feel . . . unblessed. And I look back at when there seemed to be a kind of plan, some duty in the sky. I had a dinner table, and a wife, a child, and the world so wonderfully threatened by injustices I was born to correct! How fine! Remember? When there were good people and bad people? And how easy it was to tell! The worst son of a bitch, if he loved Jews and Negroes and hated Hitler—he was a buddy. Like some kind of paradise compared to this. . . . Until I begin to look at it.

Elsie appears, a beach robe hanging from her shoulders, her arms out of the sleeves, her back to us; she is fixing her wet hair in an invisible mirror.

God, when I think of what I believed, I want to hide!

He stands, moves toward her.

. . . Yes, but I wasn't all that young! You would think a man of thirty-two would know that when a guest, changing out of a wet bathing suit in his bedroom . . .

Elsie, as he approaches, turns to him, and her robe slips off one shoulder.

and just stands there with her two bare faces hanging out . . .

ELSIE: Oh, are you through working? Why don't you swim now? The water's just right.

QUENTIN, *with a laugh of great pain, crying out:* I tell you I believed she didn't know she was naked! It's Eden! . . . Well, she was *married*! How could a woman who can tell when the Budapest String Quartet is playing off key, who refuses to wear silk stockings because the Japanese have invaded Manchuria, whose husband—my friend, a saintly professor of law—is editing my first appeal to the Supreme Court on the grass outside that window—I could see the top of his head past her tit, for God's sake! . . . Of course I understood, but it's what you allow yourself to admit! To admit what you see endangers principles!

Elsie leaves the "room" and crosses to where Louise sits. Quentin turns to them. They are talking in an intense whisper. He now approaches them from behind, halts, turns to the Listener.

You know? When two women are whispering, and they stop abruptly when you appear . . .

ELSIE and LOUISE, *turning to him after an abrupt stop to their talking:* Hi.

In the background Lou appears, reading a brief—a tender, kindly man, in shorts.

QUENTIN: . . . The subject must have been sex. And if one of them is your wife . . . she must have been talking about you.

ELSIE, *as though to get him to go:* Lou's behind the house, reading your brief. He says it's superb!

QUENTIN: I hope so. I've been kind of nervous about what he'd say.

ELSIE: I wish you'd tell him that, Quentin! Will you? Just how much his opinion means to you. It's important you tell him.

QUENTIN: I'll be glad to. *Awkwardly glancing from Louise back to her:* Nice here, isn't it?

ELSIE: It's enchanting. *Taking in Louise:* I envy you both so much!

QUENTIN: See you. Glad you could come.

ELSIE—*gets up, goes past Lou:* I want one more walk before the train, dear. Did you comb your hair today?

LOU, *closing the brief:* I think so. Quentin! This is superb! It's hardly like a brief at all; there's a majestic quality, like a classic opinion!

Chuckling, tugs Quentin's sleeve. I almost feel honored to have known you!

    Elsie is gone.

QUENTIN: I'm so glad, Lou—your opinion means . . .

LOU: Your whole career will change with this, Quentin. But do me a favor, will you?

QUENTIN: Oh, anything, Lou.

LOU: Would you offer it to Elsie to read? I know it seems an extraordinary request, but . . .

QUENTIN: No, I'd be delighted!

LOU, *secretively:* It's shaken her terribly, my being subpoenaed and all those damned headlines. Despite everything, it does affect one's whole relationship. So any gesture of respect becomes terrifically important. For example, I gave her the manuscript of my new text to read, and I've even called off publication for a while to incorporate her criticisms. It may be her psychoanalysis, but she's become remarkably acute.

QUENTIN: But I hope you don't delay any more, Lou; it'd be wonderful if you published something now. Just to show those bastards.

LOU: Yes . . .

    Glancing toward the women, he takes Quentin's arm and strolls with him.

I've been thinking of calling you about that, Quentin. You see, it's a textbook for the schools, and Elsie feels that it will only start a new attack on me.

QUENTIN: But they've investigated you, what more damage could they do?

LOU: Who knows? Another attack might knock me off the faculty. It's only Mickey's vote that saved me the last time.

QUENTIN: Really! I didn't know that.

LOU: Oh, yes, he made a marvelous speech at the Dean's meeting when I refused to testify.

QUENTIN: Well, that's Mickey.

LOU: Yes, but Elsie feels . . . I'd just be drawing down the lightning again to publish now. She even feels it's some unconscious wish for self-destruction on my part. And yet, if I put the book away, it's like

a kind of suicide to me. Everything I know is in that book....
What's your opinion?

QUENTIN: Lou, you have a right to publish; a radical past is not
leprosy. We only turned Left because it seemed the truth was there.
You mustn't be ashamed.

LOU, *in pain:* Goddamn it, yes! Except ... I never told you this,
Quentin....

QUENTIN—*comes down to the Listener:* What am I going into this
for? *Listens.* Yes—in a way it was—the day the world ended, it all
fell down, and nobody was innocent again. And yet, we never were!
What am I looking for?

LOU: When I returned from Russia and published my study of So-
viet law—*Breaks off.* I left out many things I saw. I ... lied. For a
good cause, I thought, but all that lasts is the lie. It's so strange to
me now—I have many failings, but I have never been a liar. And I
lied for the Party. Over and over, year after year. And that's why,
now ... with this book of mine, I want to be true to myself. You see,
it's no attack I fear, but being forced to defend my own incredible
lies!

Elsie appears, approaching, hearing.

ELSIE: Lou, I'm quite surprised. I thought we'd settled this.

LOU: Yes, dear, I only wanted Quentin's feeling ...

ELSIE: Your shirt's out, dear.

He quickly tucks it into his shorts. And to Quentin:

You certainly don't think he ought to publish.

QUENTIN: But the alternative seems—

ELSIE, *with a volcanic, suppressed alarm:* But, dear, that's the *situation!* Lou's not like you, Quentin; you and Mickey can function in
the rough and tumble of private practice, but Lou's a purely aca-
demic person. He's *incapable* of going out and ...

LOU, *with a difficult grin and chuckle:* Well, dear, I'm not all that delicate, I—

ELSIE—*a sudden flash of contempt; to Lou:* This is hardly the time
for illusions!

*With a smash of light Mother appears, and Father slumped in a
chair beside her.*

MOTHER: You *idiot!*

Quentin is shocked, turns quickly to Mother.
My *bonds*?

She and Father are gone. Instantly, as before, Holga appears under the tower, flowers in her hand, looking about for him.
HOLGA: Quentin?

He quickly turns his head toward her. She is gone.
QUENTIN, *alone:* How do you believe again?

Felice appears.
FELICE: I'll always bless you!

She turns and walks into the dark. The wall appears with the two light fixtures.
QUENTIN: The other night, when that girl left . . . I . . .

Turns to the wall. The fixtures light up. But he turns away, agonized.
I'll try to get to it . . .

ELSIE: Come, dear, you haven't even swum. Let's enjoy this weekend!

She walks off with Lou, kissing his cheek.
QUENTIN, *watching them go:* Then why does something seem to fall apart? Was it ever whole?

Louise now stands up from the beach chair. She turns, addresses an empty space.
LOUISE: Quentin?

QUENTIN—*he turns his eyes to the ground, then speaks to the Listener:* Wasn't that a terrifying thing, what Holga said?

LOUISE: I've decided to go into psychoanalysis.

QUENTIN, *still to Listener:* To take up your life, like an idiot child?

LOUISE: I want to talk about some things with you.

QUENTIN: But can anybody really do that?

He turns toward Louise now guiltily.
Kiss his life?

LOUISE, *as though he had not answered—speaking toward the empty space:* Quentin?

He is drawn to the spot she is concentrating her gaze on. Tension rises in him as he arrives in her line of sight and faces her.
You don't have to pick up Betty now, she enjoys playing there.
Steeling her shy self. I've got to make a decision.

QUENTIN: About what?

LOUISE, *in fear:* About everything.

QUENTIN: What do you mean?

LOUISE—*at a loss for an instant:* Sit down, will you?

> *She sits, gathering her thoughts. He hesitates, as though pained at the memory, and also because at the time he lived this it was an agony. And as he approaches his chair he speaks to the Listener.*

QUENTIN: It was like . . . a meeting. In seven years we had never had a meeting. Never, never what you'd call . . . a meeting.

LOUISE: We don't seem . . .

> *A long pause while she peers at a forming thought—*

married.

QUENTIN: We?

LOUISE—*it is sincere, what she says, but she has had to learn the words, so there is the faintest air of a formula in her way of speaking:* You don't pay any attention to me.

QUENTIN, *puzzled:* When?

LOUISE: You never did. But I never realized it till . . . recently.

QUENTIN, *to help her:* You mean like Friday night? When I didn't open the car door for you?

LOUISE: Well, that's a small thing, but it's part of what I mean, yes.

QUENTIN: But I told you; you always opened the car door for yourself.

LOUISE: I've always done everything for myself, but that doesn't mean it's right. Everybody notices it, Quentin.

QUENTIN: What?

LOUISE: The way you behave toward me. I don't . . . *exist.* People are supposed to find out about each other. I am not all this uninteresting, Quentin. Many people, men *and* women, think I *am* interesting.

QUENTIN: Well, I—*Breaks off.* I—*Breaks off.* I . . . don't know what you mean.

LOUISE: I know you don't. You have no conception of what a woman is. You think I'm some sort of . . . I don't know what I am to you.

QUENTIN: But I do pay attention—just last night I read you my whole brief.

LOUISE: Quentin, you think reading a brief to a woman is talking to her?

QUENTIN: But that's what's on my mind.

LOUISE: But if that's all on your mind what do you need a wife for?

QUENTIN: Now what kind of a question is that?

LOUISE: Quentin, that's the question!

QUENTIN—*slight pause; with fear, astonishment:* What's the question?

LOUISE: What am I to you? Do you ... do you ever *ask* me anything? Anything personal?

QUENTIN, *with rising alarm:* But Louise, what am I supposed to ask you? I *know* you!

LOUISE: No.

She stands with dangerous dignity.

You don't know me.

Pause. She proceeds now with caution.

I don't intend to be ashamed of myself any more, I used to think it was normal; or even that you don't see me because I'm not worth seeing. But I think now that you don't really see any woman. Except in some ways your mother. You do sense her feelings; you do know when she's unhappy or anxious, but not me. Or any other woman.

Elsie appears, about to drop her robe.

QUENTIN: That's not true, though. I ...

LOUISE: Elsie's noticed it too.

QUENTIN, *guiltily snapping away from the vision of Elsie:* What?

LOUISE: She's amazed at you.

QUENTIN: Why, what'd she say?

LOUISE: You don't seem to ... register the fact that a woman is *present.*

QUENTIN: Oh. *He is disarmed, confused, and silent.*

LOUISE: And you know how she admires you.

Quentin nods seriously. Suddenly he turns out the Listener and bursts into an agonized, ironical laughter. He abruptly breaks it off, and returns to silence before Louise.

Louise speaks with uncertainty; it is her first attempt at confrontation.

Quentin?

He stands in silence.

Quentin?

He is silent.

Silence is not going to solve it any more. I can't live this way. Quentin?

QUENTIN—*pause; he gathers courage:* Maybe I don't speak because the one time I did tell you my feelings you didn't get over it for six months.

LOUISE, *angered:* It wasn't six months, it was a few weeks. I did overreact, but it's understandable. You come back from a trip and tell me you'd met a woman you wanted to sleep with?

QUENTIN: That's not the way I said it.

LOUISE: It's exactly the way. And we were married a year.

QUENTIN: It is not the way I said it, Louise. It was an idiotic thing to tell you but I still say I meant it as a compliment; that I did not touch her because I realized what you meant to me. And for damn near a year you looked at me as though I were some kind of a monster who could never be trusted again.

LOUISE: Well that's in *your* mind. I've completely forgotten it.

QUENTIN: Is it only in my mind if you can still distort it this way?

LOUISE: Quentin, I am not your mother or some third party to whom you can come running with reports of your conquests!

QUENTIN: You see? This is what I mean! What conquests? How can I talk if you are going to blow everything up into a—a—

LOUISE: Quentin, I didn't bring her up, you did.

QUENTIN: Because I know you have never forgiven it, and I can't talk if I have to watch every word I say.

LOUISE, *astonished:* You mean you have to watch every word you say?

QUENTIN: Well, not every word, but—but—

LOUISE, *looking at him with new eyes:* Well, I had no idea!

QUENTIN, *pleading:* Now, look, Louise . . . I didn't mean it exactly that way!

LOUISE, *horrified:* I had no idea you were . . . dishonest with me.

QUENTIN, *drowning in guilt:* Well what did I say? What are you looking at me like that for?

With her hands thrust into her hair she rushes away, a stifled cry in her throat. He calls after her.

Louise!

Immediately to the Listener:

And why do I believe she's right? . . . That's the point! . . . Yes, now, now! It's innocence, isn't it? The innocent are always better, aren't they? Then why can't I be innocent?

Elsie appears, about to drop her robe.

Why couldn't I simply say, "Louise, your best friend is treacherous; your newfound dignity suits her purpose"? . . . No, no, it isn't only that Elsie tempted me, it's worse. If I see a sin why is it in some part mine?

Elsie vanishes as the tower appears.

Even this slaughterhouse! Could I kill Jews? Throw ice water on prisoners of war and let them freeze to death? Why does something in this place touch my shoulder like an accomplice? . . . Huh? Please, yes, if you think you know.

Mother appears. He turns to her.

In what sense treacherous?

MOTHER: What poetry he brought me! He understood me, Strauss. And two weeks after the wedding, Papa hands me the menu. To *read*!

QUENTIN: Huh! Yes! And to a little boy . . . who knows how to read; a powerful reader, that little boy!

MOTHER: I want your handwriting beautiful, darling; I want you to be . . .

QUENTIN: . . . an accomplice!

MOTHER, *turning on Father, who sits dejectedly:* My *bonds*? And you don't even tell me anything? Are you a moron?

QUENTIN—*he watches her go dark, and speaks to the Listener. The tower remains alive:* Yes, yes, I understand, but . . . Why is the world so treacherous? Shall we lay it all to mothers? You understand? The sickness is much larger than my skull; aren't there mothers who keep dissatisfaction hidden to the grave, and do not split the faith of sons until they go in guilt for what they did not do? And I'll go further—here's the final bafflement for me—is it altogether good to be not guilty for what another does?

Mickey appears coming to Quentin, who turns to him.

MICKEY: The brief is fine, kid; I swear it almost began to move me. *To Louise, grinning:* You proud of him?

LOUISE—*she starts off:* Yes! Lou and Elsie are here.

MICKEY: Oh! I didn't know. You look wonderful, Louise, look all excited!

LOUISE: Thanks! It's nice to hear.

She shyly, soundlessly laughs, glancing at Quentin, and goes.

MICKEY—*pause; his smile transforms instantly to a shy grin:* You got trouble?

QUENTIN, *embarrassed:* I don't think so. She's going into psycho-analysis.

The tower dies out.

MICKEY: You got trouble, then. *Laughs.* But she'll be more inter-esting. Although for a while she'll probably be talking about her rights.

QUENTIN: Really? That's just what she was talking about!

MICKEY—*shakes his head, laughing joyfully:* I love women! I think maybe you got married too young; I did too. Although, *you* don't fool around, do you?

QUENTIN: I don't, no.

MICKEY: Then what the hell are you so guilty about?

QUENTIN: I am?

MICKEY: She loves you, Quent.

QUENTIN: I guess so, ya.

MICKEY: Maybe you ought to— See, when it first happened to me, I set aside five minutes a day just imagining my wife as a stranger. As though I hadn't made her yet. You got to generate some respect for her mystery. Start with five minutes; I can go as long as an hour, now.

QUENTIN: Makes it seem like a game though, doesn't it?

MICKEY: Well it is, isn't it, in a way? As soon as there's two people you can't be absolutely sincere, can you? I mean she's not your rib.

QUENTIN: I guess that's right, yes.

Pause.

MICKEY: Where's Lou?

QUENTIN, *pointing:* They're down swimming. You want to swim?

MICKEY: No.

He walks to a point, looks down as over a cliff.

That dear man; look at him, he never learned how to swim, always paddled like a dog. I used to love that man. I still do.

He sits on his heels, draws in the earth.

I'm sorry you didn't get into town two weeks ago when I called you.

QUENTIN: Why, is there some . . . ?

MICKEY: Well, I called you, Quent, I called you three times wanting to talk to you.

He gets up, stands, hands in pockets, glancing at the ground.

I've been subpoenaed.

QUENTIN, *shocked:* Oh, God! The Committee?

MICKEY: Yes. I wish you'd have come into town. . . . But it doesn't matter now.

QUENTIN: I had a feeling it was something like that. I guess I . . . didn't want to know any more. I'm sorry, Mick.

To Listener:

Yes, not to see, not to see!

A long pause. They find it hard to look directly at each other. Mickey picks up a stick, gouges at it with his thumbnail.

MICKEY: I've been going through hell, Quent. It's a strange thing—to have to examine what you stand for; not theoretically, but on a life-and-death basis. A lot of things don't stand up.

QUENTIN: I guess the main thing is not to be afraid.

MICKEY: Yes. *Pause.* I don't think I am, any more. I was, two weeks ago; I shook when the marshal came into the office and handed me that pink piece of paper. I really shook. It was dreadful. My knees shook.

A pause. Both sit staring ahead. Finally, Mickey turns and looks at Quentin, who now faces him. Mickey tries to smile.

You may not be my friend any more.

QUENTIN—*tries to laugh it away, a terror rising in him:* Why?

MICKEY: I'm going to tell the truth.

Pause.

QUENTIN: How do you mean?

MICKEY: I'm . . . going to name names.

QUENTIN, *incredulously:* Why?

MICKEY: Because . . . I want to. I don't want this concealment any more. Fifteen years, wherever I go, whatever I talk about, the feeling is always there that I'm deceiving people. Like living in an occupied country, half in the dark.

QUENTIN: But you only belonged for a few months, didn't you?

MICKEY: Yes, but it was a commitment, Quent. I'm sorry we never got to talk about it; I've never really gone along with this Fifth Amendment silence, I think it's insincere; a man ought to take the rap for what he's been.

QUENTIN: But why couldn't you just tell about yourself?

MICKEY: I have. They're playing for keeps, kid; they want the names, and they mean to destroy anyone who—

QUENTIN: I think it's a mistake, Mick. All this is going to pass, and I think you'll regret it. And anyway, how can they destroy you?

MICKEY—*slight pause:* Quent, I'll be voted out of the firm if I don't testify.

QUENTIN: Oh, no! Max has always talked against this kind of thing!

MICKEY: I've had it out with Max.

QUENTIN: I can't believe it! What about DeVries?

MICKEY: DeVries was there, and Burton, and most of the others. I wish you'd have seen their faces when I told them. Men I've worked with for thirteen years. Played tennis; intimate friends, you know? And as soon as I said I had been—stones.

The tower lights.

QUENTIN, *to the Listener:* Everything is one thing! You see? I don't know what we are to one another! Or rather, rather what we ought to be!

MICKEY: Quent, I could feel their backs turning on me. It was horrible! As though—they would let me die.

Maggie appears in her bed, and her breathing is heard.

MAGGIE: Quentin?

Quentin barely glances at her and turns away, pacing up and down before the Listener. As Mickey resumes, Maggie and her deep-drawn breathing fade away.

MICKEY: I only know one thing, Quent, I want to live an open life, a straightforward, open life!

Lou enters in bathing trunks, instantly overjoyed at seeing Mickey.

LOU: Mick! I *thought* I heard your voice! *Grabs his hand.* How are you?

*Holga appears beneath the tower with flowers, and in a moment
disappears.*

QUENTIN: How do you dare make promises again? I have lived
through all the promises, you see?

MICKEY: Pretty good, Lou. I intended to call you tomorrow.

LOU: Really? I was going to call *you*; about a little problem I—*Uncertain: May* I?

MICKEY: Of course, Lou! You can always call me. I've got guests at
home. *Grasps Lou's arm.* Give my best to Elsie.

LOU, *relieved:* I'll ring you tomorrow! And thank you, Mickey!

*The gratitude seems to stab Mickey, who is already a few yards
away, and he turns back,* resolves *to turn back.*

MICKEY: What . . . was the problem, Lou?

LOU, *relieved, hurrying to him like a puppy:* Just the question of
publishing my book now. Elsie's afraid it will wake up all the sleeping dogs again. . . .

MICKEY—*pause:* But don't you have to take that chance? I think a
man's got to take the rap, Lou, for what he's done, for what he is. I
think what you hide poisons you. After all, it's your work.

LOU: I feel exactly that way! *Grabs his arm.* Golly, Mick! Why
don't we get together as we used to? I miss all that wonderful talk!
Of course I know how busy you are now, but—

MICKEY: Lou.

Pause.

LOU: Yes, Mick. I'll meet you anywhere you say!

MICKEY: Elsie coming up?

LOU: You want to see her? I could call down to the beach.

He starts off; Mickey stops him.

MICKEY: Lou.

LOU, *sensing something odd:* Yes, Mick.

QUENTIN, *facing the sky:* Dear God.

MICKEY: I've been subpoenaed.

LOU: No!

Mickey nods, looks at the ground. Lou grips his arm.

Oh, I'm terribly sorry, Mick. I was afraid of that when they called
me. But can I say something—it might ease your mind: once you're
in front of them it all gets remarkably simple!

QUENTIN: Oh, dear God!

LOU: Really, it's not as terrible as it seems to you now; everything kind of falls away excepting one's . . . one's self. One's truth.

MICKEY—*slight pause:* I've already been in front of them, Lou. Two weeks ago.

LOU: Oh! Then what do they want with you again?

MICKEY—*pause. A fixed smile on his face:* I asked to be heard again.

LOU, *puzzled, open-eyed:* Why?

MICKEY—*he carefully forms his thought:* Because I want to tell the truth.

LOU, *with the first rising of incredulous fear:* In . . . what sense? What do you mean?

MICKEY: Lou, when I left the hearing room I didn't feel I had spoken. Something else had spoken, something automatic and inhuman. I asked myself, what am I protecting by refusing to answer? Lou, you must let me finish! You must. The Party? But I despise the Party, and have for many years. Just like you. Yet there is something, something that closes my throat when I think of telling names. What am I defending? It's a dream, now, a dream of solidarity, but hasn't that died a long time ago? The fact is, I have no solidarity with the people I could name—excepting for you. And not because we were Communists together, but because we were young together. Because we—when we talked it was like—monks probably talk, like some brotherhood opposed to all the world's injustice. It's you made my throat close, just the love whenever we saw one another. But what created that love, Lou? Wasn't it a respect for truth, a hatred of hypocrisy? Therefore, in the name of that love, I ought to be true to myself now. It would be easier, in a sense, to do what you did and stick with it; I would keep your friendship, but lose myself. Because the truth, Lou, my truth, is that I think the Party *is* a conspiracy. . . . Let me finish. I think we *were* swindled; they took our lust for the right and used it for Russian purposes. And I don't think we can go on turning our backs on the truth simply because reactionaries are saying it. What I propose—is that we try to separate our love for one another from this political morass. It was not the Party we loved, it was each other's truth. And I've said nothing just now that we haven't told each other for the past five years.

LOU: Then . . . what's your proposal?

MICKEY: That we go back together. Come with me. And answer the questions. I was going to tell you this tomorrow.

LOU: Name . . . the names?

MICKEY: Yes. I've talked to all the others in the unit. They've agreed, excepting for Ward and Harry. They cursed me out, but I expected that.

LOU, *dazed:* Let me understand—you are asking my permission to name me? *Pause.* You may not mention my name. *He begins physically shaking.* And if you do it, Mickey, you are selling me for your own prosperity. If you use my name I will be dismissed. You will ruin me. You will destroy my career.

MICKEY: Lou, I think I have a right to know exactly why you—

LOU: Because if everyone broke faith there would be no civilization! That is why that Committee is the face of the Philistine! And it astounds me that you can speak of truth and justice in relation to that gang of cheap publicity hounds! Not one syllable will they get from me! Not one word from my lips! No—your eleven-room apartment, your automobile, your money are not worth this.

He strides toward the edge of the area.

MICKEY, *stiffened:* That's a lie! You can't reduce it all to money, Lou! *That is false!*

LOU, *turning on him:* There is only one truth here. You are terrified! They have bought your soul!

He starts out again.

MICKEY, *angrily, but contained:* And yours? Lou! Is it all yours, your soul?

LOU, *beginning to show tears:* How dare you speak of my—?

MICKEY, *quaking with anger:* You've got to take it if you're going to dish it out, don't you? Have you really earned this high moral one—this . . .

Elsie appears in the farthest distance, slowly coming toward them as though from a beach, her robe open, her head raised up toward the breeze, toward longing, toward the sky.

perfect integrity? I happen to remember when you came back from your trip to Russia; and I remember who made you throw your first version into my fireplace!

LOU, *almost screaming—after a glance toward Elsie:* The idea!

MICKEY: I saw you burn a true book and write another that told lies! Because she demanded it, because she terrified you, because she has taken your soul!

LOU, *shaking his fist in the air:* I condemn you!

MICKEY: But from your conscience or from hers? Who is speaking to me, Lou?

LOU: You are a monster!

He bursts into tears, walks off toward Elsie; he meets her in the near distance, says a few words, and her face shows horror. At the front of stage Mickey turns and looks across the full width toward Quentin at the farthest edge of light, and, reading Quentin's feelings:

MICKEY: I guess you'll want to get somebody else to go over your brief with you.

Quentin, indecisive, but not contradicting him, now turns to him. Good-bye, Quentin.

QUENTIN, *in a dead tone:* Good-bye, Mickey.

Mickey goes out as Elsie and Lou rush down, she in a near-hysteria. As they arrive, Louise appears, stands watching.

ELSIE: Did you hear? *Including Louise in her glance.* Did you hear? He's a *moral idiot* !

Quentin turns to her; something perhaps in his gaze or in the recesses of her mind makes her close her robe, which she holds tightly shut. And to Quentin . . .

Isn't that *incredible* ?

QUENTIN, *quietly:* Yes.

ELSIE: After such friendship! Such love between them! And for so many years!

The camp tower comes alive, and Quentin moves out of this group, slowly toward it, looking up.

LOU, *stunned:* And only this spring, brought me an expensive briefcase for my birthday!

ELSIE: And named his son Louis after you! Who can understand this?

Above, Holga appears as before, carrying flowers. She is a distance away from Quentin, who turns to her.

QUENTIN: You love me, don't you?

HOLGA: Yes.

An instant's hesitation and he turns quickly to Listener, and cries out.

QUENTIN: Is it that I'm looking for some simple-minded constancy that never is and never was?

He turns to Elsie, who is lifting Lou to his feet and kisses him.
How tenderly she lifts him up—now that he is ruined.

Elsie walks off with Lou, her arm around him, and kissing his cheek. Quentin watches them go.
Still, that could be a true kiss. Or is there no treason but only man, unblamable as trees or cats or clouds? ... Yes, I do, I see it; but if that is what we are, what will keep us safe?

Louise appears.
Or is the question foolish?

LOUISE: I had a dream. I want to tell you about it.

QUENTIN, *in pain:* Are we ever safe?

LOUISE: I was standing beside a high mountain. With my legs cut off.

He picks up a brief, looks into it.
Must you work tonight?

QUENTIN: It's Lou's case. I have a pile of stuff. *Slight pause.* Well, I can do it later. What is it?

LOUISE: Never mind.

QUENTIN—*he sits at once, as though remembering some resolution to act well:* I'm sorry, Louise. What'd you want to say?

LOUISE: I'm trying to understand why you got so angry with me at the party the other night.

QUENTIN: I wasn't *angry*; I simply felt that every time I began to talk you cut in to explain what I was about to say.

LOUISE: Well, I'd had a drink; I was a little high. I felt happy, I guess, that you weren't running for cover when everybody else was.

QUENTIN: Yes, but Max was there, and DeVries, and they don't feel they're running for cover. I only want to win Lou's case, not some moral victory over the firm. I felt you were putting me out on a limb.

LOUISE: Quentin, I saw you getting angry when I was talking about that new anti-virus vaccine.

He tries to remember, believing she is right.

What is it? Don't you want me to speak at all?

QUENTIN: That's ridiculous, Louise, why do you—

LOUISE: Because the moment I begin to assert myself it seems to threaten you. I don't think you *want* me to be happy.

QUENTIN—*there is a basic concession made by his tone of admitted bewilderment:* I tell you the truth, Louise—I don't think I feel very sure of myself any more. I feel sometimes that I don't see reality at all. I'm glad I took on Lou, but it only hit me lately that no respectable lawyer would touch him. It's like some unseen web of connection between people is simply not there. And I always relied on it, somehow; I never quite believed that people could be so easily disposed of. And it's larger than the political question. I think it's got me a little scared.

LOUISE, *with a wish for his sympathy, not accusing:* Well then, you must know how I felt when I found that letter in your suit.

QUENTIN—*he turns to her, aware:* I didn't do that to dispose of you, Louise.

   She does not reply.

I thought we'd settled about that girl.

   She still does not reply.

You mean you think I'm still . . .

LOUISE: I don't know what you're doing.

QUENTIN, *astounded:* What do you mean, you don't know?

LOUISE, *directly at him:* I said I don't know! I thought you told the truth about the other girl years ago, but after what happened again this spring—I don't know anything.

QUENTIN—*pause:* Tell me something; until this party the other night—in fact this whole year—I thought you seemed much happier. You were, weren't you?

LOUISE: Quentin, aren't you aware I've simply been staying out of your way this year?

QUENTIN, *amazed, frightened for his sense of reality:* Staying out of my way!

LOUISE: Well, can you rememer one thing I've said about myself this year?

QUENTIN, *angrily, still amazed:* I swear to God, Louise, I thought we were building something till the other night!

LOUISE: But why?

QUENTIN: Well, I can't give you a bill of particulars, but it seems pretty obvious I've been trying like hell to show what I think of you. You've seen that, haven't you?

LOUISE: Quentin, you are full of resentment; you think I'm blind?

QUENTIN: What I resent is being forever on trial, Louise. Are you an innocent bystander here? I keep waiting for some contribution you might have made to what I did, and I resent not hearing it.

LOUISE: I said I did contribute; I demanded nothing for much too long.

QUENTIN: You mean the summer before last you didn't come to me and say that if I didn't change you would divorce me?

LOUISE: I never said I was *planning* a—

QUENTIN: You said if it came down to it you would divorce me—that's not a contribution?

LOUISE: Well, it certainly ought not send a man out to play doctor with the first girl he could lay his hands on!

QUENTIN: How much shame do you want me to feel? I hate what I did. But I think I've explained it—I felt like nothing; I shouldn't have, but I did, and I took the only means I knew to—

LOUISE: This is exactly what I mean, Quentin—you are still defending it. Right now.

He is stopped by this truth.

And I know it, Quentin.

QUENTIN: And you're . . . not at all to blame, heh?

LOUISE: But how?

QUENTIN: Well, for example . . . you never turn your back on me in bed?

LOUISE: I never turned my—

QUENTIN: You have turned your back on me in bed, Louise. I am not insane!

LOUISE: Well what do you expect? Silent, cold, you lay your hand on me?

QUENTIN, *fallen:* Well, I . . . I'm not very demonstrative, I guess.

Slight pause. He throws himself on her compassion.

Louise . . . I worry about you all day. And all night.

LOUISE—*it is something, but not enough:* Well, you've got a child; I'm sure that worries you.

QUENTIN, *deeply hurt:* Is that all?

LOUISE, *with intense reasonableness:* Look, Quentin, it all comes down to a very simple thing; you want a woman to provide an . . . atmosphere, in which there are never any issues, and you'll fly around in a constant bath of praise . . .

QUENTIN: Well I wouldn't mind a little praise, what's wrong with praise?

LOUISE: Quentin, I am not a praise machine! I am not a blur and I am not your mother! I am a separate person!

QUENTIN—*he stares at her, and what lies beyond her:* I see that now.

LOUISE: It's no crime! Not if you're adult and grown-up.

QUENTIN, *quietly:* I guess not. But it bewilders me. In fact, I got the same idea when I realized that Lou had gone from one of his former students to another and none would take him . . .

LOUISE: What's Lou got to do with it? I think it's admirable that you . . .

QUENTIN: Yes, but I am doing what you call an admirable thing because I can't bear to be a separate person! I think so. I really don't want to be known as a Red lawyer; and I really don't want the newspapers to eat me alive; and if it came down to it, Lou could defend himself. But when that decent, broken man, who never wanted anything but the good of the world, sits across my desk . . . I don't know how to say that my interests are no longer the same as his, and that if he doesn't change I consign him to hell because we are separate persons.

LOUISE: You are completely confused! Lou's case has nothing—

QUENTIN, *grasping for his thought:* I am telling you my confusion! I think Mickey also became a separate person.

LOUISE: You're incredible!

QUENTIN: I think of my mother, I think she also became—

LOUISE: Are you identifying *me* with—

QUENTIN: Louise, I am asking you to explain this to me because this is when I go blind! When you've finally become a separate person, what the hell is there?

LOUISE, *with a certain unsteady pride:* Maturity.

QUENTIN: I don't know what that means.

LOUISE: It means that you know another person exists, Quentin. I'm not in analysis for nothing!

QUENTIN, *questing:* It's probably the symptom of a typical case of some kind, but I swear, Louise—if you would just once, of your own will, as right as you are—if you would come to me and say that something, something important was your fault and that you were sorry . . . it would help.

In her pride she is silent, in her refusal to be brought down again. Louise?

LOUISE: Good God! What an idiot!

She begins to weep helplessly for her life, and vanishes. Light rises on a park bench with the sound of traffic. A young Negro hurries past, neat, wearing sunglasses, on the lookout, halts to flick dust off his shined shoes, goes on. An old woman in shapeless dress carries a shopping bag and a parrot in a cage across, limping. Quentin strolls on and sits on the bench, briefcase on his lap.

QUENTIN: How few the days are that hold the mind in place; like a tapestry hanging on four or five hooks. Especially the day you stop becoming; the day you merely are. I suppose it's when the principles dissolve, and instead of the general gray of what ought to be you begin to see what is. Even the bench by the park seems alive, having held so many actual men. The word "Now" is like a bomb through the window, and it ticks.

The old woman recrosses with the parrot.

Now a woman takes a parrot for a walk. Everything suddenly has consequences; she probably worries what will happen to it when she's gone.

A plain girl in tweeds passes, reading a paperback.

And how brave a homely woman has to be! How disciplined of her, not to set fire to the museum of art.

The Negro passes, flicking dust off his shoe, comes to Quentin demanding a light for his cigarette. Quentin lights it.

And how does he keep so neat, and the bathroom on another floor? He must be furious when he shaves.

The Negro sees his girl upstage, walks off with her.

And whatever made me think that at the end of the day, I absolutely had to go home? You understand? That day when, suddenly, nothing whatsoever is ordained. Only . . . "Now," ticking away.

Maggie appears, looking about for someone.

Now there's a truth; symmetrical, lovely skin, undeniable.

MAGGIE: S'uze me, did you see a man with a big dog?

QUENTIN: No. But I saw a woman with a little bird.

MAGGIE: No, that's not him. Is this the bus stop?

QUENTIN: Ya, the sign says . . .

MAGGIE—*sits beside him:* I was standing over there and a man came with this big dog and just put the leash in my hand and walked away. So I started to go after him but the dog wouldn't move. And then this other man came and took the leash and went away. But I don't think it's really his dog. I think it's the first man's dog.

QUENTIN: But he obviously doesn't want it.

MAGGIE: But maybe he wanted for me to have it. I think the other man just saw it happening and figured he could get a free dog.

QUENTIN: Well, you want the dog?

MAGGIE: How could I keep a dog? I don't even think they allow dogs where I live. They might, but I never saw any dog. Although I'm not there much. What bus is this?

QUENTIN: Fifth Avenue. This is the downtown side. Where did you want to go?

MAGGIE—*thinks:* Well, I could go there.

QUENTIN: Where?

MAGGIE: Downtown.

QUENTIN: Lot of funny things go on, don't they?

MAGGIE: Well, he probably figured I would like a dog. Whereas I would if I had a way to keep it, but I don't even have a refrigerator.

QUENTIN: Yes. *Pause.* I guess he thought you had a refrigerator; that must be it.

She shrugs. Pause. He looks at her as she watches for the bus. He has no more to say. Louise lights up.

LOUISE: You don't talk to any woman—not like a *woman*! You think reading your brief is *talking* to me?

She goes dark. In tension Quentin leans forward, arms resting on his knees. He looks at Maggie again. Anonymous men appear, lounge about, eying her.

QUENTIN, *with an effort:* What do you do?

MAGGIE, *as though he should know:* On the switchboard.

QUENTIN: Oh, telephone operator?

MAGGIE—*laughs:* Don't you remember me?

QUENTIN, *surprised:* Me?

MAGGIE: I always sort of nod to you every morning through the window.

QUENTIN—*an instant:* Oh. In the reception room!

MAGGIE: Sure!

QUENTIN: What's your name?

MAGGIE: Maggie.

QUENTIN: Of course! You get my numbers sometimes.

MAGGIE: Did you think I just came up and started talking to you?

QUENTIN: I had no idea.

MAGGIE—*laughs:* Well what must you have thought!

QUENTIN: I didn't know what to think.

MAGGIE: I guess it's that you never saw me altogether. I mean just my head through that little window.

QUENTIN: Yes. Well, it's nice to meet all of you, finally.

MAGGIE—*laughs:* You go back to work again tonight?

QUENTIN: No, I'm just resting for a few minutes.

MAGGIE, *with a sense of his loneliness:* Oh.

She looks idly about. He glances down her body.

QUENTIN: It's a pity you have to sit behind that little window.

She laughs, gratefully. Her eye catches something.

MAGGIE, *rising:* Is that my bus down there?

QUENTIN: I'm not really sure where you want to go.

A man appears, eyes her, glances up toward the bus, back to her, staring.

MAGGIE: I wanted to find one of those discount stores; I just bought a phonograph but I only have one record. I'll see you!

She is half-backing off toward the man.

MAN: There's one on Twenty-seventh and Sixth Avenue.

MAGGIE, *turning, surprised:* Oh, thanks!

QUENTIN, *standing; moving toward her as though not to lose her to the man:* There's a record store around the corner, you know.

MAGGIE: But is it discount?

QUENTIN: Well they all discount—

MAN, *slipping his hand under her arm:* What, ten per cent? Come on, honey, I'll get you easy fifty off.

MAGGIE, *moving off on his arm:* Really? But Perry Sullivan?

MAN: Look, I'll give it to you—I'll give you two records! Come on!

MAGGIE—*she halts, suddenly aware; disengages her arm, backs:* S'uze me, I . . . I . . . forgot something.

MAN, *lathering:* Look, I'll give you ten records. *Calls off.* Hold that door! *Grabs her.* Come on!

QUENTIN, *moving toward him:* Hey!

MAN, *letting her go—to Quentin:* Ah, get lost! *He rushes off.* Hold it, hold the door!

Quentin watches the "bus" go by, then turns to her. She is absorbed in arranging her hair—but with a strangely doughy expression, removed.

QUENTIN: I'm sorry, I thought you knew him.

MAGGIE: No. I never saw him.

QUENTIN: Well . . . what were you going with him for?

MAGGIE: Well he said he knew a store.

QUENTIN—*mystified, intrigued, looks at her, then nods inconclusively:* Oh.

MAGGIE: Where's the one you're talking about?

QUENTIN: I'll have to think a minute. Let's see . . .

MAGGIE: Could I sit with you? While you're thinking?

QUENTIN: Sure.

They return to the bench. He waits till she is seated; she is aware of the politeness, glances at him as he sits. Then she looks at him fully, for some reason amazed.

That happen to you very often?

MAGGIE: Pretty often.

It is impossible to tell if she likes it or not.

QUENTIN: It's because you talk to them.

MAGGIE: But they talk to me, so I have to answer.

QUENTIN: Not if they're rude.

MAGGIE: But if they talk to me . . .

QUENTIN: Just turn your back.

MAGGIE—*she thinks about that, and indecisively:* Oh, okay. *As though remotely aware of another world, his world:* . . . Thanks, though . . . for stopping it.

QUENTIN: Well, anybody would.

MAGGIE: No, they laugh. It's a joke to them. *She laughs in pain. Slight pause.* You ... going to rest here very long?

QUENTIN: Just a few minutes. I'm on my way home. I never did this before.

MAGGIE: Oh! You look like you always did.

QUENTIN: Why?

MAGGIE: I don't know. You look like you could sit for hours, under these trees ... just thinking.

QUENTIN: No. I usually go right home. *Grinning:* I've always gone right home.

MAGGIE—*she absorbs this:* Oh. *Coming awake:* See, I'm still paying for the phonograph, whereas they don't sell records on time, you know.

QUENTIN: They're afraid they'll wear out, I guess.

MAGGIE: Oh, that must be it! I always wondered. Cause you *can* get phonographs. How'd you know that?

QUENTIN: I don't. I'm just guessing.

MAGGIE: It sounds true, though. *Laughs.* I can never guess those things! I don't know why they do anything half the time! *She laughs more deeply. He does.* I had about ten or twenty records in Washington, but my friend got sick, and I had to leave. Although maybe they're still there.

QUENTIN: Well, if you still have the apartment ...

MAGGIE: I'm not sure I do. I got a letter from them couple months ago, the Real Estate. *Pause. Thinks.* I better open it. He lived right over there on Park Avenue.

QUENTIN: Oh. Is he better?

MAGGIE: He died. *Tears come into her eyes.*

QUENTIN, *entirely perplexed:* When was this?

MAGGIE: Friday. Remember they closed the office for the day?

QUENTIN: You mean—*Astounded*—Judge Cruse?

MAGGIE: Ya.

QUENTIN, *with lingering surprise:* Oh, I didn't know that you ... He was a great lawyer. And a great judge, too.

MAGGIE, *rubbing tears:* He was very nice to me.

QUENTIN: I was at the funeral; I didn't see you, though.

MAGGIE, *with difficulty against her tears:* His wife wouldn't let me come. But I got into the hospital before he died. But as soon as I opened the door of his room the family pushed me out and ... I could hear him calling, "Maggie! Maggie!" *Pause.* They kept trying to offer me a thousand dollars. But I told them, I don't want anything, I just wanted to say good-bye to him!

She opens her purse, takes out an office envelope, opens it.

I have a little of the dirt. See? That's from his grave. His chauffeur drove me out—Alexander.

QUENTIN—*looks at the dirt, at her face:* Did he leave you very much?

MAGGIE: No, he didn't leave me anything.

She puts the envelope back, closes the purse, stares.

QUENTIN: Did you love him very much?

MAGGIE: No. But he was very nice. In fact, a couple of times I really left him.

QUENTIN: Why didn't you altogether?

MAGGIE: He didn't want me to.

QUENTIN: Oh. *Pause.* So what are you going to do now?

MAGGIE: I'd love to get that record if I knew where they had a discount.

QUENTIN: No, I mean in general.

MAGGIE: Why, they going to fire me now?

QUENTIN: Oh, I wouldn't know about that.

MAGGIE: Although I'm not worried, whereas I can always go back to hair.

QUENTIN: To where?

MAGGIE: I used to demonstrate hair preparations. *Laughs, squirts her hair with an imaginary bottle.* You know, in department stores? I was traveling even, they sent me to Boston and New Orleans and all over. *Tilting her head under his chin:* It's because I have very thick hair, you see? I have my mother's hair. And it's not broken. You notice I have no broken hair? Most women's hair is broken. Here, feel it, feel how— *She has lifted his hand to her head, and suddenly lets go of it.* Oh, s'uze me!

QUENTIN: That's all right.

MAGGIE: I just thought you might want to feel it.

QUENTIN: Sure.

MAGGIE: Go ahead. I mean if you want to.

She leans her head to him again. He touches the top of her head.

QUENTIN: It is, ya! Very soft.

MAGGIE, *proudly:* I once went from page boy to bouffant in less than ten minutes!

QUENTIN: What made you quit?

MAGGIE—*the dough comes into her eyes again:* They start sending me to conventions and all. You're supposed to entertain, you see.

QUENTIN: Oh, yes.

MAGGIE: There were parts of it I didn't like any more.

A long moment. A student goes by, reading. He looks up from his book, shyly glances at her, goes on reading. She laughs.

Aren't they sweet when they look up from their books!

She turns to him with a laugh. He looks at her warmly, smiling.

S'uze me I put your hand on my head.

QUENTIN: Oh, that's all right. . . . I'm not *that* bad. *He laughs softly, embarrassed.*

MAGGIE: You're not bad.

QUENTIN: I don't mean bad, I mean . . . shy.

MAGGIE: It's not bad to be shy. *She gives him a long look, absorbed.* I mean . . . if that's the way you are.

QUENTIN: I guess I am, then.

Pause. They look at each other.

You're very beautiful, Maggie.

She smiles, straightens as though his words had entered her.

And I wish you knew how to take care of yourself.

MAGGIE: Oh . . . *Holding out a ripped seam in her dress:* I got this torn on the bus this morning. I'm going to sew it home.

QUENTIN: I don't mean that.

She meets his eyes again—she looks chastised.

Not that I'm criticizing you. I'm not at all. Not in the slightest. You understand?

She nods, absorbed in his face. He stands.

I've got to go now.

She stands, staring at him, giving herself. He sees this. His hand moves, but it becomes a handshake.

You could look up record stores in the phone book.

MAGGIE: I think I'll take a walk in the park.

QUENTIN: You shouldn't. It's getting dark.

MAGGIE: But it's beautiful at night. I slept there one night when it was hot in my room.

QUENTIN: God, you don't want to do that! I know this park. Most of the animals are not in the zoo.

MAGGIE: Okay. I'll get a record, then. *She backs a step.* S'uze me about my hair if I embarrassed you.

QUENTIN—*laughs:* You didn't.

MAGGIE—*backing to leave, she touches the top of her head:* It's just that it's not broken.

He nods. She halts some yards away, holds out her torn seam. I'm going to sew this home.

He nods. She indicates the park, upstage.

I didn't *mean* to sleep there. I just fell asleep.

Two young guys appear, pass Quentin, slow as they pass her, and halt in the far periphery of the light, waiting for her.

QUENTIN: I understand.

MAGGIE: Well . . . see you! *Laughs.* If they don't fire me!

QUENTIN: 'Bye.

She passes the two men, who walk step for step behind her, whispering in her ear together. She doesn't turn or answer but shows no surprise.

QUENTIN—*in anguish he hurries after her:* Maggie! *He catches her arm and brings her clear of the men, takes a bill from his pocket.* Here, why don't you take a cab? It's on me. Go ahead, there's one right there. *Points and whistles.* Go on, grab it!

MAGGIE, *backing in the opposite direction from the waiting men:* Where . . . where will I tell him to go but?

QUENTIN: Just cruise in the forties—you've got enough there.

MAGGIE: Okay, 'bye! *Backing out:* You . . . you just going to rest more?

QUENTIN: I don't know.

MAGGIE, *wondrously:* Golly, that's nice!

She hurries off. He stands staring after her. Likewise, the men watch the "cab" going by, then walk off.

Lights rise on Louise reading in a chair. Quentin, clasping his briefcase behind his back, walks slowly into the area, stands a few yards from her, staring at her. She remains unaware of him, reading and smoking.

QUENTIN: Yes. She has legs, breasts, mouth, eyes. How wonderful—a woman of my own! What a miracle! In my own house!

He walks to her, bends and kisses her. She looks up at him surprised, perplexed.

Hi.

She keeps looking up at him, aware of some sealike opening in the world.

What's the matter?

She still doesn't speak.

Well, what's the matter?

LOUISE: Nothing.

She returns to her book. Mystified, disappointed, he stands watching, then opens his briefcase and begins taking out papers.

Close the door if you're going to type.

QUENTIN: I always do.

LOUISE: Not always.

QUENTIN: Almost always.

He almost laughs, he feels loose, but she won't be amused, and returns again to her book. He starts for the bedroom, halts.

How about eating out tomorrow night? Before the parents' meeting?

LOUISE: What parents' meeting?

QUENTIN: The school.

LOUISE: That was tonight.

QUENTIN, *shocked:* Really?

LOUISE: Of course. I just got back.

QUENTIN: Why didn't you remind me when I called today?

LOUISE: You knew it as well as I.

QUENTIN: But you know I often forget those things. I told you I wanted to talk to her teacher.

LOUISE, *a little more sharply:* People do what they want to do, Quentin.

QUENTIN: But Louise, I was talking to you at three o'clock this afternoon . . .

LOUISE—*an unwilling shout:* Because you said you had to work to-night!

She glares at him meaningfully; returns to her book. He stands, alarmed.

QUENTIN: I didn't work.

LOUISE, *keeping to her book: I* know you didn't work.

QUENTIN, *surprised:* How did you know?

LOUISE: Well for one thing, Max called here at seven-thirty.

QUENTIN: Max? What for?

LOUISE: Apparently the whole executive committee was in his office waiting to meet with you tonight.

His hand goes to his head; open alarm shows on his face.

He called three times, as a matter of fact.

QUENTIN: I forgot all about it! *He hurries to the phone, stops.* How is that possible? It completely—

LOUISE: Well they wouldn't be there any more now. *Pointedly:* It's ten-thirty.

QUENTIN: My God, I— How could I do that? What's his home number?

LOUISE: The book is in the bedroom.

QUENTIN: We were supposed to discuss my handling Lou's case. DeVries stayed in town tonight just to ... settle everything. And I go and walk out as though ... nothing ... *Breaks off. Picks up phone.* What's Max's number, Murray Hill 3 ... what is it?

LOUISE: The book is next to the bed.

QUENTIN: You remember it, Murray Hill 3, something.

LOUISE: It's in the book.

Pause. He looks at her. Puzzled.

QUENTIN: What are you doing?

LOUISE: I'm saying the book is in the bedroom.

QUENTIN—*slams the phone down, and, as much in fright as in anger:* But you remember his number!

LOUISE: I'm not the keeper of your phone numbers. You can remember them just as well as I.

QUENTIN: Oh, I see. *Nods ironically, starts out.*

LOUISE: Please don't use that phone, you'll wake her up.

QUENTIN—*turns:* I had no intention of calling in there.

LOUISE: I thought you might want to be private.

QUENTIN: There's nothing private about this. This concerns you as much as me. The food in your mouth and the clothes on your back.

LOUISE: Really! When did you start thinking of us?

QUENTIN: The meeting was called to decide whether I should separate from the firm until Lou's case is over—or permanently, for all I know.

Quentin goes toward the phone. She stands staring in growing fright.

Murray Hill 3 . . .

He picks it up, dials one digit.

LOUISE, *much against her will:* That's the old number.

QUENTIN: Murray Hill 3-4598.

LOUISE: It's been changed. *A moment; and finally:* Cortland 7-7098.

QUENTIN—*she is not facing him; he senses what he thinks is victory:* Thanks.

Starts again to dial, puts down the phone. She sits; there is an admission of the faintest sort of failing in her.

I don't know what to say to him.

She is silent.

We arranged for everybody to come back after dinner. It'll sound idiotic that I forgot about it.

LOUISE: You were probably frightened.

QUENTIN: But I made notes all afternoon about what I would say tonight! It's incredible!

LOUISE, *with an over-meaning:* You probably don't realize how frightened you are.

QUENTIN: I guess I don't. He said a dreadful thing today—Max. He was trying to argue me into dropping Lou and I said, "The law is the law; we can't adopt some new behavior just because there's hysteria in the country." I thought it was a perfectly ordinary thing to say but he—he's never looked at me that way—like we were suddenly standing on two distant mountains; and he said, "I don't know of any hysteria. Not in this office."

LOUISE, *without rancor:* But why does all that surprise you?

QUENTIN—*slight pause:* I don't understand exactly what you're getting at.

LOUISE: Simply that there are some issues you have to face. You tend to make relatives out of people. Max is not your father, or your brother, or anything but a very important lawyer with his own interests. He's not going to endanger his whole firm to defend a Communist. I don't know how you got that illusion.

QUENTIN: You mean—

LOUISE: I mean you can't have everything; if you feel this strongly about Lou you probably will have to resign.

QUENTIN—*pause:* You think I should?

LOUISE: That depends on how deeply you feel about Lou.

QUENTIN: I'm trying to determine that; I don't know for sure. What do you think?

LOUISE, *in anguish:* It's not my decision, Quentin.

QUENTIN, *puzzled and surprised:* But aren't you involved?

LOUISE: Of course I'm involved.

QUENTIN, *genuinely foxed:* Is it that you're not sure of how you feel?

LOUISE: I know how I feel but it is not my decision.

QUENTIN: I'm only curious how you—

LOUISE: You? Curious about me?

QUENTIN: Oh. We're not talking about what we're talking about, are we?

LOUISE, *nodding in emphasis:* You have to decide what you feel about a certain human being. For once in your life. And then maybe you'll decide what you feel about other human beings. Clearly and decisively.

QUENTIN: In other words . . . where was I tonight.

LOUISE: I don't care where you were tonight.

QUENTIN—*pause:* I sat by the park for a while. And this is what I thought. I don't sleep with other women, but I think I behave as though I do.

She is listening. He sees it, is enlivened by hope.

Maybe I invite your suspicion on myself in order to . . . to come down off some bench, to stop judging others so perfectly. Because I do judge, and harshly, too—when the fact is I'm bewildered. I even wonder if I left that letter for you to read . . . about that girl . . . in order to . . . somehow join the condemned; in some way to start being real. Can you understand that?

LOUISE: But . . . *She is digging in her heels against being taken.* Why should you be condemned if you're not still doing anything?

QUENTIN, *uneasily again:* But don't you continue to feel ashamed for something you've done in the past? You can understand that, can't you?

LOUISE: I don't do things I'll be ashamed of.

QUENTIN, *now astonished, and moving toward anger:* Really and truly?

LOUISE—*starts to rise:* I'm going to bed.

QUENTIN: I have to say it, Louise; whenever our conversations verge on you, they end. You say you want to talk, but is it only about my sins?

LOUISE: Now you listen here! You've been "at the office" one night a week since last winter. It's not my forgiveness you want, it's the end of this marriage! But you haven't the courage to say so!

QUENTIN: All right, then. *Against his own trepidation, striving for a clear conscience:* I think I won't be ashamed either. I met a girl to-night. Just happened to come by, one of the phone operators in the office. I probably shouldn't tell you this either, but I will.

She sits, slowly.

Quite stupid, silly kid. Sleeps in the park, her dress is ripped; she said some ridiculous things, but one thing struck me, she wasn't de-fending anything, upholding anything, or accusing—she was just *there,* like a tree or a cat. And I felt strangely abstract beside her. And I saw that we are killing one another with abstractions. I'm de-fending Lou because I love him, yet the society transforms that love into a kind of treason, what they call an issue, and I end up suspect and hated. Why can't we speak below the "issues"—with our real uncertainty? I walked in just now—and I had a tremendous wish to come out—to you. And you to me. It sounds absurd that this city is full of people rushing to meet one another, Louise. This city is full of lovers. . . .

LOUISE: And what did she say?

QUENTIN: I guess I shouldn't have told you about it.

LOUISE: Why not?

QUENTIN: Louise, I don't know what's permissible to say any more.

LOUISE—*nods:* You don't know how much to hide.

QUENTIN—*he angers:* All right, let's not hide anything, it would have been easy to make love to her.

Louise reddens, stiffens.

And I didn't because I thought of you, and in a new way . . . like a stranger I had never gotten to know. And by some miracle you were waiting for me, in my own home. I came into this room, Louise, full of love . . .

LOUISE: What do you want, my congratulations? You expect me to sit here and enjoy your latest conquest? You take me for a Lesbian?

QUENTIN, *perplexed:* What's a Lesbian got to do with . . .

LOUISE: Ask your friend with the torn dress. You don't imagine a real woman goes to bed with any man who happens to come along? Or that a real man goes to bed with every woman who'll have him? Especially a slut, which she obviously is?

QUENTIN: How do you know she's a—

LOUISE—*laughs:* Oh, excuse me, I didn't mean to insult her! You're unbelievable! Supposing I came home and told you I'd met a man—a man on the street I wanted to go to bed with . . .

He hangs his head, defeated.

because he made the city seem full of lovers. What would you feel? Overjoyed for my discovery?

QUENTIN—*pause; struck:* I understand. I'm sorry. I guess it would anger me too. *Slight pause.* But if you came to me with such a thing, I think I would see that you were struggling. And I would ask myself—maybe I'd even be brave enough to ask you—how *I* had failed.

LOUISE: Well, you've given me notice; I get the message.

She starts out.

QUENTIN: Louise, don't you ever doubt yourself?

She slows, but does not turn.

Is it enough to prove a case, to even win it—*Shouts*—when we are dying?

LOUISE—*turns in full possession:* I'm not dying. I'm not the one who wanted to break this up. And that's all it's about. It's all it's been about the last three years. You don't want me!

She goes out.

QUENTIN: God! Can that be true?

Mickey enters as he was in his scene, dressed in summer slacks.

MICKEY: There's only one thing I can tell you for sure, kid—don't ever be guilty.

QUENTIN: Yes! *Seeking strength, he stretches upward.* Yes! *But his conviction wavers; he turns toward the vision.* But if you had felt more guilt, maybe you wouldn't have ...

Elsie rushes into this light as before, her robe open to her tight bathing suit.

ELSIE: He's a moral idiot!

QUENTIN: Yes! That is right. And yet. ...

He turns and faces her, and she slowly, under his gaze, draws her robe together in a way to conceal her own betrayal, and she and Mickey are gone. Quentin stands staring out.

What the hell is moral? What does that really mean? And what am I ... to even ask that question? A man ought to know ... a decent man knows that like he knows his own face!

Louise enters with a folded sheet and a pillow which she tosses into the chair.

LOUISE: I don't want to sleep with you.

QUENTIN: Louise, for God's sake!

LOUISE: You are disgusting!

QUENTIN: But in the morning Betty will see ...

LOUISE: You should have thought of that.

The phone rings. He makes no move to answer.

Did you give her this number?

The phone rings again.

LOUISE: Did you give her this number? *With which she strides to the phone.* Hello! ... Oh, yes. He's here. Hold on, please. *To him:* It's Max.

For a moment, he stands touching the sheets, then looks at her, picks up the sheets, and hands them to her.

QUENTIN: I can't sleep out here; I don't want her to see it.

But she adamantly lets the sheets fall to the floor. He goes to the phone with a look of hatred.

Max? I'm sorry, the whole thing just slipped my mind. I don't know how to explain it, Max, I just went blank, I guess, I— *Pause.* The radio? No, why? *What?* When? *Long pause.* Thanks ... for letting me know. Yes, he was. Good night ... ya, see you in the morning. *Pause. He stands staring.*

LOUISE: What is it?

QUENTIN: Lou. Was killed by a subway train tonight.

LOUISE—*gasps:* How?

QUENTIN: They don't know. They say "fell or jumped."

LOUISE: He couldn't have! The crowd must have pushed him!

QUENTIN: There is no crowd at eight o'clock. It was eight o'clock.

LOUISE: But *why?* Lou *knew* himself! He knew where he *stood*! It's impossible!

QUENTIN, *staring:* Maybe it's not enough—to know yourself. Or maybe it's too much. I think he did it.

LOUISE: But *why*? It's inconceivable!

QUENTIN: When I saw him last week he said a dreadful thing. I tried not to hear it.

LOUISE: What?

QUENTIN: That I turned out to be the only friend he had.

LOUISE, *genuinely:* Why is that dreadful?

QUENTIN, *evasively, almost slyly:* It just was. *He starts moving.* I don't know why.

He arrives at the edge of the stage, tears forming in his eyes.

I didn't dare know why! But I dare now. It was dreadful because I was not his friend either, and he knew it. I'd have stuck it to the end but I hated the danger in it for myself, and he saw through my faithfulness; and he was not telling me what a friend I was, he was praying I would be— "Please be my friend, Quentin," is what he was saying to me, "I am drowning, throw me a rope!" Because I wanted out, to be a good American again, kosher again—and he saw it, and proved it in the joy . . . the joy . . . the joy I felt now that my danger had spilled out on the subway track! So it is not bizarre to me. . . .

The tower blazes into life, and he walks with his eyes up.

Holga appears with flowers.

This is not some crazy aberration of human nature to me. I can easily see the perfectly normal contractors and their cigars; the carpenters, plumbers, sitting at their ease over lunch pails, I can see them laying the pipes to run the blood out of this mansion; good fathers, devoted sons, grateful that someone else will die, not they. And how can one understand that, if one is innocent; if somewhere in the soul there is no accomplice . . .

The tower fades, Holga too. Louise brightens in light where she was standing before.

... of that joy, that joy, that joy when a burden dies ...

He moves back into the "room."

... and leaves you safe?

Maggie's breathing is heard.

MAGGIE: Quentin?

He turns in pain from it, comes to a halt on one side of the sheets and pillow lying on the floor. Louise is on the other side. He looks down at the pile.

QUENTIN: I've got to sleep; I'm very tired.

He bends to pick up the sheets. A split second later she starts to. And while he is still reaching down ...

LOUISE, *with great difficulty:* I ...

He stands with the sheets in hand, the pillow still on the floor; now he is attending her, sensing a confession.

I've always been proud you took Lou's case.

He barely nods, waiting.

It was ...

She picks up the pillow.

courageous.

She stands there with the pillow, not fully looking at him.

QUENTIN: I'm glad you feel that way.

But he makes no move. The seconds are ticking by. Neither can let down his demand for apology, for grace. With difficulty:

And that you told me. Thanks.

LOUISE: You are honest—that way. I've often told you.

QUENTIN: Recently?

LOUISE—*bridles, hands him the pillow:* Good night.

He takes the pillow; she starts away, and he feels the unwillingness with which she leaves.

QUENTIN: Louise, if there's one thing I've been trying to do it's to be honest with you.

LOUISE: No. You've been trying to arrange things, that's all—to keep the home fires burning and see the world at the same time.

QUENTIN: So that all I am is deceptive, and cunning.

LOUISE: Not all, but mostly.

QUENTIN: And there is no struggle. There is no pain. There is no struggle to find a way back to you?

LOUISE: That isn't the struggle.

QUENTIN: Then what are you doing here?

LOUISE: I . . .

QUENTIN: What the hell are you compromising yourself for if you're so goddamned honest?

On the line he starts a frustrated clench-fisted move toward her and she backs away, terrified, and strangely alive. Her look takes note of the aborted violence and she is very straight and yet ready to flee.

LOUISE: I've been waiting for the struggle to begin.

He is dumbstruck—by her sincerity, her adamance. With a straight look at him, she turns and goes out.

QUENTIN, *alone, and to himself:* Good God, can there be more? Can there be worse?

Turning to the Listener:

See, that's what's incredible to me—three years more! What did I expect to save us? Suddenly, God knows why, she'd hold out her hand and I hold out mine, and laugh, laugh it all away, laugh it all back to . . . her dear, honest face looking up to mine. . . .

Breaks off, staring.

Back to some hidden, everlasting smile that saves. That's maybe why I came; I think I still believe it. That underneath we're all profoundly friends! I can't believe this world; all this hatred isn't real to me!

Turns back to his "living room," and the sheets.

To bed down like a dog in my living room, how can that be necessary? Then go in to her, open your heart, confess the lechery, the mystery of women, say it all . . . the truth must save!

He has moved toward where she exited, now halts.

But I did that. So the truth, after all, may merely be murderous? The truth killed Lou; destroyed Mickey. Then what else is there? A workable lie? Maybe there is only one sin, to destroy your own credibility. Strength comes from a clear conscience or a dead one. Not to see one's own evil—there's power! And rightness too! So kill conscience. Kill it.

Glancing toward her exit.

Know all, admit nothing, shave closely, remember birthdays, open car doors, pursue Louise not with truth but with attention. Be uncertain on your own time, in bed be absolute. And thus, be a man . . . and join the world.

Reflectively he throws the sheet open on the couch, then stops.

And in the morning, a dagger in that dear little daughter's heart!

Flinging it toward Louise's exit.

Bitch!

Sits.

I'll say I have a cold. Didn't want to give it to Mommy.

With disgust.

Pah! Papapapapa.

Sniffs, tries to talk through his nose.

Got a cold in my dose, baby girl . . .

He groans. Pause. He stares; stalemate. A jet plane is heard. An airport porter appears, unloads two bags from a rolling cart as Holga, dressed for travel, appears opening her purse, tipping him, and now looking about for Quentin. A distant jet roars in take-off. Quentin glances at his watch, and, coming down to the chair:

Six o'clock, Idlewild.

Now he glances at Holga, who is still looking about him as in a crowd, and speaks to the Listener.

It's that the evidence is bad for promises. But how do you touch the world without a promise? And yet, I mustn't forget the way I wake; I open up my eyes each morning like a boy, even now, even now! That's as true as anything I know, but where's the evidence? Or is it simply that my heart still beats? . . . Certainly, go ahead.

He smiles and sits, following the departing Listener with his eyes; a light moves upstage, going away. He talks upstage.

You don't mind my staying? Good. I'd like to settle this. Although actually, I—*Laughs*—only came by to say hello.

He turns front. The Listener's light is gone. Alone now, he stares ahead, a different kind of relaxation on him. From the darkness high on the upper level, the sucking breathing is heard; light dimly shows Maggie, her back to us, sitting up in the "bed."

MAGGIE: Quentin?

QUENTIN, *in agony:* I'll get to it, honey.

He closes his eyes.

I'll get to it.

He stands, and as though wandering in a room he moves at random, puts a cigarette in his mouth, and strikes sparks from his lighter as darkness covers him.

CURTAIN

ACT TWO

The stage is dark. A spark is seen; a flame fires up. When the stage illuminates, Quentin is discovered lighting his cigarette—no time has passed. He continues to await the Listener's return, and walks a few steps in thought and as he does a jet plane is heard, and the garbled airport announcer's voice: ". . . from Frankfurt is now unloading at gate nine, passengers will please . . ." It becomes a watery garble and at the same moment Holga, beautifully dressed, walks onto the upper level with an airport porter, who leaves her bags and goes. She looks about as in a crowd—then, seeing "Quentin," stands on tiptoe and waves.

HOLGA: Quentin! Here! Here!
She opens her arms as he evidently approaches.
Hello!

She is gone as Louise rushes on from another point, a ribbon in her hair, a surgical mask hanging from her neck, a lab technician's smock open to show her sweater and long skirt of the thirties. A hospital attendant is mopping the floor behind her. She sees "Quentin."
LOUISE: Hello! I just got my final grades! I got an A on that paper you wrote! Ya—the one on Roosevelt. I'm a Master! *Laughs.* And guess what Halliday said. That my style has immeasurably improved! *Laughs; and now she walks with "him."* If it wasn't for the mop I'd think you were an intern in that uniform; you look well in white. *Her face falls; she halts.* Oh! Then when would you be leaving? . . . No, I'm glad, I always heard Columbia Law was the best. *Shyly:* Actually, I could try some labs in New York, it'd be cheaper

if I lived at home. . . . Well, then, I'd look for something else; anyway there are more bacteriologists than bugs these days. *With dread and shyness:* Unless you wouldn't want me to be there. *She bursts into an adoring smile.* Okay! You want a malt later? I have some money, I just sold all my textbooks! Oop! *She stops abruptly, looking down at the floor.* I'm sorry! I forgot it was wet! See you!

With a happy wave of her hand she picks her way on tiptoe over a wet floor into darkness as a door is heard opening upstage and a light moves downstage, over the floor; Quentin turns toward the returning Listener and smiles.

QUENTIN: Oh, that's all right, I didn't mind waiting. How much time do I have?

He looks at his watch, coming down to the chair. Maggie appears, above, in a lace wedding dress; Lucas, a designer, is on his knees finishing the vast hem. Carrie, a maid, stands by, holding gloves. Maggie is nervous, on the edge of life, looking into a "mirror."

Quentin sits in the chair. He looks forward now, to speak. I, ah . . .

Lucas gets up and quickly goes as . . .

MAGGIE, *in an ecstasy of fear and hope:* All right, Carrie, tell him to come in! *As though trying the angular words:* . . . My *husband*!

CARRIE, *walking a few steps to a point, halts:* You can see her now, Mister Quentin.

They are gone. He continues to the Listener.

QUENTIN: I think I can be clearer now, it shouldn't take long. I am bewildered by the death of love. And my responsibility for it.

Holga appears again, looking about for him at the airport.

This woman's on my side; I have no doubt of it. And I wouldn't want to outlive another accusation. Not hers. *He stands, agitated.* I suddenly wonder why I risk it again. Except . . . *Slight pause; he becomes still.* You ever felt you once saw yourself—absolutely true? I may have dreamed it, but I swear, I feel that somewhere along the line—with Maggie I think—for one split second I saw my life; what I had done, what had been done to me, and even what I ought to do. And that vision sometimes hangs behind my head, blind now, bleached out like the moon in the morning; and if I could only let in some necessary darkness it would shine again. I think it had to do with power.

Felice appears, about to remove the bandage.

Maybe that's why she sticks in my mind; she brings some darkness. Some dreadful element of power. *He walks around her, peering. . . .* Well, that's power, isn't it? To influence a girl to change her nose, her life? . . . It does, yes, it frightens me, and I wish to God . . .

FELICE, *raising her arm:* I'll always . . .

QUENTIN: . . . she'd stop blessing me! *He laughs uneasily, surprised at the force of his fear. . . .* Well, I suppose because there is a fraud involved; I have no such power.

Maggie suddenly appears in a "satin bed," talking into a phone.

MAGGIE, *with timid idolatry:* Hello? Is . . . How'd you know it's me? *Laughs.* You really remember me? Maggie? From that park that day? Well 'cause it's almost four years so I . . .

He comes away from her; she continues talking unheard. He halts near the chair. He glances toward a point where again Felice appears, raising her arm in blessing, and instantly disappears, and he speaks to the Listener.

QUENTIN: I do, yes, I see the similarity.

Laughter is heard as Holga appears at a "café table," an empty chair beside her.

HOLGA: I love the way you eat! You eat like a pasha, a grand duke!

QUENTIN—*looks toward her, and to Listener:* Yes, adored again! But . . . there is something different here.

As he moves toward Holga, he says to Listener:

Now keep me to my theme. I spoke of power.

He sits beside her. As he speaks now, Holga's aspect changes; she becomes moody, doesn't face him, seems hurt. And sitting beside her he tells the Listener:

We were in a café one afternoon in Salzburg, and quite suddenly, I don't know why—it all seemed to be dying between us. And I saw it all happening again. You know that moment, when you begin desperately to talk about architecture?

HOLGA: Fifteen-thirty-five. The archbishop designed it himself.

QUENTIN: Beautiful.

HOLGA, *distantly:* Yes.

QUENTIN—*as though drawing on his courage, he suddenly turns to her:* Holga. I thought I noticed your pillow was wet this morning.

HOLGA: It really isn't anything important.

QUENTIN: There are no unimportant tears. *Takes her hand, smiles.*
I know that much, anyway. Unless it doesn't concern me. Is it about
the concentration camp?

> *She wipes her eyes, unhappy with herself.*

Even during the day, sometimes, you seem about to weep.

HOLGA: I feel sometimes ... *Breaks off, then:* ... that I'm boring
you.

> *Louise appears.*

LOUISE: I am not all this uninteresting, Quentin!

> *Louise is gone.*

HOLGA: I really think perhaps we've been together too much.

QUENTIN: Except, it's only been a few weeks.

HOLGA: But I may not be all that interesting.

> *Quentin stares at her, trying to join this with his lost vision, and in
> that mood he turns out to the Listener.*

QUENTIN: The question is power, but I've lost the connection.

> *Louise appears brushing her hair.*

Yes!

> *He springs up and circles Louise.*

I tell you, there were times when she looked into the mirror and I
saw she didn't like her face, and I wanted to step between her and
what she saw. I felt guilty even for her face! But ... that day ...

> *He returns to the café table and slowly sits.*

there was some new permission ... not to take a certain blame.
There was suddenly no blame at all but that ... we're each entitled
to ... our own unhappiness.

HOLGA: I wish you'd believe me, Quentin; you have no duty here.

QUENTIN: Holga, I would go. But the truth is, I'd be looking for
you tomorrow. I wouldn't know where the hell I thought I had to
be. But there's truth in what you feel. I see it very clearly; the time
does come when I feel I must go. Not toward anything, or away
from you. But there is some freedom in the going. . . .

> *Mother appears, and she is raising her arm.*

MOTHER: Darling, there is never a depression for great people!
The first time I felt you move, I was standing on the beach at
Rockaway. . . .

> *Quentin has gotten up from the chair, and, moving toward her:*

QUENTIN: But power. Where is the—?

MOTHER: And I saw a star, and it got bright, and brighter, and brighter! And suddenly it fell, like some great man had died, and you were being pulled out of me to take his place, and be a light, a light in the world!

QUENTIN, *to Listener:* Why is there some . . . air of treachery in that?

FATHER, *suddenly appearing—to Mother:* What the hell are you talking about? We're just getting a business started again. I need him!

Quentin avidly turns from one to the other as they argue.

MOTHER: You've got Dan, you don't need him! He wants to try to get a job, go to college, maybe—

FATHER: He's got a job!

MOTHER: He means with pay! I don't want his young years going by. . . . He wants a life!

FATHER, *indicating Dan:* Why don't he "want a life"?

MOTHER: Because he's different!

FATHER: Because *he* knows what's *right* !

Indicating Mother and Quentin together:

You're two of a kind—what you "want"! Chrissake, when I was his age I was supporting six people!

He comes up to Quentin.

What are you, a stranger? *What are you?*

Quentin is peering into the revulsion of his Father's face. And he turns toward Holga in the café and back to Father.

QUENTIN: Yes, I felt a power in the going . . . and treason in it. . . . Because there's failure, and you turn your back on failure.

DAN: No, kid, don't feel that way. I just want to see him big again, but you go. I'll go back to school if things pick up.

QUENTIN, *peering at Dan:* Yes, good men stay . . . although they die there.

DAN, *indicating a book in his hand:* It's my Byron, I'll put it in your valise, and I've put in my new argyles, just don't wash them in hot water. And remember, kid, wherever you are . . .

Dan jumps onto a platform, calling. A passing train is heard.

. . . wherever you are this family's behind you! You buckle down, now. . . . I'll send you a list of books to read!

MAGGIE, *suddenly appearing on her bed; she is addressing an empty space at the foot:* But could I read them!

QUENTIN—*spins about in quick surprise:* Huh!

All the others are gone dark but he and Maggie.

MAGGIE: I mean what kind of books? 'Cause, see . . . I never really graduated high school. *She laughs nervously.* Although in Social Science he liked me so he let me keep the minutes. Except I didn't know what's a minute! *Laughs.* I like poetry, though.

QUENTIN—*breaks his stare at her, and quickly comes down to the Listener:* It's that I can't find myself in this vanity, any more. It's all contemptible! *He covers his face.*

MAGGIE, *enthralled, on the bed:* I can't hardly believe you came! Can you stay five minutes? I'm a singer now, see? In fact—*With a laugh at herself*—I'm in the top three. And for a long time I been wanting to tell you that . . . none of it would have happened to me if I hadn't met you that day.

QUENTIN: . . . Yes, I see the power she offered me; but I saw beyond it once, and there was some . . . salvation in it. . . . All right. I'll . . .

He turns to her, walking into her line of sight.

. . . try.

MAGGIE: I'm sorry if I sounded frightened on the phone but I didn't think you'd be in the office after midnight. *Laughs at herself nervously.* See, I only pretended to call you. Can you stay like five minutes?

QUENTIN, *backing into the chair:* Sure. Don't rush.

MAGGIE: That's what I mean, you know I'm rushing! Would you like a drink? Or a steak? They have two freezers here. Whereas my agent went to Jamaica, so I'm just staying here this week till I go to London Friday. It's the Palladium, like a big vaudeville house, and it's kind of an honor, but I'm a little scared to go.

QUENTIN: Why? I've heard you; you're marvelous. Especially . . .

He can't remember a title.

MAGGIE: No, I'm just flapping my wings yet. I mean if you ever heard like Ella Fitzgerald or one of those . . . But did you read what that *News* fellow wrote? He keeps my records in the 'frigerator, case they melt!

QUENTIN—*laughs with her:*—"Little Girl Blue"—it's very moving the way you do that.

MAGGIE, *surprised and pleased:* Really? 'Cause see, it's not I say to myself "I'm going to sound sexy," I just try to come *through* . . . like, in love or . . . *Laughs.* I really can't believe you're here!

QUENTIN: Why? I'm glad you called. I've often thought about you the last couple of years. All the great things happening to you gave me a secret satisfaction for some reason.

MAGGIE: Maybe 'cause you did it.

QUENTIN: Why do you say that?

MAGGIE: I don't know, just the way you looked at me . . . I didn't even have the nerve to go see an agent before that day.

QUENTIN: How did I look at you?

MAGGIE, *squinching up her shoulders, feeling for the mystery:* Like . . . out of your *self.* See, most people they . . . just look *at* you. I can't explain it! And the way you talked to me . . .

> *Louise appears.*

LOUISE: You think reading your brief is talking to me?

> *And she is gone.*

QUENTIN, *to Listener, of Louise:* Yes, I see that, but there was something more. And maybe power isn't quite the word . . .

MAGGIE: What did you mean . . . it gave you a secret satisfaction?

QUENTIN: Just that . . . like in the office, I'd hear people laughing that Maggie had the world at her feet. . . .

MAGGIE, *hurt, mystified:* They laughed!

QUENTIN: In a way.

MAGGIE, *in pain:* That's what I mean; I'm a joke to most people.

QUENTIN: No, it's that you say what you mean, Maggie. You don't seem to be upholding anything, or . . . You're not ashamed of what you are.

MAGGIE: W—what do you mean of what I am?

> *Louise appears; she is playing solitaire.*

QUENTIN, *suddenly aware he has touched a nerve:* Well . . . that you love life, and . . . It's hard to define, I—

LOUISE: The word is tart. But what did it matter as long as she praised you?

QUENTIN, *to Listener, standing, and moving within Maggie's area:* But there's truth in it—I hadn't had a woman's praise, even a girl I'd laughed at with the others . . .

MAGGIE: But you didn't, did you?

He turns to her in agony; Louise vanishes.

Laugh at me?

QUENTIN: No.

He suddenly stands and cries out to Listener:

Fraud—from the first five minutes! . . . Because—I should have agreed she *was* a joke, a beautiful piece trying to take herself seriously! Why did I lie to her, play this cheap benefactor, this . . . What? *Listens, and now, unwillingly:* Yes, that's true too; she had; a strange, surprising honor.

He turns back to her.

MAGGIE: Oh, hey? I just bought back two records I made!

QUENTIN: Bought them back how?

MAGGIE: Well, they're no good, just stupid rock-and-rolly stuff, and I start to think—*Laughs shyly*—maybe you'd turn on your radio, and I didn't want you to hear them. Is that crazy?

QUENTIN: No, but it's pretty unusual to care that much.

MAGGIE: I didn't used to, either. Honest.

QUENTIN, *mystified:* But I hardly said anything to you that day.

MAGGIE: Well, like—*Afraid she is silly*—when you told me to fix where my dress was torn?

QUENTIN: What about it?

MAGGIE: You wanted me to be . . . proud of myself. Didn't you?

QUENTIN, *surprised:* I guess I did, yes. . . . I did.

MAGGIE, *feeling she has budged him:* Would you like a drink?

QUENTIN, *relaxing:* I wouldn't mind. *Glancing around:* What's all the flowers?

MAGGIE, *pouring:* Oh, that's that dopey prince or a king or whatever he is. He keeps sending me a contract . . . whereas I get a hundred thousand dollars if we ever divorce. I'd be like a queen or something, but I only met him in El Morocco *once*! And I'm supposed to be his girl! *She laughs, handing him his drink.* I don't know why they print those things!

QUENTIN: Well, I guess everybody wants to touch you now.

MAGGIE: Cheers!

They drink; she makes a face.

I hate the taste but I love the effect! Would you like to take off your shoes? I mean just to rest.

QUENTIN: I'm okay. I thought you sounded on the phone like something frightened you.

MAGGIE, *evasively:* No. I . . . You have to go home right away?

QUENTIN: You all alone here?

MAGGIE, *with a strong evasiveness:* I don't mind that, I've always been alone. Oh, hey!

As though afraid to lose his interest, she digs into a pile of papers beside the bed, coming up with a small framed photo.

I cut your picture out of the paper last month. When you were defending that Reverend Harley Barnes in Washington? See? I framed it.

QUENTIN, *pleased and embarrassed:* What'd you do that for?

MAGGIE: It's funny how I found it. I was on the train . . .

QUENTIN: Is something frightening you, Maggie?

MAGGIE: No, don't worry! I'm just nervous you're here. See, what I did, they kept interviewing me and asking where you were born and all, and I didn't know what to answer. Whereas my father, see, he left when I was like eighteen months, and I just thought . . . if I could see him. And maybe he would like me. Or even not. Just so he'd look. I can't explain it.

QUENTIN: Maybe so you'd know who you were.

MAGGIE: Yes! So I took the train, he's got a business upstate there, and I called him from the station. And I said, "Can I see you?" And he said, "Who is it?" And I said, "It's Maggie, your daughter." Whereas he said I wasn't from him, although my mother always said I was. And he said, "I don't know who you are, see my lawyer." And I told him, "I just want you to look at me and—" And he hung up. *She laughs, lightly.* So I had time and I walked around the town and I thought maybe if I could find where he eats. And I would go in, and he'd see me and maybe . . . pick me up! *Laughs.* 'Cause my mother said he always liked beautiful girls!

QUENTIN: And then you'd tell him?

MAGGIE: I don't know. Maybe. Maybe . . . afterwards. I don't know why I tell you that . . . Oh, yes! On the train back I found this picture in the paper. And you see the way you're looking straight in the camera? That's very hard to do, you know . . . to look absolutely straight in?

QUENTIN: You mean I was looking at you.

MAGGIE: Yes! And I said, "I know who I am. I'm Quentin's friend." *Afraid she's gone too fast:* You want another drink or . . . I mean you don't have to do anything. You don't even have to see me again.

QUENTIN: Why do you say that?

MAGGIE: 'Cause I think it worries you.

QUENTIN: It does, yes.

MAGGIE: But why? I mean, can't you just be somebody's friend?

QUENTIN—*slight pause, and with resolve:* Yes. I can. It's that you're so beautiful, Maggie. I don't mean only your body and your face.

MAGGIE, *with a sudden rush of feeling:* I would do anything for you, Quentin. You—*It bursts from her*—you're like a god! S'uze me I say that but I—

QUENTIN, *with half a laugh:* Maggie, anybody would have told you to mend your dress.

MAGGIE: No, they wouldn't.

QUENTIN: What then?

MAGGIE, *in great pain:* Laugh. Or just . . . try for a quick one. You know.

QUENTIN, *to Listener:* Yes! It's all so clear: the honor! The first honor . . . was that I hadn't tried to go to bed with her! God, the hypocrisy! . . . Because, I was only afraid, and she took it for a tribute to her . . . "value"! No wonder I can't find myself here!

He has gotten to his feet in agony.

MAGGIE: Oh, hey—I christened a submarine! But you know what I did?

QUENTIN: What?

MAGGIE: I was voted the favorite of the Groton Shipyard! You know, by the workers. So the Admiral handed me the champagne bottle and I said, how come there's no workers in the ceremony, you know? And they all laughed! So I yelled down, and I got about ten of them to come up on the platform! Whereas they're the ones built it, right?

QUENTIN: That's wonderful!

MAGGIE: And you know what the Admiral said? I better watch out or I'll be a Communist. Honestly! So I said, "I don't know what's so terrible. . . . I mean they're for the poor people." Aren't they? The Communists?

QUENTIN: It's a lot more complicated, honey.

MAGGIE: But I mean, like when I was little I used to get free shoes from the Salvation Army. Although they never fit. *Embarrassed, with waning conviction:* But if the workers *do* everything why shouldn't they have the honor? Isn't that what you believe?

QUENTIN: I did, yes. But the question is whether the workers don't end up just where they are, and some new politicians on the stand.

MAGGIE: Oh. *With open longing and self-loss:* I wish I knew something!

QUENTIN: Honey, you know how to see it all with your own eyes; that's more important than all the books.

MAGGIE: But I don't know if it's true, what I see. But you do. You see and you know if it's true.

QUENTIN: What do you think I know?

MAGGIE, *some guard falling, her need rising:* Well like . . . that I was frightened.

QUENTIN: You frightened *now*? . . . You are, aren't you?

Maggie stares at him in tension; a long moment passes.

What is it, dear? You frightened to be alone here?

An involuntary half-sob escapes her. He sees she is in some great fear.

Why don't you call somebody to stay with you?

MAGGIE: I don't know anybody . . . like that.

QUENTIN—*slight pause:* Can I do anything? Don't be afraid to ask me.

MAGGIE—*in a struggle she finally says:* Would you . . . open that closet door?

QUENTIN—*he looks off, then back to her:* Just open it?

MAGGIE: Yes.

He walks into the dark periphery; she sits up warily, watching. He returns. And she lies back.

QUENTIN: Do you . . . want to tell me something?

MAGGIE: I just never know what's right to say and I—

QUENTIN: Well, say it, and find out; what are people for? I'm not going to laugh. *Sits.* What is it?

MAGGIE, *with great difficulty:* When I start to go to sleep before. And suddenly I saw smoke coming out of that closet under the door. It started to fill the whole room! *She breaks off, near weeping.*

QUENTIN—*reaches and takes her hand:* Oh, kid, that's nothing to—

MAGGIE: But it kept coming and coming!

QUENTIN: But look—you've often dreamed such things, haven't you?

MAGGIE: But I was awake!

QUENTIN: Well, it was a waking dream. It just couldn't stay down till you went to sleep. These things can be explained if you trace them back.

MAGGIE: I know. I go to an analyst.

QUENTIN: Oh . . . then tell him about it, you'll figure it out.

MAGGIE: It's when I start to call you before.

She is now absorbed in her own connections.

See, my mother . . . she used to get dressed in the closet. She was very . . . like moral, you know? But sometimes she'd smoke in there. And she'd come out—you know?—with a whole cloud of smoke around her.

QUENTIN: Well . . . possibly you felt she didn't want you to call me.

MAGGIE, *astounded:* How'd you know that?

QUENTIN: Because you said she was so moral. And here you're calling a married man.

MAGGIE: Yes! See, she tried to kill me once with a pillow on my face, whereas . . . I would turn out bad because of her . . . like her sin. And I have her hair, and the same back.

She turns half from him, showing a naked back.

'Cause I have a good back, see? Every masseur says.

QUENTIN: Yes, it is. It's beautiful. But it's no sin to call me.

MAGGIE, *shaking her head like a child—with a relieved laugh at herself:* Doesn't make me bad. Right?

QUENTIN: You're a very moral girl, Maggie.

MAGGIE, *delicately and afraid:* W—what's moral?

QUENTIN: You tell the truth, even against yourself. You're not pretending to be . . .

Turns out to the Listener, with a dread joy.

. . . innocent! Yes, that suddenly there was someone who—would not club you to death with their innocence! It's all laughable!

Felice begins to brighten, her arms raised, just as Mother appears and she is raising her arm . . .

MOTHER: I saw a star. . . .

MAGGIE: I bless you, Quentin!

Mother and Felice vanish as he turns back to Maggie, who takes up his photo.

Lot of nights when I go to sleep, I take your picture, and I bless you. You mind?

She has pressed the picture against her cheek. He bends to her, kisses her; for an instant she is unprepared, then starts to raise her arms to hold him. But he stands and backs away.

QUENTIN: I hope you sleep.

MAGGIE: I will now! *Lies back.* Honestly! I feel . . . all clear!

QUENTIN, *with a wave of his hand, backing away:* Good luck in London.

MAGGIE: And . . . what's moral, again?

QUENTIN: To live the truth.

MAGGIE: That's you!

QUENTIN: Not yet, dear; but I intend to try.

He halts. Across the room they look at one another. He walks back to her; now he bends in and she embraces him this time, offering herself, raising her body toward him. He stands, breaking it off. And as though he knows he is taking a step . . .

Don't be afraid to call me if you need any help.

She is suddenly gone. Alone, he continues the thought.

Any time . . .

Dan appears in crew-necked sweater with his book.

. . . you need anything, you call, y'hear?

DAN: This family's behind you, Quentin.

Backing into darkness, with a wave of farewell.

Any time you need anything . . .

Quentin, surprised, has turned quickly to Dan, who disappears.

QUENTIN, *to the Listener, as he still stares at the empty space Dan has left:* You know? It isn't fraud, but some . . . disguise. I came to her like Dan . . . his goodness! No wonder I can't find myself!

Felice appears, about to remove the "bandage," and he grasps for the concept.

. . . And that girl the other night.

Felice turns and goes.

When she left. It's still not clear, but suddenly those two fixtures on my wall . . .

He walks toward a "wall," looking up.
I didn't do it, but I wanted to. Like . . .
He turns and spreads his arms in crucifixion.
. . .this!
In disgust he lowers his arms.
. . . I don't know! Because she . . . *gave* me something! She . . . let me change her! As though I—*Cries out*—felt something! *He almost laughs.* What the hell am I trying to do, love *everybody*?

The line ends in self-contempt and anger. And suddenly, extremely fast, a woman appears in World War I costume—a Gibson Girl hat and veil over her face, ankle-length cloak, and in her hand a toy sailboat. She is bent over as though offering the boat to a little boy, and her voice is like a whisper, distant, obscure.
MOTHER: Quentin? Look what we brought you from Atlantic City—from the boardwalk!

The boy evidently runs away; Mother instantly is anxious and angering and rushes to a point and halts, as though calling through a closed door.
Don't lock this door! But darling, we didn't trick you, we took Dan because he's older and I wanted a rest! . . . But Fanny told you we were coming back, didn't she? Why are you running that water? Quentin, stop that water! Ike, come quick! Break down the door! Break down the door!

She has rushed off into darkness, and Quentin has started after her as though to complete the memory. He halts, and speaks to the Listener.
QUENTIN: . . . They sent me for a walk with the maid. When I came back the house was empty for a week. God, why is betrayal the only truth that sticks! . . . Yes! *He almost laughs.* "Love everybody!" And I can't even mourn my own mother. It's monstrous.

The "park bench" lights. Maggie appears in a heavy white man's sweater, a red wig over a white angora skating cap, moccasins, and sunglasses.
MAGGIE, *to the empty bench:* Hi! It's me! *Lifting the glasses.* Maggie!
QUENTIN, *looking toward Maggie:* Or mourn her, either. Is it simply grief I want? . . . No, this isn't mourning! . . . Because there's too much hatred in it!

He has come away from the adoring Maggie to the chair, shaking his head.

... No, it's not that I think I killed her. It's—

An anonymous man passes Maggie, glances, and goes on out.
MAGGIE, *to the empty bench:* See? I told you nobody recognizes me! Like my wig?

QUENTIN: ... that I can't find myself in it, it's like another man. Only the guilt comes. Yes, or the innocence!

MAGGIE, *sitting beside "him" on the bench:* When you go to Washington tonight ... you know what I could do? I could get on a different car on the same train!

QUENTIN, *to Listener:* But is it enough to tell a man he is not guilty? *Glances at her.* My name is on this man! Why can't I say "I"? *Turning toward her:* I did this. I want what I did! And I saw it once! I saw *Quentin* here! For one moment like the moon sees, I saw us both unblamed!

MAGGIE: Golly, I fell asleep the minute you left the other night! I didn't even hear you close the door! You like my wig? See? And moccasins!

Slight pause. Now he smiles.

QUENTIN: All you need is roller skates.

MAGGIE, *clapping her hands with joy:* You're funny!

QUENTIN, *half to Listener:* I keep forgetting ... *Wholly to her:* ... how beautiful you are. Your eyes make me shiver.

She is silent, adoring. He breaks it, sitting.

MAGGIE: Like to see my new apartment? There's no elevator even, or a doorman. Nobody would know. If you want to rest before you go to Washington.

He doesn't reply.

'Cause I just found out, I go to Paris after London. I'm on for two weeks, which is supposed to be unusual. But I won't be back for a while.

QUENTIN: How long will you be gone?

MAGGIE: About ... six weeks, I think.

They both arrive at the same awareness: the separation is pain. Tears are in her eyes.

Quentin?

QUENTIN: Honey . . . *Takes her hand.* Don't look for anything more from me.

MAGGIE: I'm not! See, all I thought, if I went to Washington—

QUENTIN, *with a laugh:* What about London?

MAGGIE: Oh, they'll wait. 'Cause I could register in the hotel as Miss None.

QUENTIN: N-u-n?

MAGGIE: No—"n-o-n-e"—like nothing. I made it up once, 'cause I can never remember a fake name, so I just have to think of nothing and that's me! *She laughs with joy.* I've done it.

QUENTIN: It *is* a marvelous thought. The whole government's hating me, and meanwhile back at the hotel . . .

MAGGIE: That's what I mean! Just when that committee is knocking on your head you could think of me like naked. . . .

QUENTIN: What a lovely thought.

MAGGIE: And it would make you happy.

QUENTIN, *smiling warmly at her:* And nervous. But it is a lovely thought.

MAGGIE: Because it should all be one thing, you know? Helping people, and sex. You might even argue better the next day!

QUENTIN, *with a new awareness, astonishment:* You know?—There's one word written on your forehead.

MAGGIE: What?

QUENTIN: "Now."

MAGGIE: But what else is there?

QUENTIN: A future. And I've been carrying it around all my life, like a vase that must never be dropped. So you cannot ever touch anybody, you see?

MAGGIE: But why can't you just hold it in one hand?

He laughs.

And touch with the other! I would never bother you, Quentin.

He looks at his watch, as though beginning to calculate if there might not be time.

Can't somebody just give you something? Like when you're thirsty. And you drink, and walk away, that's all.

QUENTIN: But what about you?

MAGGIE: Well . . . I would have what I gave. *Slight pause.*

QUENTIN: You're all love, aren't you?

MAGGIE: That's all I am! A person could die any minute, you know. *Suddenly:* Oh, hey! I've got a will! *She digs into her pocket and brings out a folded sheet of notepaper.* Could . . . I show it to you?

QUENTIN, *taking it:* What do you want with a will?

MAGGIE: Well I'm going to do a lot of flying now and I just got my payment yesterday. Should I tell you how much?

QUENTIN: How much?

MAGGIE: Two hundred thousand dollars.

QUENTIN: Huh! You remember we sat right here, and I gave you five dollars?

MAGGIE, *with great love:* Yes!

> *They stare at each other.*

Really, Quentin, there's not even an elevator man.

QUENTIN: You want me to look at that? Honey, I've got to do one thing at a time. *He opens the will.*

MAGGIE: I understand!

> *He starts reading the will.*

See, I'm supposed to be like a millionaire in about two years!

> *Laughs; he goes on reading.*

Is it legal if it's not typewritten?

QUENTIN—*looks at her:* Who wrote this?

MAGGIE: My agency; mostly Andy. Whereas he had to leave for London this morning to set everything up. And it was in a big rush.

> *Not comprehending, he nods and reads on.*

But he's got a copy and I've got a copy.

> *He glances at her, bewildered.*

I mean, that's what he said; that we both have copies.

> *He turns the page, reads on.*

You got a haircut. I love the back of your head, it's sweet.

> *His brows knit now as he reads.*

I'll shut up.

> *Finished reading, he stares ahead.*

Or does it have to be typed?

QUENTIN: Who's this other signature?

MAGGIE: That's Jerry Moon. He's a friend of Andy in the building business, but he knows a lot about law so he signed it for a witness. I saw him sign it. In my bedroom. Isn't it good?

QUENTIN: It leaves everything to the agency.

MAGGIE: I know, but just for temporary, till I can think of somebody to put down.

QUENTIN: But what's all the rush?

MAGGIE: Well in case Andy's plane goes down. He's got five children, see, and his—

QUENTIN: But do you feel responsible for his family?

MAGGIE: Well, no. But he did help me, he loaned me money when I—

QUENTIN: A million dollars?

MAGGIE, *with a dawning awareness:* Well, not a million. *With fear:* You mean I shouldn't?

QUENTIN: Who's your lawyer?

Two boys with bats and gloves pass, see her, walk off backward, whispering.

MAGGIE: Well, nobody. Jerry has a lawyer and he checks. I mean what's good for Andy's good for me, right?

QUENTIN—*with a certain unwillingness, even a repugnance, about interfering, he sounds neutral:* Didn't anybody suggest you get your own lawyer?

MAGGIE, *with fading conviction:* But if you trust somebody, you trust them. . . . Don't you?

QUENTIN—*a decision seizes him; he takes her hand:* Come on, I'll walk you home.

MAGGIE, *standing:* Okay! 'Cause I mean if you trust somebody!

QUENTIN: I'm sorry, honey, I can't advise you. Maybe you get something out of this that I don't understand. Let's go.

MAGGIE: No, I'm not involved with Andy. I . . . don't really sleep around with everybody, Quentin.

QUENTIN: Come on.

MAGGIE, *suddenly brightening:* 'Cause . . . I was never a prostitute. I was with a lot of men, but I never got anything. Not even for a job. I mean I'm changing. My analyst says I used to think it was like charity—sex. Like I give to those in need? *Laughs shyly.* Whereas I'm not an institution! Will you come in for a minute, too?

QUENTIN, *taking her arm:* Sure.

A small gang of boys with baseball equipment obstructs them; one of the first pair points at her.

FIRST BOY: It's Maggie, I told you!

MAGGIE, *pulling at Quentin's arm, defensively:* No, I just look like her, I'm Sarah None!

SECOND BOY: I can hear her voice!

QUENTIN: Let's go!

He tries to draw her off, but the boys grab her, and strangely, she begins accepting pencils and pieces of paper to autograph.
Hey!

CROWD: How about an autograph, Maggie?

> Whyn't you come down to the club?

> When's your next spectacular?

> Hey, Mag, I got all your records!

> Sing something!

Handing over a paper for her to sign.

> For my brother, Mag!

> Take off your sweater, Mag, it's hot out!

> How about that dance like you did on TV?

A boy wiggles sensually.

Quentin has been thrust aside; he now reaches in, grabs her, and draws her away as she walks backward, still signing, laughing with them. The boys gone, she turns to him.

MAGGIE: I'm sorry!

QUENTIN: It's like they're eating you. You like that?

MAGGIE: No, but they're just people. Could you sit down till the train? All I got so far is this French Provincial. *Taking off her sweater:* You like it? I picked it out myself. And my bed, and my record player. But it could be a nice apartment, couldn't it?

In silence Quentin takes her hand; he draws her to him; he kisses her.

Enflamed:

I love you, Quentin. I would do anything for you. And I would never bother you, I swear.

QUENTIN: You're so beautiful it's hard to look at you.

MAGGIE: You didn't even see me! *Backing away.* Why don't you just stand there and I'll come out naked! Or isn't there a later train?

QUENTIN—*pause:* Sure. There's always a later train.

He starts unbuttoning his jacket.

MAGGIE: I'll put music!

QUENTIN—*now he laughs through his words:* Yeah, put music!

She rushes into the dark, and he strives for his moment. To the Listener as he opens his jacket:

Here, it was somewhere here! . . . I don't know, a . . . a fraud!

A driving jazz comes on and she comes back, still dressed.

MAGGIE: Here, let me take off your shoes!

She drops to his feet, starting to unlace. Stiffly, with a growing horror, he looks down at her. Now shapes move in the darkness. He moves his foot away involuntarily.

QUENTIN: Maggie?

MAGGIE, *looking up from the floor, leaving off unlacing:* Yes?

He looks around in the darkness, and suddenly his Father charges forward.

FATHER: What you *want!* Always what you *want!* Chrissake, *what are you?*

Now Louise appears, reading a book, but Dan is standing beside her, almost touching her with his hand.

DAN: This family's behind you, kid.

And Mother, isolated, almost moving sensuously—and Quentin is moved, as though by them, away from Maggie.

MOTHER: Oh, what poetry he brought me, Strauss, and novels and . . .

QUENTIN—*he roars out to all of them, his fists angrily in air against them:* But where is *Quentin?*

Going toward Mother in her longing.

Yes, yes! But I know that treason! And the terror of complicity in that desire.

Turns toward Dan, who has moved alongside Father. The music breaks off.

Yes, and to not be unworthy of those loyal, failing men! But where is Quentin? Instead of taking off my clothes, this—*He bends to Maggie, raises her to her feet—*posture!

MAGGIE: Okay. Maybe when I get back we—

QUENTIN: I have to say it to you, Maggie.

To Listener.

Here it is, right here the killing fraud begins. *Pause.* You . . . have to tear up that will.

To Listener.

Can't even go to bed without a principle! But how can you speak of love, she had been chewed and spat out by a long line of grinning men! Her name floating in the stench of locker rooms and parlor-car cigar smoke! She had the truth that day, I brought the lie that she had to be "saved"! From what—except my own contempt? . . . Heh?

He is evidently caught by the Listener's contradicting him, steps closer to the chair, avidly listening.

MAGGIE, *to the empty space where Quentin was:* But I showed the will to my analyst, and he said it was okay. 'Cause a person like me has to have *somebody.*

QUENTIN: Maggie . . . honest men don't draw wills like that.

MAGGIE: But it's just for temporary. . . .

QUENTIN: Darling, if I went to Andy, and this adviser, and the analyst too, perhaps, I think they'd offer me a piece to shut up. They've got you on a table, honey, and they're carving you.

MAGGIE: But . . . I can't spend all that money anyway! I can't even *think* over twenty-five dollars!

QUENTIN: It's not the money they take, it's the dignity they destroy. You're not a piece of meat; you seem to think you owe people whatever they demand!

MAGGIE: I know. *She lowers her head with a cry, trembling with hope and shame.*

QUENTIN, *tilting up her face:* But Maggie, you're somebody! You're not a kid any more running around looking for a place to sleep! It's not only your success or that you're rich—you're straight, you're serious, you're first-class, people *mean* something to you; you don't have to go begging shady people for advice like some . . . some tramp.

With a sob of love and desperation, she slides to the floor and grasps his thighs, kissing his trousers. He watches, then suddenly lifts her and, with immense pity and joy:

Maggie, stand up!

The music flies in now, and she smiles strangely through her

tears, and with a kind of statement of her persisting nature begins un-
buttoning her blouse, her body writhing to the beat within her clothing.
And as soon as she starts her dance his head shakes . . . and to the Lis-
tener:
No, not love; to stop impersonating, that's all! To live—*Groping:*—
to live in good faith if only with my guts! To . . .
     Suddenly Dan and Father appear together; and to them:
Yes! To be "good" no more! Disguised no more! Afraid no more to
show what Quentin, Quentin, Quentin . . . is!
     Louise appears, talking.
LOUISE: You haven't even the decency to—
QUENTIN: That decency is murderous! Speak truth, not decency—I
curse the whole high administration of fake innocence! I declare it, I
am not innocent! Nor good!
     A high tribunal dimly appears; a chairman bangs his gavel once;
he is flanked by others looking down on Quentin from on high. Mag-
gie is dropping her blouse.
CHAIRMAN: But rarely Reverend Barnes cannot object to answering whether he attended the Communist-run Peace Congress in
Prague, Czechoslovakia. No—no, counsel will not be allowed to
confer with the witness, this is not a trial! Any innocent man
would be . . .
QUENTIN: And this question—innocent! How many Negroes you
allow to vote in your patriotic district? And which of your social,
political, or racial sentiments would Hitler have disapproved? And
not a trial? You fraud, your "investigators" this moment are working this man's church to hound him out of it!
HARLEY BARNES—*appears rising to his feet; he has a clerical collar:* I
decline on the grounds of the First and Fifth Amendments to the
Constitution.
QUENTIN, *with intense sorrow:* But are we sure, Harley—I ask it,
I ask it—if the tables were turned, and they were in front of you—
would you permit *them* not to answer? Hateful men that they are?
     Harley looks at him indignantly, suspiciously.
I am not sure what we are upholding any more—are we good by
merely saying no to evil? Even in a righteous "no" there's some disguise. Isn't it necessary . . . to say . . .

Harley is gone, and the tribunal. Maggie is there, snapping her fingers, letting down her hair.

. . . to finally say yes . . . to *something*?

A smile of pain and longing has come into his face, and Maggie expands now, slipping out of her skirt, dancing in place. He goes to her and grasps her body, moving with her serpentine motion.

A fact . . . a fact . . . a thing.

Maggie embraces him and then lies down on the "bed" with the imagined Quentin.

MAGGIE: Sing inside me.

Quentin moves to the chair facing the Listener; she continues on the bed behind him as he sits.

QUENTIN: Even condemned, unspeakable like all truth!

MAGGIE: Become happy.

QUENTIN, *still to Listener:* Contemptible like all truth.

MAGGIE: That's all I am.

QUENTIN: Covered like truth with slime; blind, ignorant.

MAGGIE: But nobody ever said to me, stand up!

QUENTIN: The blood's fact, the world's blind gut . . . yes!

MAGGIE: Now.

QUENTIN: To this, yes.

MAGGIE: Now . . . now.

Her recorded number ends and only the thumping needle in the empty groove is heard through the lengthening darkness. Then her voice, pillowed and soft.

MAGGIE: Quentin?

Light finds her prone on a bed, alone on the stage, a sheet partly covering her naked body. Her chin rests languidly on her hands. She glances toward a point, off.

Quenny? That soap is odorless, so you don't have to worry.

Slight pause.

It's okay! Don't rush; I love to wait for you!

Her eye falls on his shoe on the floor. She picks it up, strokes it.

I love your shoes. You have good taste!

Slight pause.

S'uze me I didn't have anything for you to eat, but I didn't know! I'll get eggs, though, case maybe in the mornings. And steaks—case at night. I mean just in case. You could have it just the way you want, just any time.

Quentin stands looking front; she speaks to empty space from the bed.

Like me?

He glances back at her adoring face, as Holga appears above in the airport, looking about for him. Maggie remains on the bed, stroking his shoe.

QUENTIN, *glancing at Maggie:* It's all true, but it isn't the truth. I know it because it all comes back too cheap; my bitterness is making me lie. I'm afraid. To make a promise. Because I don't know who'll be making it. I'm a stranger to my life.

MAGGIE—*she has lifted a tie off the floor:* Oh, your tie got all wrinkled! I'm sorry! But hey, I have a tie! *Jumping up with the sheet around her.* It's beautiful, a regular man's tie—*Catching herself:* I . . . just happen to have it!

She tries to laugh it off and goes into darkness. Holga is gone.

QUENTIN: I tell you, below this fog of tawdriness and vanity, there is a law in this disaster, and I saw it once as hard and clear as a statute. But I think I saw it . . . with some love. Or simply wonder, but not blame. It's . . . like my mother; so many of my thoughts of her degenerate into some crime; the truth is she was a light to me whenever it was dark. I loved that nut, and only love does make her real and mine. Or can one ever remember love? It's like trying to summon up the smell of roses in a cellar. You might see a rose, but never the perfume. And that's the truth of roses, isn't it—the perfume?

Maggie appears in light in a wedding dress; Carrie, the maid, is just placing a veiled hat on her head; Lucas, the designer, is on his knees hurriedly fixing the last hem. Maggie is turning herself wide-eyed in a mirror. Quentin begins to rise.

MAGGIE: Okay! Let him in, Carrie! Thanks, Lucas, but I don't want him to wait any more, the ceremony is for three! Hurry, please!

Lucas sews faster; Carrie goes to a point, calls down.

CARRIE: Mister Quentin? You can see her now.

QUENTIN: I want to see her with . . . that love again! Why is it so hard? Standing there, that wishing girl, that victory in lace. We had turned all mockery to purpose, and purpose moved around us like the natural shadows of the day!

MAGGIE, *looking ahead on the edge of life as Lucas bites off the last threads:* You won't hardly know me any more, Lucas! He saved me, I mean it! I've got a new will and I even changed my analyst, I've got a wonderful doctor now! And we're going to do all my contracts over, which I never got properly paid. And Ludwig Reiner's taking me! And he won't take even opera singers unless they're, you know, like artists! No matter how much you want to pay him. I didn't even dare but Quentin made me go—and now he took me, imagine! Ludwig Reiner!

She turns, seeing Quentin entering. An awe of the moment takes them both; Lucas goes. Carrie lightly touches Maggie's forehead and silently prays, and walks off.

QUENTIN: Oh, my darling. How perfect you are.

MAGGIE: Like me?

QUENTIN: Good God—to come home every night—to *you!*

He starts for her open-armed, laughing, but she touches his chest, excited and strangely fearful.

MAGGIE: You still don't have to do it, Quentin. I could just come to you whenever you want.

QUENTIN—*it hurts him but he tries to laugh again:* You just can't believe in something good really happening. But it's real, darling, you're my wife!

MAGGIE, *with a hush of fear on her voice:* I want to tell you something.

QUENTIN: I know enough. Come.

MAGGIE, *slipping her hand out of his:* I just want to tell you!

QUENTIN: Darling, you're always making new revelations, but that stuff doesn't matter any more.

MAGGIE, *pleased, and like a child wanting some final embrace:* But the reason I went into analysis! I never told you *that!*

QUENTIN, *smiling above his own foreboding:* All right, what?

MAGGIE: 'Cause you said we have to love what happened, didn't you? Even the bad things?

QUENTIN, *seriously now, to match her intensity:* Yes, I did.

MAGGIE: I . . . was with two men . . . the same day. *She has turned her eyes from him.* I mean the same day, see. But I didn't realize it till that night. And I got very scared. *She almost weeps now, and looks at him, subservient and oddly chastened.* I'll always love you, Quentin. But don't be afraid what people say, we could just tell them we changed our mind, and get in the car and maybe go to a motel. . . .

Anonymous men appear in the farthest distance and vanish as Quentin shakes his head.

QUENTIN: Look, darling. It wasn't you. . . . *Reaching for her hand again:* Come now.

MAGGIE: But maybe in a way it was. In a way! I don't know!

QUENTIN: Sweetheart, everyone does things that . . .

To Listener, with sudden realization:

Here, here is part of it! One part is that . . .

Back to her:

An event itself, dear, is not important; it's what you took from it. Whatever happened to you, this is what you made of it and I love this.

To Listener, rapidly:

. . . Yes! That we conspired to violate the past, and the past is holy and its horrors are holiest of all!

Turning back to Maggie:

And . . . something . . . more . . .

MAGGIE, *with hope now:* Maybe . . . it would even make me a better wife, right?

QUENTIN, *with hope against the pain:* That's the way to talk!

MAGGIE, *with gladness, seeing a fruit of the horror:* 'Cause I'm not curious! You be surprised, a lot of women, they smile and their husbands never know, but they're curious. But I *know*—I have a king, and *I know*!

A wedding march strikes up. It shatters her fragile vision; he takes her arm.

There's people who . . . going to laugh at you.

QUENTIN: Not any more, dear, they're going to see what I see. Come!

MAGGIE, *not moving with him:* What do you see? Tell me! *Bursting out of her:* 'Cause I think . . . you were ashamed once, weren't you?

QUENTIN: I see you suffering, Maggie; and once I saw it, all shame fell away.

MAGGIE: You . . . were ashamed!?

QUENTIN, *with difficulty:* Yes. But you're a victory, Maggie, for yourself and me. And somehow for everyone. *He kisses her hand.* Believe it, darling, you're like a flag to me, a kind of proof, some-how, that people can win.

MAGGIE: And you . . . you won't ever look at any other woman, right?

QUENTIN: Darling, a wife can be loved! You never saw it but . . .

MAGGIE, *with a new intensity of conflict:* Before, though—why did you kiss that Elsie?

QUENTIN: Just hello. She always throws her arms around people.

MAGGIE: But . . . why'd you let her rub her body against you?

QUENTIN—*laughs:* She wasn't rubbing her . . .

MAGGIE, *downing a much greater anxiety:* I saw it. And you stood there.

QUENTIN, *trying to laugh:* Maggie, it was a meaningless gesture.

MAGGIE: But you told me yourself that I have to look for the meaning of things, didn't you? You want me to be like I used to be? Like nothing means anything, it's all a fog? *Now pleadingly, and vaguely wronged:* I'm just trying to understand; you mustn't laugh. Why did you let her do that?

QUENTIN: She came up to me and threw her arms around me, what could I do?

MAGGIE—*a flash of contemptuous anger:* What do you mean? You just tell her to knock it off!

QUENTIN, *taken aback:* I . . . don't think you want to sound like this, honey.

MAGGIE, *frightened she has shown a forbidden side:* Sound like what?

QUENTIN, *trying to brush it away:* Darling, you're just frightened and it magnifies every threat. Come, they're waiting.

He puts her arm in his; they turn to go.

MAGGIE, *almost in tears:* Teach me, Quentin! I don't know how to be!

QUENTIN: Yes, darling. Now we start to be. Both of us.

They begin moving in processional manner toward a group of guests.

MAGGIE: It's that nobody's here ... from me. I'm like a stranger here! If my mother or my father or anybody who loved me—

QUENTIN: Be calm, dear, everyone here adores you.

Now as Maggie speaks she continues in processional tread, but he remains behind, staring at her; and she goes on with "him," her arm still held as before, but in midair now.

MAGGIE: I'm sorry if I sounded that way, but you want me to say what I feel, don't you? See, till you, I never said anything, Quentin; you like gave me my feelings to say! You don't want me just smiling, like most women, do you?

During her speech Louise has appeared.

QUENTIN, *as against the vision of Louise:* No. *Say* what you feel; the truth is on our side; always say it!

Louise is gone.

MAGGIE, *faltering, but going on:* You're not holding me!

QUENTIN, *half the stage away now, and turning toward the empty air:* I am, darling, I'm with you!

MAGGIE, *as she walks into darkness:* I'm going to be a good wife, I'm going to be a good wife. . . . Quentin, I don't feel it!

QUENTIN, *both frustrated and with an appeal to her:* I'm holding you! See everybody smiling, adoring you? Look at the orchestra guys making a V for victory! Everyone loves you, darling! Why are you sad?

Suddenly, the Wedding March is gone as from the far depths of the stage, her shape undefined, she calls out with a laugh.

MAGGIE: Surprise! You like it? They rushed it while we were away!

QUENTIN—*a slight pause; they are half a stage apart:* Yes, it's beautiful!

The dialogue is now condensed, like time swiftly passing in the mind.

MAGGIE: See how large it makes the living room? And I want to take down that other wall too! Okay?

QUENTIN, *not facing her direction; to his memory of it:* But we just finished putting those walls in.

MAGGIE: Well it's only money; I want it big, like a castle for you! You want it beautiful, don't you?

QUENTIN: It's lovely, dear, but ... maybe wait till next year with the other wall. We're behind in the taxes, darling.

MAGGIE: But we could die tomorrow! Used to say, I have one word written on my forehead—why can't it be beautiful now? I get all that money next year.

QUENTIN: But see, dear, you owe almost all of it. ...

MAGGIE: Quentin, don't hold the future like a vase—touch now, touch me! I'm here, and it's now!

QUENTIN: Okay! Tear it down! Make it beautiful! Do it now! Maybe I *am* too cautious. Forgive me.

Her voice is suddenly heard in a vocal number. He breaks into a genuine smile of joy.

Maggie, sweetheart—that's magnificent!

Now she appears, in blouse, leotards, high heels, listening and pacing. Several executives in dark suits appear, listening carefully.

MAGGIE: No! Tell me the truth! That piano's off, you're not listening!

QUENTIN: But nobody'll ever notice that.

A pianist moves near her out of the executive group.

MAGGIE: I know the difference! Don't you want me to be good? I *told* Weinstein I wanted Johnny Block but they give me this fag and he holds back my beat! Nobody listens to me, I'm a joke!

QUENTIN: All right, dear, maybe if I talked to Weinstein—

MAGGIE: No, don't get mixed up in my crummy business, you've got an important case ...

QUENTIN—*he moves to a point and demands:* Weinstein, get her Johnny Block!

The music turns over into another number and her voice, swift, sure.

There now! Listen now!

She listens in suspense; he almost struts with his power.

See? There's no reason to get upset, just tell me and I'll talk to these people any time you—

MAGGIE: Oh, thank you, darling! See? They respect you. Ask Ludwig, soon as you come in the studio my voice flies! Oh, I'm going to be a good wife, Quentin, I just get nervous sometimes that I'm—*She sits as the music goes out*—only bringing you my problems. But I want my stuff to be perfect, and all they care is if they can get rich on it.

The executives are gone.

QUENTIN: Exactly, dear—so how can you look to them for your self-respect? Come, why don't we go out for a walk? We never walk any more. *He sits on his heels beside her.*

MAGGIE: You love me?

QUENTIN: I adore you. I just wish you could find some joy in your life.

MAGGIE: Quentin, I'm a joke that brings in money.

QUENTIN: I think it's starting to change, though—you've got a great band now, and Johnny Block, and the best sound crew....

MAGGIE: Only because I fought for it. You'd think somebody'd come to me and say, Look, Maggie, you made us all this money, now we want you to develop yourself, what can we do for you?

QUENTIN: Darling, they'd be selling frankfurters if there were more money in it, how can you look to them for love?

MAGGIE, *alone, alone:* But where will I look?

QUENTIN, *thrown down:* Maggie, how can you say that?

MAGGIE—*she stands; there is an underlying suspiciousness now:* When I walked into the party you didn't even put your arms around me. I felt like one of those *wives* or something!

QUENTIN: Well, Donaldson was in the middle of a sentence and I—

MAGGIE: So what? *I walked into the room!* I hire him, he doesn't hire me!

QUENTIN: But he is directing your TV show and I was being polite to him.

MAGGIE: You don't have to be ashamed of me, Quentin. I had a right to tell him to stop those faggy jokes at my rehearsal. Just because he's cultured? I'm the one the public pays for, not Donaldson! Ask Ludwig Reiner what my value is!

QUENTIN: I married you, Maggie, I don't need Ludwig's lecture on your value.

MAGGIE, *looking at him with strange eyes—with a strange laugh:* Why ... why you so cold?

QUENTIN: I'm not cold, I'm trying to explain what happened.

MAGGIE: Well, take me in your arms, don't explain.

He takes her in his arms, kisses her, and she plaintively instructs:
Not like that. *Hold* me.

QUENTIN—*he tries to hold her tighter, then releases her:* Let's go for a walk, honey. Come on . . .

MAGGIE, *sinking:* What's the matter?

Louise appears, playing solitaire.

QUENTIN: Nothing.

MAGGIE: But Quentin . . . you should look at me more. I mean . . . like I *existed* or something. Like you used to look—out of your *self.*

Louise vanishes. Maggie moves away into darkness, deeply discouraged.

QUENTIN, *alone:* I adore you, Maggie; I'm sorry; it won't ever happen again. Never! You need more love than I thought. But I've got it, and I'll make you see it, and when you do you're going to astound the world!

A rose light floods a screen; Maggie emerges in a dressing gown, indicating an unseen window.

MAGGIE: Surprise! You like it? See the material?

QUENTIN: Oh, that's lovely! How'd you think of that?

MAGGIE: All you gotta do is close them and the sun makes the bed all rose.

QUENTIN, *striving for joy:* Yes, it's beautiful! You see? An argument doesn't mean disaster! Oh, Maggie, I never knew what love was! *Takes her in his arms.*

MAGGIE, *her spirit gradually falling:* 'Case during the day, like maybe you get the idea to come home and we make love again in daytime. *She ends sitting in a weakness; nostalgically:* Like last year, remember? In the winter afternoons? And once there was still snow on your hair. See, that's all I am, Quentin.

QUENTIN: I'll come home tomorrow afternoon.

MAGGIE: Well don't *plan* it.

He laughs, but she looks at him; her stare is piercing. His laugh dies.

QUENTIN: What is it? See, I don't want to hide things any more, darling. The truth saves, always remember that—tell me, what's bothering you?

MAGGIE, *shaking her head, seeing:* I'm not a good wife. I take up so much of your work.

QUENTIN: No, dear. I only said that because you—*Striving, against his true resentment*—you kind of implied that I didn't fight the network hard enough on that penalty, and I got it down to twenty thousand dollars. They had a right to a hundred when you didn't perform.

MAGGIE, *with rising indignation:* But can't I be sick? I was sick!

QUENTIN: I know, dear, but the doctor wouldn't sign the affidavit.

MAGGIE, *furious at him:* I had a pain in my side, for Christ's sake, I couldn't stand straight! You don't believe me, do you!

QUENTIN: Maggie, I'm only telling you the legal situation.

MAGGIE: Ask Ludwig what you should do! You should've gone in there roaring! 'Stead of a polite liberal and affidavits and—

QUENTIN, *hurt:* Don't say that, Maggie.

MAGGIE: Well, ask him! You don't know what a star's rights are! I make millions for those people!

QUENTIN: Maggie, I always thought I was a pretty good lawyer. . . .

MAGGIE: I'm not saying Ludwig is a lawyer.

QUENTIN: I know, dear, but he's always got these brave solutions but the two-three times I've tried to pin him down to specifics he gets full of oxygen.

MAGGIE: Now you're hurt! I can't *say* anything!

QUENTIN: Well, honey, I'm putting in forty per cent of my time on your problems.

MAGGIE: You are not putting—

QUENTIN, *horrified she doesn't know—an outburst:* Maggie, I keep a log; I know what I spend my time on!

> *She looks at him shaking her head; mortally wounded, tears in her eyes. She goes to a bottle and pours.*

I'm sorry, darling, but when you talk like that I feel a little . . . like a fool. Don't start drinking; please.

> *She drinks.*

Look, I don't object to the time I spend, I'm happy to do it, but—

MAGGIE: Should never gotten married. I knew it. Soon's they got married it all changes. Every man I ever knew they hate their wives.

QUENTIN: Honey, it always comes down to the same thing, don't you see? Now listen to me. *Turns her.* You're still proceeding on the basis that you're alone. That you can be disposed of. And the slightest contradiction of your wishes makes the earth tremble. But—

MAGGIE: You taught me to speak out, Quentin, and when I do you get mad.

QUENTIN: I'm not mad, I'm frustrated that you can't seem to pick up the joy we could have. My greatest happiness is when I know I've helped to make you smile, to make you—

MAGGIE: But the only reason I went to see Ludwig was so you'd be proud of me, so you could say, "See? I found her she was a little lost nut, and look, look what became of Maggie!" It's all for you, that's why I want it good!

QUENTIN: Then what are we arguing about? We want the same thing, you see?

Suddenly to Listener:

Power! Yes, the power, the power to . . . to . . . Wait a minute, I had it, and I lost it.

MAGGIE, *pouring another drink:* So maybe the best thing is if I get a lawyer . . . you know, just a stranger.

QUENTIN—*slight pause; hurt:* Okay.

MAGGIE: It's nothing against you; but see, like that girl in the orchestra, that cellist—I mean, Andy took too much but he'd have gone in there and got rid of her. I mean, you don't laugh when a singer goes off key.

QUENTIN: But she said she coughed.

MAGGIE, *furiously:* She didn't cough, she laughed! And you stand there going ho-ho-ho to her high-class jokes! Christ sake, just because she played in a symphony?

QUENTIN: Maggie, I stopped by to pick you up, I said hello to her and—

MAGGIE: I'm not finishing this tape if she's in the band tomorrow! I'm entitled to my conditions, Quentin! *Commanding:* And I don't have to plead with anybody! I want her out!

QUENTIN, *quietly:* All right. I'll call Weinstein in the morning.

MAGGIE: You won't. You're too polite.

QUENTIN: I've done it before, Maggie; three others in three different bands.

MAGGIE: Well, so what? You're my husband. You're supposed to do that. Aren't you?

QUENTIN: But I can't pretend to enjoy demanding people be fired.

MAGGIE: But if it was your daughter you'd get angry, wouldn't you? Instead of apologizing for her?

QUENTIN—*envisions it:* I guess I would, yes. I'm sorry. I'll do it in the morning.

MAGGIE, *with desperate warmth:* That's all I mean. If I want something you should ask yourself why, why does she want it, not why she shouldn't have it. That's why I don't smile, I feel I'm fighting all the time to make you *see.* You're like a little boy, you don't see the knives people hide.

QUENTIN: I see the knives, but ... It's the same thing again. You still don't believe you're not alone.

MAGGIE: Then make me believe it!

QUENTIN: I'm trying, darling, but sometimes you say a thing that cuts me down like a ... Maggie, I'm not cold to you.

MAGGIE: I didn't mean you're cold. It's just ... I've seen such terrible things, Quentin. I never told you most of it. And when you're alone all you have is what you can see. Ask my doctor—I see more than most people, 'cause I had to protect myself.

QUENTIN: But sweetheart, that's all gone. You've got a husband now who loves you.

Pause. She seems to fear greatly.

MAGGIE: But it's not all gone. When your mother tells me I'm getting fat, I know where I am—and when you don't do anything about it.

QUENTIN: But what can I do?

MAGGIE: Slap her down, that's what you do!

QUENTIN: But she says anything comes into her head, dear.

MAGGIE: She insulted me! She's jealous of me!

QUENTIN: Maggie, she adores you.

MAGGIE: What are you trying to make me think, I'm crazy?

QUENTIN: Why does everything come down to—

MAGGIE: I'm not crazy!

QUENTIN, *carefully, on eggs:* The thought never entered my mind, darling. I'll . . . talk to her.

MAGGIE, *mimicking him as though he were weak:* "I'll talk to her." She hates me!

QUENTIN: I'll tell her to apologize.

MAGGIE: But at least get a little angry!

QUENTIN: All right, I'll do it.

She drinks.

MAGGIE: I'm not going to work tomorrow.

She lies down on the "bed" as though crushed.

QUENTIN: Okay.

MAGGIE, *half springing up:* You know it's not "okay"! You're scared to death they'll sue me, why don't you say it?

QUENTIN: I'm not scared to death; it's just that you're so wonderful in this show and it's a pity to—

MAGGIE, *sitting up furiously:* All you care about is money! Don't shit me!

The anonymous men appear in the distance.

QUENTIN, *quelling a fury—his voice very level:* Maggie, don't use that language with me, will you?

MAGGIE: Calling me vulgar, that I talk like a truck driver! Well, that's where I come from. I'm for Negroes and Puerto Ricans and truck drivers!

QUENTIN: Then why do you fire people so easily?

MAGGIE—*her eyes narrowing, she is seeing him anew:* Look. You don't want me. What the hell are you doing here?

QUENTIN, *with a quavering, mountainous restraint:* I live here. And you do too, but you don't know it yet. But you're going to. I . . .

Father appears.

FATHER: Where's he going, I need him! What are you?

And he is gone.

QUENTIN: I'm here, and I stick it. And one day you're going to catch on. Now go to sleep, I'll be back in ten minutes, I'd like to take a walk.

He starts out and she comes to attention.

MAGGIE: Where are going to walk?

QUENTIN: Just around the block.

She watches him carefully. He sees her suspicion.

There's nobody else, kid; I just want to walk.

MAGGIE, *with great suspicion:* 'Kay.

He goes a few yards, halts, turns to see her taking a pill bottle and unscrewing the top.

QUENTIN, *coming back:* You can't take pills on top of whiskey, dear.

He has reached for them; she pulls them away but he grabs them again and puts them in his pocket.

That's how it happened the last time. And it's not going to happen again. Never. I'll be right back.

MAGGIE—*she pours again:* Why you wear those pants?

He turns back to her, knowing what is coming.

I told you the seat is too tight.

QUENTIN: Well, they made them too tight, but I can take a walk in them.

MAGGIE: Fags wear pants like that; I told you.

She drinks again. It is so pathological he looks with amazed eyes.

They attract each other with their asses.

QUENTIN: You calling me a fag now?

MAGGIE—*she is very drunk:* Just I've known fags and some of them didn't even know themselves that they were. And I didn't know if you knew about that.

QUENTIN: That's a hell of a way to reassure yourself, Maggie.

MAGGIE, *staggering slightly:* I'm allowed to say what I see . . .

QUENTIN: You trying to get me to throw you out? Is that what it is? So it'll get real?

MAGGIE, *pointing at him, at his control:* Wha's that suppose to be, strong and silent? I mean what is it?

She stumbles and falls. He makes no move to pick her up.

QUENTIN, *standing over her, quite knowing she is beyond understanding:* And now I walk out, huh? And it's real again, huh?

He picks her up angrily.

Is that what you want?

MAGGIE, *breaking from him:* I mean what *is it*?

She pitches forward; he catches her and roughly puts her on the bed.

Wha's the angle? I mean what is it?

She gets on her feet again.

You gonna wait till I'm old? You know what another cab driver said to me today? "I'll give you fifty dollars."

An open sob, wild and contradictory, flies out of her.

You know what's fifty dollars to a cab driver?

Her pain moves into him, his anger is swamped with it.

Go ahead, you can go; I can even walk a straight line, see? Look, see?

She walks with arms out, one foot in front of the other.

So what is it, heh? I mean what is it? I mean you want dancing? You want dancing?

QUENTIN: Please don't do that.

Breathlessly she turns on the phonograph and goes into a hip-flinging, broken ankle step around him.

MAGGIE: I mean what do you want! What is it?

He hasn't been looking at her, but beyond her, and now she starts tumbling about and he catches her and lays her down on the bed.

I mean, you gonna wait till I'm old? Or what? I mean what is it?

She lies there gasping. He stares down at her, addressing the Listener.

QUENTIN: That there is a love; limitless; a love not even of persons but blind, blind to insult, blind to the spear in the flesh, like justice blind, like . . .

Felice appears. Quentin slowly raises up his arms; holds them there. But his face is drawn together in his quest. Maggie speaks from the bed, half-asleep.

MAGGIE: Hey? Why?

Felice vanishes. He lowers his arms, peering for his answer, as . . .

I mean what do you want? Whyn't you beat it? I mean what is it?

Father appears.

FATHER: What are . . .

Quentin shakes his head, an unformed word of negation in his mouth.

Dan appears.

DAN: This family is always behind you, boy; anything you need, just . . .

Mickey appears: Quentin moves toward him.

MICKEY: ... That we both go back, Lou, you and I together; and name the names.

QUENTIN, *shaking the vision out of his head as false and crying out— as Dan and Father disappear:* No! I had it! In whose name you turn your back! I saw it clear! I saw the name!

Lou appears on high; the approaching sound of a subway train is heard and he seems to fall off a platform to the wracking squeal of brakes, crying.

LOU: Quentin!

He is gone, and Mickey is gone. Quentin's hands are a vise against his head. The tower lights as . . .

QUENTIN, *on new level of angry terror:* In whose name? In whose blood-covered name do you look into a face you loved, and say, Now, you have been found wanting, and now in your extremity you die! It had a name, it . . .

Behind his back, in the farthest extremity of the stage, hardly visible excepting as a bent-over shape, Mother appears in pre–World War I costume, calling in a strange whisper:

MOTHER: Quentin? Quentin?

She is moving rapidly through shadow. He hurries toward her, but in fear.

QUENTIN: Hah? Hah?

MOTHER: See what we brought you from Atlantic City! From the boardwalk!

A tremendous crash of surf spins him about, and Mother is gone and the light of the moon is rising on the pier.

QUENTIN: ... By the ocean. That cottage. That last night.

Maggie in a rumpled wrapper, a bottle in her hand, her hair in snags over her face, staggers out to the edge of the "pier" and stands in the sound of the surf. Now she starts to topple over the edge of the "pier" and he rushes to her and holds her in his hands. She slowly turns around and sees it's he. Now the sound of jazz from within is heard, softly.

MAGGIE: You were loved, Quentin; no man was ever loved like you.

QUENTIN, *releasing her:* Carrie tell you I called? My plane couldn't take off all day. . . .

MAGGIE, *drunk, but aware:* I was going to kill myself just now. *She walks past him. He is silent. She turns.* Or don't you believe that either?

QUENTIN, *with an absolute calm, a distance, but without hostility:* I saved you twice, why shouldn't I believe it? *Going toward her:* This dampness is bad for your throat, you oughtn't be out here.

MAGGIE—*she defiantly sits, her legs dangling:* Where've *you* been?

QUENTIN: I've been in Chicago. I told you. The Hathaway estate.

MAGGIE—*a sneer:* Estates!

QUENTIN: Well, I have to make a living before I save the world.
He goes into the bedroom, removing his jacket.

MAGGIE, *from the pier:* Didn't you hear what I told you?

QUENTIN: I heard it. I'm not coming out there, Maggie, it's too wet.
She looks out a moment, wide-eyed at the neutrality of his tone; then gets up and unsteadily comes into the room. He is taking off his tie.

MAGGIE: What's *this* all about?

QUENTIN: Just going to sleep. I'm very tired. I don't feel too hot.

MAGGIE: Tired.

QUENTIN: Yep. I can get tired too.

MAGGIE: Poor man.

QUENTIN: Not any more, no.
He sits on the bed unlacing his shoes. Sensing, she sits on a chair, the pill bottle in her hand.

MAGGIE, *like a challenge to him:* I didn't go to rehearsal today.

QUENTIN: I didn't think you did.

MAGGIE: I called Weinstein; I'm not working on his label any more and I don't care if he's got ten contracts. And I called the network; I'm not doing that stupid show, and I don't owe it to them regardless of any promise you made me make. I'm an artist and I don't have to do stupid shows no matter what contract!

QUENTIN: Maggie, I'm not your lawyer any more; tell it to—

MAGGIE: I told him. And he's getting me out of both contracts. And no arguments either.

QUENTIN: Good. I'll sleep in the living room. I've got to rest.
He starts out.

MAGGIE, *holding up the bottle:* Here, count them if you want to, I only took a few.

QUENTIN: I'm not counting pills any more, Maggie, I've given up being the policeman. But if you want to, I wish you'd tell me how many you had before I came. 'Cause they should know that in case they have to pump you out tonight.

MAGGIE, *hurt and bewildered:* What is this?

QUENTIN: Just that I can't pull on the other end of that rope any more. And I see the signs, honey, so I'm telling you in advance. The last two times when we got you out of it you thanked me for saving your life, and for days everything was warm and sweet. I'm not your analyst, but if this is how you create a happy reunion, forget it—this time I call the ambulance, so if you do wake up it'll be in the hospital, and that means the newspapers. I'm just trying to remove one of the motives, if a happy reunion is one of them—because I'm not going to be the rescuer any more. It's only fair to tell you, I just haven't got it any more. They're your pills and your life; you keep the count.

He starts out.

MAGGIE: What. . . . what's all this? Well, don't run away like a kid. What is all this?

QUENTIN—*halts; a pause:* Well . . . one thing is that I've been fired. And that's what I've been doing in Chicago. Max is there and I went to convince him that I oughtn't be let out of the firm.

MAGGIE: You're not fired.

QUENTIN: In fact, it's the second time in six months. I can't make a decision any more without something sits up inside me and busts out laughing.

MAGGIE: That my fault, heh?

QUENTIN: Maggie, I only tell it to you so you'll understand that the question is no longer whether you'll survive, but also whether I will. Because I'm backed up to the edge of the cliff, and I haven't one inch left behind me. And that's the difference tonight, Maggie. So take care what you ask me, dear, because all I've got left is the truth. You know that feeling?

They hold each other's gaze. She unscrews the bottle and takes out a pill and swallows it.

Okay.

He sits on the bed, and puts his shoes on again.

MAGGIE: What are you doing?

QUENTIN: I'll sleep at the inn tonight. I think you're safer without me here. I think I've turned into some kind of ogre to you; and I haven't the strength to try to correct it any more.

He gets his tie.

MAGGIE—*her speech thicker, but she is doped rather than drunk:* Don't . . . do that.

He looks at her lost face.

Please. Please . . . sit down.

And as she did when they first met, but in a caricature of that invitingness, she indicates a chair.

Could you . . . just while I . . . go to sleep? Please?

QUENTIN, *gently moved:* Okay, if you lie down and go to sleep.

MAGGIE: I'll . . . lie down here. See?

She quickly goes to the bed, clutching her pills, and lies down. See?

He sits facing her, a yard away. Silence.

'Member? How used talk to me till I fell asleep?

QUENTIN: I've sat beside you for days and weeks at a time, Maggie, but you never remember. I've taken you for long drives to soothe you; sailed you around the bay for hours and my office looking high and low for me, but all you remember is the bad.

MAGGIE: Could you stay . . . like five minutes?

QUENTIN—*pause; he tries not to weep:* Yes.

MAGGIE—*slight pause; suddenly she puts the pills on the floor:* See? I'm not taking any more.

He is silent.

I only had . . . about fifteen, I think. You . . . you can have the bottle if you want, even.

QUENTIN, *without rancor; explaining:* I don't want the bottle; I'm not the policeman any more.

MAGGIE: Please don't call the ambulance.

QUENTIN: Then don't take any more. I just can't go through it alone again, and I'm telling you.

MAGGIE—*slight pause:* You going back to your former wife, right?

QUENTIN: No, I've . . . *been* there.

MAGGIE: What then?

QUENTIN—*long pause:* Well, the first thing I've got to do is . . . get somebody to take care of you.

MAGGIE, *very carefully:* What do you mean, take care of me?

QUENTIN—*pause; under terrific stress he begins to touch his face, then puts his hand down:* I talked to your doctor this afternoon.

MAGGIE—*the terror growing:* About what? Thought you said your plane didn't take off.

QUENTIN: I was lying again, but there's no point to it any more. I just didn't want to have this conversation when you—

MAGGIE: I hear everything; what'd you talk to my doctor about? You going to put me somewhere? Is that it?

QUENTIN: No. But you should be supervised. And I shouldn't be with you any more. I shouldn't have been for at least a year, in fact.

MAGGIE: Well now you got what you wanted, didn't you.

QUENTIN: No, exactly the opposite. But he's trying to get a plane up here; if he can he'll spend the night with you; and you can decide with him what to do. But we shouldn't argue any more. It's between you and him.

MAGGIE, *with a knowing, determined smile:* You're not going to put *me* anywhere, mister.

QUENTIN: I've nothing to do with that, Maggie, it's you and him.

MAGGIE: Why, what'd you say to him?

QUENTIN: Maggie, you want to die and I don't know any more how to prevent it. Maybe it was just my being out in the real world for twenty-four hours again, but it struck me that I'm playing with your life out of some idiotic hope of some kind that you're suddenly going to come out of this endless spell. I think somebody ought to be with you who has no illusions of that kind, and simply watches constantly to prevent it.

MAGGIE: Maybe a little love would prevent it.

QUENTIN: But how would you know, Maggie? Not that I love you, but if I did, would you know any more? Do you know who I am? Aside from my name? I'm all the evil in the world, aren't I? All the betrayal, the broken hopes, the murderous revenge?

MAGGIE: And how'd that happen? Takes two to tango, kid.

With a sneer she opens the bottle. He stands at once.

QUENTIN: I'm not sitting here if you take anymore. Especially on top of whiskey; that's the way it happened the last time.

She spills out a few into her palm and he walks a step away.

Okay. Carrie's in her room; I've told her to look in here every few minutes, and if she sees the signs she's to call the ambulance. Good night.

MAGGIE: She won't call the ambulance, she loves me.

QUENTIN: That's why she'll call the ambulance. Which is what I would have done last year if I'd loved you instead of loving myself. I'd have done it two years ago, in fact, but I didn't know what I know now.

MAGGIE, *sneering:* What do you know now? You're spoiled. What do you know?

QUENTIN: A suicide kills two people, Maggie. That's what it's for. So I'm removing myself and perhaps it will lose its point.

She appears to consider for a moment; then carefully takes two pills and swallows them.

Right.

He walks, determined, upstage. And when he is a far distance:

MAGGIE, *on a new level; softly, and without any antagonism:* What's Lazarus?

He halts, without turning back. She looks about for him, not knowing he has left.

Quentin?

Not seeing him, she starts up off the bed; a certain alarm . . .

Quen?

He comes halfway back.

QUENTIN: Jesus raised him from the dead. In the Bible. Go to sleep now.

MAGGIE: Wha's 'at suppose to prove?

QUENTIN: The power of faith.

MAGGIE: What about those who have no faith?

QUENTIN: They only have the will.

MAGGIE: But how you get the will?

QUENTIN: You have faith.

MAGGIE: Some apples.

He smiles, turns again to go.

I want more cream puffs.

He turns back; doesn't answer.

And my birthday dress? If I'm good? Mama? I want my mother.

She sits up, looks about as in a dream, turns and sees him.

Why you standing there?

She gets out of bed, squinting, and comes up to him, peers into his face; her expression comes alive.

You ... you want music?

QUENTIN: All right, you lie down, and I'll put a little music on.

MAGGIE: No, you; you, sit down. And take off your shoes. I mean just to rest. You don't have to do anything. *She goes to the machine, turns it on; jazz.* Was I sleeping?

QUENTIN: For a moment, I think.

MAGGIE: Was she.... was anybody else here?

QUENTIN: No. Just me.

MAGGIE: Is there smoke?

QUENTIN: Your mother's dead and gone, dear, she can't hurt you any more, don't be afraid.

MAGGIE, *in a helpless voice of a child:* Where you going to put me?

QUENTIN, *his chest threatening a cry:* Nowhere, dear—he'll decide with you. He might be here tonight.

MAGGIE: See? I'll lay down. *She hurries to the bed, lies down.* See?

QUENTIN: Good.

MAGGIE: 'Member how used to talk to me till I went to sleep?

QUENTIN: Yes, dear. *He sits beside the bed.*

MAGGIE—*she struggles for lucidity, for some little pose of quiet charm:* It nice in Chicago?

QUENTIN: Yes, very nice. *The caricature of the pleasantry nearly shakes off the world.* Was it nice here?

MAGGIE—*she takes a strange, deep breath:* Ya. Some birds came. And a mouse. You ... you could have the pills if you want.

QUENTIN—*stands:* I'll have Carrie come in and take them. *He starts to move.*

MAGGIE, *clutching the bottle:* No. I won't give them to Carrie.

QUENTIN: Why do you want me to have them?

MAGGIE, *extending them:* Here.

QUENTIN—*pause:* Do you see it, Maggie? Right now? You're trying to make me the one who does it to you? I take them; and then we fight, and then I give them up, and you take the death from me. You see what's happening? You've been setting me up for a murder. Do you see it? *He moves backward.* But now I'm going away; so you're not my victim any more. It's just you, and your hand.

MAGGIE, *slowly retracting her hand, looking at it:* But ask Ludwig— I only wanted to be wonderful so you be proud, and you—

QUENTIN: And for yourself, dear, mostly for yourself. You were ambitious; it's no crime. You would have been everything you are without me.

MAGGIE, *about to weep:* You ran out of patience, right?

QUENTIN: That's right. Yes.

MAGGIE: So you lied. Right?

QUENTIN: Yes, I lied. Every day. We are all separate people.

MAGGIE: You wanted a happy whore. Right?

QUENTIN: Not a whore, but happy, yes. I didn't want too much trouble.

MAGGIE: But Jesus must have loved her. Right?

QUENTIN: Who?

MAGGIE: Lazarus?

QUENTIN—*pause; he sees, he gropes toward his vision:* That's right, yes! He . . . loved her enough to raise her from the dead. But he's God, see . . .

Felice appears, raising her arm in blessing.

. . . and God's power is love without limit. But when a man dares reach for that . . .

He has moved toward Felice, pursuing his truth.

he is only reaching for the power. Whoever goes to save another person with the lie of limitless love throws a shadow on the face of God. And God is what happened, God is what is; and whoever stands between another person and her truth is not a lover, he is . . .

He breaks off, lost, peering, and turns back to Maggie for his clue, and as Felice vanishes . . .

And then she said.

He goes back to Maggie, crying out to invoke her.

And then she said!

MAGGIE—*she is trying to wipe a film from before her thought:* But . . . but . . . will my father find me if you put me . . . No. I mean . . . what's moral?

QUENTIN, *in the tension of trying to recall:* To tell the truth.

MAGGIE: No-no . . . against yourself even.

QUENTIN: Yes.

MAGGIE—*she turns to him; her look is insane, and the truth is purified of all restraint:* Well?

 A cry is gathering in her, as though only now did she know there was no return.

I hear you. Way inside. Quentin? My love? I hear you! Tell me what happened!

 Her tears tell her sanity. He weeps facing her.

QUENTIN, *on the verge of the abyss:* Maggie, we . . . used one another.

MAGGIE, *weeping, calling:* Not me, not me!

QUENTIN: Yes, you. And I. "To live," we cried, and "Now," we cried. And loved each other's innocence as though to love enough what was not there would cover up what was. But there is an angel, and night and day he brings back to us exactly what we want to lose. And no chemical can kill him, no blindness dark enough to make him lose his way; so you must love him, he keeps truth in the world. You eat those pills like power, but only what you've done will save you. If you could only say, I have been cruel, this frightening room would open! If you could say, I have been kicked around, but I have been just as inexcusably vicious to others; I have called my husband idiot in public, I have been utterly selfish despite my generosity, I have been hurt by a long line of men but I have cooperated with my persecutors. . . .

MAGGIE—*she has been writhing, furious at this exorcism:* Son of a bitch!

QUENTIN: And I am full of hatred, I, Maggie, the sweet lover of all life—I hate the world!

MAGGIE: Get out of here!

QUENTIN: Hate women, hate men, hate all who will not grovel at my feet proclaiming my limitless love for ever and ever!

 She spills a handful of pills into her palm. He speaks desperately, trying not to physically take the pills from her.

Throw them in the sea; throw death in the sea and drink your life instead; your rotten, betrayed, hateful mockery of a life. That power is death, Maggie! Do the hardest thing of all—see our own hatred, and live!

Dumbly, she raises her hand toward her open mouth. He cannot hold back his hand and grips her wrist.

MAGGIE: What are you, goddamn judge or something? Let go. You no judge.

He lets go.

You know when I wanted to die. When I read what you wrote, judgey. Two months after we were married, judgey.

QUENTIN, *stricken, afraid, but remorseless:* Let's keep it true. It's not some words on a piece of paper destroyed us. You told me you tried to die long before you met me.

MAGGIE: So you're not even there, huh. I didn't even meet you. *Tries to laugh.* You coward. Coward!

She staggers to her feet; he finds it hard to look directly at her. A clear line of accusation momentarily seems to steady her, and with the pills in her palm she stands straight.

I was married to a king, you son of a bitch! I was looking for a fountain pen to sign some autographs. And there's his desk . . .

She is speaking toward some invisible source of justice now, telling her injury.

. . . and there's his empty chair where he sits and thinks how to help people. And there's his handwriting. I wanted to touch his handwriting. And there's some words . . .

She almost literally reads in the air, and with the same original astonishment.

"The only one I will ever love is my daughter. If I could only find an honorable way to die."

Now she turns to him.

When you gonna face that, judgey? Remember how I fell down fainted? On the new rug? 'Member? That's what killed me, judgey. Right?

She staggers up to him and into his face.

'Zat right? When you gonna face that one, kiddo?

QUENTIN—*a pause; he is struggling with her accusation and his guilt:* All right. You pour them back and I'll tell you the truth about that.

MAGGIE: You won't tell truth.

QUENTIN: I will now. *He tries to tip her hand toward the bottle, holding both her wrists.* You can hold the bottle, just pour them back.

MAGGIE, *closing her hand on the pills:* But that's why, right?

QUENTIN, *with difficulty:* We'll see. Pour them back, first.

> She lets him pour them back, but she keeps the bottle. She sits staring on the bed, holding it in two hands.

MAGGIE—*she takes a deep breath:* Liar.

QUENTIN, *in quiet tension against his own self-condemnation:* We'd had our first party in our own house. Some important people, network heads, directors . . .

MAGGIE: And you were ashamed of me. Don't lie now! You're still playing God! That's what killed me, Quentin!

QUENTIN: All right. I wasn't . . . ashamed. But . . . afraid. *Pause.* I wasn't sure if any of them . . . had had you.

MAGGIE, *astounded:* But I didn't know any of those!

QUENTIN, *not looking at her:* I didn't know. But I swear to you, I did get to where none of it meant anything to me, I couldn't imagine what I'd ever been ashamed of. But it was too late. I had written that, and I was like all the others who'd betrayed you, and I could never be trusted again.

MAGGIE, *shaking her head; it is all corroborated:* You never gave me a chance!

QUENTIN, *consumed, desperate for the slightest absolution:* I did, Maggie, but it was too late. I laid down my life for you. But it was all too late.

MAGGIE, *with a mixture of accusation but near-sympathy:* Why did you write that? *She sobs, once.*

QUENTIN: Because when the guests had gone, and you suddenly turned on me, calling me cold, remote, it was the first time I saw your eyes that way—betrayed, screaming that I'd made you feel you didn't exist.

MAGGIE: Don't mix me up with Louise!

QUENTIN: That's just it. That I could have brought two women so different to the same accusation—it closed a circle for me. And I wanted to face the worst thing I could imagine—that I could not love. And I wrote it down, like a letter . . . from myself.

> She pours pills into her hand again.

I've told you the truth. That's rock bottom. What more do you want?

She starts to raise her hand to her mouth, and he steps in and holds her wrist.

What more do you *want*?

She looks at him, her eyes unreadable.

Maggie, we've got to have some humility toward ourselves; we were both born of many errors, a human being has to forgive himself! You want me to say I killed you? All right, I killed you. Now what? What do you want?

A strange calm overtakes her. She lies back on the bed. The hostility seems to have gone.

MAGGIE: Just . . . be human. And help me. And stop arguing.

He lets her hand go; it falls to the bed.

And love me. Sit on the bed.

He sits down.

Cover me.

He covers her.

And take down the sand dune. It's not too expensive. I wanted to hear the ocean when we made love in here but we could never hear the ocean.

QUENTIN: We're nearly broke, Maggie; and that dune keeps the roof from blowing off.

MAGGIE: Then you get a new roof. You'll have them take it away, right?

He doesn't answer.

I'm cold. Lie on me.

QUENTIN: I can't do that again, not when you're like this.

MAGGIE: Please. Just till I sleep!

QUENTIN, *breaking down:* Maggie, it's a mockery. Leave me *something.*

MAGGIE: Just out of humanness! I'm cold!

Downing self-disgust, he lies down on her but holds his head away. Pause.

If you don't argue with me any more, I'll get rid of that other lawyer. 'Kay? If you don't argue? Ludwig doesn't argue.

He is silent.

And don't keep saying we're broke? And the sand dune?

The fear of his own total disintegration is growing in his face.

'Cause I love the ocean sound; like a big mother—sssh, sssh, sssh.

He slips off and stands looking down at her. Her eyes are closed.

You gonna be good now? 'Cause all I am . . . is love. And sex.

She takes a very deep, jagged breath.

Quentin reaches in carefully and tries to slip the bottle out of her hand; she grips it.

Whyn't you lie on me?

QUENTIN, *as a fact, simply:* It disgusts me.

MAGGIE: But if Lazarus . . .

QUENTIN: I am not the Savior and I am not the help. . . . You are not going to kill me, Maggie, and that's all this is for!

MAGGIE: You liar!

QUENTIN: Not any more—I am not guilty for your life! I can't be. But I am responsible for it now. And I want those pills. I don't want to fight you, Maggie. Now put them in my hand.

She looks at him; then quickly tries to swallow her handful, but he knocks some of them out—although she swallows many. He grabs for the bottle but she holds and he pulls, yanks; she goes with the force and he drags her onto the floor, trying to pry her hands open as she flails at him and tears at his face, digs at his eyes. Her strength is wild and no longer her own, and, strangely, she is smiling, almost laughing. He grabs her wrist and squeezes it with both his fists.

Drop them, you bitch! You won't kill me!

She holds on, still smiling with a profound certainty, and suddenly, clearly, he lunges for her throat and lifts her with his grip.

You won't kill me! You won't kill me!

She drops the bottle as from the farthest distance Mother rushes to a point crying out—the toy sailboat in her hand—

MOTHER: Darling, open this door! I didn't trick you! I told Fanny to tell you we'd gone as soon you got up from your nap! I didn't trick you!

Quentin springs away from Maggie, who falls back to the floor; his hands are open and in air.

Quentin, why are you running water in there?

The sound of the sea comes up. Mother backs away in horror.

Stop that water! Quentin, I'll die if you do that! I saw a star when you were born, a light, a light in the world!

He stands transfixed as Mother backs into his hand, and he begins to squeeze her throat and she to sink to the floor gasping for breath. He releases her in horror.

QUENTIN: Murder?

Mother stumbles into darkness, her hands in prayer, whispering, "I will die, I will die." He turns to Maggie, who is now getting to her hands and knees, gasping. He rushes to help her, terrified by his realization, but she flails out at him, and on one elbow looks up at him in a caricature of laughter, her eyes victorious and wild with fear.

MAGGIE: Now we both know. You tried to kill me, mister. I been killed by a lot of people, some couldn't hardly spell, but it's the same, mister. You're on the end of a long, long line, Frank.

As though to ward off the accusation he desperately reaches again to help her up, and in absolute terror she skitters away across the floor.

Stay 'way! . . . No! No—no, Frank! Don't you do that!

Cautiously, as though facing a wild, ravening beast.

Don't you do that . . . or I call Quentin if you do that.

She glances off and calls quietly, but never leaving him out of her sight.

Quentin? Qu—?

She falls unconscious, crumpled on the floor, now with deep, strange breathing. He quickly goes to her, throws her over onto her stomach, starts artificial respiration, but just as he is about to start, he stands. He calls upstage.

QUENTIN: Carrie? Carrie!

Carrie appears, praying, with open hands almost shielding her eyes. And, as though it were a final farewell:

Quick! Call the ambulance.

Carrie bends to exorcise Maggie's demons.

Stop wasting time! Call the ambulance!

Carrie hurries out.

Felice appears; he hardly glances at her, comes down to the dock, halts. Felice remains behind him.

. . . No-no, we saved her. It was just in time. For her. But not for me.

I knew why I had stayed; I packed up next morning. Her doctor tells me she had a few good months; he even thought for a while she was making it. Unless, God knows, he fell in love with her too.

He almost smiles; it is gone.

Look, I'll say it. It's really all I came to say. Barbiturates kill by suffocation. And the signal is a kind of sighing—the diaphragm is paralyzed.

With more difficulty.

And I'd noticed it when we'd begun to argue. . . . I know, it usually does subside, but if not—each second can be most precious, why waste them arguing? What can be so important to gamble her life to get?

The tower lights, fierce, implacable.

. . . My innocence, you see? To get that back you kill most easily.
. . . No, don't; I want it . . . just the way it was.

He looks up.

And all those stars, still so fixed, so fortunate! And her precious seconds squirming in my hand like bugs; and I heard. Those deep, unnatural breaths, like the footfalls of my coming peace—and knew . . . I wanted them. How is that possible—I loved that girl!

Slight pause.

And the name . . . yes, the name . . .

Louise appears, young, in her lab costume.

. . . in whose name do you ever turn your back . . .

He looks out at the audience.

. . . but in your own? In Quentin's name! Always in your own blood-covered name you turn your back!

Holga appears on the highest level.

HOLGA: But no one is innocent they did not kill!

QUENTIN: But love, is love enough? What love, what wave of pity will ever reach this knowledge—I know how to kill. . . . I know, I know . . . she was doomed in any case, but will that cure? Or is it possible . . .

He turns toward the tower, moves toward it as toward a terrible God.

. . . that this is not bizarre . . . to anyone? And I am not alone, and no man lives who would not rather be the sole survivor of this place

than all its finest victims? What is the cure? Who can be innocent
again on this mountain of skulls? I tell you what I know! My brothers died here . . .

He looks down at the fallen Maggie.

. . . but my brothers built this place; our hearts have cut these stones!
And what's the cure!

*Father and Mother and Dan appear, and Lou and Mickey; all his
people are in light now.*

. . . No, not love; I loved them all, all! And gave them willingly to
failure and to death that I might live, as they gave me and gave each
other, with a word, a look, a truth, a lie—and all in love!

HOLGA: Hello!

QUENTIN: But what will defend her?

He cries up to her.

That woman hopes!

She stands unperturbed, resolute.

Or is that . . .

Struck—to the Listener:

. . . exactly why she hopes, because she knows? What burning cities
taught her and the death of love taught me—that we are very dangerous!

Staring, seeing his vision.

And that, that's why I wake each morning like a boy—even now,
even now! I swear to you, there's something in me that could dare to
love this world again! . . . Is the knowing all? To know, and even
happily that we meet unblessed; not in some garden of wax fruit
and painted trees, that lie of Eden, but after, after the Fall, after
many, many deaths. Is the knowing all? And the wish to kill is never
killed, but with some gift of courage one may look into its face
when it appears, and with a stroke of love—as to an idiot in the
house—forgive it; again and again . . . forever?

He is evidently interrupted by the Listener, glances at his watch.

. . . Yes, I don't want to be late. Thanks for making time for me. . . .
No, it's not certainty, I don't feel that. But it does seem feasible . . .
not to be afraid. Perhaps it's all one has. I'll tell her that. . . . Yes,
she will, she'll know what I mean. Well, see you again some time.
Good luck, and thanks.

He turns upstage. He hesitates; all his people face him. He walks past Louise, pausing; but she turns her face away. He goes on and pauses beside Mother, who lowers her head in uncomprehended sorrow, and gestures as though he touched her chin and she looks up at him and dares a smile, and he smiles back. He pauses at his dejected Father and Dan, and with a look he magically makes them stand. Felice is about to raise her hand in blessing—he shakes her hand, aborting her enslavement. Mickey and Lou are standing together; he looks at them and neither of them are looking at him, but they move in behind him. Now he arrives at Maggie; she rises from the floor webbed in with demons, trying to awake. And with his life following him he climbs toward Holga, who raises her arm as though seeing him, and speaks with great love.

HOLGA: Hello!

He comes to a halt a few yards from her. A whispering goes up from all his people. He straightens against it and walks toward her, holding out his hand.

QUENTIN: Hello.

The darkness takes them all.

CURTAIN

INCIDENT AT VICHY

The Characters:

LEBEAU, a painter

BAYARD, an electrician

MARCHAND, a businessman

POLICE GUARD

MONCEAU, an actor

GYPSY

WAITER

BOY

MAJOR

FIRST DETECTIVE

OLD JEW

SECOND DETECTIVE

LEDUC, a doctor

POLICE CAPTAIN

VON BERG, a Prince

PROFESSOR HOFFMAN

FERRAND, a café proprietor

FOUR PRISONERS

INCIDENT AT VICHY

Vichy, France, 1942. A place of detention.

At the right a corridor leads to a turning and an unseen door to the street. Across the back is a structure with two grimy window panes in it—perhaps an office, in any case a private room with a door opening from it at the left.

A long bench stands in front of this room, facing a large empty area whose former use is unclear but which suggests a warehouse, perhaps, an armory, or part of a railroad station not used by the public. Two small boxes stand apart on either side of the bench.

When light begins to rise, six men and a boy of fifteen are discovered on the bench in attitudes expressive of their personalities and functions, frozen there like members of a small orchestra at the moment before they begin to play.

As normal light comes on, their positions flow out of the frieze. It appears that they do not know one another and are sitting like people thrown together in a public place, mutually curious but self-occupied. However, they are anxious and frightened and tend to make themselves small and unobtrusive. Only one, Marchand, a fairly well-dressed businessman, keeps glancing at his watch and bits of paper and calling cards he keeps in his pockets, and seems normally impatient.

Now, out of hunger and great anxiety, Lebeau, a bearded, unkempt man of twenty-five, lets out a dramatized blow of air and leans forward to rest his head on his hands. Others glance at him, then away. He is charged with the energy of fear, and it makes him seem aggressive.

LEBEAU: Cup of coffee would be nice. Even a sip.

No one responds. He turns to Bayard beside him; Bayard is his age, poorly but cleanly dressed, with a certain muscular austerity in his manner. Lebeau speaks in a private undertone.

You wouldn't have any idea what's going on, would you?

BAYARD, *shaking his head:* I was walking down the street.

LEBEAU: Me too. Something told me— Don't go outside today. So I went out. Weeks go by and I don't open my door. Today I go out. And I had no reason, I wasn't even going anywhere. *Looks left and right to the others. To Bayard:* They get picked up the same way?

BAYARD—*shrugs:* I've only been here a couple of minutes myself—just before they brought you in.

LEBEAU—*looks to the others:* Does anybody know anything?

They shrug and shake their heads. Lebeau looks at the walls, the room; then he speaks to Bayard.

This isn't a police station, is it?

BAYARD: Doesn't seem so. There's always a desk. It's just some building they're using, I guess.

LEBEAU, *glancing about uneasily, curiously:* It's painted like a police station, though. There must be an international police paint, they're always the same color everywhere. Like dead clams, and a little yellow mixed in.

Pause. He glances at the other silent men, and tries to silence himself, like them. But it's impossible, and he speaks to Bayard with a nervous smile.

You begin wishing you'd committed a crime, you know? Something definite.

BAYARD—*he is not amused, but not unsympathetic:* Try to take it easy. It's no good getting excited. We'll find out soon.

LEBEAU: It's just that I haven't eaten since three o'clock yesterday afternoon. Everything gets more vivid when you're hungry—you ever notice that?

BAYARD: I'd give you something, but I forgot my lunch this morning. Matter of fact, I was just turning back to get it when they came up alongside me. Whyn't you try to sit back and relax?

LEBEAU: I'm nervous. . . . I mean I'm nervous anyway. *With a faint, frightened laugh:* I was even nervous before the war.

His little smile vanishes. He shifts in his seat. The others wait with subdued anxiety. He notices the good clothes and secure manner of Marchand, who is at the head of the line, nearest the door. He leans forward to attract him.

Excuse me.

Marchand does not turn to him. He gives a short, sharp, low whistle. Marchand, already offended, turns slowly to him.

Is that the way they picked you up? On the street?

Marchand turns forward again without answering.

Sir?

Marchand still does not turn back to him.

Well, Jesus, pardon me for living.

MARCHAND: It's perfectly obvious they're making a routine identity check.

LEBEAU: Oh.

MARCHAND: With so many strangers pouring into Vichy this past year there're probably a lot of spies and God knows what. It's just a document check, that's all.

LEBEAU—*turns to Bayard, hopefully:* You think so?

BAYARD—*shrugs; obviously he feels there is something more to it:* I don't know.

MARCHAND, *to Bayard:* Why? There are thousands of people running around with false papers, we all know that. You can't permit such things in wartime.

The others glance uneasily at Marchand, whose sense of security is thereby confined to him alone.

Especially now with the Germans starting to take over down here you have to expect things to be more strict, it's inevitable.

A pause. Lebeau once again turns to him.

LEBEAU: You don't get any ... special flavor, huh?

MARCHAND: What flavor?

LEBEAU, *glancing at the others:* Well like ... some racial ... implication?

MARCHAND: I don't see anything to fear if your papers are all right. *He turns front, concluding the conversation.*

Again silence. But Lebeau can't contain his anxiety. He studies Bayard's profile, then turns to the man on his other side and studies his. Then, turning back to Bayard, he speaks quietly.

LEBEAU: Listen, you are . . . Peruvian, aren't you?

BAYARD: What's the matter with you, asking questions like that in here? *He turns forward.*

LEBEAU: What am I supposed to do, sit here like a dumb beast?

BAYARD, *laying a calming hand on his knee:* Friend, it's no good getting hysterical.

LEBEAU: I think we've had it. I think all the Peruvians have had it in Vichy. *Suppressing a shout:* In 1939 I had an American visa. Before the invasion. I actually had it in my hand. . . .

BAYARD: Calm down—this may all be routine.

Slight pause. Then . . .

LEBEAU: Listen . . .

He leans in and whispers into Bayard's ear. Bayard glances toward Marchand, then shrugs to Lebeau.

BAYARD: I don't know, maybe; maybe he's not.

LEBEAU, *desperately attempting familiarity:* What about you?

BAYARD: Will you stop asking idiotic questions? You're making yourself ridiculous.

LEBEAU: But I am ridiculous, aren't you? In 1939 we were packed for America. Suddenly my mother wouldn't leave the furniture. I'm here because of a brass bed and some fourth-rate crockery. And a stubborn, ignorant woman.

BAYARD: Yes, but it's not all that simple. You should try to think of why things happen. It helps to know the meaning of one's suffering.

LEBEAU: What meaning? If my mother—

BAYARD: It's not your mother. The monopolies got control of Germany. Big business is out to make slaves of everyone, that's why you're here.

LEBEAU: Well I'm not a philosopher, but I know my mother, and that's why I'm here. You're like people who look at my paintings— "What does this mean, what does that mean?" *Look* at it, don't ask what it means; you're not God, you can't tell what anything means. I'm walking down the street before, a car pulls up beside me, a man gets out and measures my nose, my ears, my mouth, the next thing I'm sitting in a police station—or whatever the hell this is here—and in the middle of Europe, the highest peak of civilization! And you know what it means? After the Romans and the Greeks and the Renaissance, and you know what this means?

BAYARD: You're talking utter confusion.

LEBEAU, *in terror:* Because I'm utterly confused! *He suddenly springs up and shouts:* Goddamnit, I want some coffee!

The Police Guard appears at the end of the corridor, a revolver on his hip; he strolls down the corridor and meets Lebeau, who has come halfway up. Lebeau halts, returns to his place on the bench, and sits. The Guard starts to turn to go up the corridor when Marchand raises his hand.

MARCHAND: Excuse me, officer, is there a telephone one can use? I have an appointment at eleven o'clock and it's quite ...

The Guard simply walks up the corridor, turns the corner, and disappears. Lebeau looks toward Marchand and shakes his head, laughing silently.

LEBEAU, *to Bayard, sotto:* Isn't it wonderful? The man is probably on his way to work in a German coal mine and he's worried about breaking an appointment. And people want realistic painting, you see what I mean? *Slight pause.* Did they measure your nose? Could you at least tell me that?

BAYARD: No, they just stopped me and asked for my papers. I showed them and they took me in.

MONCEAU, *leaning forward to address Marchand:* I agree with you, sir.

Marchand turns to him. Monceau is a bright-eyed, cheerful man of twenty-eight. His clothes were elegant, now frayed. He holds a gray felt hat on his knee, his posture rather elegant.

Vichy must be full of counterfeit papers. I think as soon as they start, it shouldn't take long. *To Lebeau:* Try to settle down.

LEBEAU, *to Monceau:* Did they measure your nose?

MONCEAU, *disapprovingly:* I think it'd be best if we all kept quiet.

LEBEAU: What is it, my clothes? How do you know, I might be the greatest painter in France.

MONCEAU: For your sake, I hope you are.

LEBEAU: What a crew! I mean the animosity!

Pause.

MARCHAND, *leaning forward to see Monceau:* You would think, though, that with the manpower shortage they'd economize on personnel. In the car that stopped me there was a driver, two French detectives, and a German official of some kind. They could easily have put a notice in the paper—everyone would have come here to present his documents. This way it's a whole morning wasted. Aside from the embarrassment.

LEBEAU: I'm not embarrassed, I'm scared to death. *To Bayard:* You embarrassed?

BAYARD: Look, if you can't be serious just leave me alone.

Pause. Lebeau leans forward to see the man sitting on the far side of Marchand. He points.

LEBEAU: Gypsy?

GYPSY, *drawing closer a copper pot at his feet:* Gypsy.

LEBEAU, *to Monceau:* Gypsies never have papers. Why'd they bother him?

MONCEAU: In his case it might be some other reason. He probably stole that pot.

GYPSY: No. On the sidewalk. *He raises the pot from between his feet.* I fix, make nice. I sit down to fix. Come police. Pfft!

MARCHAND: But of course they'll tell you anything. . . . *To Gypsy, laughing familiarly:* Right?

Gypsy laughs and turns away to his own gloom.

LEBEAU: That's a hell of a thing to say to him. I mean, would you say that to a man with pressed pants?

MARCHAND: They don't mind. In fact, they're proud of stealing. *To Gypsy:* Aren't you?

Gypsy glances at him, shrugs.

I've got a place in the country where they come every summer. I like them, personally—especially the music. *With a broad grin he sings toward the Gypsy and laughs.* We often listen to them around their campfires. But they'll steal the eyes out of your head. *To Gypsy:* Right?

Gypsy shrugs and kisses the air contemptuously. Marchand laughs with brutal familiarity.

LEBEAU: Why shouldn't he steal? How'd you get *your* money?

MARCHAND: I happen to be in business.

LEBEAU: So what have you got against stealing?

BAYARD: Are you trying to provoke somebody? Is that it?

LEBEAU: Another businessman.

BAYARD: I happen to be an electrician. But a certain amount of solidarity wouldn't hurt right now.

LEBEAU: How about some solidarity with Gypsies? Just because they don't work nine to five?

WAITER—*a small man, middle-aged, still wearing his apron:* I know this one. I've made him go away a hundred times. He and his wife stand outside the café with a baby, and they beg. It's not even their baby.

LEBEAU: So what? They've still got a little imagination.

WAITER: Yes, but they keep whining to the customers through the shrubbery. People don't like it.

LEBEAU: You know—you all remind me of my father. Always worshiped the hard-working Germans. And now you hear it all over France—we have to learn how to work like the Germans. Good God, don't you ever read history? Whenever a people starts to work hard, watch out, they're going to kill somebody.

BAYARD: That depends on how production is organized. If it's for private profit, yes, but—

LEBEAU: What are you talking about, when did the Russians start getting dangerous? When they learned how to work. Look at the Germans—for a thousand years peaceful, disorganized people— they start working and they're on everybody's back. Nobody's afraid of the Africans, are they? Because they don't work. Read the the Bible—work is a curse, you're not supposed to worship work.

MARCHAND: And how do you propose to produce anything?

LEBEAU: Well that's the problem.

Marchand and Bayard laugh.

What are you laughing at? *That is the problem!* Yes! To work without making work a god! What kind of crew is this?

The office door opens and the Major comes out. He is twenty-eight, a wan but well-built man; there is something ill about him. He walks with a slight limp, passing the line of men as he goes toward the corridor.

WAITER: Good morning, Major.

MAJOR—*startled, nods to the Waiter:* Oh. Good morning.

He continues up the corridor, where he summons the Guard around the corner—the Guard appears and they talk unheard.

MARCHAND, *sotto:* You know him?

WAITER, *proudly:* I serve him breakfast every morning. Tell you the truth, he's really not a bad fellow. Regular Army, see, not one of these S.S. bums. Got wounded somewhere, so they stuck him back here. Only came about a month ago, but he and I—

The Major comes back down the corridor. The Guard returns to his post out of sight at the corridor's end. As the Major passes Marchand . . .

MARCHAND, *leaping up and going to the Major:* Excuse me, sir.

The Major slowly turns his face to Marchand. Marchand affects to laugh deferentially.

I hate to trouble you, but I would be much obliged if I could use a telephone for one minute. In fact, it's business connected to the food supply. I am the manager of . . .

He starts to take out a business card, but the Major has turned away and walks to the door. But there he stops and turns back.

MAJOR: I'm not in charge of this procedure. You will have to wait for the Captain of Police. *He goes into the office.*

MARCHAND: I beg your pardon.

The door has been closed on his line. He goes back to his place and sits, glaring at the Waiter.

WAITER: He's not a really bad fellow.

They all look at him, eager for some clue.

He even comes at night sometimes, plays a beautiful piano. Gives himself French lessons out of a book. Always has a few nice words to say, too.

LEBEAU: Does he know that you're a . . . Peruvian?

BAYARD, *instantly:* Don't discuss that here, for God's sake! What's the matter with you?

LEBEAU: Can't I find out what's going on? If it's a general identity check it's one thing, but if—

From the end of the corridor enter First Detective with the Old Jew, a man in his seventies, bearded, carrying a large sackcloth bundle; then the Second Detective, holding the arm of Leduc; then the Police Captain, uniformed, with Von Berg; and finally the Professor in civilian clothes.

The First Detective directs the Old Jew to sit, and he does, beside the Gypsy. The Second Detective directs Von Berg to sit beside the Old Jew. Only now does the Second Detective release his hold on Leduc and indicate that he is to sit beside Von Berg.

SECOND DETECTIVE, *to Leduc:* Don't you give me any more trouble now.

The door opens and the Major enters. Instantly Leduc is on his feet, approaching the Major.

LEDUC: Sir, I must ask the reason for this. I am a combat officer, captain in the French Army. There is no authority to arrest me in French territory. The Occupation has not revoked French law in southern France.

The Second Detective, infuriated, throws Leduc back into his seat. He returns to the Professor.

SECOND DETECTIVE, *to Major, of Leduc:* Speechmaker.

PROFESSOR, *doubtfully:* You think you two can carry on now?

SECOND DETECTIVE: We got the idea, Professor. *To the Major:* There's certain neighborhoods they head for when they run away from Paris or wherever they come from. I can get you as many as you can handle.

FIRST DETECTIVE: It's a question of knowing the neighborhoods, you see. In my opinion you've got at least a couple thousand in Vichy on false papers.

PROFESSOR: You go ahead, then.

As the Second Detective turns to go with the First Detective, the Police Captain calls him.

CAPTAIN: Saint-Père.

SECOND DETECTIVE: Yes sir.

The Captain walks downstage with the Detective.

CAPTAIN: Try to avoid taking anybody out of a crowd. Just cruise around the way we did before, and take them one at a time. There are all kinds of rumors. We don't want to alarm people.

SECOND DETECTIVE: Right, sir.

The Captain gestures, and both Detectives leave up the corridor.

CAPTAIN: I am just about to order coffee. Will you gentlemen have some?

PROFESSOR: Please.

WAITER, *timidly:* And a croissant for the Major.

The Major glances quickly at the Waiter and barely smiles. The Captain, who has thrown a mystified look at the Waiter, goes into the office.

MARCHAND, *to the Professor:* I believe I am first, sir.

PROFESSOR: Yes, this way.

He goes into the office, followed by the eager Marchand.

MARCHAND, *going in:* Thank you. I'm in a dreadful hurry. . . . I was on my way to the Ministry of Supply, in fact. . . .

His voice is lost within. As the Major reaches the door, Leduc, who has been in a fever of calculation, calls to him.

LEDUC: Amiens.

MAJOR—*he halts at the door, turns to Leduc, who is at the far end of the line:* What about Amiens?

LEDUC, *suppressing his nervousness:* June ninth, 'forty. I was in the Sixteenth Artillery, facing you. I recognize your insignia, which of course I could hardly forget.

MAJOR: That was a bad day for you fellows.

LEDUC: Yes. And evidently for you.

MAJOR—*glances down at his leg:* Can't complain.

The Major goes into the office, shuts the door. A pause.

LEDUC, *to all:* What's this all about?

WAITER, *to all:* I told you he wasn't a bad guy. You'll see.

MONCEAU, *to Leduc:* It seems they're checking on identification papers.

Leduc receives the news, and obviously grows cautious and quietly alarmed. He examines their faces.

LEDUC: What's the procedure?

MONCEAU: They've just started—that businessman was the first.

LEBEAU, *to Leduc and Von Berg:* They measure your noses?

LEDUC, *sharply alarmed:* Measure noses?

LEBEAU, *putting thumb and forefinger against the bridge and tip of his nose:* Ya, they measured my nose, right on the street. I tell you what I think . . . *To Bayard:* With your permission.

BAYARD: I don't mind you talking as long as you're serious.

LEBEAU: I think it's to carry stones. It just occurred to me—last Monday a girl I know came up from Marseille—the road is full of detours. They probably need labor. She said there was a crowd of people just carrying stones. Lot of them Jews, she thought; hundreds.

LEDUC: I never heard of forced labor in the Vichy Zone. Is that going on here?

BAYARD: Where do you come from?

LEDUC—*slight pause—he decides whether to reveal:* I live in the country. I don't get into town very often. There's been no forced-labor decree, has there?

BAYARD, *to all:* Now, listen. *Everyone turns to his straight-forward, certain tone.* I'm going to tell you something, but I don't want anybody quoting me. Is that understood?

They nod. He glances at the door. He turns to Lebeau.

You hear what I said?

LEBEAU: Don't make me out some kind of an idiot. Christ's sake, I know it's serious!

BAYARD, *to the others:* I work in the railroad yards. A thirty-car freight train pulled in yesterday. The engineer is Polish, so I couldn't talk to him, but one of the switchmen says he heard people inside.

LEDUC: Inside the cars?

BAYARD: Yes. It came from Toulouse. I heard there's been a quiet roundup of Jews in Toulouse the last couple of weeks. And what's a Polish engineer doing on a train in southern France? You understand?

LEDUC: Concentration camp?

MONCEAU: Why? A lot of people have been volunteering for work in Germany. That's no secret. They're doubling the ration for anybody who goes.

BAYARD, *quietly:* The cars are locked on the outside. *Slight pause.* And they stink. You can smell the stench a hundred yards away. Babies are crying inside. You can hear them. And women. They don't lock volunteers in that way. I never heard of it.

A long pause.

LEDUC: But I've never heard of them applying the Racial Laws down here. It's still French territory, regardless of the Occupation—they've made a big point of that.

Pause.

BAYARD: The Gypsy bothers me.

LEBEAU: Why?

BAYARD: They're in the same category of the Racial Laws. Inferior.

Leduc and Lebeau slowly turn to look at the Gypsy.

LEBEAU, *turning back quickly to Bayard:* Unless he really stole that pot.

BAYARD: Well, yes, if he stole the pot then of course he—

LEBEAU, *quickly, to the Gypsy:* Hey, listen. *He gives a soft, sharp whistle. The Gypsy turns to him.* You steal that pot?

The Gypsy's face is inscrutable. Lebeau is embarrassed to press this, and more desperate.

You did, didn't you?

GYPSY: No steal, no.

LEBEAU: Look, I've got nothing against stealing. *Indicating the others:* I'm not one of these types. I've slept in parked cars, under bridges—I mean, to me all property is theft anyway so I've got no prejudice against you.

GYPSY: No steal.

LEBEAU: Look . . . I mean you're a Gypsy, so how else can you live, right?

WAITER: He steals everything.

LEBEAU, *to Bayard:* You hear? He's probably in for stealing, that's all.

VON BERG: Excuse me . . .

They turn to him.

Have you all been arrested for being Jewish?

They are silent, suspicious and surprised.

I'm terribly sorry. I had no idea.

BAYARD: I said nothing about being Jewish. As far as I know, nobody here is Jewish.

VON BERG: I'm terribly sorry.

Silence. The moment lengthens. In his embarrassment he laughs nervously.

It's only that I . . . I was buying a newspaper and this gentleman came out of a car and told me I must have my documents checked. I . . . I had no idea.

Silence. Hope is rising in them.

LEBEAU, *to Bayard:* So what'd they grab *him* for?

BAYARD—*looks at Von Berg for a moment, then addresses all:* I don't understand it, but take my advice. If anything like that happens and you find yourself on that train . . . there are four bolts halfway up the doors on the inside. Try to pick up a nail or a screwdriver, even a sharp stone—you can chisel the wood out around those bolts and the doors will open. I warn you, don't believe anything they tell you—I heard they're working Jews to death in the Polish camps.

MONCEAU: I happen to have a cousin; they sent him to Auschwitz; that's in Poland, you know. I have several letters from him saying he's fine. They've even taught him bricklaying.

BAYARD: Look, friend, I'm telling you what I heard from people who know. *Hesitates.* People who make it their business to know, you understand? Don't listen to any stories about resettlement, or that they're going to teach you a trade or something. If you're on that train get out before it gets where it's going.

Pause.

LEDUC: I've heard the same thing.

They turn to him and he turns to Bayard.

How would one find tools, you have any idea?

MONCEAU: This is so typical! We're in the French Zone, nobody has said one word to us, and we're already on a train for a concentration camp where we'll be dead in a year.

LEDUC: But if the engineer is a Pole . . .

MONCEAU: So he's a Pole, what does that prove?

BAYARD: All I'm saying is that if you have some kind of tool . . .

LEDUC: I think what this man says should be taken seriously.

MONCEAU: In my opinion you're hysterical. After all, they were picking up Jews in Germany for years before the war, they've been doing it in Paris since they came in—are you telling me all those people are dead? Is that really conceivable to you? War is war, but you still have to keep a certain sense of proportion. I mean Germans are still *people.*

LEDUC: I don't speak this way because they're Germans.

BAYARD: It's that they're Fascists.

LEDUC: Excuse me, no. It's exactly because they are people that I speak this way.

BAYARD: I don't agree with *that.*

MONCEAU—*looks at Leduc for an instant:* You must have had a peculiar life, is all I can say. I happen to have played in Germany; I know the German people.

LEDUC: I studied in Germany for five years, and in Austria and I—

VON BERG, *happily:* In Austria! Where?

LEDUC—*again he hesitates, then reveals:* The Psychoanalytic Institute in Vienna.

VON BERG: Imagine!

MONCEAU: You're a psychiatrist. *To the others:* No wonder he's so pessimistic!

VON BERG: Where did you live? I am Viennese.

LEDUC: Excuse me, but perhaps it would be wiser not to speak in . . . detail.

VON BERG, *glancing about as though he had committed a gaffe:* I'm terribly sorry . . . yes, of course. *Slight pause.* I was only curious if you knew Baron Kessler. He was very interested in the medical school.

LEDUC, *with an odd coolness:* No, I was never in that circle.

VON BERG: Oh, but he is extremely democratic. He . . . *shyly:* He is my cousin, you see. . . .

LEBEAU: You're a nobleman?

VON BERG: Yes.

LEDUC: What is your name?

VON BERG: Wilhelm Johann Von Berg.

MONCEAU, *astonished, impressed:* The prince?

VON BERG: Yes . . . forgive me, have we met?

MONCEAU, *excited by the honor:* Oh, no. But naturally I've heard your name. I believe it's one of the oldest houses in Austria.

VON BERG: Oh, that's of no importance any more.

LEBEAU, *turning to Bayard—bursting with hope:* Now, what the hell would they want with an Austrian prince?

> *Bayard looks at Von Berg, mystified.*

I mean . . . *Turning back to Von Berg:* You're Catholic, right?

VON BERG: Yes.

LEDUC: But is your title on your papers?

VON BERG: Oh, yes, my passport.

> *Pause. They sit silent, on the edge of hope, but bewildered.*

BAYARD: Were you . . . political or something?

VON BERG: No, no, I never had any interest in that direction. *Slight pause.* Of course, there is this resentment toward the nobility. That might explain it.

LEDUC: In the Nazis? Resentment?

VON BERG, *surprised:* Yes, certainly.

LEDUC, *with no evident viewpoint but with a neutral but pressing interest in drawing the nobleman out:* Really. I've never been aware of that.

VON BERG: Oh, I assure you.

LEDUC: But on what ground?

VON BERG—*laughs, embarrassed to have to even suggest he is offended:* You're not asking that seriously.

LEDUC: Don't be offended, I'm simply ignorant of that situation. I suppose I have taken for granted that the aristocracy is . . . always behind a reactionary regime.

VON BERG: Oh, there are some, certainly. But for the most part they never took responsibility, in any case.

LEDUC: That interests me. So you still take seriously the . . . the title and . . .

VON BERG: It is not a "title"; it is my name, my family. Just as you have a name, and a family. And you are not inclined to dishonor them, I presume.

LEDUC: I see. And by responsibility, you mean, I suppose, that—

VON BERG: Oh, I don't know; whatever that means. *He glances at his watch.*

Pause.

LEDUC: Please forgive me, I didn't mean to pry into your affairs. *Pause.* I'd never thought about it, and it's obvious now—they *would* want to destroy whatever power you have.

VON BERG: Oh, no, I have no power. And if I did it would be a day's work for them to destroy it. That's not the issue.

Pause.

LEDUC, *fascinated—he is drawn to some truth in Von Berg:* What is it, then? Believe me, I'm not being critical. Quite the contrary . . .

VON BERG: But these are obvious answers! *He laughs.* I have a certain . . . standing. My name is a thousand years old, and they know the danger if someone like me is perhaps . . . not vulgar enough.

LEDUC: And by vulgar you mean . . .

VON BERG: Well, don't you think Nazism . . . whatever else it may be . . . is an outburst of vulgarity? An ocean of vulgarity?

BAYARD: I'm afraid it's a lot more than that, my friend.

VON BERG, *polite, to Bayard:* I am sure it is, yes.

BAYARD: You make it sound like they have bad table manners, that's all.

VON BERG: They certainly do, yes. Nothing angers them more than a sign of any ... refinement. It is decadent, you see.

BAYARD: What kind of statement is that? You mean you left Austria because of their table manners?

VON BERG: Table manners, yes; and their adoration of dreadful art; and grocery clerks in uniform telling the orchestra what music it may not play. Vulgarity can be enough to send a man out of his country, yes, I think so.

BAYARD: In other words, if they had good taste in art, and elegant table manners, and let the orchestra play whatever it liked, they'd be all right with you.

VON BERG: But how would that be possible? Can people with respect for art go about hounding Jews? Making a prison of Europe, pushing themselves forward as a race of policemen and brutes? Is that possible for artistic people?

MONCEAU: I'd like to agree with you, Prince von Berg, but I have to say that the German audiences—I've played there—no audience is as sensitive to the smallest nuance of a performance; they sit in the theater with respect, like in a church. And nobody listens to music like a German. Don't you think so? It's a passion with them.

Pause.

VON BERG, *appalled at the truth:* I'm afraid that is true, yes. *Pause.* I don't know what to say. *He is depressed, deeply at a loss.*

LEDUC: Perhaps it isn't those people who are doing this.

VON BERG: I'm afraid I know many cultivated people who ... did become Nazis. Yes, they did. Art is perhaps no defense against this. It's curious how one takes certain ideas for granted. Until this moment I had thought of art as a ... *To Bayard:* You may be right—I don't understand very much about it. Actually, I'm essentially a musician—in an amateur way, of course, and politics has never ...

The office door opens and Marchand appears, backing out, talking to someone within. He is putting a leather document-wallet into his breast pocket, while with the other hand he holds a white pass.

MARCHAND: That's perfectly all right, I understand perfectly. Good day, gentlemen. *Holding up the pass to them:* I show the pass at the door? Thank you.

Shutting the door, he turns and hurries past the line of prisoners, and, as he passes the Boy . . .

BOY: What'd they ask you, sir?

Marchand turns up the corridor without glancing at the Boy, and as he approaches the end the Guard, hearing him, appears there. He hands the pass to the Guard and goes out. The Guard moves around the turning of the corridor and disappears.

LEBEAU, *half mystified, half hopeful:* I could have sworn he was a Jew! *To Bayard:* Didn't you think so?

Slight pause.

BAYARD—*clearly he did think so:* You have papers, don't you?

LEBEAU: Oh sure, I have good papers. *He takes rumpled documents out of his pants pocket.*

BAYARD: Well, just insist they're valid. Maybe that's what he did.

LEBEAU: I wish you'd take a look at them, will you?

BAYARD: I'm no expert.

LEBEAU: I'd like your opinion, though. You seem to know what's going on. How they look to you?

Bayard quickly hides the papers as the office door opens. The Professor appears and indicates the Gypsy.

PROFESSOR: Next. You. Come with me.

The Gypsy gets up and starts toward him. The Professor indicates the pot in the Gypsy's hand.

You can leave that.

The Gypsy hesitates, glances at the pot.

I said leave it there.

The Gypsy puts the pot down on the bench unwillingly.

GYPSY: Fix. No steal.

PROFESSOR: Go in.

GYPSY, *indicating the pot, warning the others:* That's mine.

The Gypsy goes into the office. The Professor follows him in and shuts the door. Bayard takes the pot, bends the handle off, puts it in his pocket, and sets the pot back where it was.

LEBEAU, *turning back to Bayard, indicating his papers:* What do you think?

BAYARD—*holds a paper up to the light, turns it over, gives it back to Lebeau:* Look good far as I can tell.

MONCEAU: That man did seem Jewish to me. Didn't he to you, Doctor?

LEDUC: I have no idea. Jews are not a race, you know. They can look like anybody.

LEBEAU, *with the joy of near-certainty:* He just probably had good papers. Because I know people have papers, I mean all you have to do is look at them and you know they're phony. But I mean if you have good papers, right?

Monceau has meanwhile taken out his papers and is examining them. The Boy does the same with his. Lebeau turns to Leduc.

That's true, though. My father looks like an Englishman. The trouble is I took after my mother.

BOY, *to Bayard, offering his papers:* Could you look at mine?

BAYARD: I'm no expert, kid. Anyway, don't sit there looking at them like that.

Monceau puts his away, as the Boy does. A pause. They wait.

MONCEAU: I think it's a question of one's credibility—that man just now did carry himself with a certain confidence. . . .

The Old Jew begins to pitch forward onto the floor. Von Berg catches him and with the Boy helps him back onto the seat.

LEBEAU, *with heightened nervousness:* Christ, you'd think they'd shave off their beards. I mean, to walk around with a beard like that in a country like this!

Monceau looks at his beard, and Lebeau touches it.

Well, I just don't waste time shaving, but . . .

VON BERG, *to the Old Jew:* Are you all right, sir?

Leduc bends over Von Berg's lap and feels the Old Jew's pulse. Pause. He lets his hand go, and looks toward Lebeau.

LEDUC: Were you serious? They actually measured your nose?

LEBEAU: With his fingers. That civilian. They called him "professor." *Pause. Then, to Bayard:* I think you're right; it's all a question of your papers. That businessman certainly looked Jewish. . . .

MONCEAU: I'm not so sure now.

LEBEAU, *angrily:* A minute ago you were sure, now suddenly . . . !

MONCEAU: Well, even if he wasn't—it only means it really is a general checkup. On the whole population.

LEBEAU: Hey, that's right too! *Slight pause.* Actually, I'm often taken for a gentile myself. Not that I give a damn but most of the time, I ... *To Von Berg:* How about you, they measure your nose?

VON BERG: No, they told me to get into the car, that was all.

LEBEAU: Because actually yours looks bigger than mine.

BAYARD: Will you cut that out! Just cut it out, will you?

LEBEAU: Can't I try to find out what I'm in for?

BAYARD: Did you ever think of anything beside yourself? Just because you're an artist? You people demoralize everybody!

LEBEAU, *with unconcealed terror:* What the hell am I supposed to think of? Who're you thinking of?

The office door opens. The Police Captain appears, and gestures toward Bayard.

CAPTAIN: Come inside here.

Bayard, trying hard to keep his knees from shaking, stands. Ferrand, a café proprietor, comes hurrying down the corridor with a tray of coffee things covered with a large napkin. He has an apron on. Ah, at last!

FERRAND: Sorry, Captain, but for you I had to make some fresh.

CAPTAIN, *as he goes into the office behind Ferrand:* Put it on my desk.

The door is closed. Bayard sits, wipes his face. Pause.

MONCEAU, *to Bayard, quietly:* Would you mind if I made a suggestion?

Bayard turns to him, already defensive.

You looked terribly uncertain of yourself when you stood up just now.

BAYARD, *taking offense:* Me uncertain? You've got the wrong man.

MONCEAU: Please, I'm not criticizing you.

BAYARD: Naturally I'm a little nervous, facing a room full of Fascists like this.

MONCEAU: But that's why one must seem especially self-confident. I'm quite sure that's what got that businessman through so quickly. I've had similar experiences on trains, and even in Paris when they stopped me several times. The important thing is not to look like a victim. Or even to feel like one. They can be very stupid, but they do have a sense for victims; they know when someone has nothing to hide.

LEDUC: But how does one avoid feeling like a victim?

MONCEAU: One must create one's own reality in this world. I'm an actor, we do this all the time. The audience, you know, is very sadistic; it looks for your first sign of weakness. So you must try to think of something that makes you feel self-assured; anything at all. Like the day, perhaps, when your father gave you a compliment, or a teacher was amazed at your cleverness ... Any thought—*to Bayard*—that makes you feel ... valuable. After all, you are trying to create an illusion; to make them believe you are who your papers say you are.

LEDUC: That's true, we must not play the part they have written for us. That's very wise. You must have great courage.

MONCEAU: I'm afraid not. But I have talent instead. *To Bayard:* One must show them the face of a man who is right, not a man who is suspect and wrong. They sense the difference.

BAYARD: My friend, you're in a bad way if you have to put on an act to feel your rightness. The bourgeoisie sold France; they let in the Nazis to destroy the French working class. Remember the causes of this war and you've got *real* confidence.

LEDUC: Excepting that the causes of this war keep changing so often.

BAYARD: Not if you understand the economic and political forces.

LEDUC: Still, when Germany attacked us the Communists refused to support France. They pronounced it an imperialist war. Until the Nazis turned against Russia; then in one afternoon it all changed into a sacred battle against tyranny. What confidence can one feel from an understanding that turns upside down in an afternoon?

BAYARD: My friend, without the Red Army standing up to them right now you could forget France for a thousand years!

LEDUC: I agree. But that does not require an understanding of political and economic forces—it is simply faith in the Red Army.

BAYARD: It is faith in the future; and the future is Socialist. And that is what *I* take in there with *me*.

To the others:

I warn you—I've had experience with these types. You'd better ram a viewpoint up your spine or you'll break in half.

LEDUC: I understand. You mean it's important not to feel alone, is that it?

BAYARD: None of us is alone. We're members of history. Some of us don't know it, but you'd better learn it for your own preservation.

LEDUC: That we are ... symbols.

BAYARD, *uncertain whether to agree:* Yes. Why not? Symbols, yes.

LEDUC: And you feel that helps you. Believe me, I am genuinely interested.

BAYARD: It helps me because it's the truth. What am I to them personally? Do they know me? You react personally to this, they'll turn you into an idiot. You can't make sense of this on a personal basis.

LEDUC: I agree. *Personally:* But the difficulty is—what can one be if not oneself? For example, the thought of torture or something of that sort ...

BAYARD, *struggling to live his conviction:* Well, it frightens me—of course. But they can't torture the future; it's out of their hands. Man was not made to be the slave of Big Business. Whatever they do, something inside me is laughing. Because they can't win. Impossible. *He has stiffened himself against his rising fear.*

LEDUC: So that in a sense ... you aren't here. You personally.

BAYARD: In a sense. Why, what's wrong with that?

LEDUC: Nothing; it may be the best way to hold on to oneself. It's only that ordinarily one tries to experience life, to be in spirit where one's body is. For some of us it's difficult to shift gears and go into reverse. But that's not a problem for you.

BAYARD, *solicitously:* You think a man can ever be himself in this society? When millions go hungry and a few live like kings, and whole races are slaves to the stock market—how can you be yourself in such a world? I put in ten hours a day for a few francs, I see people who never bend their backs and they own the planet....
How can my spirit be where my body is? I'd have to be an ape.

VON BERG: Then where is your spirit?

BAYARD: In the future. In the day when the working class is master of the world. *That's* my confidence ... *To Monceau:* Not some borrowed personality.

VON BERG, *wide-eyed, genuinely asking:* But don't you think ... excuse me. Are not most of the Nazis ... of the working class?

BAYARD: Well, naturally, with enough propaganda you can confuse anybody.

VON BERG: I see. *Slight pause.* But in that case, how can one have such confidence in them?

BAYARD: Who do you have confidence in, the aristocracy?

VON BERG: Very little. But in certain aristocrats, yes. And in certain common people.

BAYARD: Are you telling me that history is a question of "certain people"? Are we sitting here because we are "certain people"? Is any of us an individual to them? Class interest makes history, not individuals.

VON BERG: Yes. That seems to be the trouble.

BAYARD: Facts are not trouble. A human being has to glory in the facts.

VON BERG, *with a deep, anxious out-reaching to Bayard:* But the facts . . . Dear sir, what if the facts are dreadful? And will always be dreadful?

BAYARD: So is childbirth, so is . . .

VON BERG: But a child comes of it. What if nothing comes of the facts but endless, endless disaster? Believe me, I am happy to meet a man who is not cynical; any faith is precious these days. But to give your faith to a . . . a class of people is impossible, simply impossible—ninety-nine per cent of the Nazis are ordinary working-class people!

BAYARD: I concede it *is* possible to propagandize . . .

VON BERG, *with an untoward anxiety, as though the settlement of this issue is intimate with him:* But what can *not* be propagandized? Isn't that the . . . the only point? A few individuals. Don't you think so?

BAYARD: You're an intelligent man, Prince. Are you seriously telling me that five, ten, a thousand, ten thousand decent people of integrity are all that stand between us and the end of everything? You mean this whole world is going to hang on that thread?

VON BERG, *struck:* I'm afraid it does sound impossible.

BAYARD: If I thought that, I wouldn't have the strength to walk through the door, I wouldn't know how to put one foot in front of the other.

VON BERG—*slight pause:* Yes. I hadn't really considered it that way. But . . . you really think the working class will . . .

BAYARD: They will destroy Fascism because it is against their interest.

VON BERG—*nods:* But in that case, isn't it even more of a mystery?

BAYARD: I see no mystery.

VON BERG: But they adore Hitler.

BAYARD: How can you say that? Hitler is the creation of the capitalist class.

VON BERG, *in terrible mourning and anxiety:* But they adore him! My own cook, my gardeners, the people who work in my forests, the chauffeur, the gamekeeper—they are *Nazis*! I saw it coming over them, the love for this creature—my housekeeper dreams of him in her bed, she'd serve my breakfast like a god had slept with her; in a dream slicing my toast! I saw this adoration in my own house! That, that is the dreadful fact. *Controlling himself:* I beg your pardon, but it disturbs me. I admire your faith; all faith to some degree is beautiful. And when I know that yours is based on something so untrue—it's terribly disturbing. *Quietly:* In any case, I cannot glory in the facts; there is no reassurance there. They adore him, the salt of the earth. . . . *Staring:* Adore him.

There is a burst of laughter from within the office. He glances there, as they all do.

Strange; if I did not know that some of them in there were French, I'd have said they laugh like Germans. I suppose vulgarity has no nation, after all.

The door opens. Mr. Ferrand comes out, laughing; within, the laughter is subsiding. He waves within, closing the door. His smile drops. And as he goes past the Waiter, he glances at the door, then quickly leans over and whispers hurriedly into his ear. They all watch. Now Ferrand starts away. The Waiter reaches out and grasps his apron.

WAITER: Ferrand!

FERRAND, *brushing the Waiter's hand off his apron:* What can I do? I told you fifty times to get out of this city! Didn't I? *Starting to weep:* Didn't I?

He hurries up the corridor, wiping his tears with his apron. They all watch the Waiter, who sits there staring.

BAYARD: What? Tell me. Come on, I'm next, what'd he say?

WAITER—*whispers, staring ahead in shock:* It's not to work.

LEDUC, *leaning over toward him to hear:* What?

WAITER: They have furnaces.

BAYARD: What furnaces? . . . Talk! What is it?

WAITER: He heard the detectives; they came in for coffee just before. People get burned up in furnaces. It's not to work. They burn you up in Poland.

Silence. A long moment passes.

MONCEAU: That is the most fantastic idiocy I ever heard in my life!

LEBEAU, *to the Waiter:* As long as you have regular French papers, though . . . There's nothing about Jew on *my* papers.

WAITER, *in a loud whisper:* They're going to look at your penis.

The Boy stands up as though with an electric shock. The door of the office opens; the Police Captain appears and beckons to Bayard. The Boy quickly sits.

CAPTAIN: You can come now.

Bayard stands, assuming an artificial and almost absurd posture of confidence. But approaching the Captain he achieves an authority.

BAYARD: I'm a master electrician with the railroad, Captain. You may have seen me there. I'm classified First Priority War Worker.

CAPTAIN: Inside.

BAYARD: You can check with Transport Minister Duquesne.

CAPTAIN: You telling me my business?

BAYARD: No, but we can all use advice from time to time.

CAPTAIN: Inside.

BAYARD: Right.

Without hesitation Bayard walks into the office, the Captain following and closing the door.

A long silence. Monceau, after a moment, smooths out a rough place on the felt of his hat. Lebeau looks at his papers, slowly rubbing his beard with the back of his hand, staring in terror. The Old Jew draws his bundle deeper under his feet. Leduc takes out a nearly empty pack of cigarettes, starts to take one for himself, then silently stands, crosses the line of men, and offers it to them. Lebeau takes one.

They light up. Faintly, from the next-door building, an accordion is heard playing a popular tune.

LEBEAU: Leave it to a cop to play now.

WAITER: No, that's the boss's son, Maurice. They're starting to serve lunch.

Leduc, who has returned to his position as the last man on the bench, cranes around the corner of the corridor, observes, and sits back.

LEDUC, *quietly:* There's only one guard at the door. Three men could take him.

Pause. No one responds. Then . . .

VON BERG, *apologetically:* I'm afraid I'd only get in your way. I have no strength in my hands.

MONCEAU, *to Leduc:* You actually believe that, Doctor? About the furnaces?

LEDUC—*he thinks; then:* I believe it is possible, yes. Come, we can do something.

MONCEAU: But what good are dead Jews to them? They want free labor. It's senseless. You can say whatever you like, but the Germans are not illogical; there's no conceivable advantage for them in such a thing.

LEDUC: You can be sitting here and still speak of advantages? Is there a rational explanation for your sitting here? But you are sitting here, aren't you?

MONCEAU: But an atrocity like that is . . . beyond any belief.

VON BERG: That is exactly the point.

MONCEAU: *You* don't believe it. Prince, you can't tell me you believe such a thing.

VON BERG: I find it the most believable atrocity I have heard.

LEBEAU: But why?

Slight pause.

VON BERG: Because it *is* so inconceivably vile. That is their power. To do the inconceivable; it paralyzes the rest of us. But if that is its purpose it is not the cause. Many times I used to ask my friends—if you love your country why is it necessary to hate other countries? To be a good German why must you despise everything that is not German? Until I realized the answer. They do these things not because they are German but because they are nothing. It is the hallmark of the age—the less you exist the more important it is to make a clear impression. I can see them discussing it as a kind of ... truthfulness. After all, what *is* self-restraint but hypocrisy? If you despise Jews the most honest thing is to burn them up. And the fact that it costs money, and uses up trains and personnel—this only guarantees the integrity, the purity, the existence of their feelings. They would even tell you that only a Jew would think of the cost. They are poets, they are striving for a new nobility, the nobility of the totally vulgar. I believe in this fire; it would prove for all time that they exist, yes, and that they were sincere. You must not calculate these people with some nineteenth-century arithmetic of loss and gain. Their motives are musical, and people are merely sounds they play. And in my opinion, win or lose this war, they have pointed the way to the future. What one used to conceive a human being to be will have no room on this earth. I would try anything to get out.

A pause.

MONCEAU: But they arrested you. That German professor is an expert. There is nothing Jewish about you. . . .

VON BERG: I have an accent. I noticed he reacted when I started to speak. It is an Austrian inflection. He may think I am another refugee.

The door opens. The Professor comes out, and indicates the Waiter.

PROFESSOR: Next. You.

The Waiter makes himself small, pressing up against Lebeau. Don't be alarmed, it's only to check your papers.

The Waiter suddenly bends over and runs away—around the corner and up the corridor. The Guard appears at the end, collars him, and walks him back down the corridor.

WAITER, *to the Guard:* Felix, you know me. Felix, my wife will go crazy. Felix . . .

PROFESSOR: Take him in the office.

The Police Captain appears in the office doorway.

GUARD: There's nobody at the door.

CAPTAIN—*grabs the Waiter from the Guard:* Get in here, you Jew son-of-a-bitch. . . .

He throws the Waiter into the office; the Waiter collides with the Major, who is just coming out to see what the disturbance is. The

Major grips his thigh in pain, pushing the Waiter clear. The Waiter slides to the Major's feet, weeping pleadingly. The Captain strides over and violently jerks him to his feet and pushes him into the office, going in after him.

From within, unseen:

You want trouble? You want trouble?

The Waiter is heard crying out; there is the sound of blows struck. Quiet. The Professor starts toward the door. The Major takes his arm and leads him down to the extreme forward edge of the stage, out of hearing of the prisoners.

MAJOR: Wouldn't it be much simpler if they were just asked whether they . . .

Impatiently, without replying, the Professor goes over to the line of prisoners.

PROFESSOR: Will any of you admit right now that you are carrying forged identification papers?

Silence.

So. In short, you are all bona fide Frenchmen.

Silence. He goes over to the Old Jew, bends into his face.

Are there any Jews among you?

Silence. Then he returns to the Major.

There's the problem, Major; either we go house by house investigating everyone's biography, or we make this inspection.

MAJOR: That electrician fellow just now, though—I thought he made a point there. In fact, only this morning in the hospital, while I was waiting my turn for X-ray, another officer, a German officer, a captain, in fact—his bathrobe happened to fall open . . .

PROFESSOR: It is entirely possible.

MAJOR: It was unmistakable, Professor.

PROFESSOR: Let us be clear, Major; the Race Institute does not claim that circumcision is conclusive proof of Jewish blood. The Race Institute recognizes that a small proportion of gentiles . . .

MAJOR: I don't see any reason not to say it, Professor—I happen to be, myself.

PROFESSOR: Very well, but I certainly would never mistake you for a Jew. Any more than you could mistake a pig for a horse. Science is not capricious, Major; my degree is in racial anthropology. In any case, we can certainly separate the gentiles by this kind of examination.

He has taken the Major's arm to lead him back to the office.

MAJOR: Excuse me. I'll be back in a few minutes. *Moving to leave:* You can carry on without me.

PROFESSOR: Major; you have your orders; you are in command of this operation. I must insist you take your place beside me.

MAJOR: I think some mistake has been made. I am a line officer, I have no experience with things of this kind. My training is engineering and artillery.

Slight pause.

PROFESSOR—*he speaks more quietly, his eyes ablaze:* We'd better be candid, Major. Are you refusing this assignment?

MAJOR, *registering the threat he feels:* I'm in pain today, Professor. They are still removing fragments. In fact, I understood I was only to . . . hold this desk down until an S.S. officer took over. I'm more or less on loan, you see, from the regular Army.

PROFESSOR—*takes his arm, draws him down to the edge of the stage again:* But the Army is not exempt from carrying out the Racial Program. My orders come from the top. And my report will go to the top. You understand me.

MAJOR—*his resistance seems to fall:* I do, yes.

PROFESSOR: Look now, if you wish to be relieved, I can easily telephone General von—

MAJOR: No—no, that's all right. I . . . I'll be back in a few minutes.

PROFESSOR: This is bizarre, Major—how long am I supposed to wait for you?

MAJOR, *holding back an outburst of resentment:* I need a walk. I am not used to sitting in an office. I see nothing bizarre in it, I am a line officer, and this kind of business takes a little getting used to. *Through his teeth:* What do you find bizarre in it?

PROFESSOR: Very well.

Slight pause.

MAJOR: I'll be back in ten minutes. You can carry on.

PROFESSOR: I will not continue without you, Major. The Army's responsibility is quite as great as mine here.

MAJOR: I won't be long.

The Professor turns abruptly and strides into the office, slamming the door shut. Very much wanting to get out, the Major goes up the corridor. Leduc stands as he passes.

LEDUC: Major . . .

The Major limps past him without turning, up the corridor and out. Silence.

BOY: Mister?

Leduc turns to him.

I'd try it with you.

LEDUC, *to Monceau and Lebeau:* What about you two?

LEBEAU: Whatever you say, but I'm so hungry I wouldn't do you much good.

LEDUC: You can walk up to him and start an argument. Distract his attention. Then we—

MONCEAU: You're both crazy, they'll shoot you down.

LEDUC: Some of us might make it. There's only one man at the door. This neighborhood is full of alleyways—you could disappear in twenty yards.

MONCEAU: How long would you be free—an hour? And when they catch you they'll really tear you apart.

BOY: Please! I have to get out. I was on my way to the pawnshop. *Takes out a ring.* It's my mother's wedding ring, it's all that's left. She's waiting for the money. They have nothing in the house to eat.

MONCEAU: You take my advice, boy; don't do anything, they'll let you go.

LEDUC: Like the electrician?

MONCEAU: He was obviously a Communist. And the waiter irritated the Captain.

LEBEAU: Look, I'll try it with you but don't expect too much; I'm weak as a chicken, I haven't eaten since yesterday.

LEDUC, *to Monceau:* It would be better with another man. The boy is very light. If you and the boy rush him I'll get his gun away.

VON BERG, *to Leduc, looking at his hands:* Forgive me.

Monceau springs up, goes to a box, and sits.

MONCEAU: I am not going to risk my life for nothing. That businessman had a Jewish face. *To Lebeau:* You said so yourself.

LEBEAU, *to Leduc, appeasingly:* I did. I thought so. Look, if your papers are good, maybe that's it.

LEDUC, *to Lebeau and Monceau:* You know yourself the Germans have been moving into the Southern Zone; you see they are picking up Jews; a man has just told you that you are marked for destruction. . . .

MONCEAU—*indicates Von Berg:* They took him in. Nobody's explained it.

VON BERG: My accent . . .

MONCEAU: My dear Prince, only an idiot could mistake you for anything but an Austrian of the upper class. I took you for nobility the minute you walked in.

LEDUC: But if it's a general checkup why would they be looking at penises?

MONCEAU: There's no evidence of that!

LEDUC: The waiter's boss . . .

MONCEAU, *suppressing a nervous shout:* He overheard two French detectives who can't possibly know anything about what happens in Poland. And if they do that kind of thing, it's not the end either—I had Jew stamped on my passport in Paris and I was playing Cyrano at the same time.

VON BERG: Really! Cyrano!

LEBEAU: Then why'd you leave Paris?

MONCEAU: It was an absolutely idiotic accident. I was rooming with another actor, a gentile. And he kept warning me to get out. But naturally one doesn't just give up a role like that. But one night I let myself be influenced by him. He pointed out that I had a number of books which were on the forbidden list—of Communist literature—I mean things like Sinclair Lewis, and Thomas Mann, and even a few things by Friedrich Engels, which everybody was reading at one time. And I decided I might as well get rid of them. So we made bundles and I lived on the fifth floor of a walkup and we'd take turns going down to the street and just leaving them on benches or in doorways or anywhere at all. It was after midnight, and I was just dropping a bundle into the gutter near the Opéra, when I noticed a man standing in a doorway watching me. At that moment I realized that I had stamped my name and address in every one of those books.

VON BERG: Hah! What did you do?

MONCEAU: Started walking, and kept right on down here to the Unoccupied Zone. *An outcry of remorse:* But in my opinion, if I'd done nothing at all I might still be working!

LEDUC, *with higher urgency, but deeply sympathetic; to Monceau:* Listen to me for one moment. I beg you. There is only one man guarding that door; we may never get another chance like this again.

LEBEAU: That's another thing; if it was all that serious, wouldn't they be guarding us more heavily? I mean, that's a point.

LEDUC: That is exactly the point. They are relying on us.

MONCEAU: Relying on us!

LEDUC: Yes. To project our own reasonable ideas into their heads. It is reasonable that a light guard means the thing is not important. They rely on our own logic to immobilize ourselves. But you have just told us how you went all over Paris advertising the fact that you owned forbidden books.

MONCEAU: But I didn't do it purposely.

LEDUC: May I guess that you could no longer bear the tension of remaining in Paris? But that you wanted to keep your role in Cyrano and had to find some absolute compulsion to save your own life? It was your unconscious mind that saved you. Do you understand? You cannot wager your life on a purely rational analysis of this situation. Listen to your feelings; you must certainly *feel* the danger here. . . .

MONCEAU, *in high anxiety:* I played in Germany. That audience could not burn up actors in a furnace. *Turning to Von Berg:* Prince, you cannot tell me you believe that!

VON BERG, *after a pause:* I supported a small orchestra. When the Germans came into Austria three of the players prepared to escape. I convinced them no harm would come to them; I brought them to my castle; we all lived together. The oboist was twenty, twenty-one—the heart stopped when he played certain tones. They came for him in the garden. They took him out of his chair. The instrument lay on the lawn like a dead bone. I made certain inquiries; he is dead now. And it was even more terrible—they came and sat down and listened until the rehearsal was over. And *then* they took him. It is as though they wished to take him at exactly the moment when he was most beautiful. I know how you feel—but I tell you nothing any longer is forbidden. Nothing. *Tears are in his eyes; he turns to Leduc.* I ask you to forgive me, Doctor.

    Pause.

BOY: Will they let you go?

VON BERG, *with a guilty glance at the Boy:* I suppose. If this is all to catch Jews they will let me go.

BOY: Would you take this ring? And bring it back to my mother?

    He stretches his hand out with the ring. Von Berg does not touch it.

Number Nine Rue Charlot. Top floor. Hirsch. Sarah Hirsch. She has long brown hair . . . be sure it's her. She has a little beauty mark on this cheek. There are two other families in the apartment, so be sure it's her.

    Von Berg looks into the Boy's face. Silence. Then he turns to Leduc.

VON BERG: Come. Tell me what to do. I'll try to help you. *To Leduc:* Doctor?

LEDUC: I'm afraid it's hopeless.

VON BERG: Why?

LEDUC—*stares ahead, then looks at Lebeau:* He's weak with hunger, and the boy's like a feather. I wanted to get away, not just slaughtered. *Pause. With bitter irony:* I live in the country, you see; I haven't talked to anybody in so long, I'm afraid I came in here with the wrong assumptions.

MONCEAU: If you're trying to bait me, Doctor, forget it.

LEDUC: Would you mind telling me, are you religious?

MONCEAU: Not at all.

LEDUC: Then why do you feel this desire to be sacrificed?

MONCEAU: I ask you to stop talking to me.

LEDUC: But you are making a gift of yourself. You are the only able-bodied man here, aside from me, and yet you feel no impulse to do something? I don't understand your air of confidence.

    Pause.

MONCEAU: I refuse to play a part I do not fit. Everyone is playing the victim these days; hopeless, hysterical, they always assume the worst. I have papers; I will present them with the single idea that they must be honored. I think that is exactly what saved that businessman. You accuse us of acting the part the Germans created for us; I think you're the one who's doing that by acting so desperate.

LEDUC: And if, despite your act, they throw you into a freight car?

MONCEAU: I don't think they will.

LEDUC: But if they do. You certainly have enough imagination to visualize that.

MONCEAU: In that case, I will have done my best. I know what failure is; it took me a long time to make good; I haven't the personality for leading roles; everyone said I was crazy to stay in the profession. But I did, and I imposed my idea on others.

LEDUC: In other words, you will create yourself.

MONCEAU: Every actor creates himself.

LEDUC: But when they tell you to open your fly.

Monceau is silent, furious.

Please don't stop now; I'm very interested. How do you regard that moment?

Monceau is silent.

Believe me, I am only trying to understand this. I am incapable of penetrating such passivity; I ask you what is in your mind when you face the command to open your fly. I am being as impersonal, as scientific as I know how to be—I believe I am going to be murdered. What do you believe will happen when they point to that spot between your legs?

Pause.

MONCEAU: I have nothing to say to you.

LEBEAU: I'll tell you what I'll feel. *Indicates Von Berg.* I'll wish I was him.

LEDUC: To be someone else.

LEBEAU, *exhausted:* Yes. To have been arrested by mistake. God—to see them relaxing when they realize I am innocent.

LEDUC: You feel guilty, then.

LEBEAU—*he has gradually become closer to exhaustion:* A little, I guess. Not for anything I've done but . . . I don't know why.

LEDUC: For being a Jew, perhaps?

LEBEAU: I'm not ashamed of being a Jew.

LEDUC: Then why feel guilty?

LEBEAU: I don't know. Maybe it's that they keep saying such terrible things about us, and you can't answer. And after years and years of it, you ... I wouldn't say you believe it, but ... you do, a little. It's a funny thing—I used to say to my mother and father just what you're saying. We could have gone to America a month before the invasion. But they wouldn't leave Paris. She had this brass bed, and carpets, and draperies and all kinds of junk. Like him with his Cyrano. And I told them, "You're doing just what they want you to do!" But, see, people won't believe they can be killed. Not them with their brass bed and their carpets and their faces. . . .

LEDUC: But do you believe it? It seems to me you don't believe it yourself.

LEBEAU: I believe it. They only caught me this morning because I ... I always used to walk in the morning before I sat down to work. And I wanted to do it again. I knew I shouldn't go outside. But you get tired of believing in the truth. You get tired of seeing things clearly. *Pause.* I always collected my illusions in the morning. I could never paint what I saw, only what I imagined. And this morning, danger or no danger, I just had to get out, to walk around, to see something real, something else but the inside of my head ... and I hardly turned the corner and that motherless son-of-a-bitch of a scientist got out of the car with his fingers going for my nose. . . . *Pause.* I believe I can die. But you can get so tired ...

LEDUC: That it's not too bad.

LEBEAU: Almost, yes.

LEDUC, *glancing at them all:* So that one way or the other, with illusions or without them, exhausted or fresh—we have been trained to die. The Jew and the gentile both.

MONCEAU: You're still trying to bait me, Doctor, but if you want to commit suicide do it alone, don't involve others. The fact is there are laws and every government enforces its laws; and I want it understood that I have nothing to do with any of this talk.

LEDUC, *angering now:* Every government does not have laws condemning people because of their race.

MONCEAU: I beg your pardon. The Russians condemn the middle class, the English have condemned the Indians, Africans, and anybody else they could lay their hands on, the French, the Italians ...

every nation has condemned somebody because of his race, including the Americans and what they do to Negroes. The vast majority of mankind is condemned because of its race. What do you advise all these people—suicide?

LEDUC: What do you advise?

MONCEAU, *seeking and finding conviction:* I go on the assumption that if I obey the law with dignity I will live in peace. I may not like the law, but evidently the majority does, or they would overthrow it. And I'm speaking now of the French majority, who outnumber the Germans in this town fifty to one. These are French police, don't forget, not German. And if by some miracle you did knock out that guard you would find yourself in a city where not one person in a thousand would help you. And it's got nothing to do with being Jewish or not Jewish. It is what the world is, so why don't you stop insulting others with romantic challenges!

LEDUC: In short, because the world is indifferent you will wait calmly and with great dignity—to open your fly.

MONCEAU—*frightened and furious, he stands:* I'll tell you what I think; I think it's people like you who brought this on us. People who give Jews a reputation for subversion, and this Talmudic analysis, and this everlasting, niggling discontent.

LEDUC: Then I will tell you that I was wrong before; you didn't advertise your name on those forbidden books in order to find a reason to leave Paris and save yourself. It was in order to get yourself caught and be put out of your misery. Your heart is conquered territory, mister.

MONCEAU: If we meet again you will pay for that remark.

LEDUC: Conquered territory! *He leans forward, his head in his hands.*

BOY, *reaching over to hand the ring to Von Berg:* Will you do it? Number Nine Rue Charlot?

VON BERG, *deeply affected:* I will try.

He takes the ring. The Boy immediately stands.

LEDUC: Where are you going?

The Boy, terrified but desperate, moves on the balls of his feet to the corridor and peeks around the corner. Leduc stands, tries to draw him back.

You can't; it'll take three men to . . .

The boy shakes loose and walks rapidly up the hallway. Leduc hesitates, then goes after him.

Wait! Wait a minute! I'm coming.

The Major enters the corridor at its far end. The Boy halts, Leduc now beside him. For a moment they stand facing him. Then they turn and come down the corridor and sit, the Major following them. He touches Leduc's sleeve, and Leduc stands and follows him downstage.

MAJOR—*he is "high"—with drink and a flow of emotion:* That's impossible. Don't try it. There are sentries on both corners. *Glancing toward the office door:* Captain, I would only like to say that . . . this is all as inconceivable to me as it is to you. Can you believe that?

LEDUC: I'd believe it if you shot yourself. And better yet, if you took a few of them with you.

MAJOR, *wiping his mouth with the back of his hand:* We would all be replaced by tomorrow morning, wouldn't we?

LEDUC: We might get out alive, though; you could see to that.

MAJOR: They'd find you soon.

LEDUC: Not me.

MAJOR, *with a manic amusement, yet deeply questioning:* Why do you deserve to live more than I do?

LEDUC: Because I am incapable of doing what you are doing. I am better for the world than you.

MAJOR: It means nothing to you that I have feelings about this?

LEDUC: Nothing whatever, unless you get us out of here.

MAJOR: And then what? Then what?

LEDUC: I will remember a decent German, an honorable German.

MAJOR: Will that make a difference?

LEDUC: I will love you as long as I live. Will anyone do that now?

MAJOR: That means so much to you—that someone love you?

LEDUC: That I be worthy of someone's love, yes. And respect.

MAJOR: It's amazing; you don't understand anything. Nothing of that kind is left, don't you understand that yet?

LEDUC: It is left in me.

MAJOR, *more loudly, a fury rising in him:* There are no persons any more, don't you see that? There will never be persons again. What do I care if you love me? Are you out of your mind? What am I, a dog that I must be loved? You—*turning to all of them*—goddamned Jews!

The door opens; the Professor and the Police Captain appear. Like dogs, Jew-dogs. Look at him—*indicating the Old Jew*—with his paws folded. Look what happens when I yell at him. Dog! He doesn't move. Does he move? Do you see him moving? *He strides to the Professor and takes him by the arm.* But we move, don't we? We measure your noses, don't we, Herr Professor, and we look at your cocks, we keep moving continually!

PROFESSOR, *with a gesture to draw him aside:* Major . . .

MAJOR: Hands off, you civilian bastard.

PROFESSOR: I think . . .

MAJOR, *drawing his revolver:* Not a word!

PROFESSOR: You're drunk.

The Major fires into the ceiling. The prisoners tense in shock.

MAJOR: Everything stops now.

He goes in thought, revolver cocked in his hand, and sits beside Lebeau.

Now it is all stopped.

His hands are shaking. He sniffs in his running nose. He crosses his legs to control them, and looks at Leduc, who is still standing.

Now you tell me. You tell me. Now nothing is moving. You tell me. Go ahead now.

LEDUC: What shall I tell you?

MAJOR: Tell me how . . . how there can be persons any more. I have you at the end of this revolver—*indicates the Professor*—he has me—and somebody has him—and somebody has somebody else. Now tell me.

LEDUC: I told you.

MAJOR: I won't repeat it. I am a man of honor. What do you make of that? I will not tell them what you advised me to do. What do you say—damned decent of me, isn't it . . . not to repeat your advice?

Leduc is silent. The Major gets up, comes to Leduc. Pause.

You are a combat veteran.

LEDUC: Yes.

MAJOR: No record of subversive activities against the German authority.

LEDUC: No.

MAJOR: If you were released, and the others were kept ... would you refuse?

Leduc starts to turn away. The Major nudges him with the pistol, forcing him face to face.

Would you refuse?

LEDUC: No.

MAJOR: And walk out of that door with a light heart?

LEDUC—*he is looking at the floor now:* I don't know. *He starts to put his trembling hands into his pockets.*

MAJOR: Don't hide your hands. I am trying to understand why you are better for the world than me. Why do you hide your hands? Would you go out that door with a light heart, run to your woman, drink a toast to your skin? ... Why are you better than anybody else?

LEDUC: I have no duty to make a gift of myself to your sadism.

MAJOR: But I do? To others' sadism? Of myself? I have that duty and you do not? To make a gift of myself?

LEDUC—*looks at the Professor and the Police Captain, glances back at the Major:* I have nothing to say.

MAJOR: That's better.

He suddenly gives Leduc an almost comradely push and nearly laughs. He puts his gun away, turns swaying to the Professor and with a victorious shout:

Next!

The Major brushes past the Professor into the office. Lebeau has not moved.

PROFESSOR: This way.

Lebeau stands up, starts sleepily toward the corridor, turns about, and moves into the office, the Professor following him.

CAPTAIN, *to Leduc:* Get back there.

Leduc returns to his seat. The Captain goes into the office; the door shuts. Pause.

MONCEAU: You happy now? You got him furious. You happy?

The door opens; the Captain appears, beckoning to Monceau.

CAPTAIN: Next.

Monceau gets up at once; taking papers out of his jacket, he fixes a smile on his face and walks with erect elegance to the Captain and with a slight bow, his voice cheerful:

MONCEAU: Good morning, Captain.

He goes right into the office; the Captain follows, and shuts the door. Pause.

BOY: Number Nine Rue Charlot. Please.

VON BERG: I'll give it to her.

BOY: I'm a minor. I'm not even fifteen. Does it apply to minors?
Captain opens the door, beckons to the Boy.

BOY, *standing:* I'm a minor. I'm not fifteen until February ...

CAPTAIN: Inside.

BOY, *halting before the Captain:* I could get my birth certificate for you.

CAPTAIN, *prodding him along:* Inside, inside.

They go in. The door shuts. The accordion is heard again from next door. The Old Jew begins to rock back and forth slightly, praying softly. Von Berg, his hand trembling as it passes down his cheek, stares at the Old Jew, then turns to Leduc on his other side. The three are alone now.

VON BERG: Does he realize what is happening?

LEDUC, *with an edgy note of impatience:* As much as anyone can, I suppose.

VON BERG: He seems to be watching it all from the stars. *Slight pause.* I wish we could have met under other circumstances. There are a great many things I'd like to have asked you.

LEDUC, *rapidly, sensing the imminent summons:* I'd appreciate it if you'd do me a favor.

VON BERG: Certainly.

LEDUC: Will you go and tell my wife?

VON BERG: Where is she?

LEDUC: Take the main highway north two kilometers. You'll see a small forest on the left and a dirt road leading into it. Go about a kilometer until you see the river. Follow the river to a small mill. They are in the tool shed behind the wheel.

VON BERG, *distressed:* And ... what shall I say?

LEDUC: That I've been arrested. And that there may be a possibility I can ... *Breaks off.* No, tell her the truth.

VON BERG, *alarmed:* What do you mean?

LEDUC: The furnaces. Tell her that.

VON BERG: But actually ... that's only a rumor, isn't it?

LEDUC—*turns to him—sharply:* I don't regard it as a rumor. It should be known. I never heard of it before. It must be known. Just take her aside—there's no need for the children to hear it, but tell her.

VON BERG: It's only that it would be difficult for me. To tell such a thing to a woman.

LEDUC: If it's happening you can find a way to say it, can't you?

VON BERG—*hesitates; he senses Leduc's resentment:* Very well. I'll tell her. It's only that I have no great . . . facility with women. But I'll do as you say. *Pause. He glances to the door.* They're taking longer with that boy. Maybe he *is* too young, you suppose?

Leduc does not answer. Von Berg seems suddenly hopeful.

They would stick to the rules, you know. . . . In fact, with the shortage of physicians you suppose they—

He breaks off.

I'm sorry if I said anything to offend you.

LEDUC, *struggling with his anger:* That's all right.

Slight pause. His voice is trembling with anger.

It's just that you keep finding these little shreds of hope and it's a little difficult.

VON BERG: Yes, I see. I beg your pardon. I understand.

Pause. Leduc glances at the door; he is shifting about in high tension.

Would you like to talk of something else, perhaps? Are you interested in . . . in music?

LEDUC, *desperately trying to control himself:* It's really quite simple. It's that you'll survive, you see.

VON BERG: But I can't help that, can I?

LEDUC: That only makes it worse! I'm sorry, one isn't always in control of one's emotions.

VON BERG: Doctor, I can promise you—it will not be easy for me to walk out of here. You don't know me.

LEDUC—*he tries not to reply; then:* I'm afraid it will only be difficult because it is so easy.

VON BERG: I think that's unfair.

LEDUC: Well, it doesn't matter.

VON BERG: It does to me. I . . . I can tell you that I was very close to suicide in Austria. Actually, that is why I left. When they murdered my musicians—not that alone, but when I told the story to many of my friends there was hardly any reaction. That was almost worse. Do you understand such indifference?

LEDUC—*he seems on the verge of an outbreak:* You have a curious idea of human nature. It's astounding you can go on with it in these times.

VON BERG, *with hand on heart:* But what is left if one gives up one's ideals? What *is* there?

LEDUC: Who are you talking about? You? Or me?

VON BERG: I'm terribly sorry. . . . I understand.

LEDUC: Why don't you just stop talking. I can't listen to anything. *Slight pause.* Forgive me. I do appreciate your feeling. *Slight pause.* I see it too clearly, perhaps—I know the violence inside these people's heads. It's difficult to listen to amelioration, even if it's well-meant.

VON BERG: I had no intention of ameliorating—

LEDUC: I think you do. And you must; you will survive, you will have to ameliorate it; just a little, just enough. It's no reflection on you. *Slight pause.* But, you see, this is why one gets so furious. Because all this suffering is so pointless—it can never be a lesson, it can never have a meaning. And that is why it will be repeated again and again forever.

VON BERG: Because it cannot be shared?

LEDUC: Yes. Because it cannot be shared. It is total, absolute, waste.

He leans forward suddenly, trying to collect himself against his terror. He glances at the door.

How strange—one can even become impatient.

A groan as he shakes his head with wonder and anger at himself. Hm!—what devils they are.

VON BERG, *with an overtone of closeness to Leduc:* You understand now why I left Vienna. They can make death seductive. It is their worst sin. I had dreams at night—Hitler in a great flowing cloak, almost like a gown, almost like a woman. He was beautiful.

LEDUC: Listen—don't mention the furnaces to my wife.

VON BERG: I'm glad you say that, I feel very relieved, there's really no point . . .

LEDUC, *in a higher agony as he realizes:* No, it's . . . it's . . . You see there was no reason for me to be caught here. We have a good hide-out. They'd never have found us. But she has an exposed nerve in one tooth and I thought I might find some codeine. Just say I was arrested.

VON BERG: Does she have sufficient money?

LEDUC: You could help her that way if you like. Thank you.

VON BERG: The children are small?

LEDUC: Two and three.

VON BERG: How dreadful. How dreadful. *He looks with a glance of fury at the door.* Do you suppose if I offered him something? I can get hold of a good deal of money. I know so little about people—I'm afraid he's rather an idealist. It could infuriate him more.

LEDUC: You might try to feel him out. I don't know what to tell you.

VON BERG: How upside down everything is—to find oneself wishing for a money-loving cynic!

LEDUC: It's perfectly natural. We have learned the price of idealism.

VON BERG: And yet can one wish for a world without ideals? That's what's so depressing—one doesn't know what to wish for.

LEDUC, *in anger:* You see, I knew it when I walked down the road, I knew it was senseless! For a goddamned toothache! So what, so she doesn't sleep for a couple of weeks! It was perfectly clear I shouldn't be taking the chance.

VON BERG: Yes, but if one loves someone . . .

LEDUC: We are not in love any more. It's just too difficult to separate in these times.

VON BERG: Oh, how terrible.

LEDUC, *more softly, realizing a new idea:* Listen . . . about the furnaces . . . don't mention that to her. Not a word, please. *With great self-contempt:* God, at a time like this—to think of taking vengeance on her! What scum we are! *He almost sways in despair.*

Pause. Von Berg turns to Leduc; tears are in his eyes.

VON BERG: There is nothing, is that it? For you there is nothing?

LEDUC, *flying out at him suddenly:* Well what do you propose? Excuse me, but what in hell are you talking about?

The door opens. The Professor comes out and beckons to the Old

Jew. He seems upset, by an argument he had in the office, possibly.
Next.

The Old Jew does not turn to him.
You hear me, why do you sit there?

He strides to the Old Jew and lifts him to his feet brusquely. The man reaches down to pick up his bundle, but the Professor tries to push it back to the floor.
Leave that.

With a wordless little cry, the Old Jew clings to his bundle.
Leave it!

The Professor strikes at the Old Jew's hand, but he only holds on tighter, uttering his wordless little cries. The Police Captain comes out as the Professor pulls at the bundle.
Let go of that!

The bundle rips open. A white cloud of feathers blows up out of it. For an instant everything stops as the Professor looks in surprise at the feathers floating down. The Major appears in the doorway as the feathers settle.
CAPTAIN: Come on.

The Captain and the Professor lift the Old Jew and carry him past the Major into the office. The Major with deadened eyes glances at the feathers and limps in, closing the door behind him.

Leduc and Von Berg stare at the feathers, some of which have fallen on them. They silently brush them off. Leduc picks the last one off his jacket, opens his fingers, and lets it fall to the floor.

Silence. Suddenly a short burst of laughter is heard from the office.

VON BERG, *with great difficulty, not looking at Leduc:* I would like to be able to part with your friendship. Is that possible?

Pause.

LEDUC: Prince, in my position one gets the habit of looking at oneself quite impersonally. It is not you I am angry with. In one part of my mind it is not even this Nazi. I am only angry that I should have been born before the day when man has accepted his own nature; that he is *not* reasonable, that he is full of murder, that his ideals are only the little tax he pays for the right to hate and kill with a clear conscience. I am only angry that, knowing this, I still deluded myself. That there was not time to truly make part of myself what I know, and to teach others the truth.

VON BERG, *angered, above his anxiety:* There are ideals, Doctor, of another kind. There are people who would find it easier to die than stain one finger with this murder. They exist. I swear it to you. People for whom everything is *not* permitted, foolish people and ineffectual, but they do exist and will not dishonor their tradition. *Desperately:* I ask your friendship.

> *Again laughter is heard from within the office. This time it is louder. Leduc slowly turns to Von Berg.*

LEDUC: I owe you the truth, Prince; you won't believe it now, but I wish you would think about it and what it means. I have never analyzed a gentile who did not have, somewhere hidden in his mind, a dislike if not a hatred for the Jews.

VON BERG, *clapping his ears shut, springing up:* That is impossible, it is not true of me!

LEDUC, *standing, coming to him, a wild pity in his voice:* Until you know it is true of you you will destroy whatever truth can come of this atrocity. Part of knowing who we are is knowing we are not someone else. And Jew is only the name we give to that stranger, that agony we cannot feel, that death we look at like a cold abstraction. Each man has his Jew; it is the other. And the Jews have their Jews. And now, now above all, you must see that you have yours—the man whose death leaves you relieved that you are not him, despite your decency. And that is why there is nothing and will be nothing—until you face your own complicity with this . . . your own humanity.

VON BERG: I deny that. I deny that absolutely. I have never in my life said a word against your people. Is that your implication? That I have something to do with this monstrousness! I have put a pistol to my head! To my head!

> *Laughter is heard again.*

LEDUC, *hopelessly:* I'm sorry; it doesn't really matter.

VON BERG: It matters very much to me. Very much to me!

LEDUC, *in a level tone full of mourning; and yet behind it a howling horror:* Prince, you asked me before if I knew your cousin, Baron Kessler.

Von Berg looks at him, already with anxiety.
Baron Kessler is a Nazi. He helped to remove all the Jewish doctors from the medical school.
Von Berg is struck; his eyes glance about.
You were aware of that, weren't you?
Half-hysterical laughter comes from the office.
You must have heard that at some time or another, didn't you?
VON BERG, *stunned, inward-seeing:* Yes. I heard it. I . . . had forgotten it. You see, he was . . .
LEDUC: . . . Your cousin. I understand.
They are quite joined; and Leduc is mourning for the Prince as much as for himself, despite his anger.
And in any case, it is only a small part of Baron Kessler to you. I understand it. But it is all of Baron Kessler to me. When you said his name it was with love; and I'm sure he must be a man of some kindness, with whom you can see eye to eye in many things. But when I hear that name I see a knife. You see now why I say there is nothing, and will be nothing, when even you cannot really put yourself in my place? Even you! And that is why your thoughts of suicide do not move me. It's not your guilt I want, it's your responsibility—that might have helped. Yes, if you had understood that Baron Kessler was in part, in some part, in some small and frightful part—doing your will. You might have done something then, with your standing, and your name and your decency, aside from shooting yourself!
VON BERG, *in full horror, his face upthrust, calling:* What can ever save us? *He covers his face with his hands.*
The door opens. The Professor comes out.
PROFESSOR, *beckoning to the Prince:* Next.
Von Berg does not turn, but holds Leduc in his horrified, beseeching gaze. The Professor approaches the Prince.
Come!
The Professor reaches down to take Von Berg's arm. Von Berg angrily brushes away his abhorrent hand.
VON BERG: *Hände weg!*
The Professor retracts his hand, immobilized, surprised, and for a moment has no strength against his own recognition of authority. Von

Berg turns back to Leduc, who glances up at him and smiles with warmth, then turns away.

Von Berg turns toward the door and, reaching into his breast pocket for a wallet of papers, goes into the office. The Professor follows and closes the door.

Alone, Leduc sits motionless. Now he begins the movements of the trapped; he swallows with difficulty, crosses and recrosses his legs. Now he is still again and bends over and cranes around the corner of the corridor to look for the guard. A movement of his foot stirs up feathers. The accordion is heard outside. He angrily kicks a feather off his foot. Now he makes a decision; he quickly reaches into his pocket, takes out a clasp knife, opens the blade, and begins to get to his feet, starting for the corridor.

The door opens and Von Berg comes out. In his hand is a white pass. The door shuts behind him. He is looking at the pass as he goes by Leduc, and suddenly turns, walks back, and thrusts the pass into Leduc's hand.

VON BERG, *in a strangely angered whisper, motioning him out:* Take it! Go!

Von Berg sits quickly on the bench, taking out the wedding ring. Leduc stares at him, a horrified look on his face. Von Berg hands him the ring.

Number Nine Rue Charlot. Go.

LEDUC, *in a desperate whisper:* What will happen to you?

VON BERG, *angrily waving him away:* Go, go!

Leduc backs away, his hands springing to cover his eyes in the awareness of his own guilt.

LEDUC—*a plea in his voice:* I wasn't asking you to do this! You don't owe me this!

VON BERG: Go!

Leduc, his eyes wide in awe and terror, suddenly turns and strides up the corridor. At the end of it the Guard appears, hearing his footsteps. He gives the Guard the pass and disappears.

A long pause. The door opens. The Professor appears.

PROFESSOR: Ne— *He breaks off. Looks about, then, to Von Berg:* Where's your pass?

Von Berg stares ahead. The Professor calls into the office.

Man escaped!

He runs up the corridor, calling.
Man escaped! Man escaped!

The Police Captain rushes out of the office. Voices are heard outside calling orders. The accordion stops. The Major hurries out of the office. The Police Captain rushes past him.

CAPTAIN: What? *Glancing back at Von Berg, he realizes and rushes up the corridor, calling:* Who let him out! Find that man! What happened?

The voices outside are swept away by a siren going off. The Major has gone to the opening of the corridor, following the Police Captain. For a moment he remains looking up the corridor. All that can be heard now is the siren moving off in pursuit. It dies away, leaving the Major's rapid and excited breaths, angry breaths, incredulous breaths.

Now he turns slowly to Von Berg, who is staring straight ahead. Von Berg turns and faces him. Then he gets to his feet. The moment lengthens, and lengthens yet. A look of anguish and fury is stiffening the Major's face; he is closing his fists. They stand there, forever incomprehensible to one another, looking into each other's eyes.

At the head of the corridor four new men, prisoners, appear. Herded by the Detectives, they enter the detention room and sit on the bench, glancing about at the ceiling, the walls, the feathers on the floor, and the two men who are staring at each other so strangely.

CURTAIN

THE PRICE

The Characters:

VICTOR FRANZ

ESTHER FRANZ

GREGORY SOLOMON

WALTER FRANZ

AUTHOR'S PRODUCTION NOTE

A fine balance of sympathy should be maintained in the playing of the roles of Victor and Walter. The actor playing Walter must not regard his attempts to win back Victor's friendship as mere manipulation. From entrance to exit, Walter is attempting to put into action what he has learned about himself, and sympathy will be evoked for him in proportion to the openness, the depth of need, the intimations of suffering with which the role is played.

This admonition goes beyond the question of theatrics to the theme of the play. As the world now operates, the qualities of both brothers are necessary to it; surely their respective psychologies and moral values conflict at the heart of the social dilemma. The production must therefore withhold judgment in favor of presenting both men in all their humanity and from their own viewpoints. Actually, each has merely proved to the other what the other has known but dared not face. At the end, demanding of one another what was forfeited to time, each is left touching the structure of his life.

The play can be performed with an intermission, as indicated at the end of Act One, if circumstances require it. But an unbroken performance is preferable.

THE PRICE

ACT ONE

New York.

Two windows are seen at the back of the stage. Daylight filters through their sooty panes, which have been X'd out with fresh white-wash to prepare for the demolition of the building.

Now daylight seeps through a skylight in the ceiling, grayed by the grimy panes. The light from above first strikes an overstuffed arm-chair in center stage. It has a faded rose slipcover. Beside it on its right, a small table with a filigreed radio of the Twenties on it and old newspapers; behind it a bridge lamp. At its left an old wind-up Victrola and a pile of records on a low table. A white cleaning cloth and a mop and pail are nearby.

The room is progressively seen. The area around the armchair alone appears to be lived-in, with other chairs and a couch related to it. Outside this area, to the sides and back limits of the room and up the walls, is the chaos of ten rooms of furniture squeezed into this one.

There are four couches and three settees strewn at random over the floor; armchairs, wingbacks, a divan, occasional chairs. On the floor and stacked against the three walls up to the ceiling are bureaus, armoires, a tall secretary, a breakfront, a long, elaborately carved serving table, end tables, a library table, desks, glass-front bookcases, bow-front glass cabinets, and so forth. Several long rolled-up rugs and some shorter ones. A long sculling oar, bedsteads, trunks. And over-head one large and one smaller crystal chandelier hang from ropes, not connected to electric wires. Twelve dining-room chairs stand in a row along a dining-room table at left.

There is a rich heaviness, something almost Germanic, about the furniture, a weight of time upon the bulging fronts and curving chests marshalled against the walls. The room is monstrously crowded and dense, and it is difficult to decide if the stuff is impressive or merely over-heavy and ugly.

An uncovered harp, its gilt chipped, stands alone downstage, right. At the back, behind a rather make-shift drape, long since faded, can be seen a small sink, a hotplate, and an old icebox. Up right, a door to the bedroom. Down left, a door to the corridor and stairway, which are unseen.

We are in the attic of a Manhattan brownstone soon to be torn down.

From the down-left door, Police Sergeant Victor Franz enters in uniform. He halts inside the room, glances about, walks at random a few feet, then comes to a halt. Without expression, yet somehow stilled by some emanation from the room, he lets his gaze move from point to point, piece to piece, absorbing its sphinxlike presence.

He moves to the harp with a certain solemnity, as toward a coffin, and, halting before it, reaches out and plucks a string. He turns and crosses to the dining-room table and removes his gun belt and jacket, hanging them on a chair which he has taken off the table, where it had been set upside down along with two others.

He looks at his watch, waiting for time to pass. Then his eye falls on the pile of records in front of the phonograph. He raises the lid of the machine, sees a record already on the turntable, cranks, and sets the tone arm on the record. Gallagher and Shean sing. He smiles at the corniness.

With the record going he moves to the long sculling oar which stands propped against furniture and touches it. Now he recalls something, reaches in behind a chest, and takes out a fencing foil and mask. He snaps the foil in the air, his gaze held by memory. He puts the foil and mask on the table, goes through two or three records on the pile, and sees a title that makes him smile widely. He replaces the Gallagher and Shean record with this. It is a Laughing Record—two men trying unsuccessfully to get out a whole sentence through their wild hysteria.

He smiles. Broader. Chuckles. Then really laughs. It gets into him; he laughs more fully. Now he bends over with laughter, taking an unsteady step as helplessness rises in him.

Esther, his wife, enters from the down-left door. His back is to her. A half-smile is already on her face as she looks about to see who is laughing with him. She starts toward him, and he hears her heels and turns.

ESTHER: What in the world is that?

VICTOR, *surprised:* Hi! *He lifts the tone arm, smiling, a little embarrassed.*

ESTHER: Sounded like a party in here!

He gives her a peck.

Of the record: What *is* that?

VICTOR, *trying not to disapprove openly:* Where'd you get a drink?

ESTHER: I told you. I went for my checkup. *She laughs with a knowing abandonment of good sense.*

VICTOR: Boy, you and that doctor. I thought he told you not to drink.

ESTHER—*laughs:* I had one! One doesn't hurt me. Everything's normal anyway. He sent you his best. *She looks about.*

VICTOR: Well, that's nice. The dealer's due in a few minutes, if you want to take anything.

ESTHER, *looking around with a sigh:* Oh, dear God—here it is again.

VICTOR: The old lady did a nice job.

ESTHER: Ya—I never saw it so clean. *Indicating the room:* Make you feel funny?

VICTOR—*shrugs:* No, not really—she didn't recognize me, imagine?

ESTHER: Dear boy, it's a hundred and fifty years. *Shaking her head as she stares about:* Huh.

VICTOR: What?

ESTHER: Time.

VICTOR: I know.

ESTHER: There's something different about it.

VICTOR: No, it's all the way it was. *Indicating one side of the room:* I had my desk on that side and my cot. The rest is the same.

ESTHER: Maybe it's that it always used to seem so pretentious to me, and kind of bourgeois. But it does have a certain character. I think some of it's in style again. It's surprising.

VICTOR: Well, you want to take anything?

ESTHER, *looking about, hesitates:* I don't know if I want it around. It's all so massive ... where would we put any of it? That chest is lovely. *She goes to it.*

VICTOR: That was mine. *Indicating one across the room:* The one over there was Walter's. They're a pair.

ESTHER, *comparing:* Oh ya! Did you get hold of him?

VICTOR—*rather glances away, as though this had been an issue:* I called again this morning—he was in consultation.

ESTHER: Was he in the office?

VICTOR: Ya. The nurse went and talked to him for a minute—it doesn't matter. As long as he's notified so I can go ahead.

She suppresses comment, picks up a lamp.

That's probably real porcelain. Maybe it'd go in the bedroom.

ESTHER, *putting the lamp down:* Why don't I meet you somewhere? The whole thing depresses me.

VICTOR: Why? It won't take long. Relax. Come on, sit down; the dealer'll be here any minute.

ESTHER, *sitting on a couch:* There's just something so damned rotten about it. I can't help it; it always was. The whole thing is infuriating.

VICTOR: Well, don't get worked up. We'll sell it and that'll be the end of it. I picked up the tickets, by the way.

ESTHER: Oh, good. *Laying her head back:* Boy, I hope it's a good picture.

VICTOR: Better be. Great, not good. Two-fifty apiece.

ESTHER, *with sudden protest:* I don't care! I want to go somewhere. *She aborts further response, looking around.* God, what's it all about? When I was coming up the stairs just now, and all the doors hanging open ... It doesn't seem possible ...

VICTOR: They tear down old buildings every day in the week, kid.

ESTHER: I know, but it makes you feel a hundred years old. I hate empty rooms. *She muses.* What was that screwball's name?—rented the front parlor, remember?—repaired saxophones?

VICTOR, *smiling:* Oh—Saltzman. *Extending his hand sideways:* With the one eye went out that way.

ESTHER: Ya! Every time I came down the stairs, there he was waiting for me with his four red hands! How'd he ever get all those beautiful girls?

VICTOR—*laughs:* God knows. He must've smelled good.

She laughs, and he does.

He'd actually come running up here sometimes; middle of the afternoon—"Victor, come down quick, I got extras!"

ESTHER: And you did, too!

VICTOR: Why not? If it was free, you took it.

ESTHER, *blushing:* You never told me that.

VICTOR: No, that was before you. Mostly.

ESTHER: You dog.

VICTOR: So what? It was the Depression.

She laughs at the non sequitur.

No, really—I think people were friendlier; lot more daytime screwing in those days. Like the McLoughlin sisters—remember, with the typing service in the front bedroom? *He laughs.* My father used to say, "In that typing service it's two dollars a copy."

She laughs. It subsides.

ESTHER: And they're probably all dead.

VICTOR: I guess Saltzman would be—he was well along. Although—*He shakes his head, laughs softly in surprise.* Jeeze, he wasn't either. I think he was about . . . my age now. Huh!

Caught by the impact of time, they stare for a moment in silence.

ESTHER—*gets up, goes to the harp:* Well, where's your dealer?

VICTOR, *glancing at his watch:* It's twenty to six. He should be here soon.

She plucks the harp.

That should be worth something.

ESTHER: I think a lot of it is. But you're going to have to bargain, you know. You can't just take what they say . . .

VICTOR, *with an edge of protest: I* can bargain; don't worry, I'm not giving it away.

ESTHER: Because they *expect* to bargain.

VICTOR: Don't get depressed already, will you? We didn't even start. *I* intend to bargain, I know the score with these guys.

ESTHER—*withholds further argument, goes to the phonograph; firing up some slight gaiety:* What's this record?

VICTOR: It's a Laughing Record. It was a big thing in the Twenties.

ESTHER, *curiously:* You remember it?

VICTOR: Very vaguely. I was only five or six. Used to play them at parties. You know—see who could keep a straight face. Or maybe they just sat around laughing; I don't know.

ESTHER: That's a wonderful idea!

Their relation is quite balanced, so to speak; he turns to her.

VICTOR: You look good.

She looks at him, an embarrassed smile.

I mean it.—I *said* I'm going to bargain, why do you . . . ?

ESTHER: I believe you.—This is the suit.

VICTOR: Oh, is that it! And how much? Turn around.

ESTHER, *turning:* Forty-five, imagine? He said nobody'd buy it, it was too simple.

VICTOR, *seizing the agreement:* Boy, women are dumb; that is really handsome. See, I don't mind if you get something for your money, but half the stuff they sell is such crap . . . *Going to her:* By the way, look at this collar. Isn't this one of the ones you just bought?

ESTHER, *examining it:* No, that's an older one.

VICTOR: Well, even so. *Turning up a heel:* Ought to write to Consumers Union about these heels. Three weeks—look at them!

ESTHER: Well, you don't walk straight.—You're not going in uniform, I hope.

VICTOR: I could've murdered that guy! I'd just changed, and McGowan was trying to fingerprint some bum and he didn't want to be printed; so he swings out his arm just as I'm going by, right into my container.

ESTHER, *as though this symbolized:* Oh, God . . .

VICTOR: I gave it to that quick cleaner, he'll try to have it by six.

ESTHER: Was there cream and sugar in the coffee?

VICTOR: Ya.

ESTHER: He'll never have it by six.

VICTOR, *assuagingly:* He's going to try.

ESTHER: Oh, forget it.

Slight pause. Seriously disconsolate, she looks around at random.

VICTOR: Well, it's only a movie . . .

ESTHER: But we go out so rarely—why must everybody know your salary? I want an evening! I want to sit down in a restaurant without some drunken ex-cop coming over to the table to talk about old times.

VICTOR: It happened twice. After all these years, Esther, it would seem to me . . .

ESTHER: I know it's unimportant—but like that man in the museum; he really did—he thought you were the sculptor.

VICTOR: So I'm a sculptor.

ESTHER, *bridling:* Well, it was nice, that's all! You really do, Vic—you look distinguished in a suit. Why not? *Laying her head back on the couch:* I should've taken down the name of that scotch.

VICTOR: All scotch is chemically the same.

ESTHER: I know; but some is better.

VICTOR, *looking at his watch:* Look at that, will you? Five-thirty sharp, he tells me. People say anything. *He moves with a heightened restlessness, trying to down his irritation with her mood. His eye falls on a partly opened drawer of a chest, and he opens it and takes out an ice skate.* Look at that, they're still good! *He tests the edge with his fingernail; she merely glances at him.* They're even sharp. We ought to skate again sometime. *He sees her unremitting moodiness.* Esther, I said I would bargain!—You see?—you don't know how to drink; it only depresses you.

ESTHER: Well, it's the kind of depression I enjoy!

VICTOR: Hot diggity dog.

ESTHER: I have an idea.

VICTOR: What?

ESTHER: Why don't you leave me? Just send me enough for coffee and cigarettes.

VICTOR: Then you'd *never* have to get out of bed.

ESTHER: I'd get out. Once in a while.

VICTOR: I got a better idea. Why don't you go off for a couple of weeks with your doctor? Seriously. It might change your viewpoint.

ESTHER: I wish I could.

VICTOR: Well, do it. He's got a suit. You could even take the dog—especially the dog. *She laughs.* It's not funny. Every time you go out for one of those walks in the rain I hold my breath what's going to come back with you.

ESTHER, *laughing:* Oh, go on, you love her.

VICTOR: I love her! You get plastered, you bring home strange animals, and I "love" them! I do not love that goddamned dog!

She laughs with affection, as well as with a certain feminine defiance.

ESTHER: Well, I want her!

VICTOR—*pause:* It won't be solved by a dog, Esther. You're an intelligent, capable woman, and you can't lay around all day. Even something part-time, it would give you a place to go.

ESTHER: I don't need a place to go. *Slight pause.* I'm not quite used to Richard not being there, that's all.

VICTOR: He's gone, kid. He's a grown man; you've got to do something with yourself.

ESTHER: I can't go to the same place day after day. I never could and I never will. Did you *ask* to speak to your brother?

VICTOR: I asked the nurse. Yes. He couldn't break away.

ESTHER: That son of a bitch. It's sickening.

VICTOR: Well, what are you going to do? He never had that kind of feeling.

ESTHER: What feeling? To come to the phone after sixteen years? It's common decency. *With sudden intimate sympathy:* You're furious, aren't you?

VICTOR: Only at myself. Calling him again and again all week like an idiot ... To hell with him, I'll handle it alone. It's just as well.

ESTHER: What about his share?

He shifts; pressed and annoyed.

I don't want to be a pest—but I think there could be some money here, Vic.

He is silent.

You're going to raise that with him, aren't you?

VICTOR, *with a formed decision:* I've been thinking about it. He's got a right to his half, why should he give up anything?

ESTHER: I thought you'd decided to put it to him?

VICTOR: I've changed my mind. I don't really feel he owes me anything, I can't put on an act.

ESTHER: But how many Cadillacs can he drive?

VICTOR: That's why he's got Cadillacs. People who love money don't give it away.

ESTHER: I don't know why you keep putting it like charity. There's such a thing as a moral debt. Vic, you made his whole career possible. What law said that only he could study medicine—?

VICTOR: Esther, please—let's not get back on that, will you?

ESTHER: I'm not back on anything—you were even the better student. That's a real debt, and he ought to be made to face it. He could never have finished medical school if you hadn't taken care of Pop. I mean we ought to start talking the way people talk! There could be some real money here.

VICTOR: I doubt that. There are no antiques or—

ESTHER: Just because it's ours why must it be worthless?

VICTOR: Now what's that for?

ESTHER: Because that's the way we think! We do!

VICTOR, *sharply:* The man won't even come to the phone, how am I going to—?

ESTHER: Then you write him a letter, bang on his door. This *belongs* to you!

VICTOR, *surprised, seeing how deadly earnest she is:* What are you so excited about?

ESTHER: Well, for one thing it might help you make up your mind to take your retirement.

A slight pause.

VICTOR, *rather secretively, unwillingly:* It's not the money been stopping me.

ESTHER: Then what is it?

He is silent.

I just thought that with a little cushion you could take a month or two until something occurs to you that you want to do.

VICTOR: It's all I think about right now, I don't have to quit to think.

ESTHER: But nothing seems to come of it.

VICTOR: Is it that easy? I'm going to be fifty. You don't just start a whole new career. I don't understand why it's so urgent all of a sudden.

ESTHER—*laughs:* All of a sudden! It's all I've been talking about since you became eligible—I've been saying the same thing for three years!

VICTOR: Well, it's not three years—

ESTHER: It'll be three years in March! It's *three years.* If you'd gone back to school then you'd almost have your Master's by now; you might have had a chance to get into something you'd love to do. Isn't that true? Why can't you make a move?

VICTOR—*pause. He is almost ashamed:* I'll tell you the truth. I'm not sure the whole thing wasn't a little unreal. I'd be fifty-three, fifty-four by the time I could start doing anything.

ESTHER: But you always knew that.

VICTOR: It's different when you're right on top of it. I'm not sure it makes any sense now.

ESTHER, *moving away, the despair in her voice:* Well ... this is exactly what I tried to tell you a thousand times. It makes the same sense it ever made. But you might have twenty more years, and that's still a long time. Could do a lot of interesting things in that time. *Slight pause.* You're so young, Vic.

VICTOR: I am?

ESTHER: Sure! I'm not, but you are. God, all the girls goggle at you, what do you want?

VICTOR—*laughs emptily:* It's hard to discuss it, Es, because I don't understand it.

ESTHER: Well, why not talk about what you don't understand? Why do you expect yourself to be an authority?

VICTOR: Well, one of us is got to stay afloat, kid.

ESTHER: You want me to pretend everything is great? I'm bewildered and I'm going to act bewildered! *It flies out as though long suppressed:* I've asked you fifty times to write a letter to Walter—

VICTOR, *like a repeated story:* What's this with Walter again? What's Walter going to—?

ESTHER: He is an important scientist, and that hospital's building a whole new research division. I saw it in the paper, it's his hospital.

VICTOR: Esther, the man hasn't called me in sixteen years.

ESTHER: But neither have you called him!

He looks at her in surprise.

Well, you haven't. That's also a fact.

VICTOR, *as though the idea were new and incredible:* What would I call him for?

ESTHER: Because, he's your brother, he's influential, and he could help— Yes, that's how people do, Vic! Those articles he wrote had a real idealism, there was a genuine human quality. I mean people do change, you know.

VICTOR, *turning away:* I'm sorry, I don't need Walter.

ESTHER: I'm not saying you have to approve of him; he's a selfish bastard, but he just might be able to put you on the track of something. I don't see the humiliation.

VICTOR, *pressed, irritated:* I don't understand why it's all such an emergency.

ESTHER: Because I don't know where in hell I am, Victor! *To her surprise, she has ended nearly screaming. He is silent. She retracts.* I'll do anything if I know why, but all these years we've been saying, once we get the pension we're going to start to live.... It's like pushing against a door for twenty-five years and suddenly it opens ... and we stand there. Sometimes I wonder, maybe I misunderstood you, maybe you like the department.

VICTOR: I've hated every minute of it.

ESTHER: I did everything wrong! I swear, I think if I demanded more it would have helped you more.

VICTOR: That's not true. You've been a terrific wife—

ESTHER: I don't think so. But the security meant so much to you I tried to fit into that; but I was wrong. God—just before coming here, I looked around at the apartment to see if we could use any of this—and it's all so ugly. It's worn and shabby and tasteless. And I have good taste! I know I do! It's that everything was always temporary with us. It's like we never were anything, we were always about-to-be. I think back to the war when any idiot was making so much money—that's when you should have quit, and I knew it, I knew it!

VICTOR: That's when I wanted to quit.

ESTHER: I only had one drink, Victor, so don't—

VICTOR: Don't change the whole story, kid. I wanted to quit, and you got scared.

ESTHER: Because you said there was going to be a Depression after the war.

VICTOR: Well, go to the library, look up the papers around 1945, see what they were saying!

ESTHER: I don't care! *She turns away—from her own irrationality.*

VICTOR: I swear, Es, sometimes you make it sound like we've had no life at all.

ESTHER: God—my mother was so right! I can never believe what I see. I knew you'd never get out if you didn't during the war—I saw it happening, and I said nothing. You know what the goddamned trouble is?

VICTOR, *glancing at his watch, as he senses the end of her revolt:* What's the goddamned trouble?

ESTHER: We can never keep our minds on money! We worry about it, we talk about it, but we can't seem to *want* it. I do, but you don't. I really do, Vic. I want it. Vic? *I want money!*

VICTOR: Congratulations.

ESTHER: You go to hell!

VICTOR: I wish you'd stop comparing yourself to other people, Esther! That's all you're doing lately.

ESTHER: Well, I can't help it!

VICTOR: Then you've got to be a failure, kid, because there's always going to be somebody up ahead of you. What happened? I have a certain nature; just as you do—I didn't change—

ESTHER: But you have changed. You've been walking around like a zombie ever since the retirement came up. You've gotten so vague—

VICTOR: Well, it's a decision. And I'd like to feel a little more certain about it. . . . Actually, I've even started to fill out the forms a couple of times.

ESTHER, *alerted:* And?

VICTOR, *with difficulty—he cannot understand it himself:* I suppose there's some kind of finality about it that . . . *He breaks off.*

ESTHER: But what else did you expect?

VICTOR: It's stupid; I admit it. But you look at that goddamned form and you can't help it. You sign your name to twenty-eight years and you ask yourself, Is that all? Is that it? And it is, of course. The trouble is, when I think of starting something new, that number comes up—five oh—and the steam goes out. But I'll do something. I will! *With a greater closeness to her now:* I don't know what it is; every time I think about it all—it's almost frightening.

ESTHER: What?

VICTOR: Well, like when I walked in here before ... *He looks around.* This whole thing—it hit me like some kind of craziness. Piling up all this stuff here like it was made of gold. *He half-laughs, almost embarrassed.* I brought up every stick; damn near saved the carpet tacks. *He turns to the center chair.* That whole way I was with him—it's inconceivable to me now.

ESTHER, *with regret over her sympathy:* Well ... you loved him.

VICTOR: I know, but it's all words. What was he? A busted businessman like thousands of others, and I acted like some kind of a mountain crashed. I tell you the truth, every now and then the whole thing is like a story somebody told me. You ever feel that way?

ESTHER: All day, every day.

VICTOR: Oh, come on—

ESTHER: It's the truth. The first time I walked up those stairs I was nineteen years old. And when you opened that box with your first uniform in it—remember that? When you put it on the first time?— how we laughed? If anything happened you said you'd call a cop! *They both laugh.* It was like a masquerade. And we were right. That's when we were right.

VICTOR, *pained by her pain:* You know, Esther, every once in a while you try to sound childish and it—

ESTHER: I mean to be! I'm sick of the— Oh, forget it, I want a drink. *She goes for her purse.*

VICTOR, *surprised:* What's that, the great adventure? Where are you going all of a sudden?

ESTHER: I can't stand it in here, I'm going for a walk.

VICTOR: Now you cut out this nonsense!

ESTHER: I am not an alcoholic!

VICTOR: You've had a good life compared to an awful lot of people! You trying to turn into a goddamned teenager or something?

ESTHER, *indicating the furniture:* Don't talk childishness to me, Victor—not in this room! You let it lay here all these years because you can't have a simple conversation with your own brother, and I'm childish? You're still eighteen years old with that man! I mean I'm stuck, but I admit it!

VICTOR, *hurt:* Okay. Go ahead.

ESTHER—*she can't quite leave:* You got a receipt? I'll get your suit. *He doesn't move. She makes it rational:* I just want to get out of here.

VICTOR—*takes out a receipt and gives it to her. His voice is cold:* It's right off Seventh. The address is on it. *He moves from her.*

ESTHER: I'm coming back right away.

VICTOR, *freeing her to her irresponsibility:* Do as you please, kid. I mean it.

ESTHER: You were grinding your teeth again last night. Did you know that?

VICTOR: Oh! No wonder my ear hurts.

ESTHER: I wish I had a tape recorder. I mean it, it's gruesome; sounds like a lot of rocks coming down a mountain. I wish you could hear it, you wouldn't take this self-sufficient attitude.

He is silent, alarmed, hurt. He moves upstage as though looking at the furniture.

VICTOR: It's okay. I think I get the message.

ESTHER, *afraid—she tries to smile and goes back toward him:* Like what?

VICTOR—*moves a chair and does a knee bend and draws out the chassis of an immense old radio:* What other message is there?

Slight pause.

ESTHER, *to retrieve the contact:* What's that?

VICTOR: Oh, one of my old radios that I made. Mama mia, look at those tubes.

ESTHER, *more wondering than she feels about radios:* Would that work?

VICTOR: No, you need a storage battery. . . . *Recalling, he suddenly looks up at the ceiling.*

ESTHER, *looking up:* What?

VICTOR: One of my batteries exploded, went right through there someplace. *He points.* There! See where the plaster is different?

ESTHER, *striving for some spark between them:* Is this the one you got Tokyo on?

VICTOR, *not relenting, his voice dead:* Ya, this is the monster.

ESTHER, *with a warmth:* Why don't you take it?

VICTOR: Ah, it's useless.

ESTHER: Didn't you once say you had a lab up here? Or did I dream that?

VICTOR: Sure, I took it apart when Pop and I moved up here. Walter had that wall, and I had this. We did some great tricks up here.

    She is fastened on him.

He avoids her eyes and moves waywardly. I'll be frank with you, kid—I look at my life and the whole thing is incomprehensible to me. I know all the reasons and all the reasons and all the reasons, and it ends up—nothing. *He goes to the harp, touches it.* It's strange, you know? I forgot all about it—we'd work up here all night sometimes, and it was often full of music. My mother'd play for hours down in the library. Which is peculiar, because a harp is so soft. But it penetrates, I guess.

ESTHER: You're dear. You are, Vic. *She starts toward him, but he thwarts her by looking at his watch.*

VICTOR: I'll have to call another man. Come on, let's get out of here. *With a hollow, exhausted attempt at joy:* We'll get my suit and act rich!

ESTHER: Vic, I didn't mean that I—

VICTOR: Forget it. Wait, let me put these away before somebody walks off with them. *He takes up the foil and mask.*

ESTHER: Can you still do it?

VICTOR, *his sadness, his distance clinging to him:* Oh no, you gotta be in shape for this. It's all in the thighs—

ESTHER: Well, let me see, I never saw you do it!

VICTOR, *giving the inch:* All right, but I can't get down far enough any more. *He takes position, feet at right angles, bouncing himself down to a difficult crouch.*

ESTHER: Maybe you could take it up again.

VICTOR: Oh no, it's a lot of work, it's the toughest sport there is. *Resuming position:* Okay, just stand there.

ESTHER: Me?

VICTOR: Don't be afraid. *Snapping the tip:* It's a beautiful foil, see how alive it is? I beat Princeton with this. *He laughs tiredly and makes a tramping lunge from yards away; the button touches her stomach.*

ESTHER, *springing back:* God! Victor!

VICTOR: What?

ESTHER: You looked beautiful.

He laughs, surprised and half-embarrassed—when both of them are turned to the door by a loud, sustained coughing out in the corridor. The coughing increases.

Enter Gregory Solomon. In brief, a phenomenon; a man nearly ninety but still straight-backed and the air of his massiveness still with him. He has perfected a way of leaning on his cane without appearing weak.

He wears a worn fur-felt black fedora, its brim turned down on the right side like Jimmy Walker's—although much dustier—and a shapeless topcoat. His frayed tie has a thick knot, askew under a curled-up collar tab. His vest is wrinkled, his trousers baggy. A large diamond ring is on his left index finger. Tucked under his arm, a wrung-out leather portfolio. He hasn't shaved today.

Still coughing, catching his breath, trying to brush his cigar ashes off his lapel in a hopeless attempt at businesslike decorum, he is nodding at Esther and Victor and has one hand raised in a promise to speak quite soon. Nor has he failed to glance with some suspicion at the foil in Victor's hand.

VICTOR: Can I get you a glass of water?

Solomon gestures an imperious negative, trying to stop coughing.

ESTHER: Why don't you sit down?

Solomon gestures thanks, sits in the center armchair, the cough subsiding.

You sure you don't want some water?

SOLOMON, *in a Russian-Yiddish accent:* Water I don't need; a little blood I could use. Thank you. *He takes deep breaths, his attention on Victor, who now puts down the foil.* Oh boy. That's some stairs.

ESTHER: You all right now?

SOLOMON: Another couple steps you'll be in heaven. Ah—excuse me, Officer, I am looking for a party. The name is . . . *He fingers in his vest.*

VICTOR: Franz.

SOLOMON: That's it, Franz.

VICTOR: That's me.

Solomon looks incredulous.

Victor Franz.

SOLOMON: So it's a policeman!

VICTOR, *grinning:* Uh huh.

SOLOMON: What do you know! *Including Esther:* You see? There's only one beauty to this lousy business, you meet all kinda people. But I never dealt with a policeman. *Reaching over to shake hands:* I'm very happy to meet you. My name is Solomon, Gregory Solomon.

VICTOR, *shaking hands:* This is my wife.

ESTHER: How do you do.

SOLOMON, *nodding appreciatively to Esther:* Very nice. *To Victor:* That's a nice-looking woman. *He extends his hands to her.* How do you do, darling. Beautiful suit.

ESTHER—*laughs:* The fact is, I just bought it!

SOLOMON: You got good taste. Congratulations, wear it in good health. *He lets go her hand.*

ESTHER: I'll go to the cleaner, dear. I'll be back soon. *With a step toward the door—to Solomon:* Will you be very long?

SOLOMON, *glancing around at the furniture as at an antagonist:* With furniture you never know, can be short, can be long, can be medium.

ESTHER: Well, you give him a good price now, you hear?

SOLOMON: Ah ha! *Waving her out:* Look, you go to the cleaner, and we'll take care everything one hundred per cent.

ESTHER: Because there's some very beautiful stuff here. I know it, but he doesn't.

SOLOMON: I'm not sixty-two years in the business by taking advantage. Go, enjoy the cleaner.

She and Victor laugh.

ESTHER, *shaking her finger at him:* I hope I'm going to like you!

SOLOMON: Sweetheart, all the girls like me, what can I do?

ESTHER, *still smiling—to Victor as she goes to the door:* You be careful.

VICTOR, *nodding:* See you later.

　She goes.

SOLOMON: I like her, she's suspicious.

VICTOR, *laughing in surprise:* What do you mean by that?

SOLOMON: Well, a girl who believes everything, how you gonna trust her?

　Victor laughs appreciatively.

I had a wife . . . *He breaks off with a wave of the hand.* Well, what's the difference? Tell me, if you don't mind, how did you get my name?

VICTOR: In the phone book.

SOLOMON: You don't say! The phone book.

VICTOR: Why?

SOLOMON, *cryptically:* No-no, that's fine, that's fine.

VICTOR: The ad said you're a registered appraiser.

SOLOMON: Oh yes. I am registered, I am licensed, I am even vaccinated.

　Victor laughs.

Don't laugh, the only thing you can do today without a license is you'll go up the elevator and jump out the window. But I don't have to tell you, you're a policeman, you know this world. *Hoping for contact:* I'm right?

VICTOR, *reserved:* I suppose.

SOLOMON, *surveying the furniture, one hand on his thigh, the other on the chair arm in a naturally elegant position:* So. *He glances about again, and with an uncertain smile:* That's a lot of furniture. This is all for sale?

VICTOR: Well, ya.

SOLOMON: Fine, fine. I just like to be sure where we are. *With a weak attempt at a charming laugh:* Frankly, in this neighborhood I never expected such a load. It's very surprising.

VICTOR: But I said it was a whole houseful.

SOLOMON, *with a leaven of unsureness:* Look, don't worry about it, we'll handle everything very nice. *He gets up from the chair and goes to one of the pair of chiffoniers which he is obviously impressed with. He looks up at the chandeliers. Then straight at Victor:* I'm not mixing in, Officer, but if you wouldn't mind—what is your connection? How do you come to this?

VICTOR: It was my family.

SOLOMON: You don't say. Looks like it's standing here a long time, no?

VICTOR: Well, the old man moved everything up here after the '29 crash. My uncles took over the house and they let him keep this floor.

SOLOMON, *as though to emphasize that he believes it: I* see. *He walks to the harp.*

VICTOR: Can you give me an estimate now, or do you have to—?

SOLOMON, *running a hand over the harp frame:* No-no, I'll give you right away, I don't waste a minute, I'm very busy. *He plucks a string, listens. Then bends down and runs a hand over the sounding board:* He passed away, your father?

VICTOR: Oh, long time ago—about sixteen years.

SOLOMON, *standing erect:* It's standing here sixteen years?

VICTOR: Well, we never got around to doing anything about it, but they're tearing the building down, so . . . It was very good stuff, you know—they had quite a little money.

SOLOMON: Very good, yes . . . I can see. *He leaves the harp with an estimating glance.* I was also very good; now I'm not so good. Time, you know, is a terrible thing. *He is a distance from the harp and indicates it.* That sounding board is cracked, you know. But don't worry about it, it's still a nice object. *He goes to an armoire and strokes the veneer.* It's a funny thing—an armoire like this, thirty years you couldn't give it away; it was a regular measles. Today all of a sudden, they want it again. Go figure it out. *He goes to one of the chests.*

VICTOR, *pleased:* Well, give me a good price and we'll make a deal.

SOLOMON: Definitely. You see, I don't lie to you. *He is pointing to the chest.* For instance, a chiffonier like this I wouldn't have to keep it a week. *Indicating the other chest:* That's a pair, you know.

VICTOR: I know.

SOLOMON: That's a nice chairs, too. *He sits on a dining-room chair, rocking to test its tightness.* I like the chairs.

VICTOR: There's more stuff in the bedroom, if you want to look.

SOLOMON: Oh? *He goes toward the bedroom.* What've you got here? *He looks into the bedroom, up and down.* I like the bed. That's a very nice carved bed. That I can sell. That's your parents' bed?

VICTOR: Yes. They may have bought that in Europe, if I'm not mistaken. They used to travel a good deal.

SOLOMON: Very handsome, very nice. I like it. *He starts to return to the center chair, eyes roving the furniture.* Looks a very nice family.

VICTOR: By the way, that dining-room table opens up. Probably seat about twelve people.

SOLOMON, *looking at the table:* I know that. Yes. In a pinch even fourteen. *He picks up the foil.* What's this? I thought you were stabbing your wife when I came in.

VICTOR, *laughing:* No, I just found it. I used to fence years ago.

SOLOMON: You went to college?

VICTOR: Couple of years, ya.

SOLOMON: That's very interesting.

VICTOR: It's the old story.

SOLOMON: No, listen— What happens to people is always the main element to me. Because when do they call me? It's either a divorce or somebody died. So it's always a new story. I mean it's the same, but it's different. *He sits in the center chair.*

VICTOR: You pick up the pieces.

SOLOMON: That's very good, yes. I pick up the pieces. It's a little bit like you, I suppose. You must have some stories, I betcha.

VICTOR: Not very often.

SOLOMON: What are you, a traffic cop, or something . . . ?

VICTOR: I'm out in Rockaway most of the time, the airports.

SOLOMON: That's Siberia, no?

VICTOR, *laughing:* I like it better that way.

SOLOMON: You keep your nose clean.

VICTOR, *smiling:* That's it. *Indicating the furniture:* So what do you say?

SOLOMON: What I say? *Taking out two cigars as he glances about:* You like a cigar?

VICTOR: Thanks, I gave it up long time ago. So what's the story here?

SOLOMON: I can see you are a very factual person.

VICTOR: You hit it.

SOLOMON: Couldn't be better. So tell me, you got some kind of paper here? To show ownership?

VICTOR: Well, no, I don't. But ... *He half-laughs.* I'm the owner, that's all.

SOLOMON: In other words, there's no brothers, no sisters.

VICTOR: I have a brother, yes.

SOLOMON: Ah hah. You're friendly with him. Not that I'm mixing in, but I don't have to tell you the average family they love each other like crazy, but the minute the parents die is all of a sudden a question who is going to get what and you're covered with cats and dogs—

VICTOR: There's no such problem here.

SOLOMON: Unless we're gonna talk about a few pieces, then it wouldn't bother me, but to take the whole load without a paper is a—

VICTOR: All right, I'll get you some kind of statement from him; don't worry about it.

SOLOMON: That's definite; because even from high-class people you wouldn't believe the shenanigans—lawyers, college professors, television personalities—five hundred dollars they'll pay a lawyer to fight over a bookcase it's worth fifty cents—because you see, everybody wants to be number one, so . . .

VICTOR: I said I'd get you a statement. *He indicates the room.* Now what's the story?

SOLOMON: All right, so I'll tell you the story. *He looks at the dining-room table and points to it.* For instance, you mention the dining-room table. That's what they call Spanish Jacobean. Cost maybe twelve, thirteen hundred dollars. I would say—1921, '22. I'm right?

VICTOR: Probably, ya.

SOLOMON—*clears his throat:* I see you're an intelligent man, so before I'll say another word, I ask you to remember—with used furniture you cannot be emotional.

VICTOR—*laughs:* I haven't opened my mouth!

SOLOMON: I mean you're a policeman, I'm a furniture dealer, we both know this world. Anything Spanish Jacobean you'll sell quicker a case of tuberculosis.

VICTOR: Why? That table's in beautiful condition.

SOLOMON: Officer, you're talking reality; you cannot talk reality with used furniture. They don't like that style; not only they don't like it, they hate it. The same thing with that buffet there and that . . . *He starts to point elsewhere.*

VICTOR: You only want to take a few pieces, is that the ticket?

SOLOMON: Please, Officer, we're already talking too fast—

VICTOR: No-no, you're not going to walk off with the gravy and leave me with the bones. All or nothing or let's forget it. I told you on the phone it was a whole houseful.

SOLOMON: What're you in such a hurry? Talk a little bit, we'll see what happens. In a day they didn't build Rome. *He calculates worriedly for a moment, glancing again at the pieces he wants. He gets up, goes and touches the harp.* You see, what I had in mind—I would give you such a knockout price for these few pieces that you—

VICTOR: That's *out.*

SOLOMON, *quickly:* Out.

VICTOR: I'm not running a department store. They're tearing the building down.

SOLOMON: Couldn't be better! We understand each other, so—*with his charm*—so there's no reason to be emotional. *He goes to the records.* These records go? *He picks up one.*

VICTOR: I might keep three or four.

SOLOMON, *reading a label:* Look at that! Gallagher and Shean!

VICTOR, *with only half a laugh:* You're not going to start playing them now!

SOLOMON: Who needs to play? I was on the same bill with Gallagher and Shean maybe fifty theaters.

VICTOR, *surprised:* You were an actor?

SOLOMON: An actor! An acrobat; my whole family was acrobats. *Expanding with this first opening:* You never heard "The Five Solomons"—may they rest in peace? I was the one on the bottom.

VICTOR: Funny—I never heard of a Jewish acrobat.

SOLOMON: What's the matter with Jacob, he wasn't a wrestler?—wrestled with the Angel?

Victor laughs.

Jews been acrobats since the beginning of the world. I was a horse them days: drink, women, anything—on-the-go, on-the-go, nothing ever stopped me. Only life. Yes, my boy. *Almost lovingly putting down the record:* What do you know, Gallagher and Shean.

VICTOR, *more intimately now, despite himself; but with no less persistence in keeping to the business:* So where are we?

SOLOMON—*glancing off, he turns back to Victor with a deeply concerned look:* Tell me, what's with crime now? It's up, hey?

VICTOR: Yeah, it's up, it's up. Look, Mr. Solomon, let me make one thing clear, heh? I'm not sociable.

SOLOMON: You're not.

VICTOR: No, I'm not; I'm not a businessman, I'm not good at conversations. So let's get to a price, and finish. Okay?

SOLOMON: You don't want we should be buddies.

VICTOR: That's exactly it.

SOLOMON: So we wouldn't be buddies! *He sighs.* But just so you'll know me a little better—I'm going to show you something. *He takes out a leather folder which he flips open and hands to Victor.* There's my discharge from the British navy. You see? "His Majesty's Service."

VICTOR, *looking at the document:* Huh! What were you doing in the British Navy?

SOLOMON: Forget the British Navy. What does it say the date of birth?

VICTOR: "Eighteen ..." *Amazed, he looks up at Solomon.* You're almost ninety?

SOLOMON: Yes, my boy. I left Russia sixty-five years ago, I was twenty-four years old. And I smoked all my life. I drinked, and I loved every woman who would let me. So what do I need to steal from you?

VICTOR: Since when do people need a reason to steal?

SOLOMON: I never saw such a man in my life!

VICTOR: Oh yes you did. Now you going to give me a figure or—?

SOLOMON—*he is actually frightened because he can't get a hook into*

Victor and fears losing the good pieces: How can I give you a figure? You don't trust one word I say!

VICTOR, *with a strained laugh:* I never saw you before, what're you asking me to trust you?!

SOLOMON, *with a gesture of disgust:* But how am I going to start to talk to you? I'm sorry; here you can't be a policeman. If you want to do business a little bit you gotta believe or you can't do it. I'm . . . I'm . . . Look, forget it. *He gets up and goes to his portfolio.*

VICTOR, *astonished:* What are you doing?

SOLOMON: I can't work this way. I'm too old every time I open my mouth you should practically call me a thief.

VICTOR: Who called you a thief?

SOLOMON, *moving toward the door:* No—I don't need it. I don't want it in my shop. *Wagging a finger into Victor's face:* And don't forget it—I never gave you a price, and look what you did to me. You see? I never gave you a price!

VICTOR, *angering:* Well, what did you come here for, to do me a favor? What are you talking about?

SOLOMON: Mister, I pity you! What is the matter with you people! You're worse than my daughter! Nothing in the world you believe, nothing you respect—how can you live? You think that's such a smart thing? That's so hard, what you're doing? Let me give you a piece of advice—it's not that you can't believe nothing, that's not so hard—it's that you still got to believe it. *That's* hard. And if you can't do that, my friend—you're a dead man! *He starts toward the door.*

VICTOR, *chastened despite himself:* Oh, Solomon, come on, will you?

SOLOMON: No-no. You got a certain problem with this furniture but you don't want to listen so how can I talk?

VICTOR: I'm listening! For Christ's sake, what do you want me to do, get down on my knees?

SOLOMON, *putting down his portfolio and taking out a wrinkled tape measure from his jacket pocket:* Okay, come here. I realize you are a factual person, but some facts are funny. *He stretches the tape measure across the depth of a piece.* What does that read? *Then turns to Victor, showing him.*

VICTOR—*comes to him, reads:* Forty inches. So?

SOLOMON: My boy, the bedroom doors in a modern apartment

house are thirty, thirty-two inches maximum. So you can't get this in—

VICTOR: What about the old houses?

SOLOMON, *with a desperation growing:* All I'm trying to tell you is that my possibilities are smaller!

VICTOR: Well, can't I ask a question?

SOLOMON: I'm giving you architectural facts! Listen—*Wiping his face, he seizes on the library table, going to it.* You got there, for instance, a library table. That's a solid beauty. But go find me a modern apartment with a library. If they would build old hotels, I could sell this, but they only build new hotels. People don't live like this no more. This stuff is from another world. So I'm trying to give you a modern viewpoint. Because the price of used furniture is nothing but a viewpoint, and if you wouldn't understand the viewpoint is impossible to understand the price.

VICTOR: So what's the viewpoint—that it's all worth nothing?

SOLOMON: That's what you said, I didn't say that. The chairs is worth something, the chiffoniers, the bed, the harp—

VICTOR—*turns away from him:* Okay, let's forget it, I'm not giving you the cream—

SOLOMON: What're you jumping!

VICTOR, *turning to him:* Good God, are you going to make me an offer or not?

SOLOMON, *walking away with a hand at his temple:* Boy, oh boy, oh boy. You must've arrested a million people by now.

VICTOR: Nineteen in twenty-eight years.

SOLOMON: So what are you so hard on me?

VICTOR: Because you talk about everything but money and I don't know what the hell you're up to.

SOLOMON, *raising a finger:* We will now talk money. *He returns to the center chair.*

VICTOR: Great. I mean you can't blame me—every time you open your mouth the price seems to go down.

SOLOMON, *sitting:* My boy, the price didn't change since I walked in.

VICTOR, *laughing:* That's even better! So what's the price?

Solomon glances about, his wit failed, a sunk look coming over his face.

What's going on? What's bothering you?

SOLOMON: I'm sorry, I shouldn't have come. I thought it would be a few pieces but . . . *Sunk, he presses his fingers into his eyes.* It's too much for me.

VICTOR: Well, what'd you come for? I told you it was the whole house.

SOLOMON, *protesting:* You called me so I came! What should I do, lay down and die? *Striving again to save it:* Look, I want very much to make you an offer, the only question is . . . *He breaks off as though fearful of saying something.*

VICTOR: This is a hell of a note.

SOLOMON: Listen, it's a terrible temptation to me! But . . . *As though throwing himself on Victor's understanding:* You see, I'll tell you the truth; you must have looked in a very old phone book; a couple of years ago already I cleaned out my store. Except a few English andirons I got left, I sell when I need a few dollars. I figured I was eighty, eighty-five, it was time already. But I waited—and nothing happened—I even moved out of my apartment. I'm living in the back of the store with a hotplate. But nothing happened. I'm still practically a hundred per cent—not a hundred, but I feel very well. And I figured maybe you got a couple nice pieces—not that the rest can't be sold, but it could take a year, year and half. For me that's a big bet. *In conflict, he looks around.* The trouble is I love to work; I love it, but—*Giving up:* I don't know what to tell you.

VICTOR: All right, let's forget it then.

SOLOMON, *standing:* What're you jumping?

VICTOR: Well, are you in or out!

SOLOMON: How do I know where I am! You see, it's also this particular furniture—the average person he'll take one look, it'll make him very nervous.

VICTOR: Solomon, you're starting again.

SOLOMON: I'm not bargaining with you!

VICTOR: Why'll it make him nervous?

SOLOMON: Because he knows it's never gonna break.

VICTOR, *not in bad humor, but clinging to his senses:* Oh come on, will you? Have a little mercy.

SOLOMON: My boy, you don't know the psychology! If it wouldn't break there is no more possibilities. For instance, you take—*crosses to table*—this table . . . Listen! *He bangs the table.* You can't move it. A man sits down to such a table he knows not only he's married, he's got to stay married—there is no more possibilities.

Victor laughs.

You're laughing, I'm telling you the factual situation. What is the key word today? Disposable. The more you can throw it away the more it's beautiful. The car, the furniture, the wife, the children—everything has to be disposable. Because you see the main thing today is—shopping. Years ago a person, he was unhappy, didn't know what to do with himself—he'd go to church, start a revolution—*something.* Today you're unhappy? Can't figure it out? What is the salvation? Go shopping.

VICTOR, *laughing:* You're terrific, I have to give you credit.

SOLOMON: I'm telling you the truth! If they would close the stores for six months in this country there would be from coast to coast a regular massacre. With this kind of furniture the shopping is over, it's finished, there's no more possibilities, you *got* it, you see? So you got a problem here.

VICTOR, *laughing:* Solomon, you are one of the greatest. But I'm way ahead of you, it's not going to work.

SOLOMON, *offended:* What "work"? I don't know how much time I got. What is so terrible if I say that? The trouble is, you're such a young fella you don't understand these things—

VICTOR: I understand very well, I know what you're up against. I'm not so young.

SOLOMON, *scoffing:* What are you, forty? Forty-five?

VICTOR: I'm going to be fifty.

SOLOMON: Fifty! You're a baby boy!

VICTOR: Some baby.

SOLOMON: My God, if I was fifty . . . ! I got married I was seventy-five.

VICTOR: Go on.

SOLOMON: What are you talking? She's still living by Eighth Avenue over there. See, that's why I like to stay liquid, because I don't want her to get her hands on this. . . . Birds she loves. She's living there with maybe a hundred birds. She gives you a plate of soup it's got feathers. I didn't work all my life for them birds.

VICTOR: I appreciate your problems, Mr. Solomon, but I don't have to pay for them. *He stands.* I've got no more time.

SOLOMON, *holding up a restraining hand—desperately:* I'm going to buy it! *He has shocked himself, and glances around at the towering masses of furniture.* I mean I'll ... *He moves, looking at the stuff.* I'll have to live, that's all, I'll make up my mind! I'll buy it.

VICTOR—*he is affected as Solomon's fear comes through to him:* We're talking about everything now.

SOLOMON, *angrily:* Everything, everything! *Going to his portfolio:* I'll figure it up, I'll give you a very nice price, and you'll be a happy man.

VICTOR, *sitting again:* That I doubt.

Solomon takes a hard-boiled egg out of the portfolio.

What's this now, lunch?

SOLOMON: You give me such an argument, I'm hungry! I'm not supposed to get too hungry.

VICTOR: Brother!

SOLOMON—*cracks the shell on his diamond ring:* You want me to starve to death? I'm going to be very quick here.

VICTOR: Boy—I picked a number!

SOLOMON: There wouldn't be a little salt, I suppose.

VICTOR: I'm not going running for salt now!

SOLOMON: Please, don't be blue. I'm going to knock you off your feet with the price, you'll see. *He swallows the egg. He now faces the furniture, and, half to himself, pad and pencil poised:* I'm going to go here like an IBM. *He starts estimating on his pad.*

VICTOR: That's all right, take it easy. As long as you're serious.

SOLOMON: Thank you. *He touches the hated buffet:* Ay, yi, yi. All right, well ... *He jots down a figure. He goes to the next piece, jots down another figure. He goes to another piece, jots down a figure.*

VICTOR, *after a moment:* You really got married at seventy-five?

SOLOMON: What's so terrible?

VICTOR: No, I think it's terrific. But what was the point?

SOLOMON: What's the point at twenty-five? You can't die twenty-six?

VICTOR, *laughing softly:* I guess so, ya.

SOLOMON: It's the same like secondhand furniture, you see; the whole thing is a viewpoint. It's a mental world. *He jots down another figure for another piece.* Seventy-five I got married, fifty-one, and twenty-two.

VICTOR: You're kidding.

SOLOMON: I wish! *He works, jotting his estimate of each piece on the pad, opening drawers, touching everything. Peering into a dark recess, he takes out a pencil flashlight, switches it on, and begins to probe with the beam.*

VICTOR—*he has gradually turned to watch Solomon, who goes on working:* Cut the kidding now—how old are you?

SOLOMON, *sliding out a drawer:* I'm eighty-nine. It's such an accomplishment?

VICTOR: You're a hell of a guy.

SOLOMON, *smiling with the encouragement and turning to Victor:* You know, it's a funny thing. It's so long since I took on such a load like this—you forget what kind of life it puts into you. To take out a pencil again ... it's a regular injection. Frankly, my telephone you could use for a ladle, it wouldn't interfere with nothing. I want to thank you. *He points at Victor.* I'm going to take good care of you, I mean it. I can open that?

VICTOR: Sure, anything.

SOLOMON, *going to an armoire:* Some of them had a mirror ... *He opens the armoire, and a rolled-up fur rug falls out. It is about three by five.* What's this?

VICTOR: God knows. I guess it's a rug.

SOLOMON, *holding it up:* No-no—that's a lap robe. Like for a car.

VICTOR: Say, that's right, ya. When they went driving. God, I haven't seen that in—

SOLOMON: You had a chauffeur?

VICTOR: Ya, we had a chauffeur.

Their eyes meet. Solomon looks at him as though Victor were coming into focus. Victor turns away. Now Solomon turns back to the armoire.

SOLOMON: Look at that! *He takes down an opera hat from the shelf within.* My God! *He puts it on, looks into the interior mirror.* What a world! *He turns to Victor:* He must've been some sporty guy!

VICTOR, *smiling:* You look pretty good!

SOLOMON: And from all this he could go so broke?

VICTOR: Why not? Sure. Took five weeks. Less.

SOLOMON: You don't say. And he couldn't make a comeback?

VICTOR: Well some men don't bounce, you know.

SOLOMON—*grunts:* Hmm! So what did he do?

VICTOR: Nothing. Just sat here. Listened to the radio.

SOLOMON: But what did he do? What—?

VICTOR: Well, now and then he was making change at the Automat. Toward the end he was delivering telegrams.

SOLOMON, *with grief and wonder:* You don't say. And how much he had?

VICTOR: Oh . . . couple of million, I guess.

SOLOMON: My God. What was the matter with him?

VICTOR: Well, my mother died around the same time. I guess that didn't help. Some men just don't bounce, that's all.

SOLOMON: Listen, I can tell you bounces. I went busted 1932; then 1923 they also knocked me out; the panic of 1904, 1898 . . . But to lay down like *that* . . .

VICTOR: Well, you're different. He believed in it.

SOLOMON: What he believed?

VICTOR: The system, the whole thing. He thought it was his fault, I guess. You—you come in with your song and dance, it's all a gag. You're a hundred and fifty years old, you tell your jokes, people fall in love with you, and you walk away with their furniture.

SOLOMON: That's not nice.

VICTOR: Don't shame me, will ya?—What do you say? You don't need to look any more, you know what I've got here.

Solomon is clearly at the end of his delaying resources. He looks about slowly; the furniture seems to loom over him like a threat or a promise. His eyes climb up to the edges of the ceiling, his hands grasping one another.

What are you afraid of? It'll keep you busy.

Solomon looks at him, wanting even more reassurance.

SOLOMON: You don't think it's foolish?

VICTOR: Who knows what's foolish? You enjoy it—

SOLOMON: Listen, I love it—

VICTOR:—so take it. You plan too much, you end up with nothing.

SOLOMON, *intimately:* I would like to tell you something. The last few months, I don't know what it is—she comes to me. You see, I had a daughter, she should rest in peace, she took her own life, a suicide. . . .

VICTOR: When was this?

SOLOMON: It was . . . 1916—the latter part. But very beautiful, a lovely face, with large eyes—she was pure like the morning. And lately, I don't know what it is—I see her clear like I see you. And every night practically, I lay down to go to sleep, so she sits there. And you can't help it, you ask yourself—what happened? What *happened*? Maybe I could have said something to her . . . maybe I *did* say something . . . it's all . . . *He looks at the furniture.* It's not that I'll die, you can't be afraid of that. But . . . I'll tell you the truth—a minute ago I mentioned I had three wives . . . *Slight pause. His fear rises.* Just this minute I realize I had four. Isn't that terrible? The first time was nineteen, in Lithuania. See, that's what I mean—it's impossible to know what is important. Here I'm sitting with you . . . and . . . and . . . *He looks around at the furniture.* What for? Not that I don't want it, I want it, but . . . You see, all my life I was a terrible fighter—you could never take nothing from me; I pushed, I pulled, I struggled in six different countries, I nearly got killed a couple times, and it's . . . It's like now I'm sitting here talking to you and I tell you it's a dream, it's a dream! You see, you can't imagine it because—

VICTOR: I know what you're talking about. But it's not a dream—it's that you've got to make decisions before you know what's involved, but you're stuck with the results anyway. Like I was very good in science—I loved it. But I had to drop out to feed the old man. And I figured I'd go on the Force temporarily, just to get us through the Depression, then go back to school. But the war came, we had the kid, and you turn around and you've racked up fifteen years on the pension. And what you started out to do is a million miles away. Not that I regret it all—we brought up a terrific boy, for one thing; nobody's ever going to take that guy. But it's like you were saying—it's impossible to know what's important. We always agreed, we stay out of the rat race and live our own life. That was important. But you shovel the crap out the window, it comes back in under the door—it all ends up she wants, she wants. And I can't really blame her—there's just no respect for anything but money.

SOLOMON: What've you got against money?

VICTOR: Nothing, I just didn't want to lay down my life for it. But I think I laid it down another way, and I'm not even sure any more what I was trying to accomplish. I look back now, and all I can see is a long, brainless walk in the street. I guess it's the old story; do anything, but just be sure you win. Like my brother; years ago I was living up here with the old man, and he used to contribute five dollars a month. A *month*! And a successful surgeon. But the few times he'd come around, the expression on the old man's face—you'd think God walked in. The respect, you know what I mean? The respect! And why not? Why not?

SOLOMON: Well, sure, he had the power.

VICTOR: Now you said it—if you got that you got it all. You're even lovable! *He laughs.* Well, what do you say? Give me the price.

SOLOMON—*slight pause:* I'll give you eleven hundred dollars.

VICTOR—*slight pause:* For everything?

SOLOMON, *in a breathless way:* Everything.

  Slight pause. Victor looks around at the furniture.

I want it so I'm giving you a good price. Believe me, you will never do better. I want it; I made up my mind.

  Victor continues staring at the stuff. Solomon takes out a common envelope and removes a wad of bills.

Here . . . I'll pay you now. *He readies a bill to start counting it out.*

VICTOR: It's that I have to split it, see—

SOLOMON: All right . . . so I'll make out a receipt for you and I'll put down six hundred dollars.

VICTOR: No-no . . . *He gets up and moves at random, looking at the furniture.*

SOLOMON: Why not? He took from you so take from him. If you want, I'll put down four hundred.

VICTOR: No, I don't want to do that. *Slight pause.* I'll call you tomorrow.

SOLOMON, *smiling:* All right; with God's help if I'm there tomorrow I'll answer the phone. If I wouldn't be . . . *Slight pause.* Then I wouldn't be.

VICTOR, *annoyed, but wanting to believe:* Don't start that again, will you?

SOLOMON: Look, you convinced me, so I want it. So what should I do?

VICTOR: *I* convinced *you?*

SOLOMON, *very distressed:* Absolutely you convinced me. You saw it—the minute I looked at it I was going to walk out!

VICTOR, *cutting him off, angered at his own indecision:* Ah, the hell with it. *He holds out his hand.* Give it to me.

SOLOMON, *wanting Victor's good will:* Please, don't be blue.

VICTOR: Oh, it all stinks. *Jabbing forth his hand:* Come on.

SOLOMON, *with a bill raised over Victor's hand—protesting:* What stinks? You should be happy. Now you can buy her a nice coat, take her to Florida, maybe—

VICTOR, *nodding ironically:* Right, right! We'll all be happy now. Give it to me.

Solomon shakes his head and counts bills into his hand. Victor turns his head and looks at the piled walls of furniture.

SOLOMON: There's one hundred; two hundred; three hundred; four hundred . . . Take my advice, buy her a nice fur coat your troubles'll be over—

VICTOR: I know all about it. Come on.

SOLOMON: So you got there four, so I'm giving you . . . five, six, seven . . . I mean it's already in the Bible, the rat race. The minute she laid her hand on the apple, that's it.

VICTOR: I never read the Bible. Come on.

SOLOMON: If you'll read it you'll see—there's always a rat race, you can't stay out of it. So you got there seven, so now I'm giving you . . .

A man appears in the doorway. In his mid-fifties, well-barbered; hatless, in a camel's-hair coat, very healthy complexion. A look of sharp intelligence on his face.

Victor, seeing past Solomon, starts slightly with shock, withdrawing his hand from the next bill which Solomon is about to lay in it.

VICTOR, *suddenly flushed, his voice oddly high and boyish:* Walter!

WALTER—*enters the room, coming to Victor with extended hand and with a reserve of warmth but a stiff smile:* How are you, kid?

Solomon has moved out of their line of sight.

VICTOR—*shifts the money to his left hand as he shakes:* God, I never expected you.

WALTER, *of the money—half-humorously:* Sorry I'm late. What are you doing?

VICTOR, *fighting a treason to himself, thus taking on a strained humorous air:* I . . . I just sold it.

WALTER: Good! How much?

VICTOR, *as though absolutely certain now he has been had:* Ah . . . eleven hundred.

WALTER, *in a dead voice shorn of comment:* Oh. Well, good. *He turns rather deliberately—but not overly so—to Solomon:* For everything?

SOLOMON—*comes to Walter, his hand extended; with an energized voice that braves everything:* I'm very happy to meet you, Doctor! My name is Gregory Solomon.

WALTER—*the look on his face is rather amused, but his reserve has possibilities of accusation:* How do you do?

He shakes Solomon's hand, as Victor raises his hand to smooth down his hair, a look of near-alarm for himself on his face.

CURTAIN

ACT TWO

The action is continuous. As the curtain rises Walter is just releasing Solomon's hand and turning about to face Victor. His posture is reserved, stiffened by traditional control over a nearly fierce curiosity. His grin is disciplined and rather hard, but his eyes are warm and combative.

WALTER: How's Esther?

VICTOR: Fine. Should be here any minute.

WALTER: Here? Good! And what's Richard doing?

VICTOR: He's at M.I.T.

WALTER: No kidding! M.I.T.!

VICTOR, *nodding:* They gave him a full scholarship.

WALTER, *dispelling his surprise:* What do you know. *With a wider smile, and embarrassed warmth:* You're proud.

VICTOR: I guess so. They put him in the Honors Program.

WALTER: Really. That's wonderful.—You don't mind my coming, do you?

VICTOR: No! I called you a couple of times.

WALTER: Yes, my nurse told me. What's Richard interested in?

VICTOR: Science. So far, anyway. *With security:* How're yours?

WALTER—*moving, he breaks the confrontation:* I suppose Jean turned out best—but I don't think you ever saw her.

VICTOR: I never did, no.

WALTER: The *Times* gave her quite a spread last fall. Pretty fair designer.

VICTOR: Oh? That's great. And the boys? They in school?

WALTER: They often are. *Abruptly laughs, refusing his own embarrassment:* I hardly see them, Vic. With all the unsolved mysteries in the world they're investigating the guitar. But what the hell . . . I've given up worrying about them. *He walks past Solomon, glancing at the furniture:* I'd forgotten how much he had up here. There's your radio!

VICTOR, *smiling with him:* I know, I saw it.

WALTER, *looking down at the radio, then upward to the ceiling through which the battery once exploded. Both laugh. Then he glances with open feeling at Victor:* Long time.

VICTOR, *fending off the common emotion:* Yes. How's Dorothy?

WALTER, *cryptically:* She's all right, I guess. *He moves, glancing at the things, but again with suddenness turns back.* Looking forward to seeing Esther again. She still writing poetry?

VICTOR: No, not for years now.

SOLOMON: He's got a very nice wife. We met.

WALTER, *surprised; as though at something intrusive:* Oh? *He turns back to the furniture.* Well. Same old junk, isn't it?

VICTOR, *downing a greater protest:* I wouldn't say that. Some of it isn't bad.

SOLOMON: One or two very nice things, Doctor. We came to a very nice agreement.

VICTOR, *with an implied rebuke:* I never thought you'd show up; I guess we'd better start all over again—

WALTER: Oh, no-no, I don't want to foul up your deal.

SOLOMON: Excuse me, Doctor—better you should take what you want now than we'll argue later. What did you want?

WALTER, *surprised, turning to Victor:* Oh, I didn't want anything. I came by to say hello, that's all.

VICTOR: I see. *Fending off Walter's apparent gesture with an over-quick movement toward the oar:* I found your oar, if you want it.

WALTER: Oar?

  Victor draws it out from behind furniture. A curved-blade sweep. Hah! *He receives the oar, looks up its length, and laughs, hefting it.* I must have been out of my mind!

SOLOMON: Excuse me, Doctor; if you want the oar—

WALTER, *standing the oar before Solomon, whom he leaves holding on to it:* Don't get excited, I don't want it.

SOLOMON: No. I was going to say—a personal thing like this I have no objection.

WALTER, *half-laughing:* That's very generous of you.

VICTOR, *apologizing for Solomon:* I threw in everything—I never thought you'd get here.

WALTER, *with a strained over-agreeableness:* Sure, that's all right. What are you taking?

VICTOR: Nothing, really. Esther might want a lamp or something like that.

SOLOMON: He's not interested, you see; he's a modern person, what are you going to do?

WALTER: You're not taking the harp?

VICTOR, *with a certain guilt:* Well, nobody plays . . . You take it, if you like.

SOLOMON: You'll excuse me, Doctor—the harp, please, that's another story . . .

WALTER—*laughs—archly amused and put out:* You don't mind if I make a suggestion, do you?

SOLOMON: Doctor, please, don't be offended, I only—

WALTER: Well, why do you interrupt? Relax, we're only talking. We haven't seen each other for a long time.

SOLOMON: Couldn't be better; I'm very sorry. *He sits, nervously pulling his cheek.*

WALTER, *touching the harp:* Kind of a pity—this was Grandpa's wedding present, you know.

VICTOR, *looking with surprise at the harp:* Say—that's right!

WALTER, *to Solomon:* What are you giving him fo this?

SOLOMON: I didn't itemize—one price for everything. Maybe three hundred dollars. That sounding board is cracked, you know.

VICTOR, *to Walter:* You want it?

SOLOMON: Please, Victor, I hope you're not going to take that away from me. *To Walter:* Look, Doctor, I'm not trying to fool you. The harp is the heart and soul of the deal. I realize it was your mother's harp, but like I tried to tell—*to Victor*—you before—*to Walter*—with used furniture you cannot be emotional.

WALTER: I guess it doesn't matter. *To Victor:* Actually, I was wondering if he kept any of Mother's evening gowns, did he?

VICTOR: I haven't really gone through it all—

SOLOMON, *raising a finger, eagerly:* Wait, wait, I think I can help you. *He goes to an armoire he had earlier looked into, and opens it.*
WALTER, *moving toward the armoire:* She had some spectacular—
SOLOMON, *drawing out the bottom of a gown elaborately embroidered in gold:* Is this what you mean?
WALTER: Yes, that's the stuff!

Solomon blows dust off and hands him the bottom of the gown. Isn't that beautiful! Say, I think she wore this at my wedding! *He takes it out of the closet, holds it up.* Sure! You remember this?
VICTOR: What do you want with it?

WALTER, *drawing out another gown off the rack:* Look at this one! Isn't that something? I thought Jeannie might make something new out of the material, I'd like her to wear something of Mother's.
VICTOR—*a new, surprising idea:* Oh! Fine, that's a nice idea.
SOLOMON: Take, take—they're beautiful.
WALTER, *suddenly glancing about as he lays the gowns across a chair:* What happened to the piano?
VICTOR: Oh, we sold that while I was still in school. We lived on it for a long time.
WALTER, *very interestedly:* I never knew that.
VICTOR: Sure. And the silver.
WALTER: Of course! Stupid of me not to remember that. *He half-sits against the back of a couch. His interest is avid, and his energy immense.* I suppose you know—you've gotten to look a great deal like Dad.
VICTOR: *I* do?
WALTER: It's very striking. And your voice is very much like his.
VICTOR: I know. It has that sound to me, sometimes.
SOLOMON: So, gentlemen . . . *He moves the money in his hand.*
VICTOR, *indicating Solomon:* Maybe we'd better settle this now.
WALTER: Yes, go ahead! *He walks off, looking at the furniture.*
SOLOMON, *indicating the money Victor holds:* You got there seven—
WALTER, *oblivious of Solomon; unable, so to speak, to settle for the status quo:* Wonderful to see you looking so well.
VICTOR—*the new interruption seems odd; observing more than speaking:* You do too, you look great.
WALTER: I ski a lot; and I ride nearly every morning. . . . You

know, I started to call you a dozen times this year—*He breaks off. Indicating Solomon:* Finish up, I'll talk to you later.

SOLOMON: So now I'm going to give you—*A bill is poised over Victor's hand.*

VICTOR, *to Walter:* That price all right with you?

WALTER: Oh, I don't want to interfere. It's just that I dealt with these fellows when I split up Dorothy's and my stuff last year, and I found—

VICTOR, *from an earlier impression:* You're not divorced, are you?

WALTER, *with a nervous shot of laughter:* Yes!

Esther enters on his line; she is carrying a suit in a plastic wrapper.

ESTHER, *surprised:* Walter! For heaven's sake!

WALTER, *eagerly jumping up, coming to her, shaking her hand:* How are you, Esther!

ESTHER, *between her disapproval and fascinated surprise:* What are *you* doing here?

WALTER: You've hardly changed!

ESTHER, *with a charged laugh, conflicted with herself:* Oh, go on now! *She hangs the suit on a chest handle.*

WALTER, *to Victor:* You son of a gun, she looks twenty-five!

VICTOR, *watching for Esther's reaction:* I know!

ESTHER, *flattered, and offended, too:* Oh stop it, Walter! *She sits.*

WALTER: But you do, honestly; you look marvelous.

SOLOMON: It's that suit, you see? What did I tell you, it's a very beautiful suit.

Victor laughs a little as Esther looks conflicted by Solomon's compliment.

ESTHER, *with mock-affront—to Victor:* What are you laughing at? It is. *She is about to laugh.*

VICTOR: You looked so surprised, that's all.

ESTHER: Well, I'm not used to walking into all these compliments! *She bursts out laughing.*

WALTER, *suddenly recalling—eagerly:* Say! I'm sorry I didn't know I'd be seeing you when I left the house this morning—I'd have brought you some lovely Indian bracelets. I got a whole boxful from Bombay.

ESTHER, *still not focused on Walter, sizing him up:* How do you come to—?

WALTER: I operated on this big textile guy and he keeps sending me things. He sent me this coat, in fact.

ESTHER: I was noticing it. That's gorgeous material.

WALTER: Isn't it? Two gallstones.

ESTHER, *her impression lingering for the instant:* How's Dorothy?— Did I hear you saying you were—?

WALTER, *very seriously:* We're divorced, ya. Last winter.

ESTHER: I'm sorry to hear that.

WALTER: It was coming a long time. We're both much better off— we're almost friendly now. *He laughs.*

ESTHER: Oh, stop that, you dog.

WALTER, *with naive excitement:* It's true!

ESTHER: Look, I'm for the woman, so don't hand me that. *To Victor—seeing the money in his hand:* Have you settled everything?

VICTOR: Just about, I guess.

WALTER: I was just telling Victor—*to Victor:* when we split things up I—*to Solomon:* you ever hear of Spitzer and Fox?

SOLOMON: Thirty years I know Spitzer and Fox. Bert Fox worked for me maybe ten, twelve years.

WALTER: They did my appraisal.

SOLOMON: They're good boys. Spitzer is not as good as Fox, but between the two you're in good hands.

WALTER: Yes. That's why I—

SOLOMON: Spitzer is vice president of the Appraisers' Association.

WALTER: I see. The point I'm making—

SOLOMON: I used to be president.

WALTER: Really.

SOLOMON: Oh yes. I made it all ethical.

WALTER, *trying to keep a straight face—and Victor as well:* Did you?

Victor suddenly bursts out laughing, which sets off Walter and Esther, and a warmth springs up among them.

SOLOMON, *smiling, but insistent:* What's so funny? Listen, before me was a jungle—you wouldn't laugh so much. I put in all the rates, what we charge, you know—I made it a profession, like doctors, lawyers—used to be it was a regular snakepit. But today, you got nothing to worry—all the members are hundred per cent ethical.

WALTER: Well, that was a good deed, Mr. Solomon—but I think you can do a little better on this furniture.

ESTHER, *to Victor, who has money in his hand:* How much has he offered?

VICTOR, *embarrassed, but braving it quite well:* Eleven hundred.

ESTHER, *distressed; with a transcendent protest:* Oh, I think that's . . . isn't that very low? *She looks to Walter's confirmation.*

WALTER, *familiarly:* Come on, Solomon. He's been risking his life for you every day; be generous—

SOLOMON, *to Esther:* That's a real brother! Wonderful. *To Walter:* But you can call anybody you like—Spitzer and Fox, Joe Brody, Paul Cavallo, Morris White—I know them all and I know what they'll tell you.

VICTOR, *striving to retain some assurance; to Esther:* See, the point he was making about it—

SOLOMON, *to Esther, raising his finger:* Listen to him because he—

VICTOR, *to Solomon:* Hold it one second, will you? *To Esther and Walter:* Not that I'm saying it's true, but he claims a lot of it is too big to get into the new apartments.

ESTHER, *half-laughing:* You believe that?

WALTER: I don't know, Esther, Spitzer and Fox said the same thing.

ESTHER: Walter, the city is full of big, old apartments!

SOLOMON: Darling, why don't you leave it to the boys?

ESTHER, *suppressing an outburst:* I wish you wouldn't order me around, Mr. Solomon! *To Walter, protesting:* Those two bureaus alone are worth a couple of hundred dollars!

WALTER, *delicately:* Maybe I oughtn't interfere—

ESTHER: Why? *Of Solomon:* Don't let him bulldoze you—

SOLOMON: My dear girl, you're talking without a basis—

ESTHER, *slashing:* I don't like this kind of dealing, Mr. Solomon! I just don't like it! *She is near tears. A pause. She turns back to Walter:* This money is very important to us, Walter.

WALTER, *chastised:* Yes. I . . . I'm sorry, Esther. *He looks about.* Well . . . if it was mine—

ESTHER: Why? It's yours as much as Victor's.

WALTER: Oh no, dear—I wouldn't take anything from this.

Pause.

VICTOR: No, Walter, you get half.

WALTER: I wouldn't think of it, kid. I came by to say hello, that's all.

Pause.

ESTHER—*she is very moved:* That's terrific, Walter. It's ... Really, I ...

VICTOR: Well, we'll talk about it.

WALTER: No-no, Vic, you've earned it. It's yours.

VICTOR, *rejecting the implication:* Why have I earned it? You take your share.

WALTER: Why don't we discuss it later? *To Solomon:* In my opinion—

SOLOMON, *to Victor:* So now you don't even have to split. *To Victor and Walter:* You're lucky they're tearing the building down—you got together, finally.

WALTER: I would have said a minimum of three thousand dollars.

ESTHER: That's exactly what I had in mind! *To Solomon:* I was going to say thirty-five hundred dollars.

WALTER, *to Victor; tactfully:* In that neighborhood.

Silence. Solomon sits there holding back comment, not looking at Victor, blinking with protest. Victor thinks for a moment; then turns to Solomon, and there is a wide discouragement in his voice.

VICTOR: Well? What do you say?

SOLOMON, *spreading out his hands helplessly, outraged:* What can I say? It's ridiculous. Why does he give you three thousand? What's the matter with five thousand, ten thousand?

WALTER, *to Victor, without criticism:* You should've gotten a couple of other estimates, you see, that's always the—

VICTOR: I've been calling you all week for just that reason, Walter, and you never came to the phone.

WALTER, *blushing:* Why would that stop you from—?

VICTOR: I didn't think I had the right to do it alone—the nurse gave you my messages, didn't she?

WALTER: I've been terribly tied up—and I had no intention of taking anything for myself, so I assumed—

VICTOR: But how was I supposed to know that?

WALTER, *with open self-reproach:* Yes. Well, I ... I beg your pardon. *He decides to stop there.*

SOLOMON: Excuse me, Doctor, but I can't understand you; first it's a lot of junk—

ESTHER: Nobody called it a lot of junk!

SOLOMON: He called it a lot of junk, Esther, when he walked in here.

Esther turns to Walter, puzzled and angry.

WALTER, *reacting to her look; to Solomon:* Now just a minute—

SOLOMON: No, please. *Indicating Victor:* This is a factual man, so let's be factual.

ESTHER: Well, that's an awfully strange thing to say, Walter.

WALTER, *intimately:* I didn't mean it in that sense, Esther—

SOLOMON: Doctor, please. You said junk.

WALTER, *sharply—and there is an over-meaning of much greater anger in his tone:* I didn't mean it in that sense, Mr. Solomon! *He controls himself—and, half to Esther:* When you've been brought up with things, you tend to be sick of them. . . . *To Esther:* That's all I meant.

SOLOMON: My dear man, if it was Louis Seize, Biedermeier, something like that, you wouldn't get sick.

WALTER, *pointing to a piece, and weakened by knowing he is exaggerating:* Well, there happens to be a piece right over there in Biedermeier style!

SOLOMON: Biedermeier "style"! *He picks up his hat.* I got a hat it's in Borsolino style but it's not a Borsolino. *To Victor:* I mean he don't have to charge me to make an impression.

WALTER, *striving for an air of amusement:* Now what's that supposed to mean?

VICTOR, *with a refusal to dump Solomon:* Well, what basis *do* you go on, Walter?

WALTER, *reddening but smiling:* I don't know . . . it's a feeling, that's all.

ESTHER—*there is ridicule:* Well, on what basis do you take eleven hundred, dear?

VICTOR, *angered; his manly leadership is suddenly in front:* I simply felt it was probably more or less right!

ESTHER, *as a refrain:* Oh God, here we go again. All right, throw it away—

SOLOMON, *indicating Victor:* Please, Esther, he's not throwing nothing away. This man is no fool! *To Walter as well:* Excuse me, but this is not right to do to him!

WALTER, *bridling, but retaining his smile:* You going to teach me what's right now?

ESTHER, *to Victor, expanding Walter's protest:* Really! I mean.

VICTOR—*obeying her protest for want of a certainty of his own, he touches Solomon's shoulder:* Mr. Solomon ... why don't you sit down in the bedroom for a few minutes and let us talk?

SOLOMON: Certainly, whatever you say. *He gets up.* Only please, you made a very nice deal, you got no right to be ashamed. . . . *To Esther:* Excuse me, I don't want to be personal.

ESTHER—*laughs angrily:* He's fantastic!

VICTOR, *trying to get him moving again:* Whyn't you go inside?

SOLOMON: I'm going; I only want you to understand, Victor, that if it was a different kind of man—*turning to Esther:* I would say to you that he's got the money in his hand, so the deal is concluded.

WALTER: He can't conclude any deal without me, Solomon, I'm half owner here.

SOLOMON, *to Victor:* You see? What did I ask you the first thing I walked in here? "Who is the owner?"

WALTER: Why do you confuse everything? I'm not making any claim, I merely—

SOLOMON: Then how do you come to interfere? He's got the money; I know the law!

WALTER, *angering:* Now you stop being foolish! Just stop it! I've got the best lawyers in New York, so go inside and sit down.

VICTOR, *as he turns back to escort Solomon:* Take it easy, Walter, come on, cut it out.

ESTHER, *striving to keep a light, amused tone:* Why? He's perfectly right.

VICTOR, *with a hard glance at her, moving upstage with Solomon:* Here, you better hold onto this money.

SOLOMON: No, that's yours; you hold . . .

   He sways. Victor grasps his arm. Walter gets up.

WALTER: You all right?

SOLOMON—*dizzy, he grasps his head:* Yes, yes, I'm . . .

WALTER, *coming to him:* Let me look at you. *He takes Solomon's wrists, looks into his face.*

SOLOMON: I'm only a little tired, I didn't take my nap today.

WALTER: Come in here, lie down for a moment. *He starts Solomon toward the bedroom.*

SOLOMON: Don't worry about me, I'm . . . *He halts and points back at his portfolio, leaning on a chest.* Please, Doctor, if you wouldn't mind—I got a Hershey's in there.

Walter hesitates to do his errand.

Helps me.

Walter unwillingly goes to the portfolio and reaches into it.

I'm a very healthy person, but a nap, you see, I have to have a . . .

Walter takes out an orange.

Not the orange—on the bottom is a Hershey's.

Walter takes out a Hershey bar.

That's a boy.

WALTER—*returns to him and helps him to the bedroom:* All right, come on . . . easy does it . . .

SOLOMON, *as he goes into the bedroom:* I'm all right, don't worry. You're very nice people.

Solomon and Walter exit into the bedroom. Victor glances at the money in his hand, then puts it on a table, setting the foil on it.

ESTHER: Why are you being so apologetic?

VICTOR: About what?

ESTHER: That old man. Was that his first offer?

VICTOR: Why do you believe Walter? He was obviously pulling a number out of a hat.

ESTHER: Well, I agree with him. Did you try to get him to go higher?

VICTOR: I don't know how to bargain and I'm not going to start now.

ESTHER: I wish you wouldn't be above everything, Victor, we're not twenty years old. We need this money.

He is silent.

You hear me?

VICTOR: I've made a deal, and that's it. You know, you take a tone sometimes—like I'm some kind of an incompetent.

ESTHER—*gets up, moves restlessly:* Well anyway, you'll get the whole amount.—God, he's certainly changed. It's amazing.

VICTOR, *without assent:* Seems so, ya.

ESTHER, *wanting him to join her:* He's so human! And he laughs!
VICTOR: I've seen him laugh.
ESTHER, *with a grin of trepidation:* Am I hearing something or is that my imagination?
VICTOR: I want to think about it.
ESTHER, *quietly:* You're not taking his share?
VICTOR: I said I would like to think . . .

    Assuming he will refuse Walter's share, she really doesn't know what to do or where to move, so she goes for her purse with a quick stride.

VICTOR, *getting up:* Where you going?
ESTHER, *turning back on him:* I want to know. Are you or aren't you taking his share?
VICTOR: Esther, I've been calling him all week; doesn't even bother to come to the phone, walks in here and smiles and I'm supposed to fall into his arms? I can't behave as though nothing ever happened, and you're not going to either! Now just take it easy, we're not dying of hunger.
ESTHER: I don't understand what you think you're upholding!
VICTOR, *outraged:* Where have you been?!
ESTHER: But he's doing exactly what you thought he should do! What do you *want*?
VICTOR: Certain things have happened, haven't they? I can't turn around this fast, kid. He's only been here ten minutes, I've got twenty-eight years to shake off my back. . . . Now sit down, I want you here. *He sits.*

    She remains standing, uncertain of what to do.

Please. You can wait a few minutes for your drink.
ESTHER, *in despair:* Vic, it's all blowing away.
VICTOR, *to diminish the entire prize:* Half of eleven hundred dollars is five-fifty, dear.
ESTHER: I'm not talking about money.

    Voices are heard from the bedroom.

He's obviously making a gesture, why can't you open yourself a little? *She lays her head back.* My mother was right—I can never believe anything I see. But I'm going to. That's all I'm going to do. What I see.

A chair scrapes in the bedroom.

VICTOR: Wipe your cheek, will you?

Walter enters from the bedroom.

How is he?

WALTER: I think he'll be all right. *Warmly:* God, what a pirate! *He sits.* He's eighty-nine!

ESTHER: I don't believe it!

VICTOR: He is. He showed me his—

WALTER, *laughing:* Oh, he show you that too?

VICTOR, *smiling:* Ya, the British Navy.

ESTHER: *He* was in the British Navy?

VICTOR, *building on Walter's support:* He's got a discharge. He's not altogether phony.

WALTER: I wouldn't go that far. A guy that age, though, still driving like that . . . *As though admitting Victor was not foolish:* There *is* something wonderful about it.

VICTOR, *understating: I* think so.

ESTHER: What do you think we ought to do, Walter?

WALTER—*slight pause. He is trying to modify what he believes is his overpowering force so as not to appear to be taking over. He is faintly smiling toward Victor:* There is a way to get a good deal more out of it. I suppose you know that, though.

VICTOR: Look, I'm not married to this guy. If you want to call another dealer we can compare.

WALTER: You don't have to do that; he's a registered appraiser.— You see, instead of selling it, you could make it a charitable contribution.

VICTOR: I don't understand.

WALTER: It's perfectly simple. He puts a value on it—let's say twenty-five thousand dollars, and—

ESTHER, *fascinated with a laugh:* Are you kidding?

WALTER: It's done all the time. It's a dream world but it's legal. He estimates its highest retail value, which could be put at some such figure. Then I donate it to the Salvation Army. I'd have to take ownership, you see, because my tax rate is much higher than yours so it would make more sense if I took the deduction. I pay around fifty per cent tax, so if I make a twenty-five-thousand-dollar contribution I'd be saving around twelve thousand in taxes. Which we could split however you wanted to. Let's say we split it in half, I'd give you six thousand dollars. *A pause.* It's really the only sensible way to do it, Vic.

ESTHER—*glances at Victor, but he remains silent:* Would it be costing you anything?

WALTER: On the contrary—it's found money to me. *To Victor:* I mentioned it to him just now.

VICTOR, *as though this had been the question:* What'd he say?

WALTER: It's up to you. We'd pay him an appraisal fee—fifty, sixty bucks.

VICTOR: Is he willing to do that?

WALTER: Well, of course he'd rather buy it outright, but what the hell—

ESTHER: Well, that's not his decision, is it?

VICTOR: No . . . it's just that I feel I did come to an agreement with him and I—

WALTER: Personally, I wouldn't let that bother me. He'd be making fifty bucks for filling out a piece of paper.

ESTHER: That's not bad for an afternoon.

   Pause.

VICTOR: I'd like to think about it.

ESTHER: There's not much time, though, if you want to deal with *him.*

VICTOR, *cornered:* I'd like a few minutes, that's all.

WALTER, *to Esther:* Sure . . . let him think it over. *To Victor:* It's perfectly legal, if that's what's bothering you. I almost did it with my stuff but I finally decided to keep it. *He laughs.* In fact, my own apartment is so loaded up it doesn't look too different from this.

ESTHER: Well, maybe you'll get married again.

WALTER: I doubt that very much, Esther.—I often feel I never should have.

ESTHER, *scoffing:* Why!

WALTER: Seriously. I'm in a strange business, you know. There's too much to learn and far too little time to learn it. And there's a price you have to pay for that. I tried awfully hard to kid myself but there's simply no time for people. Not the way a woman expects, if she's any kind of woman. *He laughs.* But I'm doing pretty well alone!

VICTOR: How would I list an amount like that on my income tax?

WALTER: Well . . . call it a gift.

Victor is silent, obviously in conflict. Walter sees the emotion.

Not that it is, but you could list it as such. It's allowed.

VICTOR: I see. I was just curious how it—

WALTER: Just enter it as a gift. There's no problem.

With the first sting of a vague resentment, Walter turns his eyes away. Esther raises her eyebrows, staring at the floor. Walter lifts the foil off the table—clearly changing the subject.

You still fence?

VICTOR, *almost gratefully pursuing this diversion:* No, you got to join a club and all that. And I work weekends often. I just found it here.

WALTER, *as though to warm the mood:* Mother used to love to watch him do this.

ESTHER, *surprised, pleased:* Really?

WALTER: Sure, she used to come to all his matches.

ESTHER, *to Victor, somehow charmed:* You never told me that.

WALTER: Of course; she's the one made him take it up. *He laughs to Victor.* She thought it was elegant!

VICTOR: Hey, that's right!

WALTER, *laughing at the memory:* He did look pretty good too! *He spreads his jacket away from his chest.* I've still got the wounds! *To Victor, who laughs:* Especially with those French gauntlets she—

VICTOR, *recalling:* Say. . . ! *Looking around with an enlivened need:* I wonder where the hell . . . *He suddenly moves toward a bureau.* Wait, I think they used to be in . . .

ESTHER, *to Walter: French* gauntlets?

WALTER: She brought them from Paris. Gorgeously embroidered. He looked like one of the musketeers.

Out of the drawer where he earlier found the ice skate, Victor takes a pair of emblazoned gauntlets.

VICTOR: Here they are! What do you know!

ESTHER, *reaching her hand out:* Aren't they beautiful!

He hands her one.

VICTOR: God, I'd forgotten all about them. *He slips one on his hand.*

WALTER: Christmas, 1929.

VICTOR, *moving his hand in the gauntlet:* Look at that, they're still soft . . . *To Walter—a little shy in asking:* How do you remember all this stuff?

WALTER: Why not? Don't you?

ESTHER: He doesn't remember your mother very well.

VICTOR: I remember her. *Looking at the gauntlet:* It's just her face; somehow I can never *see* her.

WALTER, *warmly:* That's amazing, Vic. *To Esther:* She adored him.

ESTHER, *pleased:* Did she?

WALTER: Victor? If it started to rain she'd run all the way to school with his galoshes. Her Victor—my God! By the time he could light a match he was already Louis Pasteur.

VICTOR: It's odd . . . like the harp! I can almost hear the music . . . But I can never see her face. Somehow. *For a moment, silence, as he looks across at the harp.*

WALTER: What's the problem?

Pause. Victor's eyes are swollen with feeling. He turns and looks up at Walter, who suddenly is embarrassed and oddly anxious.

SOLOMON—*enters from the bedroom. He looks quite distressed. He is in his vest, his tie is open. Without coming downstage:* Please, Doctor, if you wouldn't mind I would like to . . . *He breaks off, indicating the bedroom.*

WALTER: What is it?

SOLOMON: Just for one minute, please.

Walter stands. Solomon glances at Victor and Esther and returns to the bedroom.

WALTER: I'll be right back. *He goes rather quickly up and into the bedroom.*

A pause. Victor is sitting in silence, unable to face her.

ESTHER, *with delicacy and pity, sensing his conflicting feelings:* Why can't you take him as he is?

He glances at her.

Well you can't expect him to go into an apology, Vic—he probably sees it all differently, anyway.

He is silent. She comes to him.

I know it's difficult, but he is trying to make a gesture, I think.

VICTOR: I guess he is, yes.

ESTHER: You know what would be lovely? If we could take a few weeks and go to like ... out-of-the-way places ... just to really break it up and see all the things that people do. You've been around such mean, petty people for so long and little ugly tricks. I'm serious—it's not romantic. We're much too suspicious of everything.

VICTOR, *staring ahead:* Strange guy.

ESTHER: Why?

VICTOR: Well, to walk in that way—as though nothing ever happened.

ESTHER: Why not? What can be done about it?

VICTOR—*slight pause:* I feel I have to say something.

ESTHER, *with a slight trepidation, less than she feels:* What can you say?

VICTOR: You feel I ought to just take the money and shut up, heh?

ESTHER: But what's the point of going backwards?

VICTOR, *with a self-bracing tension:* I'm not going to take this money unless I talk to him.

ESTHER, *frightened:* You can't bear the thought that he's decent.

He looks at her sharply.

That's all it is, dear. I'm sorry, I have to say it.

VICTOR, *without raising his voice:* I can't bear that he's *decent*!

ESTHER: You throw this away, you've got to explain it to me. You can't go on blaming everything on him or the system or God knows what else! You're free and you can't make a move, Victor, and that's what's driving me crazy! *Silence. Quietly:* Now take this money.

He is silent, staring at her.

You take this money! Or I'm washed up. You hear me? If you're stuck it doesn't mean I have to be. Now that's it.

Movements are heard within the bedroom. She straightens. Victor smooths down his hair with a slow, preparatory motion of his hand, like one adjusting himself for combat.

WALTER—*enters from the bedroom, smiling, shaking his head. Indi-*

cating the bedroom: Boy—we got a tiger here. What is this between you, did you know him before?

VICTOR: No. Why? What'd he say?

WALTER: He's still trying to buy it outright. *He laughs.* He talks like you added five years by calling him up.

VICTOR: Well, what's the difference, I don't mind.

WALTER, *registering the distant rebuke:* No, that's fine, that's all right. *He sits. Slight pause.* We don't understand each other, do we?

VICTOR, *with a certain thrust, matching Walter's smile:* I am a little confused, Walter . . . yes.

WALTER: Why is that?

Victor doesn't answer at once.

Come on, we'll all be dead soon!

VICTOR: All right, I'll give you one example. When I called you Monday and Tuesday and again this morning—

WALTER: I've explained that.

VICTOR: But I don't make phone calls to pass the time. Your nurse sounded like I was a pest of some kind . . . it was humiliating.

WALTER—*oddly, he is over-upset:* I'm terribly sorry, she shouldn't have done that.

VICTOR: I know, Walter, but I can't imagine she takes that tone all by herself.

WALTER, *aware now of the depth of resentment in Victor:* Oh no—she's often that way. I've never referred to you like that.

Victor is silent, not convinced.

Believe me, will you? I'm terribly sorry. I'm overwhelmed with work, that's all it is.

VICTOR: Well, you asked me, so I'm telling you.

WALTER: Yes! You should! But don't misinterpret that. *Slight pause. His tension has increased. He braves a smile.* Now about this tax thing. He'd be willing to make the appraisal twenty-five thousand. *With difficulty:* If you'd like, I'd be perfectly willing for you to have the whole amount I'd be saving.

Slight pause.

ESTHER: Twelve thousand?

WALTER: Whatever it comes to.

Pause. Esther slowly looks to Victor.

You must be near retirement now, aren't you?

ESTHER, *excitedly:* He's past it. But he's trying to decide what to do.

WALTER: Oh. *To Victor—near open embarrassment now:* It would come in handy, then, wouldn't it?

Victor glances at him as a substitute for a reply.

I don't need it, that's all, Vic. Actually, I've been about to call you for quite some time now.

VICTOR: What for?

WALTER—*suddenly, with a strange quick laugh, he reaches and touches Victor's knee:* Don't be suspicious!

VICTOR, *grinning:* I'm just trying to figure it out, Walter.

WALTER: Yes, good. All right. *Slight pause.* I thought it was time we got to know one another. That's all.

Slight pause.

VICTOR: You know, Walter, I tried to call you a couple of times before this about the furniture—must be three years ago.

WALTER: I was sick.

VICTOR, *surprised:* Oh . . . Because I left a lot of messages.

WALTER: I was quite sick. I was hospitalized.

ESTHER: What happened?

WALTER—*slight pause. As though he were not quite sure whether to say it:* I broke down.

Slight pause.

VICTOR: I had no idea.

WALTER: Actually, I'm only beginning to catch up with things. I was out of commission for nearly three years. *With a thrust of success:* But I'm almost thankful for it now—I've never been happier!

ESTHER: You seem altogether different!

WALTER: I think I am, Esther. I live differently, I think differently. All I have now is a small apartment. And I got rid of the nursing homes—

VICTOR: What nursing homes?

WALTER, *with a removed self-amusement:* Oh, I owned three nursing homes. There's big money in the aged, you know. Helpless, desperate children trying to dump their parents—nothing like it. I even pulled out of the market. Fifty per cent of my time now is in City hospitals. And I tell you, I'm alive. For the first time. I do medicine, and that's it. *Attempting an intimate grin:* Not that I don't soak the rich occasionally, but only enough to live, really. *It is as though this was his mission here, and he waits for Victor's comment.*

VICTOR: Well, that must be great.

WALTER, *seizing on this minute encouragement:* Vic, I wish we could talk for weeks, there's so much I want to tell you. . . . *It is not rolling quite the way he would wish and he must pick examples of his new feelings out of the air.* I never had friends—you probably know that. But I do now, I have good friends. *He moves, sitting nearer Victor, his enthusiasm flowing.* It all happens so gradually. You start out wanting to be the best, and there's no question that you do need a certain fanaticism; there's so much to know and so little time. Until you've eliminated everything extraneous—*he smiles*—including people. And of course the time comes when you realize that you haven't merely been specializing in something—something has been specializing in you. You become a kind of instrument, an instrument that cuts money out of people, or fame out of the world. And it finally makes you stupid. Power can do that. You get to think that because you can frighten people they love you. Even that you love them.—And the whole thing comes down to fear. One night I found myself in the middle of my living room, dead drunk with a knife in my hand, getting ready to kill my wife.

ESTHER: Good Lord!

WALTER: Oh ya—and I nearly made it too! *He laughs.* But there's one virtue in going nuts—provided you survive, of course. You get to see the terror—not the screaming kind, but the slow, daily fear you call ambition, and cautiousness, and piling up the money. And really, what I wanted to tell you for some time now—is that you helped me to understand that in myself.

VICTOR: Me?

WALTER: Yes. *He grins warmly, embarrassed.* Because of what you did. I could never understand it, Vic—after all, you *were* the better student. And to stay with a job like that through all those years seemed . . . *He breaks off momentarily, the uncertainty of Victor's reception widening his smile.* You see, it never dawned on me until I got sick—that you'd made a choice.

VICTOR: A choice, how?

WALTER: You wanted a real life. And that's an expensive thing; it costs. *He has found his theme now; sees he has at last touched something in Victor. A breath of confidence comes through now.* I know I may sound terribly naive, but I'm still unused to talking about anything that matters. Frankly, I didn't answer your calls this week because I was afraid. I've struggled so long for a concept of myself and I'm not sure I can make it believable to you. But I'd like to. *He sees permission to go on in Victor's perplexed eyes:* You see, I got to a certain point where . . . I dreaded my own work; I finally couldn't cut. There are times, as you know, when if you leave someone alone he might live a year or two; while if you go in you might kill him. And the decision is often . . . not quite, but almost . . . arbitrary. But the odds are acceptable, provided you think the right thoughts. Or don't think at all, which I managed to do till then. *Slight pause. He is no longer smiling; instead, a near-embarrassment is on him.* I ran into a cluster of misjudgments. It can happen, but it never had to me, not one on top of the other. And they had one thing in common; they'd all been diagnosed by other men as inoperable. And quite suddenly the . . . the whole prospect of my own motives opened up. Why had I taken risks that very competent men had declined? And the quick answer, of course, is—to pull off the impossible. Shame the competition. But suddenly I saw something else. And it was terror. In dead center, directing my brains, my hands, my ambition—for thirty years.

Slight pause.

VICTOR: Terror of what?

Pause.

WALTER, *his gaze direct on Victor now:* Of it ever happening to me—*he glances at the center chair*—as it happened to him. Overnight, for no reason, to find yourself degraded and thrown-down. *With the faintest hint of impatience and challenge:* You know what I'm talking about, don't you?

Victor turns away slightly, refusing commitment.

Isn't that why you turned your back on it all?

VICTOR, *sensing the relevancy to himself now:* Partly. Not altogether, though.

WALTER: Vic, we were both running from the same thing. I

thought I wanted to be tops, but what it was was untouchable. I ended in a swamp of success and bankbooks, you on civil service. The difference is that you haven't hurt other people to defend yourself. And I've learned to respect that, Vic; you simply tried to make yourself useful.

ESTHER: That's wonderful—to come to such an understanding with yourself.

WALTER: Esther, it's a strange thing; in the hospital, for the first time since we were boys, I began to feel ... like a brother. In the sense that we shared something. *To Victor:* And I feel I would know how to be friends now.

VICTOR—*slight pause; he is unsure:* Well fine. I'm glad of that.

WALTER—*sees the reserve but feels he has made headway and presses on a bit more urgently:* You see, that's why you're still so married. That's a very rare thing. And why your boy's in such good shape. You've lived a real life. *To Esther:* But you know that better than I.

ESTHER: I don't know what I know, Walter.

WALTER: Don't doubt it, dear—believe me, you're fortunate people. *To Victor:* You know that, don't you?

VICTOR, *without looking at Esther:* I think so.

ESTHER: It's not quite as easy as you make it, Walter.

WALTER—*hesitates, then throws himself into it:* Look, I've had a wild idea—it'll probably seem absurd to you, but I wish you'd think about it before you dismiss it. I gather you haven't decided what to do with yourself now? You're retiring ... ?

VICTOR: I'll decide one of these days, I'm still thinking.

WALTER, *nervously:* Could I suggest something?

VICTOR: Sure, go ahead.

WALTER: We've been interviewing people for the new wing. For the administrative side. Kind of liaison people between the scientists and the board. And it occurred to me several times that you might fit in there.

Slight pause.

ESTHER, *with a release of expectation:* That would be wonderful!

VICTOR—*slight pause. He glances at her with suppression, but his voice betrays excitement:* What could I do there, though?

WALTER, *sensing Victor's interest:* It's kind of fluid at the moment, but there's a place for people with a certain amount of science who—

VICTOR: I have no degree, you know.

WALTER: But you've had analytic chemistry, and a lot of math and physics, if I recall. If you thought you needed it you could take some courses in the evenings. I think you have enough background.—How would you feel about that?

VICTOR, *digging in against the temptation:* Well . . . I'd like to know more about it, sure.

ESTHER, *as though to press him to accept:* It'd be great if he could work in science, it's really the only thing he ever wanted.

WALTER: I know; it's a pity he never went on with it. *Turning to Victor:* It'd be perfectly simple, Vic, I'm chairman of the committee. I could set it all up—

Solomon enters. They turn to him, surprised. He seems about to say something, but in fear changes his mind.

SOLOMON: Excuse me, go right ahead. *He goes nervously to his portfolio, reaching into it—which was not his original intention.* I'm sorry to disturb you. *He takes out an orange and starts back to the bedroom, then halts, addressing Walter:* About the harp. If you'll make me a straight out-and-out sale, I would be willing to go another fifty dollars. So it's eleven fifty, and between the two of you nobody has to do any favors.

WALTER: Well, you're getting warmer.

SOLOMON: I'm a fair person! So you don't have to bother with the appraisal and deductions, all right? *Before Walter can answer:* But don't rush, I'll wait. I'm at your service. *He goes quickly and worriedly into the bedroom.*

ESTHER, *starting to laugh; to Victor:* Where did you *find* him?

WALTER: —that wonderful? He "made it all ethical!"

Esther bursts out laughing, and Walter with her, and Victor manages to join. As it begins to subside, Walter turns to him.
What do you say, Vic? Will you come by?

The laughter is gone. The smile is just fading on Victor's face. He looks at nothing, as though deciding. The pause lengthens, and lengthens still. Now it begins to seem he may not speak at all. No one knows how to break into his puzzling silence. At last he turns to

Walter with a rather quick movement of his head as though he had made up his mind to take the step.

VICTOR: I'm not sure I know what you want, Walter.

   Walter looks shocked, astonished, almost unbelieving. But Victor's gaze is steady on him.

ESTHER, *with a tone of the conciliator shrouding her shock and protest:* I don't think that's being very fair, is it?

VICTOR: Why is it unfair? We're talking about some pretty big steps here. *To Walter:* Not that I don't appreciate it, Walter, but certain things have happened, haven't they? *With a half laugh:* It just seems odd to suddenly be talking about—

WALTER, *downing his resentment:* I'd hoped we could take one step at a time, that's all. It's very complicated between us, I think, and it seemed to me we might just try to—

VICTOR: I know, but you can understand it would be a little confusing.

WALTER—*unwillingly, anger peaks his voice:* What do you find confusing?

VICTOR—*considers for a moment, but he cannot go back:* You must have some idea, don't you?

WALTER: This is a little astonishing, Victor. After all these years you can't expect to settle everything in one conversation, can you? I simply felt that with a little good will we . . . we . . . *He sees Victor's adamant poise.* Oh, the hell with it. *He goes abruptly and snatches up his coat and one of the evening gowns.* Get what you can from the old man, I don't want any of it. *He goes and extends his hand to Esther, forcing a smile.* I'm sorry, Esther. It was nice seeing you anyway.

   Sickened, she accepts his hand.

Maybe I'll see you again, Vic. Good luck. *He starts for the door. There are tears in his eyes.*

ESTHER, *before she can think:* Walter?

   Walter halts and turns to her questioningly. She looks to Victor helplessly. But he cannot think either.

WALTER: I don't accept this resentment, Victor. It simply baffles me. I don't understand it. I just want you to know how I feel.

ESTHER, *assuaging:* It's not resentment, Walter.

VICTOR: The whole thing is a little fantastic to me, that's all. I haven't cracked a book in twenty-five years, how do I walk into a research laboratory?

ESTHER: But Walter feels that you have enough background—

VICTOR, *almost laughing over his quite concealed anger at her:* I know less chemistry than most high-school kids, Esther. *To Walter:* And physics, yet! Good God, Walter. *He laughs.* Where you been?

WALTER: I'm sure you could make a place for yourself—

VICTOR: What place? Running papers from one office to another?

WALTER: You're not serious.

VICTOR: Why? Sooner or later my being your brother is not going to mean very much, is it? I've been walking a beat for twenty-eight years, I'm not qualified for anything technical. What's this all about?

WALTER: Why do you keep asking what it's about? I've been perfectly open with you, Victor!

VICTOR: I don't think you have.

WALTER: Why! What do you think I'm—?

VICTOR: Well, when you say what you said a few minutes ago, I—

WALTER: What did I say?!

VICTOR, *with a resolutely cool smile:* What a pity it was that I didn't go on with science.

WALTER, *puzzled:* What's wrong with that?

VICTOR, *laughing:* Oh, Walter, come on, now!

WALTER: But I feel that. I've always felt that.

VICTOR, *smiling still, and pointing at the center chair; a new reverberation sounds in his voice:* There used to be a man in that chair, staring into space. Don't you remember that?

WALTER: Very well, yes. I sent him money every month.

VICTOR: You sent him five dollars every month.

WALTER: I could afford five dollars. But what's that got to do with you?

VICTOR: What it's got to do with me!

WALTER: Yes, I don't see that.

VICTOR: Where did you imagine the rest of his living was coming from?

WALTER: Victor, that was your decision, not mine.

VICTOR: My decision!

WALTER: We had a long talk in this room once, Victor.

VICTOR, *not recalling:* What talk?

WALTER, *astonished:* Victor! We came to a complete understanding—just after you moved up here with Dad. I told you then that I was going to finish my schooling come hell or high water, and I advised you to do the same. In fact, I warned you not to allow him to strangle your life. *To Esther:* And if I'm not mistaken I told you the same at your wedding, Esther.

VICTOR, *with an incredulous laugh:* Who the hell was supposed to keep him alive, Walter?

WALTER, *with a strange fear, more than anger:* Why did anybody have to? He wasn't sick. He was perfectly fit to go to work.

VICTOR: Work? In 1936? With no skill, no money?

WALTER—*outburst:* Then he could have gone on welfare! Who *was* he, some exiled royalty? What did a hundred and fifty million other people do in 1936? He'd have survived, Victor. Good God, you must know that by now, don't you?!

Slight pause.

VICTOR—*suddenly at the edge of fury, and caught by Walter's voicing his own opinion, he turns to Esther:* I've had enough of this, Esther; it's the same old thing all over again, let's get out of here. *He starts rapidly upstage toward the bedroom.*

WALTER, *quickly:* Vic! Please! *He catches Victor, who frees his arm.* I'm not running him down. I loved him in many ways—

ESTHER, *as though conceding her earlier position:* Vic, listen—maybe you *ought* to talk about it.

VICTOR: It's all pointless! The whole thing doesn't matter to me! *He turns to go to the bedroom.*

WALTER: He exploited you!

Victor halts, turns to him, his anger full in his face.

Doesn't that matter to you?

VICTOR: Let's get one thing straight, Walter—I am nobody's victim.

WALTER: But that's exactly what I've tried to tell you. I'm not trying to condescend.

VICTOR: Of course you are. Would you be saying any of this if I'd made a pile of money somewhere? *Dead stop.* I'm sorry, Walter, I can't take that. I made no choice; the icebox was empty and the man was sitting there with his mouth open. *Slight pause.* I didn't start this, Walter, and the whole thing doesn't interest me, but when you talk about making choices, and I should have gone on with science, I have to say something.—Just because you want things a certain way doesn't make them that way. *He has ended at a point distant from Walter.*

A slight pause.

WALTER, *with affront mixed into his trepidation:* All right then . . . How do *you* see it?

VICTOR: Look, you've been sick, Walter, why upset yourself with all this?

WALTER: It's important to me!

VICTOR, *trying to smile—and in a friendly way:* But why? It's all over the dam. *He starts toward the bedroom again.*

ESTHER: I think he's come to you in good faith, Victor.

He turns to her angrily, but she braves his look.

I don't see why you can't consider his offer.

VICTOR: I said I'd consider it.

ESTHER, *restraining a cry:* You know you're turning it down! *In a certain fear of him, but persisting:* I mean what's so dreadful about telling the truth, can it be any worse than this?

VICTOR: What "truth?" What are you—?

Solomon suddenly appears from the bedroom.

ESTHER: For God's sake, *now* what?

SOLOMON: I just didn't want you to think I wouldn't make the appraisal; I will, I'll do it—

ESTHER, *pointing to the bedroom:* Will you please leave us alone!

SOLOMON, *suddenly, his underlying emotion coming through; indicating Victor:* What do you want from him! He's a policeman! I'm a dealer, he's a doctor, and he's a policeman, so what's the good you'll tear him to pieces?!

ESTHER: Well, one of us has got to leave this room, Victor.

SOLOMON: Please, Esther, let me . . . *Going quickly to Walter:* Doctor, listen to me, take my advice—stop it. What can come of this? In the first place, if you take the deduction how do you know in two, three years they wouldn't come back to you, whereby they disallow it? I don't have to tell you, the Federal Government is not reliable. I understand very well you want to be sweet to him—*to Esther*—but can be two, three years before you'll know how sweet they're going to allow him. *To Victor and Walter:* In other words, what I'm trying to bring out, my boys, is that—

ESTHER: —you want the furniture.

SOLOMON, *shouting at her:* Esther, if I didn't want it I wouldn't buy it! But what can they settle here? It's still up to the Federal Government, don't you see? If they can't settle nothing they should stop it right now! *With a look of warning and alarm in his eyes:* Now please—do what I tell you! I'm not a fool! *He walks out into the bedroom, shaking.*

WALTER, *after a moment:* I guess he's got a point, Vic. Why don't you just sell it to him; maybe then we can sit down and talk sometime. *Glancing at the furniture:* It isn't really a very conducive atmosphere.—Can I call you?

VICTOR: Sure.

ESTHER: You're both fantastic. *She tries to laugh.* We're giving this furniture away because nobody's able to say the simplest things. You're incredible, the both of you.

WALTER, *a little shamed:* It isn't that easy, Esther.

ESTHER: Oh, what the hell—I'll say it. When he went to you, Walter, for the five hundred he needed to get his degree—

VICTOR: Esther! There's no—

ESTHER: It's one of the things standing between you, isn't it? Maybe Walter can clear it up. I mean . . . Good God, is there never to be an end? *To Walter, without pause:* Because it stunned him, Walter. He'll never say it, but—*she takes the plunge*—he hadn't the slightest doubt you'd lend it to him. So when you turned him down—

VICTOR, *as though it wearies him:* Esther, he was just starting out—

ESTHER, *in effect, taking her separate road:* Not the way you told me! Please let me finish! *To Walter:* You already had the house in Rye, you were perfectly well established, weren't you?

VICTOR: So what? He didn't feel he could—

WALTER, *with a certain dread, quietly:* No, no, I . . . I could have spared the money . . . *He sits slowly.* Please, Vic—sit down, it'll only take a moment.

VICTOR: I just don't see any point in—

WALTER: No—no; maybe it's just as well to talk now. We've never talked about this. I think perhaps we have to. *Slight pause. Toward Esther:* It *was* despicable; but I don't think I can leave it quite that way. *Slight pause.* Two or three days afterward—*to Victor*—after you came to see me, I phoned to offer you the money. Did you know that?

Slight pause.

VICTOR: Where'd you phone?

WALTER: Here. I spoke to Dad.

Slight pause. Victor sits.

I saw that I'd acted badly, and I—

VICTOR: You didn't act badly—

WALTER, *with a sudden flight of his voice:* It was frightful!! *He gathers himself against his past.* We'll have another talk, won't we? I wasn't prepared to go into all this. . . .

Victor is expressionless.

In any case . . . when I called here he told me you'd joined the Force. And I said—he mustn't permit you to do a thing like that. I said—you had a fine mind and with a little luck you could amount to something in science. That it was a terrible waste. Etcetera. And his answer was—"Victor wants to help me. I can't stop him."

Pause.

VICTOR: You told him you were ready to give me the money?

WALTER: Victor, you remember the . . . the helplessness in his voice. At that time? With Mother recently gone and everything shot out from under him?

VICTOR, *persisting:* Let me understand that, Walter; did you tell—?

WALTER, *in anguish, but hewing to himself:* There are conversations, aren't there, and looking back it's impossible to explain why you said or didn't say certain things? I'm not defending it, but I would like to be understood, if that's possible. You all seemed to need each other more, Vic—more than I needed them. I was never able to feel your kind of . . . faith in him; that . . . confidence. His selfishness—which was perfectly normal—was always obvious to me, but you never seemed to notice it. To the point where I used to blame myself for a lack of feeling. You understand? So when he said that you wanted to help him, I felt somehow that it'd be wrong for me to try to break it up between you. It seemed like interfering.

VICTOR: I see.—Because he never mentioned you'd offered the money.

WALTER: All I'm trying to convey is that . . . I was never indifferent; that's the whole point. I did call here to offer the loan, but he made it impossible, don't you see?

VICTOR: I understand.

WALTER, *eagerly:* Do you?

VICTOR: Yes.

WALTER, *sensing the unsaid:* Please say what you think. It's absurd to go on this way. What do you want to say?

VICTOR—*slight pause:* I think it was all . . . very convenient for you.

WALTER, *appalled:* That's all?

VICTOR: I think so. If you thought Dad meant so much to me—and I guess he did in a certain way—why would five hundred bucks break us apart? I'd have gone on supporting him; it would have let me finish school, that's all.—It doesn't make any sense, Walter.

WALTER, *with a hint of hysteria in his tone:* What makes sense?

VICTOR: You didn't give me the money because you didn't want to.

WALTER, *hurt and quietly enraged—slight pause:* It's that simple.

VICTOR: That's what it comes to, doesn't it? Not that you had any obligation, but if you want to help somebody you do it, if you don't you don't. *He sees Walter's growing frustration and Esther's impatience.* Well, why is that so astonishing? We do what we want to do, don't we? *Walter doesn't reply. Victor's anxiety rises.* I don't understand what you're bringing this all up for.

WALTER: You don't feel the need to heal anything.

VICTOR: I wouldn't mind that, but how does this heal anything?

ESTHER: I think he's been perfectly clear, Victor. He's asking your friendship.

VICTOR: By offering me a job and twelve thousand dollars?

WALTER: Why not? What else can I offer you?

VICTOR: But why do you have to offer me anything?

Walter is silent, morally checked.

It sounds like I have to be saved, or something.

WALTER: I simply felt that there was work you could do that you'd enjoy and I—

VICTOR: Walter, I haven't got the education, what are you talking about? You can't walk in with one splash and wash out twenty-eight years. There's a price people pay. I've paid it, it's all gone, I haven't got it any more. Just like you paid, didn't you? You've got no wife, you've lost your family, you're rattling around all over the place? Can you go home and start all over again from scratch? This is where we are; now, right here, now. And as long as we're talking, I have to tell you that this is not what you say in front of a man's wife.

WALTER, *glancing at Esther, certainty shattered:* What have I said . . . ?

VICTOR, *trying to laugh:* We don't need to be saved, Walter! I've done a job that has to be done and I think I've done it straight. You talk about being out of the rat race, in my opinion, you're in it as deep as you ever were. Maybe more.

ESTHER—*stands:* I want to go, Victor.

VICTOR: Please, Esther, he's said certain things and I don't think I can leave it this way.

ESTHER, *angrily:* Well, what's the difference?

VICTOR, *suppressing an outburst:* Because for some reason you don't understand *anything* any more! *He is trembling as he turns to Walter.* What are you trying to tell me—that it was all unnecessary? Is that it?

> *Walter is silent.*

Well, correct me, is that the message? Because that's all I get out of this.

WALTER, *toward Esther:* I guess it's impossible—

VICTOR, *the more strongly because Walter seems about to be allied with Esther:* What's impossible? . . . What do you *want,* Walter!

WALTER—*in the pause is the admission that he indeed has not leveled yet. And there is fear in his voice:* I wanted to be of some use. I've learned some painful things, but it isn't enough to know; I wanted to act on what I know.

VICTOR: Act—in what way?

WALTER, *knowing it may be a red flag, but his honor is up:* I feel . . . I could be of help. Why live, only to repeat the same mistakes again and again? I didn't want to let the chance go by, as I let it go before.

Victor is unconvinced.

And I must say, if this is as far as you can go with me, then you're only defeating yourself.

VICTOR: Like I did before.

Walter is silent.

Is that what you mean?

WALTER—*hesitates, then with frightened but desperate acceptance of combat:* All right, yes; that's what I meant.

VICTOR: Well, that's what I thought.—See, there's one thing about the cops—you get to learn how to listen to people, because if you don't hear right sometimes you end up with a knife in your back. In other words, I dreamed up the whole problem.

WALTER, *casting aside his caution, his character at issue:* Victor, my five hundred dollars was not what kept you from your degree! You could have left Pop and gone right on—he was perfectly fit.

VICTOR: And twelve million unemployed, what was that, my neurosis? I hypnotized myself every night to scrounge the outer leaves of lettuce from the Greek restaurant on the corner? The good parts we cut out of rotten grapefruit . . . ?

WALTER: I'm not trying to deny—

VICTOR, *leaning into Walter's face:* We were eating garbage here, buster!

ESTHER: But what is the point of—

VICTOR, *to Esther:* What are you trying to do, turn it all into a dream? *To Walter:* And perfectly fit! What about the inside of his head? The man was ashamed to go into the street!

ESTHER: But Victor, he's gone now.

VICTOR, *with a cry—he senses the weakness of his position:* Don't tell me he's gone now! *He is wracked, terribly alone before her.* He was here then, wasn't he? And a system broke down, did I invent that?

ESTHER: No, dear, but it's all different now.

VICTOR: What's different now? We're a goddamned army holding this city down and when it blows again you'll be thankful for a roof over your head! *To Walter:* How can you say that to me? I could have left him with your five dollars a month? I'm sorry, you can't brainwash me—if you got a hook in your mouth don't try to stick it into mine. You want to make up for things, you don't come around

to make fools out of people. I didn't invent my life. Not altogether.
You had a responsibility here and you walked on it. . . . You can go.
I'll send you your half.

*He is across the room from Walter, his face turned away. A long
pause.*

WALTER: If you can reach beyond anger, I'd like to tell you something. Vic? *Victor does not move.* I know I should have said this
many years ago. But I did try. When you came to me I told you—remember I said, "Ask Dad for money"? I did say that.

Pause.

VICTOR: What are you talking about?

WALTER: He had nearly four thousand dollars.

ESTHER: When?

WALTER: When they were eating garbage here.

Pause.

VICTOR: How do you know that?

WALTER: He'd asked me to invest it for him.

VICTOR: Invest it.

WALTER: Yes. Not long before he sent you to me for the loan.

Victor is silent.

That's why I never sent him more than I did. And if I'd had the
strength of my convictions I wouldn't have sent him that!

*Victor sits down in silence. A shame is flooding into him which he
struggles with. He looks at nobody.*

VICTOR, *as though still absorbing the fact:* He actually had it? In the
bank?

WALTER: Vic, that's what he was living on, basically, till he died.
What we gave him wasn't enough; you know that.

VICTOR: But he had those jobs—

WALTER: Meant very little. He lived on his money, believe me. I
told him at the time, if he would send you through I'd contribute
properly. But here he's got you running from job to job to feed
him—I'm damned if I'd sacrifice when he was holding out on you.
You can understand that, can't you?

*Victor turns to the center chair and, shaking his head, exhales a
blow of anger and astonishment.*

Kid, there's no point getting angry now. You know how terrified he was that he'd never earn anything any more. And there was just no reassuring him.

VICTOR, *with protest—it is still nearly incredible:* But he saw I was supporting him, didn't he?

WALTER: For how long, though?

VICTOR, *angering:* What do you mean, how long? He could see I wasn't walking out—

WALTER: I know, but he was sure you would sooner or later.

ESTHER: He was waiting for him to walk out.

WALTER—*fearing to inflame Victor, he undercuts the obvious answer:* Well . . . you could say that, yes.

ESTHER: I knew it! God, when do I believe what I see!

WALTER: He was terrified, dear, and . . . *To Victor:* I don't mean that he wasn't grateful to you, but he really couldn't understand it. I may as well say it, Vic—I myself never imagined you'd go that far.

Victor looks at him. Walter speaks with delicacy in the face of a possible explosion.

Well, you must certainly see now how extreme a thing it was, to stick with him like that? And at such cost to you?

Victor is silent.

ESTHER, *with sorrow:* He sees it.

WALTER, *to erase it all, to achieve the reconciliation:* We could work together, Vic. I know we could. And I'd love to try it. What do you say?

There is a long pause. Victor now glances at Esther to see her expression. He sees she wants him to. He is on the verge of throwing it all up. Finally he turns to Walter, a new note of awareness in his voice.

VICTOR: Why didn't you tell me he had that kind of money?

WALTER: But I did when you came to me for the loan.

VICTOR: To "ask Dad"?

WALTER: Yes!

VICTOR: But would I have come to you if I had the faintest idea he had four thousand dollars under his ass? It was meaningless to say that to me.

WALTER: Now just a second . . . *He starts to indicate the harp.*

VICTOR: Cut it out, Walter! I'm sorry, but it's kind of insulting. I'm not five years old! What am I supposed to make of this? You knew he had that kind of money, and came here many times, you sat here, the two of you, watching me walking around in this suit? And now you expect me to—?

WALTER, *sharply:* You certainly knew he had *something,* Victor!

VICTOR: What do you want here? What do you want here!

WALTER: Well, all I can tell you is that *I* wouldn't sit around eating garbage with *that* staring me in the face! *He points at the harp.* Even then it was worth a couple of hundred, maybe more! Your degree was right there. Right there, if nothing else.

Victor is silent, trembling.

But if you want to go on with this fantasy, it's all right with me. God knows, I've had a few of my own.

He starts for his coat.

VICTOR: Fantasy.

WALTER: It's a fantasy, Victor. Your father was penniless and your brother a son of a bitch, and you play no part at all. I said to ask him because you could see in front of your face that he had some money. You knew it then and you certainly know it now.

VICTOR: You mean if he had a few dollars left, that—?

ESTHER: What do you mean, a few dollars?

VICTOR, *trying to retract:* I didn't know he—

ESTHER: But you knew he had something?

VICTOR, *caught; as though in a dream where nothing is explicable:* I didn't say that.

ESTHER: Then what are you saying?

VICTOR, *pointing at Walter:* Don't you have anything to say to *him?*

ESTHER: I want to understand what you're saying! You knew he had money left?

VICTOR: Not four thousand dol—

ESTHER: But enough to make out?

VICTOR, *crying out in anger and for release:* I couldn't nail him to the wall, could I? He said he had nothing!

ESTHER, *stating and asking:* But you knew better.

VICTOR: I don't know what I knew! *He has called this out, and his voice and words surprise him. He sits staring, cornered by what he senses in himself.*

ESTHER: It's a farce. It's all a goddamned farce!

VICTOR: Don't. Don't say that.

ESTHER: Farce! To stick us into a furnished room so you could send him part of your pay? Even after we were married, to go on sending him money? Put off having children, live like mice—and all the time you knew he ...? Victor, I'm trying to understand you. Victor?—Victor!

VICTOR, *roaring out, agonized:* Stop it! Silence. *Then:* Jesus, you can't leave everything out like this. The man was a beaten dog, ashamed to walk in the street, how do you demand his last buck—?

ESTHER: You're still saying that? The man had *four thousand dollars*!

He is silent.

It was all an act! Beaten dog!—he was a calculating liar! And in your heart you knew it!

He is struck silent by the fact, which is still ungraspable.

No wonder you're paralyzed—you haven't believed a word you've said all these years. We've been lying away our existence all these years; down the sewer, day after day after day ... to protect a miserable cheap manipulator. No wonder it all seemed like a dream to me—it *was;* a goddamned nightmare. I knew it was all unreal, I knew it and I let it go by. Well, I can't any more, kid. I can't watch it another day. *I'm* not ready to die. *She moves toward her purse.*

She sits. Pause.

VICTOR—*not going to her; he can't. He is standing yards from her.* This isn't true either.

ESTHER: We are dying, that's what's true!

VICTOR: I'll tell you what happened. You want to hear it? *She catches the lack of advocacy in his tone, the simplicity. He moves from her, gathering himself, and glances at the center chair, then at Walter.* I did tell him what you'd said to me. I faced him with it. *He doesn't go on; his eyes go to the chair.* Not that I "faced" him, I just told him—"Walter said to ask you." *He stops; his stare is on the center chair, caught by memory; in effect, the last line was addressed to the chair.*

WALTER: And what happened?

Pause.

VICTOR, *quietly:* He laughed. I didn't know what to make of it. Tell you the truth—*to Esther*—I don't think a week has gone by that I haven't seen that laugh. Like it was some kind of a wild joke—because we *were* eating garbage here. *He breaks off.* I didn't know what I was supposed to do. And I went out. I went—*he sits, staring*—over to Bryant Park behind the public library. *Slight pause.* The grass was covered with men. Like a battlefield; a big open-air flophouse. And not bums—some of them still had shined shoes and good hats, busted businessmen, lawyers, skilled mechanics. Which I'd seen a hundred times. But suddenly—you know?—I *saw* it. *Slight pause.* There was no mercy. Anywhere. *Glancing at the chair at the end of the table:* One day you're the head of the house, at the head of the table, and suddenly you're shit. Overnight. And I tried to figure out that laugh.—How could he be holding out on me when he loved me?

ESTHER: Loved . . .

VICTOR, *his voice swelling with protest:* He loved me, Esther! He just didn't want to end up on the grass! It's not that you don't love somebody, it's that you've got to survive. We know what that feels like, don't we!

She can't answer, feeling the barb.

We do what we have to do. *With a wide gesture including her and Walter and himself:* What else are we talking about here? If he did have something left it was—

ESTHER: *"If "* he had—

VICTOR: What does that change! I know I'm talking like a fool, but what does that change? He couldn't believe in anybody anymore, and it was unbearable to me! *The unlooked-for return of his old feelings seems to anger him. Of Walter:* He'd kicked him in the face; my mother—*he glances toward Walter as he speaks; there is hardly a pause*—the night he told us he was bankrupt, my mother . . . It was right on this couch. She was all dressed up—for some affair, I think. Her hair was piled up, and long earrings? And he had his tuxedo on . . . and made us all sit down; and he told us it was all gone. And she vomited. *Slight pause. His horror and pity twist in his voice.* All over his arms. His hands. Just kept on vomiting, like thirty-five years coming up. And he sat there. Stinking like a sewer. And a look came onto his face. I'd never seen a man look like that. He was sitting there, letting it dry on his hands. *Pause. He turns to Esther.* What's the difference what you know? Do *you* do everything you know?

She avoids his eyes, his mourning shared.

Not that I excuse it; it was idiotic, nobody has to tell me that. But you're brought up to believe in one another, you're filled full of that crap—you can't help trying to keep it going, that's all. I thought if I stuck with him, if he could see that somebody was still ... *He breaks off; the reason strangely has fallen loose. He sits.* I can't explain it; I wanted to ... stop it from falling apart. I ... *He breaks off again, staring.*

Pause.

WALTER, *quietly:* It won't work, Vic.

Victor looks at him, then Esther does.

You see it yourself, don't you? It's not that at all. You see that, don't you?

VICTOR, *quietly, avidly:* What?

WALTER, *with his driving need:* Is it really that something fell apart? Were we really brought up to believe in one another? We were brought up to succeed, weren't we? Why else would he respect me so and not you? What fell apart? What was here to fall apart?

Victor looks away at the burgeoning vision.

Was there ever any love here? When he needed her, she vomited. And when you needed him, he laughed. What was unbearable is not that it all fell apart, it was that there was never anything here.

Victor turns back to him, fear on his face.

ESTHER, *as though she herself were somehow moving under the rays of judgment:* But who ... who can ever face that, Walter?

WALTER, *to her:* You have to! *To Victor:* What you saw behind the library was not that there was no mercy in the world, kid. It's that there was no love in this house. There was no loyalty. There was nothing here but a straight financial arrangement. That's what was unbearable. And you proceeded to wipe out what you saw.

VICTOR, *with terrible anxiety:* Wipe out—

WALTER: Vic, I've been in this box. I wasted thirty years protecting myself from that catastrophe. *He indicates the chair:* And I only got out alive when I saw that there was no catastrophe, there had never been. They were never lovers—she said a hundred times that her marriage destroyed her musical career. I saw that nothing fell here, Vic—and he doesn't follow me any more with that vomit on his hands. I don't look high and low for some betrayal any more; my days belong to *me* now, I'm not afraid to risk believing someone. All I ever wanted was simply to do science, but I invented an efficient, disaster-proof, money-maker. You—*to Esther, with a warm smile:* He could never stand the sight of blood. He was shy, he was sensitive ... *To Victor:* And what do you do? March straight into the most violent profession there is. We invent ourselves, Vic, to wipe out what we know. You invent a life of self-sacrifice, a life of duty; but what never existed here cannot be upheld. You were not upholding something, you were denying what you knew they were. And denying yourself. And that's all that is standing between us now—an illusion, Vic. That I kicked them in the face and you must uphold them against me. But I only saw then what you see now—there was nothing here to betray. I am not your enemy. It is all an illusion and if you could walk through it, we could meet ... *His reconciliation is on him.* You see why I said before, that in the hospital—when it struck me so that we ... we're brothers. It was only two seemingly different roads out of the same trap. It's almost as though—*he smiles warmly, uncertain still*—we're like two halves of the same guy. As though we can't quite move ahead—alone. You ever feel that?

Victor is silent.

Vic?

Pause.

VICTOR: Walter, I'll tell you—there are days when I can't remember what I've got against you. *He laughs emptily, in suffering.* It hangs in me like a rock. And I see myself in a store window, and my hair going, I'm walking the streets—and I can't remember why. And you can go crazy trying to figure it out when all the reasons disappear—when you can't even hate any more.

WALTER: Because it's unreal, Vic, and underneath you know it is.

VICTOR: Then give me something real.

WALTER: What can I give you?

VICTOR: I'm not blaming you now, I'm asking you. I can understand you walking out. I've wished a thousand times I'd done the same thing. But, to come here through all those years knowing what you knew and saying nothing . . . ?

WALTER: And if I said—Victor, if I said that I did have some wish to hold you back? What would that give you now?

VICTOR: Is that what you wanted? Walter, tell me the truth.

WALTER: I wanted the freedom to do my work. Does that mean I stole your life? *Crying out and standing:* You made those choices, Victor! And that's what you have to face!

VICTOR: But, what do you face? You're not turning me into a walking fifty-year-old mistake—we have to go home when you leave, we have to look at each other. What do *you* face?

WALTER: I have offered you everything I know how to!

VICTOR: I would know if you'd come to give me something! I would know that!

WALTER, *crossing for his coat:* You don't want the truth, you want a monster!

VICTOR: You came for the old handshake, didn't you! The okay!
      Walter halts in the doorway.
And you end up with the respect, the career, the money, and the best of all, the thing that nobody else can tell you so you can believe it—that you're one hell of a guy and never harmed anybody in your life! Well, you won't get it, not till I get mine!

WALTER: And you? You never had any hatred for me? Never a wish to see me destroyed? To destroy me, to destroy me with this saintly self-sacrifice, this mockery of sacrifice? What will you give me, Victor?

VICTOR: I don't have it to give you. Not any more. And you don't have it to give me. And there's nothing to give—I see that now. I just didn't want him to end up on the grass. And he didn't. That's all it was, and I don't need anything more. I couldn't work with you, Walter. I can't. I don't trust you.

WALTER: Vengeance. Down to the end. *To Esther:* He is sacrificing his life to vengeance.

ESTHER: Nothing was sacrificed.

WALTER, *to Victor:* To prove with your failure what a treacherous son of a bitch I am!—to hang yourself in my doorway!

ESTHER: Leave him, Walter—please, don't say any more!

WALTER—*humiliated by her. He is furious. He takes an unplanned step toward the door:* You quit; both of you. *To Victor as well:* You lay down and quit, and that's the long and short of all your ideology. It is all envy!

Solomon enters, appehensive, looks from one to the other.

And to this moment you haven't the guts to face it! But your failure does not give you moral authority! Not with me! I *worked* for what I made and there are people walking around today who'd have been dead if I hadn't. Yes. *Moving toward the door, he points at the center chair.* He was smarter than all of us—he saw what you wanted and he gave it to you! *He suddenly reaches out and grabs Solomon's face and laughs.* Go ahead, you old mutt—rob them blind, they love it! *Letting go, he turns to Victor.* You will never, never again make me ashamed! *He strides toward the doorway. A gown lies on the dining table, spread out, and he is halted in surprise at the sight of it.*

Suddenly Walter sweeps it up in his hands and rushes at Victor, flinging the gown at him with an outcry. Victor backs up at his wild approach.

VICTOR: Walter!

The flicker of a humiliated smile passes across Walter's face. He wants to disappear into air. He turns, hardly glancing at Victor, makes for the door, and, straightening, goes out.

VICTOR—*starts hesitantly to the door:* Maybe he oughtn't go into the street like that—

SOLOMON, *stopping him with his hand:* Let him go.

Victor turns to Solomon uncertainly.

What can you do?

ESTHER: Whatever you see, huh.

Solomon turns to her, questioningly.

You believe what you see.

SOLOMON, *thinking she was rebuking him:* What then?

ESTHER: No—it's wonderful. Maybe that's why you're still going.

Victor turns to her. She stares at the doorway.

I was nineteen years old when I first walked up those stairs—if that's believable. And he had a brother, who was the cleverest, most wonderful young doctor . . . in the world. As he'd be soon. Somehow, some way. *She turns to the center chair.* And a rather sweet, inoffensive gentleman, always waiting for the news to come on. . . . And next week, men we never saw or heard of will come and smash it all apart and take it all away.—So many times I thought—the one thing he wanted most was to talk to his brother, and that if they could— But he's come and he's gone. And I still feel it—isn't that terrible? It always seems to me that one little step more and some crazy kind of forgiveness will come and lift up everyone. When do you stop being so . . . foolish?

SOLOMON: I had a daughter, should rest in peace, she took her own life. That's nearly fifty years. And every night I lay down to sleep, she's sitting there. I see her clear like I see you. But if it was a miracle and she came to life, what would I say to her? *He turns back to Victor, paying out.* So you got there seven; so I'm giving you eight, nine, ten, eleven—*he searches, finds a fifty*—and there's a fifty for the harp. Now you'll excuse me—I got a lot of work here tonight. *He gets his pad and pencil and begins carefully listing each piece.*

VICTOR—*folds the money:* We could still make the picture, if you like.

ESTHER: Okay.

He goes to his suit and begins to rip the plastic wrapper off.
Don't bother.

He looks at her.

She turns to Solomon. Good-bye, Mr. Solomon.

SOLOMON—*looks up from his pad:* Good-bye, dear. I like that suit, that's very nice. *He returns to his work.*

ESTHER: Thank you. *She walks out with her life.*

VICTOR—*buckles on his gun belt, pulls up his tie:* When will you be taking it away?

SOLOMON: With God's help if I'll live, first thing in the morning.

VICTOR, *of the suit:* I'll be back for this later, then. And there's my foil, and the mask, and the gauntlets. *Puts on his uniform jacket.*

SOLOMON, *continuing his work:* Don't worry, I wouldn't touch it.

VICTOR, *extending his hand:* I'm glad to have met you, Solomon.

SOLOMON: Likewise. And I want to thank you.

VICTOR: What for?

SOLOMON, *with a glance at the furniture:* Well . . . who would ever believe I would start such a thing again . . . ? *He cuts himself off.* But go, go, I got a lot of work here.

VICTOR, *starting to the door, putting his cap on:* Good luck with it.

SOLOMON: Good luck you can never know till the last minute, my boy.

VICTOR, *smiling:* Right. Yes. *With a last look around at the room.* Well . . . bye-bye.

SOLOMON, *as Victor goes out:* Bye-bye, bye-bye.

He is alone. He has the pad and pencil in his hand, and he takes the pencil to start work again. But he looks about, and the challenge of it all oppresses him and he is afraid and worried. His hand goes to his cheek, he pulls his flesh in fear, his eyes circling the room.

His eye falls on the phonograph. He goes, inspects it, winds it up, sets the tone arm on the record, and flicks the starting lever. The Laughing Record plays. As the two comedians begin their routine, his depressed expression gives way to surprise. Now he smiles. He chuckles, and remembers. Now a laugh escapes, and he nods his head in recollection. He is laughing now, and shakes his head back and forth as though to say, "It still works!" And the laughter, of the record and his own, increase and combine. He holds his head, unable to stop laughing, and sits in the center chair. He leans back sprawling in the chair, laughing with tears in his eyes, howling helplessly to the air.

SLOW CURTAIN

THE CREATION OF THE WORLD AND OTHER BUSINESS

The Characters:

GOD   ANGELS:
ADAM   Raphael
                     Azrael
EVE   Chemuel

LUCIFER   CAIN

                     ABEL

THE CREATION OF THE WORLD
AND OTHER BUSINESS

ACT ONE

Music.

A night sky full of stars. Day spreads its pristine light, forming shadows in the contrasting sunlight. It is Paradise, the ultimate Garden—which is to say that it is all an impression of color rather than terrestrial details of plants and vines. Only one such feature stands apart; from the left, reaching out like an inverted, finger-spread hand, is a tree branch with golden leaves, from which hangs—an apple.

God appears on his throne above the acting level. He is deep in thought as he tries to visualize the inevitable future.

Now, as light spreads, the caw of a crow sounds, the dawn-welcoming chatter of monkeys, the hee-hawing ass, the lion's echoing roar, seals barking, pigs grunting, the loon's sudden laughter—all at once in free cacophony.

And as they subside and day is full, one of the shadows moves—a man, Adam, who reaches up above his head and plucks a fig and, propped up against a rock, crosses his legs and idly chews. He is in every way a man and naked, but his skin is imprinted with striped and speckled shadows, an animated congealment of light and color and darkness.

God emerges behind and to one side of him. He looks about, at the weather, up at the sky. Then He turns and looks down at Adam, who gradually feels His presence, and with only the slightest start of surprise. . . .

ADAM: Oh! Good morning, God!
GOD: Good morning, Adam. Beautiful day.

ADAM: Oh, perfect, Lord. But they all are.

GOD: I've turned up the breeze a little. . . .

ADAM: I just noticed that. *Holds up a hand to feel it.* This is exactly right now. Thanks, Lord.

GOD: I'm very pleased with the way you keep the garden. I see you've pruned the peach tree.

ADAM: I had to, Lord. An injured branch was crying all night. Are we going to name more things today?

GOD: I have something else to discuss with you this morning, but I don't see why we couldn't name a few things first. *He points.* What would you call that?

ADAM: That? I'd call that a lion.

GOD: Lion. Well, that sounds all right. And that?

ADAM: That? Ahhh . . . lamb?

GOD, *trying the word:* Lamb.

ADAM: I don't know what it is today—everything seems to start with L.

GOD: I must say that *looks* like a lamb. And that?

ADAM: L, L, L . . . That should be—ah . . . labbit?

GOD, *cocking His head doubtfully:* Labbit doesn't seem—

ADAM, *quickly:* You're right, that's wrong. See, I was rushing.

GOD: Slow down, we have all the time in the world.

ADAM: Actually, that looks like something that should begin with an R. . . . Rabbit!

GOD: Rabbit sounds much better.

ADAM, *happily:* Rabbit, rabbit!—oh, sure, that's much better.

GOD: How about that?

ADAM: I've been wondering about that. I have a feeling it should have a name that goes up and down, like . . . ka . . . ka . . .

GOD: Yes? Go on. . . . *Ka* what?

ADAM, *undulantly:* Ca-ter-pill-ar.

GOD: What an amazing creature you've turned out to be; I would never have thought of "Caterpillar" in a million years. That'll be enough for today. I imagine you've noticed by this time that all the animals live in pairs—there are male and female?

ADAM: I'm so glad you mentioned that.

GOD: Oh, it disturbs you?

ADAM: Oh no, Lord, nothing disturbs me.

GOD: I'm glad to see that you've settled for perfection.

ADAM: It just seemed odd that, of all the creatures, only I am alone. But I'm sure you have your reasons.

GOD: Actually, Adam—and I know this won't shake your confidence—but now and then I do something and, quite frankly, it's only afterwards that I discover the reasons. Which, of course, is just as well. In your case it was extremely experimental. I had just finished the chimpanzee and had some clay left over. And I—well, just played around with it, and by golly there you were, the spitting image of me. In fact, that is probably why I feel such a special closeness to you: you sprang out of my instinct rather than some design. And that is probably why it never occurred to me to give you a wife, you see.

ADAM: Oh, I see. What would it look like? Or don't you know yet?

GOD: Supposing I improvise something and see how it strikes you.

ADAM: All right. But would I have to—like, talk to it all the time?

GOD: What in the world gave you an idea like that?

ADAM: Well, these lions and monkeys and mice—they're all constantly talking to each other. And I so enjoy lying on my back and just listening to the lilacs budding.

GOD: You mean you'd rather remain alone?

ADAM: I don't know! I've never had anybody.

GOD: Well, neither have I, so I'm afraid I can't help you there. Why don't we just try it and see what happens?

ADAM: Of course, Lord, anything you say.

GOD: Lie down, then, and I'll put you to sleep.

ADAM: Yes, Lord.

He lies down. God feels his rib cage.

GOD: I'll take out a bottom rib. This one here. You'll never know the difference.

ADAM, *starting up:* Is that—fairly definite?

GOD: Oh, don't worry, I shouldn't have put it in in the first place, but I wanted to be extra sure. Now close your eyes.

ADAM, *lying back nervously:* Yes, sir. . . . *Starts up again.* Is this also going to be experimental, or—I mean how long are we going to keep her?

GOD: Now look, son, you don't have to hang around her every minute. If it gets too much, you just walk off by yourself.

ADAM: Oh, good. *Starts lying down, then sits up nervously.* I just wondered.

GOD: Sleep, Adam! *He ceremonially lowers his hands on Adam's rib. Something stirs on the periphery, rising from the ground. Music.*

> This is now bone of thy bones,
> And flesh of thy flesh;
> She shall be called ... Woman,
> Because she was taken out of Man.

Wake up, Adam. *Adam opens his eyes and sits up. Eve moves out of the darkness, and they look at each other. Her skin too is covered with shadow-marks. God walks around her, inspecting her.* Hmmmm. Very nice. *To Adam:* What do you say? *Music dies off.*

ADAM, *nervously:* Well ... she certainly is *different.*

GOD: Is that all?

ADAM: Oh, Lord, she's perfect! *But he is still uneasy.*

GOD: I think so too.

ADAM: Me too.

GOD: Huh! I don't know how I do it! What would you like to call her?

ADAM: Eve.

GOD: Eve! Lovely name. *Takes her hand.* Now dear, you will notice many different kinds of animals in this garden. Each has its inborn rule. The bee will not eat meat; the elephant will not sing and fish have no interest in flowers.—Those are apples on that tree; you will not eat them.

EVE: Why?

ADAM: That's the rule!

GOD: Be patient, Adam, she's very new. *To Eve:* Perhaps the day will come when I can give you a fuller explanation; for the moment, we'll put it this way. That is the Tree of Knowledge, Knowledge of Good and Evil. All that you have here springs from my love for you; out of love for me you will not eat of that tree or you will surely die. Not right away, but sometime. Now tell me, Eve—when you look at that tree, what do you think of?

EVE, *looks up at the tree:* ... God?

ADAM: She got it!

GOD: That's exactly the point, dear. *Takes both their hands.* Now be glad of one another. And remember—if you eat of that tree you shall surely die. Not right away, but sometime. If you stay clear of it, everything will go on just as it is, forever. Eve?

EVE: Yes, Lord.

GOD: Adam?

ADAM: Yes, Lord.

GOD: It is all yours, my children, till the end of time.

He walks away and vanishes. Adam and Eve turn from God and face each other. They smile tentatively. Examine each other's hands, breasts. He sniffs her. Sniffs closer.

ADAM: You smell differently than I do.

EVE: You do too.

He kisses her lips. Then she kisses his. They smile. He gives a little wave.

ADAM: Well . . . maybe I'll see you again sometime. I feel like lying down over there.

EVE: I do too!

ADAM, *halting:* You do?

She stretches out.

EVE: I think I have the same thoughts you do.

ADAM, *deciding to test this:* Are you a little thirsty?

EVE: Mmhm.

ADAM: Me too. And a little hungry?

EVE: Mmhm.

ADAM: Well, that's nice. Here, want a fig?

EVE: I just felt like a fig! *They chew.*

ADAM: We can go swimming later, if you like.

EVE: Fine! That's just what I was thinking. *They lie in silence.*

ADAM: Beautiful, isn't it?

EVE: Oh, ya. Is it all right to ask—

ADAM: What?

EVE:—what you do all day?

ADAM: Well, up till recently I've been naming things. But that's practically over now. See that up there? *She looks up.* I named that a pomegranate.

EVE: Pomewhat?

ADAM: Pomegranate.

EVE: That doesn't look like a pomegranate.

ADAM: Of course it's a pomegranate. *He fetches her one.* Here, eat one, you'll see. As you're spitting out the seeds it feels like "pomegranate, pomegranate, pomegranate." *She bites into it. As she spits out seeds.* Granate, granate, granate. . . .

EVE, *chewing, spitting out seeds:* Say . . . you're right, you're right.

ADAM: That's better.

EVE—*she suddenly plucks something out of his hair and holds it between her fingers:* What's this?

ADAM: That? That's a prndn. *He scratches himself.* It's one of the first things I named.

EVE: This you named a prndn?

ADAM, *with a tingle of alarm:* Now look, woman, once a thing is named, it's *named.*

EVE, *hurt, surprised:* Oh.

ADAM—*conviction failing, he turns back to her:* Why? What should I call it?

EVE: Well, to *me,* this is a louse.

ADAM: Saaay! No wonder I woke up full of L's this morning! *With a happy laugh, she eats the louse.* Isn't it marvelous how we both have exactly the same thoughts, pretty near!

EVE, *chewing:* Yes. *He stares ahead, considering for a moment, then, to show off, he spreads his arms and stands on one foot.* So what do you do all day?

ADAM: Sometimes I do this. Or this. *He rolls onto his head and does a headstand. She watches for a moment. His headstand collapses.* Why? Do you have something in mind?

EVE: I think I do, but I don't know what it is. Say, that bush!

ADAM: What about it?

EVE: I just saw it growing!

ADAM: Oh, sure. Listen . . . do you hear?

EVE: Yes. What is that sound?

ADAM: That's the sound of sunset.

EVE: And that crackling?

ADAM: A shadow is moving across dry leaves.

EVE: What is that piping sound?

ADAM: Two trout are talking in the river.

EVE, *looking upward:* Something has exhaled.

ADAM: God is sighing.

EVE: Something is rising and falling.

ADAM: That's the footsteps of an angel walking through the vines. Come, I'll show you the pool.

EVE, *getting up:* I was just thinking that!

ADAM: Good for you! I'll teach you to ride my alligators! *With a comradely arm over her shoulder he walks her out, as angels Chemuel, Azrael, and Raphael enter on the platform.*

CHEMUEL: Did you ever see anything so sweet?

RAPHAEL: Look at him putting a plum in her mouth! How lovely! *God enters on the platform.*

CHEMUEL: She's adorable! Lord, you've done it again. *God, however, has left the group and stands in deep thought, apart.* Everybody! Halllllll-elujah!

ANGELS, *singing Handel:* Hallelujah, hallelujah . . .

A full-blown orchestra and mighty chorus erupt from the air in accompaniment.

GOD, *motioning them out:* Excuse me! A little later, perhaps. I'd like a few words with Lucifer.

CHEMUEL, *kissing God's hand, as they leave:* Congratulations, Lord!

RAPHAEL: We'll bring the full chorus tonight!

Alone, God looks down at the earth, as Lucifer enters.

GOD: All right, go ahead, say it.

LUCIFER: Nothing for me to say, Lord. *He points below.* You see it as well as I.

GOD, *looking down, shaking His head:* What did I do wrong?

LUCIFER: Why look at it that way? They're beautiful, they help each other, they praise You every few minutes—

GOD: Lucifer, they don't multiply.

LUCIFER: Maybe give them a few more years. . . .

GOD: But there's no sign of anything. Look at them—the middle of a perfect, moonlit night, and they're playing handball.

LUCIFER: Well, You wanted them innocent.

GOD: Every once in a while, though, he does seem to get aroused.

LUCIFER: Aroused, yes, but what's the good if he doesn't get it in the right place? And when he does, she walks off to pick a flower or something.

GOD: I can't figure that out. *Pause. They stare down.*

LUCIFER: Of course, You could always—*He breaks off.*

GOD: What?

LUCIFER: Look, I don't want to mix in, and then You'll say I'm criticizing everything—

GOD: I don't know why I stand for your superciliousness.

LUCIFER: At least I don't bore You like the rest of these spirits.

GOD: Sometimes I'd just as soon you did. What have you got in mind?

LUCIFER: Now, remember, You asked me.

GOD: What have you got in mind!

LUCIFER: You see? You're mad already.

GOD, *roaring furiously:* I am not mad!

LUCIFER: All right, all right. You could take her back and restring her insides. Reroute everything, so wherever he goes in it connects to the egg.

GOD: No-no-no, I don't want to fool with that. She's perfect now; I'm not tearing her apart again. Out of the question.

LUCIFER: Well, then, You've only got one other choice. You've got to thin out the innocence down there. *God turns to him suspiciously.* See? You're giving me that look again; whatever I say, You turn it into some kind of a plot. Like when You made that fish with the fur on. Throw him in the ocean, and all the angels run around screaming hosannas. *I* come and tell You the thing's drowned, and You're insulted.

GOD: Yes. But I—I've stopped making fish with fur any more.

LUCIFER: But before I can penetrate with a fact I've got to go through hell.

GOD—*He suddenly points down:* He's putting his arm around her. *Lucifer looks down.* Lucifer! *They both stretch over the edge to see better.* Lucifer!! *Suddenly His expression changes to incredulity, then anger, and He throws up His hands in futile protest.* Where in the world does he get those stupid ideas!

LUCIFER, *still looking down:* Now he's going to sleep.

GOD: Oh, dear, dear, dear, dear. *He sits disconsolately.*

LUCIFER: Lord, the problem down there is that You've made it all so perfect. Everything they look at is not only good, it's equally good. The sun is good, rats are good, fleas are good, the moon, lions, athlete's foot—every single thing is just as good as every other thing. Because, naturally, You created everything, so everything's as attractive as everything else.

GOD: What's so terrible about perfection? Except that you can't stand it?

LUCIFER: Well, simply—if You want him to go into her, into the right place, and stay there long enough, You'll have to make that part better.

GOD: I am not remaking that woman.

LUCIFER: It's not necessary. All I'm saying is that sex has to be made not just good, but—well, terrific. Right now he'd just as soon pick his nose. In other words, You've got to rivet his attention on that one place.

GOD: How would I do that?

LUCIFER: Well, let's look at it. What is the one thing that makes him stop whatever he's doing and pay strict attention?

GOD: What?

LUCIFER: You, Lord. Soon as You appear, he, so to speak, comes erect. Give sex that same sort of holiness in his mind, the same sort of hope that is never discouraged and never really fulfilled, the same fear of being unacceptable. Make him feel toward sex as he feels toward You, and You're in—*unbeschreiblich!* Between such high promise and deadly terror, he won't be able to think of anything else.

Pause.

GOD: How?

LUCIFER: Well ... *He hesitates a long moment, until God slowly turns to him with a suspicious look.* All right, look—there's no way around it, I simply have to talk about those apples.

GOD, *stamps His foot and stands, strides up and down, trying to control His temper:* Lucifer!

LUCIFER: I refuse to believe that man's only way to demonstrate his love for God is to refuse to eat some fruit! That kind of game is simply unworthy of my father!

GOD, *angered:* Really now!

LUCIFER: Forgive me, sir, but I am useless to you if I don't speak my mind. May I tell you why *I* think You planted that tree in the garden? *God is silent, but consenting, even if unwillingly.* Objectively speaking, it *is* senseless. You wanted Adam's praise for everything You made, absolutely innocent of any doubt about Your goodness. Why, then, plant a fruit which can only make him wise, sophisticated, and analytical? May I continue? *God half-willingly nods.* He certainly will begin to question everything if he eats an apple, but why is that necessarily bad? *God looks surprised, angering.* He'll not only marvel that the flower blooms, he will ask why and discover chlorophyll—and bless You for chlorophyll. He'll not only praise You that food makes him strong, he will discover his bile duct and praise You for his pancreas. He may lose his innocence, but the more he learns of Your secrets, the more reasons he will have to praise You. And that is why, quite without consciously knowing it, You planted that tree there. It was Your fantastic inner urge to magnify Your glory to the last degree. In six words, Lord, You wanted full credit for everything.

GOD: He must never eat those apples.

LUCIFER: Then why have You tempted him? What is the point?

GOD: I wanted him to wake each morning, look at that tree, and say, "For God's sake I won't eat these apples." Not even one.

LUCIFER: Fine. But with that same absence of curiosity he is not investigating Eve.

GOD: But the other animals manage.

LUCIFER: Their females go into heat, and the balloon goes up. But Eve is ready almost any time, and that means no time. It's part of that whole dreadful uniformity down there.

GOD: They are my children; I don't want them to know evil.

LUCIFER: Why call it evil? One apple, and he'll know the difference between good and better. And once he knows that, he'll be all over her. *He looks down.* Look, he's kissing a tree. You see? The damned fool has no means of discriminating.

GOD, *looking down:* Well, he should kiss trees too.

LUCIFER: Fine. If that's the way You feel, You've got Adam and Eve, and it'll be a thousand years before you're a grandfather. *He stands.* Think it over. I'd be glad to go down and—*God gives him a look.* I'm only trying to help!

GOD: Lucifer, I'm way ahead of you.

LUCIFER: Lord, that's inevitable.

GOD: Stay away from that tree.

LUCIFER, *with a certain evasiveness:* Whatever You say, sir. May I go now?

GOD, *after a pause:* Don't have the illusion that I am in conflict about this; I mean, don't decide to go down there and do Me a favor, or something. I know perfectly well why I put that tree there.

LUCIFER, *surprised:* Really!

GOD: Yes, really. I am in perfect control over my unconscious, friend. It was not to tempt Adam; it's I who was tempted. I finished him and I saw he was beautiful, and for a moment I loved him beyond anything I had ever made—and I thought, maybe I should let him see through the rose petal to its chemistry, the formation of amino acids to the secrets of life. His simple praise for surfaces made me impatient to show him the physics of My art, which would raise him to a god.

LUCIFER: Why'd You change Your mind?

GOD: Because I thought of what became of you. The one angel who really understands biology and physics, the one I loved before all the rest and took such care to teach—and you can't take a breath without thinking how to overthrow Me and take over the universe!

LUCIFER: Lord, I only wanted them to know more, the more to praise You!

GOD: The more they know, the less they will need Me, Lucifer; you know that as well as I! And that's all you're after, to grind away their respect for Me. "Give them an apple!" If it weren't for the Law of the Conservation of Energy I would destroy you! Don't go near that tree or those dear people—not in any form, you hear? They are innocent, and innocent they will remain till I turn out the lights forever!

God goes out. Lucifer is alone.

LUCIFER: Now what is He *really* saying? He put it there to tempt *Himself*! Therefore He's not of one mind about innocence; and how could He be when innocence blinds Adam to half the wonders He has made? I will help the Lord. Yes, that's the only way to put it; I'm His helper. I open up the marvels He dares not show, and thereby magnify His glory. In short, I disobey what He says and carry out what He means, and if that's evil, it's only to do good. Strange—I never felt so close to my creator as I do right now! Once Adam eats, he'll multiply, and Lucifer completes the lovely world of God! Oh, praise the Lord who gave me all this insight! My fight with Him is over! Now evil be my good, and Eve and Adam multiply in blessed sin! Make way, dumb stars, the world of man begins!

He exits as light rises on Paradise, where Eve is bent over from the waist, examining a—to us invisible—turtle. Adam enters. His attention is caught by her raised buttocks, and he approaches, halts, and stares—then looks off, puzzled by an idea he can't quite form in his mind. Giving it up, he asks . . .

ADAM: You want to play volleyball?

Lucifer enters.

LUCIFER: Good evening.

ADAM: Good evening. *He nervously nudges Eve, who now stands up. Something in Lucifer moves something in her.*

EVE: Oh!

Lucifer exchanges a deep glance with her, then moves, glancing about, and then turns back to Adam.

LUCIFER: Had enough?

EVE: Enough of what?

LUCIFER: You don't imagine, do you, that God intended you to lie around like this forever?

ADAM: We're going swimming later.

LUCIFER: Swimming! What about making something of yourselves?

ADAM: Making some . . . ?

LUCIFER, *with a quick glance about for God:* I'm a little short of time, Adam. By the way, my name is Lucifer. The archangel?

ADAM, *impressed:* Ohhh! I'm very pleased to meet you. This is my wife, Eve.

EVE: How do you do?

LUCIFER, *taking her hand with a little pressure:* Awfully nice to meet you, Eve. Tell me, you ever hold your breath?

ADAM: Oh, sure, she does that a lot. Show him, Eve. *She inhales and holds it.* She can do that till she turns blue. *Eve lets out the air.*

EVE: I can really turn blue if I want to.

LUCIFER: And why does that happen?

ADAM: Because God makes it.

LUCIFER: But how, dear?

ADAM: How should she know?

LUCIFER: But God *wants* her to know.

ADAM: But why didn't He tell us?

LUCIFER: He's trying to tell you; that's why I've come; I am the Explainer. Adam, the fact is that God gives His most important commands through His silences. For example, there is nothing He feels more passionate about than that you begin to multiply.

EVE: Really?

LUCIFER: Of course. That's why that tree is there.

EVE: We multiply with the tree?

LUCIFER: No, but if you eat the fruit you'll know how. He just can't bring Himself to say it, you see.

EVE: Is that so!

ADAM: Now, wait a minute, excuse me. We're not even supposed to *think* about that tree.

EVE: Say, that's right. In fact, lately, that's practically all I do is go around not thinking about it.

LUCIFER: Oh, you find that's getting difficult?

EVE: No, but it takes up so much time.

ADAM: It's because we'll die if we eat those things. *Lucifer reaches up, takes the apple.* You better watch out, they're not good for you— Don't! *Lucifer bites into the apple, chews. They watch him, wide-eyed.* Oh, I know why, it's that you're an angel!

LUCIFER: You could be too.

ADAM, *worried:* Angels?

LUCIFER: Absolutely. Now listen carefully, because this is fairly deep and I may have to leave any minute. You know by now why the Lord put you in this lovely garden.

ADAM: To praise everything.

LUCIFER: Right. Now what if I told you that there are a number of things you've been leaving out?

ADAM, *shocked:* Oh, no! I praise absolutely everything.

LUCIFER, *pointing to his penis:* And what about this thing here? Do you praise Him for that?

ADAM, *looking down at himself:* Well, not in particular, but I include it in.

LUCIFER: But how can you when you don't know what it's for?

EVE: He pees that way.

LUCIFER: Pees! That is so incidental it's not even worth mentioning. *To Adam:* You have no idea, do you?

ADAM: Well . . . ahh . . .

LUCIFER: Yes?

ADAM: I'm only guessing, but sometimes it makes me feel—

LUCIFER: Feel what?

ADAM: Well . . . kind of sporty?

LUCIFER: Adam! God has made you in His image, given you His body. How dare you refuse to understand the very best part of it? Now you will eat this apple.

ADAM: Angel, please—I really don't feel I should.

LUCIFER, *holding the apple to Adam's tightly shut lips:* You must! Could I make this offer without God's permission?

EVE: Say, that's right!

LUCIFER: Of course it's right! I mean nothing happens He doesn't want to happen—*n'est-ce pas?* Now, you take one bite, and I promise you will understand everything. Adam, open your mouth and you will become—*he glances quickly about, lowers his voice*—like God.

ADAM: Like *God*! You should never say a thing like that!

LUCIFER: You're not even living like animals!

ADAM: I don't want to hear any more! He said it in plain Hebrew, don't eat those apples, and that's it! I'm going swimming. Eve?

EVE, *extending her hand to Lucifer:* Very nice to have met you.

LUCIFER, *slowly running his eyes from her feet to her face:* Likewise.

A strange sensation emanates from his eyes, and she slowly looks down at her body.

ADAM: Eve?

She unwillingly breaks from Lucifer, and they leave. Lucifer looks at the apple in his hand and takes a big bite. He stands there chewing thoughtfully. Offstage a splash is heard. A pause. Eve returns, glancing behind her, and hurries to Lucifer.

EVE: There's only one thing I wonder if you could tell me.

LUCIFER: I love questions, my dear. What is it?

EVE—*she looks down at herself, pointing:* Why has he got that thing and I don't?

LUCIFER: Isn't it funny? I knew you were going to ask that question.

EVE: Well, I mean, is it going to grow on later?

LUCIFER: Never.

EVE: Why?

LUCIFER, *offering her his apple:* Take a bite, Eve, and everything will clear up.

EVE—*she accepts the apple, looks at it:* It smells all right.

LUCIFER: Of course. It *is* all right.

EVE: Maybe just a little bite.

LUCIFER: Better make it medium. You have an awful lot to learn, dear.

EVE: Well . . . here goes! *She bites and chews, her eyes widening, her body moving sinuously. A dread sound fills the air. She approaches him.*

LUCIFER, *retreating:* 'Fraid I've got to leave, dear.

EVE: You going *now*?

LUCIFER: Oh, yes, right now! But I'll be around.

He hurries off, glancing behind with trepidation. She stands there staring. She feels her body, her breasts, her face, awakening to herself. She starts her hand down to her genitals and inhales a surprised breath. Adam enters. The sound goes silent.

ADAM: Where were you? Come on, the water's perfect! . . . Eve? *She turns to him.* What's the matter? *She sensuously touches his arm and puts it around her.* What are you doing? *She smashes her lips against his.* What is this? *She holds her apple before his face.*

EVE: Eat it.

ADAM: Eve!

EVE: It's marvelous! Please, a bite, a bite!

ADAM: But God said—

EVE: I'm God.

ADAM: You're what?

EVE: He is in me! He'll be in you! I never felt like this! I am the best thing that ever happened! Look at me! Adam, don't you see me?

ADAM: Well, sure, I—

EVE: You're not looking at me!

ADAM: Of course I'm looking at you!

EVE: But you're not *seeing* me! You don't see anything!

ADAM: Why? I see the trees, the sky—

EVE: You wouldn't see anything else if you were seeing me.

ADAM: How's that possible?

EVE: Say "Ahh."

ADAM: Ahh.

She suddenly pushes the apple into his mouth.

EVE: Chew! Swallow!

He chews. The dread sound again. She watches. He looks down at his penis. Then to her. Then up at her face, astonished. He starts to reach for her.

VOICE OF GOD, *echoing through the theater on the PA system:* WHERE ART THOU! *They both retract, glancing desperately around. They rush about, trying to hide from each other.* WHERE ART THOU!

ADAM: Here, quick! Put something on! *He hands her a leaf, which she holds in front of her.* Gee, you know you look even better with that leaf on—

EVE, *looking off:* He's coming!

They disappear. God enters.

GOD: Where art thou?

ADAM, *still unseen:* Here, Lord. *God turns, looking around. Adam emerges. He is wearing a large leaf. Nervously apologizing.* I heard Thy voice in the garden and I was afraid, because I was naked; and I hid myself. *Eve emerges.*

GOD: Who told thee that thou wast naked?

ADAM: Who told me?

GOD: Who told thee! You didn't know you were naked!

ADAM, *appalled, looking down at himself:* Say, that's right.

GOD, *mimicking him:* "Say, that's right." You ate the apple!

ADAM: She made me.

EVE: I couldn't help it. A snake came. *To Adam:* Wasn't he a snake?

ADAM: Like a snake, ya.

GOD: That son of a ...*Calling out:* Lucifer, I get my hands on you ...!

EVE: But why'd You put the tree here if You . . . ?

GOD: *You're* questioning *Me*! Who the hell do you think you are? I put the tree here so there would be at least one thing you shouldn't think about! So, unlike the animals, you should exercise a little self-control.

EVE: Oh!

GOD: "Oh," she says. I'll give you an "Oh" that you'll wish you'd never been born! But first I'm going to fix it between you and snakes. Serpent, because thou hast done this,

> Thou art cursed above all cattle,
>
> And above every beast of the field;
>
> And I will put enmity between thee and woman—
>
> That means all women will hate snakes.
>
> Or almost all.

You see? It's already impossible to make an absolute statement around here! You bad girl, look what you did to Me!

EVE, *covering her face:* I'm ashamed.

GOD: Ashamed! You don't know the half of it.

> I will greatly multiply thy sorrow and thy conception;
>
> In sorrow thou shalt bring forth children—

EVE: Oh God!

GOD: And thy desire shall be to thy husband

> And he shall rule over thee.

No more equals, you hear? He's the boss forever. Pull up your leaf.

He turns to Adam. And as for you, schmuck!

> Cursed is the ground for thy sake,
>
> In sorrow shalt thou eat of it all the days of thy life.
>
> Thorns and thistles shall it bring forth to thee;
>
> No more going around just picking up lunch.
>
> In the sweat of thy face shalt thou eat bread,
>
> Till thou return unto the ground;
>
> Yes, my friend, now there is time and age and death,
>
> No more living forever. You got it?
>
> For dust thou art.
>
> And unto dust shalt thou return.

ADAM—*he sobs:* What am I doing? What's this water?

GOD: You're weeping, my son, those are your first tears;

> There will be more before you're finished.
> Now you have become as one of us,
> A little lower than the angels,
> Because now you know good and evil.
> Adam and Eve? Get out of the Garden.

ADAM: Out where?

GOD, *pointing:* There!

ADAM: But that's a desert!

GOD: Right! It wasn't good enough for you here? Go and see how you make out on your own.

ADAM: God. Dear God, isn't there any way we can get back in? I don't want to be ashamed, I don't want to be so full of sadness. It was so wonderful here, we were both so innocent!

GOD: Out! You know too much to live in Eden.

ADAM: But I am ignorant!

GOD: Knowing you are ignorant is too much to know.
> The lion and the elephant, the spider and the mouse—
> They will remain, but they know My perfection
> Without knowing it. You ate what I forbade,
> You yearned for what you were not
> And thus laid a judgment on My work.
> I Am What I Am What I Am, but it was not enough;
> The warmth in the sand, the coolness of water,
> The coming and going of day and night—
> It was not enough to live in these things.
> You had to have power, and power is in you now,
> But not Eden any more. Listen, Adam. Listen, Eve.
> Can you hear the coming of night?

ADAM—*surprised, he raises his hand:* Why . . . no!

GOD: Can you hear the sound of shadows on the leaves?

EVE, *with immense loss and wonder:* No!

> *God turns his back on them, hurt, erect.*

EVE: Where is the voice of the trout talking in the river?

ADAM: Where are the footsteps of angels walking through the vines?

> *On the verge of weeping, they are turning to catch the sounds they knew, deaf to the world. Light is playing on them as instruments are*

heard playing a lugubrious tune. They dejectedly leave Paradise.

A sad bassoon solo emerges, played by Raphael. God, hands behind his back, turns to Raphael, Chemuel, and Azrael, who enter together.

GOD: That is the most depressing instrument I have ever heard.

RAPHAEL, *the bassoonist, protesting:* But You invented it, Lord.

GOD: I can't imagine how I could have thought of such a thing.

CHEMUEL: It was just after Eve ate the apple. You were very down. And You said, "I think I will invent the bassoon."

GOD: Well, put it away, Raphael.

AZRAEL: Look at Adam and Even down there. All they do any more is screw.

CHEMUEL: Maybe we ought to talk about something cheerful.

GOD: Do that, yes.

Pause. The angels think.

CHEMUEL: I think the Rocky Mountains are the best yet! *God turns to him, pained.* I mean the way they go up.

RAPHAEL: And then the way they go down.

GOD: I'm afraid that Lucifer was the only one of you who knew how to carry on a conversation.

AZRAEL, *a fierce fellow, deep-throated:* I would like to kill Adam and Eve.

GOD: That's natural, Azrael, as the Angel of Death, but I'm not ready for that yet.

AZRAEL: They like to swim; I could drown them. Or push them over a cliff—

GOD, *pained:* Don't say those things, stop it.

AZRAEL: I have to say, Lord, I warned You at the time: You mustn't make a creature that looks like You, or You'll *never* let me kill him.

CHEMUEL: It was such a pleasure with the lions and the gorillas.

GOD: Yes, but—*He looks down at the earth*—when they're good it makes me feel so marvelous.

AZRAEL: But how often are they good?

GOD: I know, but when they praise My name and all that. There's nothing like it. When they send up those hallelujahs from Notre Dame—

AZRAEL: Notre Dame!

RAPHAEL: Lord, Notre Dame isn't for six thousand years.

GOD: I know, but I'm looking forward. *He stands, shocked, His eye caught by something below.* Look at that! How do they think up such positions?

AZRAEL: I don't understand why You let them go on offending You like this. You called back other mistakes—the fish with fur who drowned—

CHEMUEL: And the beetle who hiccupped whenever it snowed.

AZRAEL: Why don't You let me go down and wipe them out?

GOD: They are the only ones who need Me.

CHEMUEL: Sure! Give them a chance.

GOD: I'll never forget the first time I realized what I meant to them. It was the first time Adam laid her down and went into her. She closed her eyes, and she began to breathe so deeply I thought she'd faint, or die, or explode. And suddenly she cried out, "Oh dear God!" I have never heard My name so genuinely praised.

AZRAEL: I find the whole spectacle disgusting.

GOD: I know. It's the worst thing that ever happened. *He is in conflict, staring.* It can't go on this way; I must have it out with Lucifer.

ALL: Lucifer!

GOD, *energetically:* I have never before been in conflict with Myself. Look at it; My poor, empty Eden; the ripened peach falls uneaten to the ground, and My two idiotic darlings roam the desert scrounging for a crust. It has definitely gone wrong. And not one of you has an idea worth talking about. Clear away; I must decide.

CHEMUEL: Decide what, Lord?

GOD: I don't know yet, but a decision is definitely rising in Me. And that was the one thing Lucifer always knew—the issue. Go. *Chemuel throws up his hands.*

ALL, *singing:* Hallelujah, hallelujah . . .

　　The angels are walking out.

GOD: One more.

ALL: Hallelujah!

　　They go. God is alone. He concentrates. Lucifer appears.

LUCIFER, *wary, looking for cues to God's attitude:* Thank You, Father. I have been waiting. I am ready to face my ordeal.

GOD: Lucifer, I have been struggling to keep from destroying you. The Law of the Conservation of Energy does not protect an angel from being broken into small pieces and sprinkled over the Atlantic Ocean.

LUCIFER: Wouldn't that just spread him around, though?

GOD: What restrains me is a feeling that somewhere in the universe a stupendous event has occurred. For an instant it made Me terribly happy. I thought it might be the icecaps, but they're not really working out.

LUCIFER: Trouble?

GOD: There is a definite leak.

LUCIFER: Can You repair it?

GOD: I've decided to let them run. It will mean a collection of large lakes across North America, and some in Europe.

LUCIFER: Oh, Father, surely You planned it that way.

GOD: I see now that I probably did; but frankly I wasn't thinking of the lakes; I simply felt there should be icecaps on both poles. But that's the way it is—one thing always leads to another.

LUCIFER: Then you must already know the fantastic news I've brought You.

GOD, *staring for his thought:* I undoubtedly do. *At a loss:* Happy news.

LUCIFER: Glorious.

GOD: I knew it! In the very midst of all my disappointments I suddenly felt a sort of . . . hopeful silence.

LUCIFER: The silent seed of Adam squirming into Eve's ovarian tube.

GOD, *striking His forehead:* Aaaaah! Of course! And the ovum?

LUCIFER: Has been fertilized.

GOD: And has attached itself . . .

LUCIFER: To the womb. It is holding on nicely.

GOD: Then so far—

LUCIFER: So good. I can't see any reason to worry.

GOD, *clapping His hands:* My first upright pregnancy! *Worried:* Maybe she ought to lie down more.

LUCIFER: Lord, she could stand on her head and not lose it.

GOD: And how is she feeling?

LUCIFER: I thought I'd ask You about that. She is slightly nauseated in the mornings.

GOD: That is partly disgust with herself. At least I hope so. But it is also the blood supply diverting to the womb.

LUCIFER: I never thought of that! In any case, it works.

GOD: How utterly, utterly superb.

LUCIFER: Oh, dear Father, ever since my interview with Eve I've been terrified You'd never speak to me again. And now when I so want to thank You properly, all metaphor, simile, and image scatter before this victory of ours. *God becomes alert.* Like the firm cheek of Heaven, the wall of her womb nuzzles the bud of the first son of man.

GOD: Say that again?

LUCIFER: Like the firm—

GOD: No, before that.

   Slight pause.

LUCIFER: But surely it was all according to plan?

GOD, *peering at him:* According to . . . ?

LUCIFER: It was supposed to happen through me. Of course, I am perfectly aware that I merely acted as Your agent.

GOD: Not on your life! They would have made it in Paradise, clean and innocent, and with My blessing instead of My curse!

LUCIFER: But the fact is, they were not making it!

GOD: They might have by accident!

LUCIFER: Father, I can't believe a technicality is more important then this service to Your cause!

GOD: Technicality! I am going to condemn you, Lucifer.

LUCIFER: Dear God, for what? For making You a grandfather?

GOD: I forbade that apple! Nobody violates a Commandment, I don't care how good it comes out!

LUCIFER: You mean the letter of the law is more important than the survival of the human race? *God is silent. A smile breaks onto Lucifer's face.* This is a test, isn't it? You're testing me? *God is inscrutable.* That's all right, don't answer. Now I will confess myself and prove that I finally understand my part in the Plan.

GOD: What Plan? What are you talking about?

LUCIFER: Your hidden Plan for operating the world. All my life, sir, I've had the feeling that I was somehow . . . a *useless* angel. I look at Azrael, so serious and grave, perfect for the Angel of Death. And our sweet Chemuel—exactly right for the Angel of Mercy. But when I tried to examine *my* character, I could never find any. Gorgeous profile, superb intelligence, but what was Lucifer *for*? Am I boring You?

GOD: Not at all.

LUCIFER, *worried:* How do you mean that? *God simply looks at him.* Good, good—don't make it easy for me. I will now explain about the apple. You see, I'd gone down there to help you, but she took one bite and that innocent stare erupted with such carnal appetite that I began to wonder, was it possible I had actually done something—*He breaks off.*

GOD: Evil?

LUCIFER: Oh, that terrible word! But now I will face it! *The desperate yet joyful confession.* Father, I've *always* had certain impulses that mystified me. If I saw my brother angels soaring upwards, my immediate impulse was to go down. A raspberry cane bends to the right, I'd find myself leaning left. Others praise the forehead, I am drawn to the ass. Holes—I don't want to leave anything out—I adore holes. Every hole is precious to me. I'll go even further—in excrement, decay, the intestine of the world is my stinking desire. You ever hear anything so straightforwardly disgusting? I tell you I have felt so worthless, I was often ready to cut my throat. But Eve is pregnant now, and I see the incredible, hidden truth.

GOD: Which is?

LUCIFER: How can I be rotten? How else but through my disobedience was Eve made pregnant with mankind? How dare I hate myself? Not only am I not rotten—I am God's corrective symmetry, that festering embrace which keeps His world from impotent virtue. And once I saw that, I saw Your purpose working through me and I nearly wept with self-respect. And I fell in love—with both of us. *Slight pause. God is motionless.* Well, that's—the general idea, right?

GOD: Lucifer, you are a degenerate! You are a cosmic pervert!

LUCIFER: But God in Heaven, who made me this way?

God whacks him across the face; Lucifer falls to his knees.

GOD: Don't you ever, ever say that.

LUCIFER: Adonoi elohaenu, adonoi echaud. Father, I know Your anger is necessary, but my love stands fast!

GOD: Love! The only love you know is for yourself! You think I haven't seen you standing before a mirror whole years at a time!

LUCIFER: I have, Lord, admiring Your handiwork.

GOD: How can you lie like this and not even blush!

LUCIFER: All right! *He stands up. Now* I will tell You the Truth! *At the pinnacle:* Lord, I am ready to take my place beside the throne.

GOD: Beside the *what?*

UCIFER: Why, the throne, Lord. At Your right hand. If not the right, then the left. I can suggest a title: Minister of Excremental Matters. I can walk with a limp, now watch this. *He walks, throwing one leg out spastically.*

GOD: What is this?

LUCIFER: And I do a tic, You see? *He does a wild tic as he walks crazily.*

GOD: What are you doing?

LUCIFER: I'll stutter, too. *Horribly:* Whoo, wha—munnnn—

GOD: What is this?

LUCIFER: I'll wear a hunch back and masturbate incessantly, eternal witness that God loves absolutely everything He made! What a *lesson!* But before You answer—the point, the far-reaching ultimate, is that this will change the future. Do you remember the future, Lord?

GOD: Of course I remember the future.

LUCIFER: It is a disaster; it is one ghastly war after another down through the centuries.

GOD: You can never change the future. The past, yes, but not the future.

LUCIFER: How do you change the past?

GOD: Why, the past is always changing—nobody remembers anything. But the future can no more be turned away than the light flowing off the moon.

LUCIFER: Unless we stood together, Lord, You immaculate on Your throne, absolutely good, and I beside You, perfectly evil. Father and son, the two inseparable buddies. *God is caught by it.* There could never, never be war! You see it, I can see You see it! If good and evil stand as one, what'll they have to fight about? What army could ever mobilize if on all the flags was written: "For God and Country and the Stinking Devil"? Without absolute righteousness there can never be a war! We will flummox the generals! Father, you are a handshake away from a second Paradise! Peace on earth to the end of time. *God is peering, feverish.* And that, sir, is your entire plan for me as I see it.

GOD: In other words, I would no longer be absolutely right.

LUCIFER: Just in public, sir. Privately, of course—*a gesture connecting them*—we know what's what.

GOD: We do.

LUCIFER: Oh, Lord, I have no thought of . . . actually—

GOD: Sharing power.

LUCIFER: God forbid. I'm speaking purely of the image.

GOD: But in reality . . .

LUCIFER: Nothing's changed. You're good, and I'm bad. It's just that to the public—

GOD: We will appear to be—

LUCIFER: Yes.

GOD: Equal.

LUCIFER: Not morally equal. Just equally real. Because if I'm sitting beside You in Heaven—

GOD: Then I must love you.

LUCIFER: Exactly. And if God can love the Devil, He can love absolutely anybody.

GOD: *That's* certainly true, yes.

LUCIFER: So people would never come to hate themselves, and there's the end of guilt. Another Eden, and everybody innocent again.

    Pause.

GOD: Operationally speaking—

LUCIFER: Yes.

GOD: Yes *sir.*

LUCIFER: Yes sir. Excuse me.

GOD: In cases of lying, cheating, fornication, murder, and so on— you mean they are no longer to be judged?

LUCIFER: Oh, on the contrary! Between the two of us *no one* will escape the judgment of Heaven. I'll judge the bad people, and you judge the good.

GOD: But who would try to be good if it's just as good to be bad?

LUCIFER: And will the bad be good for fear of your judgment? So you may as well let them be bad and the good be good, and either way they'll all love God because they'll know that God ... loves ... me. Sir, I am ready to take my place. Between the two of us we'll have mankind mousetrapped.

GOD: Yes. *Slight pause.* There is only one problem.

LUCIFER: But basically that's the Plan, isn't it?

GOD: There is a problem.

LUCIFER: What's that?

GOD, *looking straight at him:* I don't love you.

LUCIFER, *shocked—he can hardly speak:* You can't mean that.

GOD: Afraid I do.

LUCIFER: Well. *He gives a deflated laugh.* This is certainly a surprise.

GOD: I see that. And it is fundamentally why we can never sit together. Nothing is real to you. Except your appetite for distinction and power. I've been waiting for some slightest sign of repentance for what you did to Paradise, but there's nothing, is there? Instead, I'm to join you in a cosmic comedy where good and evil are the same. It doesn't occur to you that I am unable to share the bench with the very incarnation of all I despise?

LUCIFER: I can't believe You'd let Your feelings stand in the way of peace.

GOD: But that is why I am perfect—I *am* my feelings.

LUCIFER: You don't think that's a limitation?

GOD: It certainly is. I am perfectly limited. Where evil begins, I end. When good loves evil, it is no longer good, and if God could love the Devil, then God has died. And that is precisely what you're after, isn't it?!

LUCIFER: I am after peace! Beteween us and mankind!

GOD: Then let there be war! Better ten thousand years of war than I should rule one instant with the help of unrighteousness!

LUCIFER: Lord God, I am holding out my hand!

GOD, *rising:*

Go to Hell! Now thou art fallen in all thy beauty.
As the rain doth fall and green the grass
And the fish out of water suffocates,
So dost thy fall prove that there are consequences.
Now die in Heaven, Lucifer, and live in Hell
That man may ever know how good and evil separate!

LUCIFER: Lord? *He is upright, stern.* You will not take my hand?

GOD: Never! Never, never, never!

LUCIFER: Then I will take the world. *He exits.*

GOD, *calling:* And if you ever do, I will burn it, I will flood it out, I will leave it a dead rock spinning in silence! For I am the Lord, and the Lord is good and only good!

ANGELS' VOICES, *singing loudly and sharply:* Blessed is the Lord my God, Glory, glory, glory!

God sits, cleaved by doubt. He turns His head, looking about.

GOD: Why do I miss him? *He stares ahead.* How strange.

CURTAIN

ACT TWO

Darkness. The sound of a high wind. It dies off. A starry sky.

In the starlight, Adam and Eve are discovered asleep, but apart. He snores contentedly, she lies in silence on her back, her very pregnant belly arching up.

Lucifer, in black now, rises from the ground. He scans the sky for any sign of God, then looks down at the two people. In deep thought he walks to the periphery and sits, his chin on his fist, staring.

Overhead a bird begins to sing. He looks up.

LUCIFER: Oh, shut up. *The birdsong effloresces gloriously.* Will you get out of here? Go! Glorify the Lord some place else! *Flapping of wings. He follows the bird's flight overhead with his gaze.* Idiot. *Depressed, he stares ahead.* Everything I see throws up the same irrational lesson. The hungriest bird sings best. What a system! That deprivation should make music—is anarchy! And what is greatness in God's world? A peaceful snake lies dozing in the sun with no more dignity than a long worm; but let him arch his head to strike— and there, by God, is a *snake*! Yes! I have reasoned, pleaded, argued, when only murder in this world makes majesty—God's included. Was He ever Godlier, ever more my king than when He murdered my hopes? And will I ever be more than a ridiculous angel—*he turns to Adam and Eve*—until I murder His? *He stands, goes to Eve, looks down at her.* Where is His dearest hope in all the world—but in that belly? *He suddenly raises his foot to stomp her, then retracts.* No. N-no. Let her do it. Make her do it. *He looks skyward.* Oh, the shock, the shock! If she refused the Lord the fruit of man because He made the world unreasonable! *He inspires himself, slowly sinks to the ground, and insinuates into Eve's ear:* This is a dream. *He ceremoniously lifts his hand and with his middle finger touches her forehead.* I enter the floor of thy skull. *He bends and kisses her belly.* Now, woman, help me save the world from the anarchy of God. *She inhales sensuously, and her knee rises, her cloak falling away, exposing a bare thigh.* Your time has come, dear woman. *He slides his hand along her thigh.*

EVE, *exhaling pleasurably:* Aaaaaahhh!

LUCIFER: Sssh! Don't wake up; the only safe place to have this conversation is inside your head. Am I clear in your mind? Do you remember me?

EVE: Oh, yes! When our fingers touched around the apple—

LUCIFER: Flesh to naked flesh!

EVE: And I awoke and saw myself! How beautiful I was! *She opens her eyes.*

LUCIFER: What in the world has happened to you? How'd you get so ugly?

EVE, *covering her face:* I can't stand myself!

LUCIFER: When I think how you looked in Paradise—*she weeps*—Why did you let yourself go?

EVE: Can you help me, angel? Something's got into my belly, and it keeps getting bigger.

LUCIFER: No idea what it is?

EVE: Well . . . I *have* been eating a lot of clams lately.

LUCIFER: Clams.

EVE: Sometimes it even squirms. *Lucifer looks away in thought.* Isn't that it?

LUCIFER, *turning back to her:* Like to have it out?

EVE, *clapping her hands:* Could I?

LUCIFER: But are you sure you won't change your mind afterwards?

EVE: No! I want to be as I was. Please, angel, take thy power and drive it out.

LUCIFER: Lie back, dear.

EVE: Oh, thank you, angel, I will adore you forever!

LUCIFER, *starting to spread her knees:* I certainly hope so. Now just try to relax. . . .

EVE, *on her back, facing the sky, her arms stretched upward:* Oh, won't the Lord be happy when He sees me looking good again! *Lucifer removes his hands, instantly turning away to think. She, on her back, can't see what he is doing.* Is anything happening?

LUCIFER, *drawing her upright:* Woman, I don't want you hating me in the morning; now listen, and I will waken your mind as once I awakened your body in Paradise.

EVE: By the way, I've been wanting to ask you: did you ever come to me again—*after* Paradise?

LUCIFER, *evasively:* Why do you ask?

EVE: Near twilight, once, I was lying on my stomach, looking at my face in a pool; and suddenly a strange kind of weight pressed down on my back, and it pressed and pressed until we seemed to go tumbling out like dragonflies above the water. And in my ear a voice kept whispering. "This is God's will, darling. . . ."

LUCIFER: Which it was, at the time.

EVE, *marveling:* It was you!

LUCIFER: All me. About nine months ago.

EVE, *gleefully:* Oh, angel, that was glorious! Come, make me beautiful again! *She starts to lie back; he stops her.*

LUCIFER: You will have it out, Eve, but it's important there be no recriminations afterwards, so I'm going to tell you the truth. I have been thrown out of Heaven.

EVE: How's that possible? You're an *angel*!

LUCIFER: Dear girl, we are dealing with a spirit to whom nothing is sacred.

EVE: But why? What did you do?

LUCIFER: What He could not do. *He breaks off.*

EVE: What?

LUCIFER, *taking the plunge:* I caused you to multiply.

EVE: You mean—*she looks down at her belly*—I'm multiplying?

LUCIFER: What you have in your belly . . . is a man.

EVE: A man! *Overjoyed, she rolls back onto the ground.* In me!

LUCIFER: Remember what you said! You want it out!

EVE, *sitting up:* How is God feeling about me? Does He know?

LUCIFER: All right, then. Yes, He knows and He is ecstatic!

EVE: Oh, praise the Lord!

LUCIFER, *furiously:* Quadruple hallelujahs!

EVE: Glory to Him in the highest!

LUCIFER: Precisely. *Jabbing his finger at her:* And now I'll bet your agony begins!

EVE, *with a shock of pain:* Aaaahhhhh!

LUCIFER: Why'd you stop praising Him? *She yells in pain.* Where's the hallelujah!?

EVE: What is happening to me?

LUCIFER: What're you complaining about? You praise God, and this is what you get for it!

EVE: But why?

LUCIFER: Don't you remember Him cursing you out of Paradise?

EVE: And this—

LUCIFER: Is it, honey.

EVE, *pointing to the sleeping Adam:* But he ate the apple too!

LUCIFER: Right. And he looks better than ever.

EVE, *furiously pounding her hands on the ground:* WHY?

LUCIFER, *grabbing her face, driving his point home:* Because this is the justice of the world He made, and only you can change that world!

EVE: Angel . . . it's getting worse.

LUCIFER: Oh, it'll get worse than this, dear.

EVE: It can't get worse!

LUCIFER: Oh, yes, it can, because He's perfect, and when He makes something worse, it's *perfectly* worse!

EVE: Oh God, what have I done!

LUCIFER: You multiplied with my help, not with His, and your agony is His bureaucratic revenge. Now listen to me—

EVE: I can't stand any more! *Lashing about on the ground.* Where's a rock, I'll kill him! *With clawed hands she starts for Adam.*

LUCIFER: He is as innocent as you!

EVE, *bursting into helpless tears:* This is not *right*!

LUCIFER: Oh, woman, to hear that word at last from other lips than mine! It is not right, no—it is chaos. Eve, you are the only voice of reason God's insane world can ever have, for in you alone His chaos shows its claws. *In poena veritas*—the only truth is pain. Now mount it and take your power.

EVE: What power? I'm a grain of dust.

LUCIFER: He is pacing up and down in Heaven waiting for this child. You have in your belly the crown of God.

EVE: The crown . . . ?

LUCIFER: His highest honor is your gratitude for the agony He is giving you. He is a maniac! *He takes her hand.* You can refuse. You must deny this crown to chaos. Kill it. *He is behind her, his lips to her ear, his hand on her belly.*

> Let the serpent in again, and we'll murder him,
> And so teach the Lord His first humility.

He slips around in front of her, starting to press her back to the ground.

> Crown His vengeance on thee not with life
> But with a death; a lump of failure
> Lay before the Lord a teaching, woman—

EVE, *in conflict, resisting his pressure to lie down: I* teach God?

LUCIFER:

> Teach God, yes!—that if men must be born
> Only in the pain of unearned sin,
> Then there will be no men at all!
> Open to me!

He tries to spread her legs. She reaches uncertainly to his face, while trying to fend his hands off.

EVE: Angel, I'm afraid!

LUCIFER: Hold still! *He is on top of her to pin her down.*

EVE: I don't think I can do that!

LUCIFER: Open up, you bitch! *He violently tries to spread her knees; she breaks free, skittering away on the ground.*

EVE: I can't! I mustn't! I won't! *Sexually infuriated, he starts again for her.* I want him! *Adam turns over. Lucifer springs out of her line of sight so that she is looking around at empty space, holding her belly. In short, she has only now awakened in the dream's hangover. Day is dawning.* Where am I? *The baaing of sheep is heard.*

LUCIFER:

The dream ends here, a dark rehearsal of the coming day;
This day you must decide—to crown unreason with thy gift of life,
Or with a tiny death teach justice. *He bends and kisses her.*
I understand thee, woman—I alone.
Call any time at all.

Intimately, pointing into her face: You know what I mean.

Adams sits up. Lucifer goes. Day dawns. Adam stares at Eve, as she sits there. Now she brings her body forward and wipes her eyes.

ADAM: What a night! I don't think I slept five minutes. *She gives him a look.* Did you?

EVE, *after a slight pause, guiltily:* I slept very well, yes.

Disturbed, inward, she gets up, begins gathering pieces of wood for the fire. The baaing of sheep is heard.

ADAM, *looking around:* Say! *She stops moving, looks at him.* The wind! It finally stopped! See? I told you I'd find a place that's not windy!

A blast of howling wind makes them both huddle into their clothes. It dies off. She gets out some figs, places them in a bowl.

EVE: There's your figs.

ADAM: Could it be, you suppose, that everywhere but in Paradise it's just naturally windy? *He bites into a fig.*

EVE: I just don't know, Adam.

ADAM—*he spits out sand:* They're sandy.

EVE: Well, it's windy.

He leans his head on his fist disconsolately.

ADAM: What a way to live! At least if I knew how long it was going to last—

EVE: I still don't understand what's so wrong about digging a hole. We could sit in it and keep out of the wind. Like the groundhogs.

ADAM: I wish you'd stop trying to change the rules! We're not groundhogs. If He meant us to live in holes, He would have given us claws.

EVE: But if He meant us to live in a windstorm, He'd have put our eyes in our armpits. *Another blast of wind; then it dies.*

ADAM: Aren't you eating anything?

EVE: I don't feel like it.

ADAM: You know something? You don't look so green today.

EVE, *faintly hopeful, a little surprised at his interest:* I don't?

ADAM: All your color came back. What happened? *He slides over to her, looking quizzically and somewhat excitedly into her face.* You look beautiful, Eve.

EVE—*she laughs nervously:* Well, I can't imagine why!

ADAM, *pushing her back, starting to open her cloak:* It's amazing! I haven't seen you look this way since Paradise! *His hand on her swollen belly stops him.* Oh, excuse me.

EVE, *grasping his hand:* That's all right!

ADAM, *getting up, sliding his hand out of hers:* I forgot that thing. *He stands, looks around.* What a funny morning!

EVE: Why do you always look around like that?

ADAM, *after a slight pause:* I miss God.

EVE, *looking down in sorrow:* I'm sorry, Adam. *Sheep are heard again.*

ADAM, *looking off:* It is just that I'm never really sure what to do next. That grass is giving out; we'll have to move this afternoon.

EVE: I don't think I can walk very far.

ADAM: Goddamn clams . . .

EVE: I'm always out of breath, Adam. This thing has gotten very heavy.

ADAM: Does it still move?

EVE: It's doing it now. Would you like to feel it?

ADAM, *touching her belly:* Huh!

EVE: It's almost like a little foot pressing.

ADAM: A foot! No. *He presses his stomach.* I have the same thing sometimes.

EVE, *with sudden hope:* You too? Let me feel it! *She feels his stomach.* I don't feel anything.

ADAM: Well, it stopped. I can't remember—did He say to kill clams before eating?

EVE: But they squash so.

ADAM: I'm not sure we're supposed to eat live things. I can't remember half the things He said any more.

EVE, *tentatively, with some trepidation:* Can I talk to you about that? I'm not sure any more it is those clams.

ADAM: Don't worry, it's the clams. Sits down and eats maybe fifty clams, and suddenly it's not the clams.

EVE: Well, I *like* clams. Especially lately.

ADAM: I like eggs.

EVE: Adam, dear, there's something I feel I should tell you.

ADAM: I had three delicious eggs last— *He breaks off, recalling.* No, no, that was a dream!

EVE, *startled:* You dreamed?

ADAM: Why, did you?

EVE, *quickly:* Tell me yours first.

ADAM: I ... was in Paradise. Huh! Remember those breakfasts there?

EVE: I wasn't there long enough for breakfast. I was born just before lunch. And I never even got that.

ADAM: Pity you missed it. What a dream! Everything was just the way it used to be. I woke up, and there He was—

EVE: God.

ADAM: Yes. And He brought a tray—and about six beautifully scrambled eggs.

EVE, *with guilt and hunger:* Ohhhh!

ADAM: And no sand whatsoever. I guess it was Sunday because there was also a little tray of warm croissants.

EVE, *sadly charmed:* And then?

ADAM: Same as always—I named a few things. And then we took a nice nap. And angels were playing some soft music. *He hums, trying to recall the tune.* How perfect it all was!

EVE: Until I showed up.

ADAM: Yes. *He looks about with a heightened longing, and, seeing this, she weeps.*

EVE: I don't know why He made me!

ADAM: Well, don't cry, maybe we'll find out some day. I'll round up the sheep. *He starts out.*

EVE—*trying not to call him, she does:* Adam!

ADAM, *halting:* You'll just have to walk. That thing might go away if you get some exercise. *He moves to go.*

EVE: An angel came.

ADAM: When?

EVE: Last night.

ADAM—*happily astounded, he rushes to her:* Which one?

EVE, *fearfully:* It was, ah ...

ADAM: Chemuel?

EVE: No, not Chemuel.

ADAM: Raphael? Michael?

EVE, *holding her forehead:* No.

ADAM: Well, what'd he look like? Short or tall?

EVE: Quite tall.

ADAM: It wasn't God, was it?

EVE: Oh, not God.

ADAM: What'd he want?

EVE: I—I can't remember it clearly.

ADAM: Was it about getting back into Paradise?

EVE: Well, no. . . .

ADAM: About what we're supposed to do next?

EVE: Not exactly. . . .

ADAM: Why didn't you wake me up?

EVE: I couldn't move!

ADAM: You mean God sends an angel down, and you can't even remember what he said?

EVE: It was about this—*she touches her belly*—thing.

ADAM, *disbelieving; in fact, with disappointment:* About that?

EVE—*she looks up at him:* Would you sit down, Adam? I think I know what we're supposed to do now. *He senses something strange, sits on his heels.* He came through the mist. Like the mist on the sea. Smoke rose from his hair, and his hands smoked.

   Lucifer materializes; motionless, he stands in his terrible beauty at the periphery.

ADAM, *with wonder:* Ahhh!

EVE: And he said— *She breaks off in fear as she feels the attraction of the Evil One.*

ADAM: What?

   A blast of wind. They huddle. It dies. She has remained staring ahead. Now she turns to him.

EVE: That angel opened my eyes, Adam. I see it all very clearly now—with you the Lord was only somewhat disappointed, but with me He was furious. *Lucifer gravely nods.* And his curse is entirely on me. It is the reason why you've hardly changed out here in the world; but I bleed, and now I am ugly and swollen up like a frog. And I never dream of Paradise, but you do almost every night, and you seem to expect to find it over every hill. And that is right—I think now that you belong in Eden. But not me. And as long as I am with you, you will never find it again. *Slight pause.* Adam, I haven't the power to move from this place, and this is the proof that I must stay here, and you—go back to Paradise.

ADAM, *in conflict with his wishes:* Alone?

EVE: He would lead you there if you walked away alone. You are thirsting for Eden, and the Lord knows that.

ADAM: But so are you.

EVE: Eden is not in me any more.

Lucifer seems to expand with joy.

ADAM: Eve!

EVE: I disgust Him! I am abominable to Him!

ADAM: But the Lord said we are to cleave to one another. I don't think I'm *supposed* to go.

EVE, *bursting into tears, as much with pity for him as with her own indignation:* But you don't like me any more either!

ADAM, *pointing at her belly:* That thing—that thing is what I cannot bear! It turns my stomach! I can't seem to get near you any more! Every time I turn around I'm bumping into it! *She cries louder, turns to find herself face to face with Lucifer.* I don't understand you. Do you *like* that thing?

EVE, *turning back to him from the tempting angel:* I—I don't know!

ADAM: Because if it moves it's alive, and if it's alive we could just hit it! *She gasps, holding her belly.* There, you see? You like it! And this is why I don't know where I am any more! I told you when it started, if you jumped up and down—

EVE: I did jump!

ADAM: You did not jump. You went like that. *He makes a few measly hops.*

EVE: I jumped as hard as I could!

ADAM: I think you're taking *care* of that thing! *Jealously.* You know what's in there, don't you?

EVE, *crying out:* I love thee, husband, and I know this thing will be thy curse!

ADAM: Woman, you will tell me what is in thy belly!

EVE, *clapping her hands over her eyes:* It is a death!

Pause.

ADAM: Whose death?

Pause. Eve lowers her hands, staring ahead.

EVE: Its own.

Pause.

ADAM: Who told thee?

EVE: Lucifer.

ADAM: You're seeing Lucifer again?

EVE: I screamed, but you didn't hear me!

ADAM: Well, I was sleeping!

EVE: You're always sleeping! Every time that son of a bitch comes around, you're someplace else! I would never have touched that apple in the first place if you hadn't left me alone with him!

ADAM: Well, I was *swimming*!

EVE: If you're not swimming, you're sleeping!

ADAM: You mean I can't turn my back for a minute on my own *wife*?

EVE: I couldn't help it, it was like a dream!

ADAM: I don't know how a decent woman can dream about the Devil.

EVE: Adam—he's not all bad.

ADAM: He's not all . . . ! *Light dawns in his head.* Ohhhh! No wonder you looked so juicy when you woke up! I want to know what's so good about him!

EVE, *clapping her hands to her ears:* I can't stand any more!

ADAM, *furiously:* God said I am thy master, woman, and you are going to tell me what went on here! No wonder I haven't been able to get near you. There's been something strange about you for months!

EVE: There is a man in my belly, Adam.

ADAM, *chilled with astonishment, wonder, fear:* A man!

EVE: He told me.

Long pause.

ADAM: How could a man fit in there?

EVE: Well . . . small. To start off with. Like the baby monkeys and the little zebras—

ADAM: Zebras! He's got you turning us into animals now? No human being has been born except grown-up! I may be confused about a lot of things, but I know facts!

EVE: But it's what God said—we were to go forth and multiply.

ADAM, *striking his chest indignantly:* If we're going to multiply, it'll be through me! Same as it always was! What am I going to do with you? After everything he did to us with his goddamned lies, you still—

EVE: Husband, he told me to do with it exactly what you have told me to do with it.

ADAM, *struck:* What I . . . ?

EVE: He told me it is a man and he told me to kill it. What the Devil hath spoken, thou hast likewise spoken.

Silence. Neither moves. One sheep baas, like a sinister snarl. A sudden surge of wind, which quickly dies.

ADAM, *tortured:* But I had no idea it was a man when I said that.

EVE, *holding her belly, with a long gaze beyond them both:* Adam . . . I believe I am meant to bring out this man—alone.

ADAM, *furiously, yet unable to face her directly:* Are you putting me with that monster?

EVE: But why do you all want him dead!

ADAM: I forbid you to say that again! I am not Lucifer! *A heartbroken cry escapes him.* Eve! *He sinks to his knees. He curls up in ignominy, then prostrates himself before her, flat out on the ground, pressing his lips to her foot.* Forgive me! *He weeps. Wind blasts. It dies.*

EVE—*a new thought interrupts her far-off gaze, and she looks at his prostrate body:* Will you dig us a hole?

ADAM—*he joyously scrambles up and kisses her hand:* A hole!

EVE: It needn't be too big—

ADAM: What do you mean? I'll dig you the biggest hole you ever saw in your life! Woman . . . *With a cry of gratitude he sweeps her into his arms.* Woman, thou art my salvation!

EVE: Oh, my darling, that's so good to hear!

ADAM: How I thirst for thee! My doe, my rabbit . . .

EVE: My five-pointed buck, my thundering bull!

ADAM, *covering his crotch:* Oh, Eve, thy forgiveness hath swelled me like a ripened ear of corn.

EVE: Oh, how sweet. Then I will forgive thee endlessly.

Lucifer shows alarm and rising anger.

ADAM: Say, now, the Lord will probably expect me to think of a name for him. Or do you want to? *He indicates her belly.*

EVE: No, you. You're so good at names.

ADAM—*he thinks, paces:* Well, let's see . . .

EVE: I'll be quiet. *She watches him with pleasure.* It ought to be something clear and clean and—something for a *handsome* man.

ADAM: Y'know, when I saw the first giraffe—it may not fit, but it went through my mind at the time.

EVE: What?

ADAM: Frank?

EVE: Don't you think that's a little too, ah . . . ?

ADAM: I guess so, yes. Maybe it ought to begin with A.

EVE, *simultaneously:* . . . to begin with an A.

  They point at each other and laugh.

ADAM: I mean because he's the first.

EVE: He's the first.

  They laugh again.

EVE: Isn't it marvelous that we both have the same thoughts . . .

ADAM: Both have the same thoughts.

EVE, *in the clear:* . . . again!

ADAM, *lifting his arms thankfully:* What a God we have!

EVE: How perfectly excellent is the Lord!

  Lucifer throws up his hands and goes into darkness, holding his head.

ADAM, *suddenly looking down at the ground, astonished:* Eve?

EVE: What, my darling?

ADAM: Is this grass growing?

EVE, *looking about quickly at the ground:* I believe it is!

ADAM, *looking front:* Look at the pasture! It's up to their bellies!

EVE: Adam, the wind . . . !

  They look up and around. There is silence.

ADAM: Woman, we must have done something right! *He looks upward.* I think He loves us again.

EVE—*her hands shoot up, open-palmed, her eyes wide with terror:* Sssh!

ADAM: Could it possibly be . . .

EVE, *a hand moving toward her belly:* Ssh, sh!

ADAM: . . . that the curse is *over?* *She grips her belly. She suddenly rushes right and is stopped by a wild, curling cry of a high-screaming French horn. He is oblivious to the sound.* What are you doing? *She turns and rushes upstage; he is starting after her, and she is stopped short by a whining blow on a timpani and a simultaneous snarling trumpet blast. He nearly catches her, but she gets away and is rushing left and is stopped by a pair of cacophonic flutes. He catches her now.* Eve! *She wrenches free of him—and she shows terror of him; and for an instant they are two yards apart, he uncomprehending, she in deadly fear of him. Protesting:* It's Adam. I am thy husband!

She rushes to a point and halts, crying upwards.

EVE: *Chemuuuuu-ellll!* Merciful sweet angel, take me out of myself! *She is seized by her agony and rolls over and over along the ground, as a massive cacophonic music flares up. Adam is put off, unmanned, afraid to touch her. She slams her hands on the ground as she writhes on her back.* God! Oh, God!

ADAM: Maybe it'll get better.

EVE: It will get worse. And when it gets worse it—*she sits up, recalling*—will get perfectly worse.... *A contraction.* Oh, God! *Stretching on her side, hands outstretched:* I call on any angel whatsoever!

ADAM, *calling upward:* Chemuel, come! Bring mercy!

EVE: Help me, demon! Come to me, Lucifer!

ADAM, *clapping his ears shut:* Aiiiii!

EVE, *as though whipped, submissively begging:* Take out this agony! Demon, I am awake! Still me, angel! Take him out of my flesh!

ADAM, *falling to his knees:* God in Heaven, she is out of her mind!

EVE: I am *in* my mind—He never gave me a chance!

ADAM: Lord, give her a chance!

EVE: No, He loves this! God, if this is Thy pleasure, then I owe Thee nothing any more, and I call, I call, I call for—*A seizure; with each call she pounds the earth.* God. Oh, God. Oh, God. God—damn—you—God!

ADAM, *curled up in terror:* Aiiii!

Lucifer appears at the periphery.

EVE: Still me, demon . . . take this out! Don't waste another minute! Not a minute more! He is bursting me! Kill him! Kill him!

Lucifer takes a step toward her and is halted by trumpets: a single melodious chord. She faints. Adam tries to rise and, seeing her, he faints too. God enters. A step behind Him are Azrael, Angel of Death, and Chemuel, Angel of Mercy.

GOD, *standing over her, looking down:* Now bend, Azrael, and blow thy cold death across her lip. *Azrael bends and exhales over her face. Eve shudders as with icy cold and gasps in air, still asleep.* That's enough. Chemuel, in thy compassion, drive anguish to the corner of her mind, and seal it up. *Chemuel kneels, kisses her once. Eve exhales with relief. God walks a few yards away and sits.* Go away, Death. *Azrael stands fast.* Go, Azrael. And wait her need. *Azrael exits unwillingly.* Chemuel, in thy mercy, deliver Eve. *Chemuel reaches, lays his hand on her swollen belly, and with a short pull removes the swelling; clutching it to his breast, he starts to lean to kiss her again.* That's enough. *Chemuel hesitates, glancing up at God.* Go, Chemuel, and wait her need. *Chemuel stands and goes out.* Now in thy slumber let us reason together. *Adam and Eve sit up, their eyes shut in sleep.* Behold the stranger thine agony hath made. *A youth of sixteen appears, his eyes shut, his arms drawn in close to his body, his hands clasping his forward-tilted head. He moves waywardly, like a windblown leaf, and as he at last approaches Eve, he halts some feet away as God speaks again.* Here is the first life of thy life, woman. And it is fitting that the first letter stand before his name. But seeing that in thy extremity thou hast already offered his life to Lucifer; and seeing, Adam, that in your ignorance you have likewise threatened him with murder—*He loses his calm*—all of which amazes Me and sets My teeth on edge—*He breaks off, gritting His teeth*—I am nevertheless mindful that this child—*He turns to the youth*—is innocent. So we shall try again. And rather than call him Abel, who was in jeopardy, he shall be Cain, for his life's sake. *He stands.* Now Cain is born!

Cain lies down, coiled beside Eve. She sits up, opens her eyes, and looks down at Cain.

EVE, *joyfully surprised:* Ahhh!

ADAM, *waking quickly, seeing Cain:* What's that?

EVE: It is . . .

GOD: Cain. Thy son.

Both gasp, surprised by His presence.

EVE—*she suddenly feels her flat belly and with a cry prostrates before God:* I see I have been favored of Thee, O Lord!

GOD, *indicating the inert Cain:* Here is thine innocence returned to thee, which thou so lightly cast away in Eden. Now protect him from the worm of thine own evil, which this day hath uncovered in thee. Look in My face, woman.

EVE, *covering her eyes:* I dare not, for I doubted Thy goodness!

GOD: And will you doubt Me any more?

EVE: Never, never, never!

GOD: Then lift up thine eyes.

She slowly dares to face Him on her knees.

EVE: I have gotten a man from the Lord.

GOD: Thou art the mother of mankind.

EVE: And generations unknown to me shall spring from my loins.

He extends His hand. She rests hers on it and rises.

> I am the river abounding in fish,
> I am the summer sun arousing the bee,
> As the rising moon is held in her place
> By Thine everlasting mind, so am I held
> In Thine esteem.

GOD: Eve, you are my favorite girl!

An angelic waltz strikes up. God sweeps Eve in a glorious dance all over the stage. Adam, happiness on his face, makes light and abortive attempts to cut in. God and Eve exit, dancing, Adam trailing behind and calling.

ADAM: Eve! Look at Him dance! *Laughing, bursting with joy, he waltzes out after them.*

Lucifer, alone with Cain coiled up nearby, looks off toward the party and shakes his head.

LUCIFER: You've got to hand it to Him. *He turns front, staring.* What a system! *Now he looks down at Cain.* So this is Cain. *He crouches over Cain.* With the kiss of Lucifer begin thy life; let my nature coil around thine own. And on thy shoulders may I climb the throne. *He bends and kisses him.*

CURTAIN

ACT THREE

The family discovered asleep. A primitive shelter is suggested, hanging skins, and a cooking area in one corner. God is seated on a rock. He is thoughtfully watching them. He shakes his head, baffled, then raises a hand.

GOD: Azrael! *Azrael lights up behind the left screen.* Angel of Death, I have work for you today. The time has come when the human race will spread across the earth. But these people have all but forgotten God. They eat to live and live to eat. By what law shall the multitudes be governed when even now my name is hardly mentioned any more? *Stands, looking down at the people.* Therefore, when this dawn comes, you will blow visions of death into their dreams. But be careful not to kill anybody; you are only to remind them that they cannot live forever. And having seen death, I hope they'll think of God again, and begin to face their terrible responsibilities. *Azrael starts to raise his arms.* Not yet!—wait till dawn. I want them to remember what they've dreamed when they awake. *To the people:* Dear people, I shall be watching every move you make today. *He exits. Lucifer comes up out of the trap. Looks about, notices a golden bowl and picks it up.*

LUCIFER: Every time I come up here they've got more junk. What a race—a little prosperity and they don't even need the Devil.

EVE, *awakening:* What spirit art thou?

LUCIFER: It's me, honey.

EVE: Why don't you just go to hell and stay there?

LUCIFER: Darling, I'm terribly worried about your soul! A beautiful, intelligent woman like you can't waste her life just cooking and doing the house. You simply have no idea what you're missing!

EVE: I have absolutely everything I ever dreamed of, Angel. . . .

LUCIFER: But don't you want to broaden your horizons?

EVE: No! *She lies back down.*

LUCIFER: Whatever you say, darling. Sweet dreams, pretty girl. *Comes away from her.* For all the bad I've done I might as well have stayed in heaven. Only bad trouble will make them call to me for help. I'll break them apart!—or they'll turn the whole earth into this smug suburb of Heaven. Now let's see—Cain is jealous of his brother; suppose we start from there. . . . *He leaps to Cain when the light of dawn glows and Azrael appears behind the screen. Lucifer hides to observe him. Sotto.* Azrael? What's this about? *Azrael raises his caped arms menacingly.* My God, is somebody going to die? *Azrael blows three loud, short breaths. The people instantly groan. Azrael vanishes. Lucifer comes down to the people.* Groaning! Did he blow dreams into them?

ADAM—*sits up:* What a dream! *She turns to him expectantly.* I think I saw . . . something die.

EVE, *against her fear:* Maybe a sheep.

ADAM: No. It had a face.

LUCIFER: But none of them is old or sick—how do they die?

EVE: A *person's* face?

ADAM: Yes. And there was blood.

EVE: Blood!

LUCIFER: Blood?—Is he setting them up for a murder?—Of course! What better way to make them guilty and put the fear of God back into them! What a mistake I nearly made—I've got to keep them out of trouble, not get them into it.

CAIN, *sitting up:* What a dream!

ADAM AND EVE: What!

CAIN: I think I saw something die.

LUCIFER: And here's my opening at last! I'll stop this killing and they'll love me for it, and hate the Lord who has to have a death and their remorse! Oh, this is beautiful! But which one kills, and who's supposed to die? *He continuously moves around the periphery and sometimes in among them, searchingly, awaiting his opening.*

ABEL, *sitting up:* What a dream!

ADAM: That's enough. Eve, make breakfast.

ABEL: I was flying across the sky. . . .

EVE: But that's a wonderful dream!

ABEL: And then I fell. . . . *Mystified:* And an angel kissed me.

CAIN, *instantly—an exhale of recognition, his finger raised:* Ohhhhh! *All turn to him as he points to Abel.* I remember now. He died. *Eve gasps.*

EVE: Don't say that! *She gets up and goes to Abel and, holding his head in her arms, kisses him. Adam moves her aside, and he kisses him.*

LUCIFER: It's Abel dies? But who kills him?

CAIN, *kisses Abel:* I saw thee on the ground, thy face crushed, and a blood-covered flail . . . rolling away.

ADAM: All right, now wait a minute.

CAIN, *turning to Adam:* How is it that he dies in my sleep? *Turning to Abel:* You haven't done anything, have you?

ABEL, *to Eve:* The minute anything happens he always blames me!

EVE: You two stop fighting.

ADAM: Now pay attention. Nobody ever dreamed of death before, so I don't want to hear any arguments of any kind whatsoever today.

LUCIFER: Good man! *To Eve:* Brighten it up.

EVE: I'll make a nice breakfast!

CAIN: Father. *Adam turns to him, sensing his strange intensity.* When you decided to leave Paradise, did God . . . ?

EVE: What's Paradise got to do with this?

CAIN: I wish we could talk about it, Mother! Didn't God give you any instructions when you left? I mean, how do we know we're saying the right prayers. Or maybe we don't pray enough.

ADAM: Oh, no. I'm sure He'd let us know if we were doing something wrong.

CAIN: But maybe that's what the dream was for.

ADAM, *struck by this:* Say!

CAIN: Because lately when I'm out in the fields chopping weeds—it suddenly seems so strange . . .

EVE, *impatiently:* What, dear?

CAIN: Did God order you to make me the farmer and Abel to tend the sheep?

ADAM: You can't expect Him to go into those kind of details, Cain. He just felt it was time we went out in the world and multiplied, that's all.

CAIN: Father, I've never understood why you couldn't have stayed in the Garden and multiplied.

EVE: In the *Garden!*

ADAM: Oh, no, boy—

EVE: That's not something you do in the *Garden,* darling.

CAIN: Well, what did He say, exactly, when you left?

ADAM: He said to get out—

EVE: Not "Get out!"

ADAM, *quickly:* No, no, not "Get out!"

EVE: I think he's overtired.

CAIN: I am not overtired! Why do you always make everything ridiculous? I'm not talking about sheep or farming; I'm talking about what God wants us to *do!*

ABEL: If you think He wants me to farm, I'll be glad to switch.

CAIN, *to Adam with a laugh:* He's going to farm!

ADAM, *laughing:* God help us!

ABEL, *protesting:* Why!

CAIN: With your sense of responsibility, we'd be eating thistle soup!

EVE, *touching Abel:* He's just more imaginative.

LUCIFER: Will you just shut up?

CAIN: Imaginative!

ABEL: Have I ever lost a sheep?

CAIN: How *could* you lose them? They always end up in my corn.

ABEL: Cain, that only happened once!

CAIN, *with raw indignation:* Go out there and sweat the way I do and tell me it only happened once!

EVE: He's just younger!

CAIN: And I'm older, and I'll be damned if I plant another crop until he fences those sheep!

LUCIFER: Stop this!

EVE, *to Adam:* Stop this!

CAIN: Why must you always take his side?

EVE: But how can he build a fence?

CAIN: The same way I plant a crop, Mother! By bending his back! Abel, I'm warning you, if you ever again—

ADAM: Boys, boys!

ABEL, *turning away:* If he wants a fence, I think he should build it.

CAIN: *I* should build it! Are the corn eating the sheep or the sheep eating the corn?

ABEL: It's not natural for me to build a fence.

CAIN: Not natural! You've been talking to God lately?

ABEL: I don't know anything about God. But it's the nature of sheep to move around, and it's the nature of corn to stay in one place. So the fence should fence the thing that stays in one place and not the thing that moves around.

ADAM: That's logical, Cain.

CAIN: In other words, the work belongs to me and the whole wide world belongs to him!

ADAM, *at a loss:* No, that's not fair either.

ABEL, *angering, to Adam:* Well, I can't fence the mountains, can I? I can't fence the rivers where they go to drink. *To Cain:* I know you work harder, Cain, but I didn't decide that. I've even thought sometimes that it is unfair, and maybe we should change places for a while—

CAIN: You wouldn't last a week.

ABEL, *crying out:* Then what am I supposed to do? *Cain is close, staring into his face, a tortured expression in his eyes which puzzles Abel.* Why is he looking like that? *Suddenly Cain embraces Abel, hugging him close.*

ADAM: Attaboy!

EVE, *puzzled and alarmed:* Cain?

CAIN—*he lets Abel go and moves a few steps, staring:* I don't know what's happening to me.

ADAM: Abel, shake his hand. Go on, make up. You're both sorry.

ABEL, *holding out his hand:* Cain?

LUCIFER, *victoriously to Heaven:* Why don't you give up?

   Cain has just raised his hand to approach Abel when a large snake is dropped in their midst from Heaven. Eve screams. Lucifer rushes and flings it out of sight.

LUCIFER: Scat! Get out of here!

EVE: It flew in and flew out!

ADAM: A flying snake?

Instantly the high howling of several coyotes is heard, and the family turns in all directions, as though toward an invading force.

LUCIFER, *off to one side, looking up to Heaven:* Father, this is *low*!

ADAM, *looking about at the air:* Something is happening. *To Eve, who is staring about:* I think . . . I'd better tell them. *She covers her eyes in trepidation.* Eve? Maybe we're supposed to, now.

EVE, *lowering her hands:* All right. Then maybe everything will be as it was again.

ADAM: Boys? Maybe you'd better sit down, boys.

ABEL: Tell what, Pa?

They all sit except Eve, who remains standing, staring about apprehensively.

ADAM: About the question of leaving Paradise—I don't want you to think that we tried to mislead you or anything like that.

EVE, *pleadingly to Cain:* It's just everything was going so good, you see?

ADAM, *with a glance around at the air:* But it looks like something is happening, so maybe we better get this settled.

ABEL: What, Pa?

ADAM: We . . . didn't exactly *decide* to go, y'see. We were ah—*he blinks away a tear*—told to leave.

CAIN: *Told?*

ABEL: Why, Pa?

ADAM, *fumbling:* Why? Well . . . *He turns helplessly to Eve.* Why?

EVE: We just didn't fit in, you see. I mean if a person doesn't fit in—

ADAM: If we're going to tell it, we better tell it.

EVE: But the way you're telling it, it sounds like it was all my fault!

ADAM: I didn't say anything yet!

EVE: Well, when are you going to say it?

ADAM, *setting himself:* Well—as we told you before, I was alone with God for a long time, and then—

ABEL: He made Mama.

ADAM: Right.

ABEL, *with a big smile:* And you liked her right away, heh?

CAIN: Of course he did.

ADAM: She was gorgeous. Of course, there wasn't much choice. *He laughs.*

EVE: Ha. Ha. Ha.

ADAM: Well, anyway, I believe I mentioned there was this tree—with an apple—

ABEL: Of good and evil.

ADAM: Right.

CAIN: Which you're never allowed to eat under any circumstances.

ADAM: Right. Well, the thing is, you see—we ate it.

ABEL—*thrilled and scared, he laughs:* You ate it!

CAIN: I thought you said you—

ADAM: No, we ate it.

ABEL, *more scared now:* Not Mama, though.

ADAM: Mama too.

> *Cain goes to a lyre and, turning his back on them, he plays. They watch him for a moment, aware of his intense feeling.*

ABEL, *avidly:* And then what happened?

> *Cain strums as loud as he can, then stops.*

ADAM, *with a worried glance at Cain:* Well, the next thing—I looked at her, y'see. And there was something funny. I didn't know what it was. And then I realized. She was naked.

> *Cain now turns to them.*

CAIN AND ABEL: Mama?

EVE: Well, *he* was too.

CAIN—*shocked, he drops the lyre:* Mama!

LUCIFER, *holding his head:* Ohhh!

EVE: We didn't know it, darling!

CAINE: How could you not know you were naked?

EVE: Well, we were like children; like you, like Abel. You remember, when Abel was a baby and ran around—

CAIN, *outraged, accusing:* But you weren't a baby!

EVE, *to Adam, at a loss:* Aren't you going to say anything?

ABEL, *explaining for Adam:* Well, they were like animals.

CAIN, *pained, horrified:* Don't you say a thing like that!

ADAM, *to Cain:* Well, I told you—I could smell water?

ABEL: Sure! And they could hear the trout talking.

CAIN: But you never said you were actually . . . *animals.*

ADAM: Now just a minute, Cain. That was the way God wanted it—

CAIN: I can't believe that! God could never have wanted my mother going around without any clothes on!

ADAM, *angrily, standing:* You mean *I* wouldn't let her put her clothes on?

EVE, *going to him:* Darling, we were innocent!

CAIN, *furiously:* You were naked and innocent? Don't you understand that that's why He threw you out?

EVE: But He loved us most when we were naked. He only got mad when we knew we were. *Slight pause.*

CAIN, *swept by this truth:* No wonder we dreamed of death!

EVE: Why?

CAIN: We've been saying all the wrong prayers. We shouldn't be thanking God—we should be begging His forgiveness. We've been living as though we were innocent. We've been living as though we were blessed!

EVE: But we are, darling.

CAIN: We are cursed, Mother!

EVE, *furiously to Adam:* You should never have told him!

CAIN: Why did you lie to us?

ADAM: Now just a minute . . .

CAIN, *accusingly:* I always *knew* there was something you weren't saying!

ADAM: Just a minute! *Slight pause.* We didn't want to frighten you, that's all. But maybe now you're old enough to understand.—He did curse us when He threw us out. And part of the curse is that we will have to die.

CAIN: *We're* going to die?

ABEL: Like the sheep, you mean?

ADAM: Sheep, birds, everything.

CAIN: You and Mama, too? You mean we wouldn't see you any more?

EVE: Don't worry about it, darling. I'm sure we have a long, long time yet.

CAIN: You mean before He got angry you would never die?

ADAM: Far as I know—yes.

CAIN: Oh, my God—then He must have been absolutely furious with you.

EVE: I'm sure He's forgiven us, dear, or we wouldn't have you and everything so wonderful—

CAIN, *sinking to his knees:* Listen to me! I tell you we have been warned. Now we must do what has never been done.

EVE: Do what?

CAIN: We must give this day—not to the animals or the crops; this day we must give to God. I tell you—*he looks upward tenderly*—if we will open up our sins to Him and cleanse ourselves, he might show his face and tell us we are supposed to live. Father, Mother, Abel—come and pray with me.

ADAM, *to Eve:* Well—a prayer wouldn't hurt.

EVE, *recalling:* Maybe he's right. Maybe it'll all be sweet again. *Going to her knees:* What should we pray, darling?

Cain faces Heaven. Adam goes to his knees. And finally Abel.

CAIN: Almighty God, seeing that our parents were thrown out of Paradise for their transgressions against Thee, we, Cain and Abel, beseech Thy forgiveness. Let this family live, let us be innocent again! Now each one, give up the sin.

Adam and Eve shut their eyes and concentrate. Abel watches them, then leans over to Eve.

ABEL, *with a glance at the praying Cain:* Does this mean I'm building a fence?

CAIN, *eyes shut:* It seems to me that when a person dies in his brother's dream he ought to pray!

ADAM: I saw it too, Abel—you were dead. I think you'd better pray.

Pause. All heads are lowered. Lucifer stands up. He comes down to them and sits next to Abel.

ABEL, *softly:* Mother!

EVE: Sssh!

ABEL: Someone has come.

ADAM: I don't see anybody.

A slight pause. They contemplate, but Abel is glancing apprehensively toward Lucifer.

ABEL: Who are thou?

The family turns quickly to him, astonished, Lucifer being invisible to all but Abel.

LUCIFER: I am what you fear in your heart is true—your brother is dangerous. Tell him you'll build the fence. *Abel reacts in refusal.* This man is inconsolable!

ABEL: Why?

LUCIFER: She loves you best, Abel.

ABEL: But Cain is loved!

EVE: How sweet! *To Adam:* Did you hear?

LUCIFER: Cain has her respect, but her love has gone to you. Tell him you'll build it if you care to live! This man is murderous. *Now Abel turns with new eyes to Cain.*

ABEL: About the fence—

CAIN: Yes?

ABEL: You're right. It's not the corn that eat the sheep but the sheep that eat the corn—

LUCIFER: Attaboy!

EVE, *to Adam, happily:* Listen!

ABEL: So I will build the fence around the sheep.

EVE, *to Adam:* Do you hear!

ADAM: Marvelous.

CAIN: Where would you build it?

ABEL: Well—anywhere out of the way. In the valley?

CAIN: I need the valley.

ABEL: Oh ... On the hillside?

CAIN: I'll need the hillside. I'm planning to set out quite a large vineyard this spring.

ABEL: Where would you suggest, then?

CAIN: There is very rich pasture across the mountain.

ABEL: That's ... pretty far away, though, isn't it?

CAIN: I don't think it's all that far.

LUCIFER: Agree! Agree!

ABEL, *swallowing his resentment:* All right, Cain.

LUCIFER: I know how you feel, son, but lying is better than dying.

EVE, *affected by Abel's anguish:* Cain, dear, I want you to tell him you didn't mean that before—

LUCIFER: Abel, shut her up—

EVE, *to Cain, insistently:* You won't make him go so far away to pasture, will you?

LUCIFER: She is killing you, word by loving word!

ABEL: I don't mind, Mother. In fact—

LUCIFER: I *like* long walks.

ABEL: I *like* long walks.

EVE: But you *agreed* to build the fence! *To Cain:* Why must you humiliate him?

Cain slams his hands down on the ground and springs up furiously, goes to a big rock and picks it up.

LUCIFER, *to Abel:* Watch out! Don't your back on him! *Abel quickly turns to watch his brother.*

EVE: What are you doing?

Cain places the boulder on top of another.

CAIN: What has never been done. It has come to me to make an offering to the Lord.

LUCIFER, *shaking a fist at Heaven:* Don't you ever give up?

EVE, *vastly relieved:* That's a wonderful idea!

ADAM: Say, now! That sounds very good, Cain.

EVE: You think He'll come?

ADAM: He might. The way Cain loves Him, He might just stop by. *To Cain, with his expertise:* Take the best of thy corn and the first of thy wheat, and a little parsley—He always rather liked parsley.

Cain finds a flat stone and sets it on top of the altar he is constructing. Eve immediately takes a broom and starts sweeping the area.

EVE: What about some grapes?

ADAM, *calling to Cain:* Grapes too!

CAIN: The grapes aren't too good this year—

EVE: You'd better not, then.

ADAM, *all excited:* Don't listen to her; it doesn't matter if they're not too good, it's the feeling behind it. Because He's fair, Cain, you'll see. And here's another thing. We've got to praise Him more. We haven't been praising Him enough.

EVE: Praise God! Praise the Lord!

ADAM: Will you wait! *To Cain:* Hurry up, get the stuff. *Cain rushes back to load a tray with his crops.*

EVE, *clasping her hands together feverishly:* He's going to come! I feel it, I tell you I feel it!

ADAM, *supervising Cain, calling:* I'd throw in a few onions. *To Eve:* Loved a good onion.

EVE: It's going to be like it was again! *She rushes to Abel.* Push back your hair, darling. Adam, there's dirt on your cheek. *Adam brushes it off. Abel fixes his hair. Cain turns to them now with a tray loaded with vegetables and fruit. Silence for an instant; then Eve suddenly is swept forward to him.* Would you mind, darling? *She picks an apple off the tray.* No apples. *She hides the apple in her clothes.*

CAIN, *in tension:* Is it all right, Pa?

Adam comes forward, inspects the tray. Silence.

ADAM: This looks absolutely beautiful, Cain. Now, when you see His face, regard the right eye. Because that's the one He loves you with. The left one squints, y'see, because that's the one He judges with. So watch the right eye and don't be frightened.

CAIN: I love Him, Father.

ADAM: I know that, Cain, and now you will know His love for thee. *He kisses Cain, who turns and tensely starts for the altar.*

EVE: Cain!

He halts. She comes to him, elevated within. She kisses the offering. Then she kisses him. He turns again to the altar. Abel steps before him. They stare at one another. Now Cain leans and kisses him. Then he carefully sets the offering on the altar and steps back. All go to their knees before the altar, as—

EVE, *to Adam, tentatively:* I think Abel ought to make an offering too.

Abel sits up, and Adam considers this. Cain remains bowed. Lucifer cries out, rushing about before Abel.

LUCIFER: Don't! Under no circumstances must you get into this competition!

CAIN: It was my idea, Mother. Can't he do it another time?

EVE: It was just a suggestion. You don't have to get angry.

ABEL, *struck by his vision:* Maybe He would come because of me. . . .

LUCIFER: What are *you* guilty about? Just because your mother loves you best? Lie back and enjoy it.

ABEL: But it is not fair to Cain, and I can't bear that any more! I want God to bring us peace!

LUCIFER: And what if it turns out God also loves you best? Is *that* fair to Cain?

ABEL: But—Cain would have to accept *that*!

LUCIFER: Boy, even with God's help, nobody can be Number One and good at the same time. Don't compete!

ABEL: Get thee behind me! *He draws his knife and rushes upstage.*

EVE, *to Adam:* He's going to do it! *Calling to Abel, who is exiting:* Pick a nice fat lamb, darling!

LUCIFER, *as he rushes upstage after Abel:* Abel! Don't call down God!

Cain is still on his knees, staring ahead. Eve feels his anguish.

EVE: He'll come now, dear, and He'll bless you both, as I do *But Cain refuses to turn to her; she sees his hurt.* I love thee, Cain, I always loved thee from the hour of thy conception!

LUCIFER, *looks to Heaven:* What a genius that old fart is—with one dream of death he's got them all guilty! By God, I'll free them now or never—with the truth! *He exits.*

Abel enters, holding before him a slab of wood loaded with the flesh and entrails of a lamb, his hands dripping blood. Adam instantly goes to him, smears his own hand, and snaps the blood into the air toward the sky.

ADAM: The blood is the life, and the life is the Lord's.

EVE—*she looks up at the sky:*

>   Now, Maker, show Thyself and spread Thy peace
>   On all of us, my Abel and my Cain.

She and Adam kiss Abel from his right and left. He sets his offering on the altar. The deep bellow of a bull is heard.

ALL: Aiee!

The bellowing resounds again, and now a figure rises behind the altar, a man with the head of a bull. At the right they all prostrate themselves on the ground.

LUCIFER:

>   A second time I come with thine awakening, Mankind!
>   Nobody's guilty any more!
>   And for your progeny now and forever
>   I declare one massive, eternal, continuous parole!

From here on out there is no sin or innocence
But only Man. *He flings off his mask.*
Now claim thy birthright! *He leaps, stands away from the altar,
welcoming arms outflung.*
Total freedom!

EVE, *leaps up:* Thank God!

ADAM, *springing to his feet:* That's the Devil!

LUCIFER: There are two Gods, Adam—in Heaven, God; and God on earth is me!

ADAM: Slaughter him! *He starts for Lucifer, and the boys stand. Eve throws herself before Lucifer to shield him.* Woman!

EVE: I believe this angel!

ADAM: This is the enemy!

EVE: I won't deny it any more—this spirit makes me happy!

ADAM, *to the altar:* Lord, show Thy face, my wife is going to Hell!

EVE: Adam! *She raises her hand gently toward him.*

Where has all our old contentment gone?
You were so long in Paradise
With God, that all your dreams go there,
But the only home I ever had is on this dust,
This windy world,
And here I am condemned. I know God rules in Heaven,
But in the name of peace, I have to speak the truth:
Except for one short dance—*she nearly weeps*—
God never showed me any kindness.

ADAM: Woman!

EVE:

I see it, husband!
This God is mine—I know it!
For only this one frees me of my sin.

ADAM: There is one God!

EVE: No—two! One for me and one for—*A strange light blossoms around the altar, and, seeing it, she breaks off and like the others backs away. Lucifer rushes down to her.*

LUCIFER: Let's end this war! Dance with me, woman. Show God your love and end this stupid war!

A wild music explodes, then diminishes as Lucifer pulls her to

himself, and in conflict she breaks and with arms spread calls to Abel.
EVE: Abel! Cain! *Rushing to them, grabbing them:* Love! Love, my darlings!

ADAM: I forbid this! God's coming!

EVE—*clamping both their heads to her, she calls out to Adam and Heaven:* Is God not pleased if peace comes in? *She springs from them and then turns back invitingly to them.* Let hate go out and love come in!

LUCIFER:

Now save yourselves with music and the truth!

Be what you are and as you are.

Give God to Adam, boys—and I will give you Eve!

The music flies up: Eve begins to dance—awkwardly at first, and Lucifer grabs her, awakens her again, and her body loosens, writhes; then she flies to Abel, who is embarrassed but quickly learns, and now she flies to Cain, who is stiff at first, but Lucifer helps him loosen up, and finally she is whirling among the three of them, kissing them in turn, her hands flowing over their bodies and theirs over hers—and suddenly Cain explodes into a prancing step, flapping his arms like a giant mating bird. Eve is astonished, innocently laughs, but in a sweep he pulls her down and climbs onto her. The truth is out—fuck her, Cain, and save the world! *Adam rushes to separate them. Lucifer grabs him.* Shame! How can you be so selfish! *And with Cain on his stunned but compliant mother and Abel trying to hold out till Cain is done—God appears behind the altar.*

Adam roars a gigantic, horrified roar. Silence. Cain rolls off Eve and sits looking up at the Presence. Eve sits up. Adam prostrates himself.

ADAM: Glory to God in the highest!

LUCIFER: Good morning, sir. *With an ironic gesture toward the crew.* May I introduce you to mankind? I don't believe I need labor the point—to the naked eye how pious and God-fearing they were; but with a moment's instruction and the right kind of music, a bear would blush at their morality. Dear Father, what are we fighting about? Truly, Lord, what is Man beyond his appetite? *Extends his hand.* Come, make peace; share Heaven—I the God of what-they-are, and you in charge of their improvement. In you let them find their hopes, in me their pleasure, and shut the gates of Hell forever. Sir, I am ready to take my place.

Striving against anger, God turns his head to each of the people in turn. Then He looks down at the offerings and picks out an onion.

GOD: Peace, children, on this first Sabbath. Whose is this?

LUCIFER: You'll accept those offerings when the filth in their hearts stinks to Heaven!

GOD: Whose is this?

CAIN, *with uncertainty:* That was mine, Lord.

GOD: Do you want me to taste it?

LUCIFER: You saw him on his mother!

GOD: Cain?

CAIN, *his eyes averted:* If it please Thee.

GOD: Why?

CAIN: It's . . . my *onion*, sir.

GOD: Then you still have respect for an onion?

CAIN: Lord, it's my work, my labor; it is the best of all I've made.

GOD, *with angry eyes:* And were you not the best that I had made?

Cain looks up, aware, and lowers his eyes in shame. God bites the onion, chews it.

GOD: That . . . is a good onion, Cain. *Cain falls to his knees weeping.* And this is Abel's meat?

ABEL: It's mine, sir, yes.

GOD: Mutton.

EVE: Oh, no, sir—lamb.

GOD—*He glances at her, then with high interest leans and inhales the delicious scent:* Ohhh, yes.

ABEL, *encouraged:* My youngest, fattest lamb, Lord. I hope it will please Thee.

EVE: I usually sprinkle it with salt and pepper first. . . .

GOD: You might try rubbing a bud of garlic over it.

EVE: Oh, I will!

ADAM: Do that next time, definitely.

EVE: Oh, yes, Adam!

Now God picks up a piece of meat. All grow tense. Abel raises his head to watch. God puts the meat in His mouth and chews, His eyes opening wider with the taste.

GOD: What in the world do you feed your flock?

ABEL, *joyously:* I find the sweetest grass, sir!

CAIN: And corn. *God turns to him. Abel, tense, turns to him.*

GOD, *understanding:* Oh, yes. I see. *He turns slowly to Abel.* Abel? Rise. *Abel springs to his feet.* Young man, this is undoubtedly the sweetest, most delicious, delicate, and profoundly *satisfying* piece of meat I have ever tasted since the world began.

Adam, filled with glory, comes to Abel and shakes his hand.

ADAM: Boy, this is our proudest moment.

EVE—*unable to hold back, she starts for Abel:* Darling! *She grabs Abel's face, kisses him on the lips, and turns up to God.* There is one God now and forever, there is no other on earth or in Heaven!

GOD: And don't you forget it, either. *Turning to Lucifer, who is staring at the ground:* I seem to have forgotten what you were saying. What was that all about, fallen angel?

LUCIFER, *bitterly:* About the truth, sir—my mistake. But this isn't over yet!

GOD, *steps down from the altar:* Come, children, and walk a little way with me, and we shall talk a while together of life and earth and Heaven. Come, Adam. *He takes Adam by the hand.* Eve? *She comes to him, enthralled, and gives him her hand.* Abel? Cain?

CAIN: Lord, there's still my corn. You haven't tasted my corn.

GOD: Oh, I can see it's all very nice. You have done quite well, Cain. Keep it up. *With which He walks into light with Adam, and Abel following behind.*

EVE, *beckoning:* Cain? *Seeing his shock:* Darling, he loved your vegetables. Come.

Cain seems to hardly hear her and takes a few dead steps following her. She goes, and he comes to a halt. Lucifer starts for him, then halts as he sees his strange expression.

LUCIFER: Now control yourself, boy. Cain?

CAIN: He never even tasted my corn.

LUCIFER: You mustn't get excited.

CAIN, *with the undercurrent of dangerous laughter:* But do you know what goes into an ear of corn? I planted twice this year; the floods washed my seeds away the first time. *His eyes fall on a flask beside the altar.* And my wine. *Going to the flask:* I was going to offer ... *He suddenly kicks down the altar.*

LUCIFER: Listen to me—*For good measure Cain sends all the food flying with another kick.* We've got to get serious!

CAIN: Cain, serious? That's all over, Devil, now Cain starts to *live!* *He starts throwing everyone out of the shelter.*

LUCIFER: What's this, now?

CAIN: This is my house! Mine! *He faces Lucifer.* No one enters here but Cain any more. They have God, and I have this farm—and before I'm finished, my fences will stretch out to cover the earth!

LUCIFER: Adam will never agree to leave this house—

CAIN: Oh, he'll agree, all right—*he strides to his flail and brandishes it*—once I explain it to him! *He whips the flail with a whoosh, and, holding it up:* There's the only wisdom I will ever need again! *A deep hum sounds in the earth, like a dynamo.*

LUCIFER: Listen! *Cain freezes.* He has set a moaning in the earth. *Daylight changes to night; stars appear.* Look! *Both look up at the night sky.*

> He is giving you a night at noon,
> Darkening your mind to kill for him!

Frightened, Cain turns from the sky to the flail in his hand and throws it down guiltily.

> Don't let him use you. Go away. Hide yourself.

CAIN: I, hide? I was the one who thought of the offerings; from me this Sabbath came! Let them hide! I want nothing from anyone any more!

LUCIFER: But God wants a murder from you.

CAIN, *astonished:* God . . . wants . . . ?

LUCIFER: He has designed your vengeance, boy. He's boiling your blood in his hand.

CAIN: But why?

LUCIFER:

> So He may stand above your crime, the blameless God,
> The only assurance of Mankind, and His power is safe.
> Come now,
> We'll hide you till this anger's gone.

He leads Cain a few yards; Cain moves as though being carried, staring into Lucifer's face.

ABEL'S VOICE, *calling from a distance:* Cain? Where are you? Come on!

Cain swerves about toward the voice.

LUCIFER: Don't stop!

CAIN—*a cry, as though from his bowel, to the sky:* How is Abel the favorite of God?

LUCIFER:

God has no favorites! *He grasps Cain's astounded face.*

Man's a mirror to Him, Cain,

In which He looks to see His praise.

CAIN: But I have praised Him! And Abel only played His flute!

LUCIFER: So where is good and where is evil?

God wants power, not morals!

ABEL'S VOICE, *closer now, calling:* Cain! We're all waiting for you!

LUCIFER, *grabbing for him:* Come!

CAIN: I have to face him first! *He breaks from Lucifer, facing in the direction of Abel's voice.*

LUCIFER:

Then face him with indifference.

Kill love, Cain, kill whatever in you cares;

Murder now is but another sort of praise to God!

Don't praise Him with a death!

ABEL, *closer yet:* Cain?

CAIN:

His voice is like silver, like his life,

And mine is the voice of the ox, the driven beast!

LUCIFER: Indifference, Cain!

Abel enters.

ABEL: Aren't you coming? God is sitting by the river, telling all about Paradise—come on! *Cain stares front.*

LUCIFER, *facing front:* I swear this, Cain—if man will not kill man, God is unnecessary! Walk away and you're free! *Cain starts to walk away.*

ABEL: Brother! God wants you there!

CAIN, *halting:* Wants *me*?

LUCIFER: Swallow it and walk!

ABEL: Of course—he loves you, Cain. He was just saying how you do everything He wants.

CAIN: Then, by God, I order you out of here and your mother and father, and never come back!

ABEL: Brother!—I've as much right here as you. *He moves toward Cain.*

CAIN: Are you even so sure of his blessing that you come to me?

ABEL: You'll not hurt me, Cain.

CAIN: Why? Am I thy servant? *He sweeps up his flail.* Am I thy fool? Run from me!

ABEL: *Astonished at the flail, he starts to back away.* Brother! God loves us both!

CAIN: You are dead to me, Abel—run!

ABEL, *halts:* I will not! Come to the Lord!

CAIN, *moving toward him, raising the flail:* Run for your life!

ABEL: Brother, let God calm you!

CAIN, *whirling about, flail raised, he calls to the air:* Save us, Lord . . . !

ABEL, *rushing to him:* Come to Him!

CAIN— *he turns on Abel, calling to God:* Now save us! *He strikes at Abel, who dodges and runs.*

ABEL, *screaming:* Mother!

CAIN—*pursuing him, he strikes Abel down:* Save us! *He strikes him again on the ground.* Save us!

LUCIFER: Cain! How can you love God so!

GOD, *calling from off:* Cain! Where art thou!

Cain flings the flail away like an alien thing that somehow got into his hand. God enters rapidly, behind Him Eve and Adam.

GOD: Where is thy brother?

Cain is silent.

EVE: Where is Abel?

ADAM: Where is he?

GOD: Where is Abel, thy brother?

CAIN, *with a new, dead indifference:* I know not. Am I my brother's keeper?

GOD: The voice of thy brother's blood crieth unto me from the ground.

EVE—*seeing the corpse, like a sigh at first:* Ahhh.

ADAM, *wide-eyed:* Ohhh. *The sigh repeatedly emanating from her, she halts, looking down at the corpse. Adam comes and faces it.* Ohhhh.

EVE—*she goes down beside the corpse, keening.* Abel? Wake, my darling!

ADAM: Abel? *Calls.* Abel!

GOD: What hast thou done!

CAIN, *with a bitter, hard grin, plus a certain intimate, familiar tone:* What had to be done. As the Lord surely knew when I laid before Him the fruit of my sweat—for which there was only Thy contempt.

GOD: But why contempt? Didn't I approve of your offering?

CAIN: As I would "approve" my ox. Abel's lamb was not "approved," it was adored, like his life!

GOD, *indignantly:* But I *like* lamb! *Cain is dumfounded.* I don't deny it, I like lamb better than onions.

LUCIFER: Surely there can be no accounting for taste.

CAIN: And this is Your justice?

GOD: Justice!

CAIN, *with a bitter laugh:* Yes, justice! Justice!

GOD: When have I ever spoken that word?

CAIN: You mean our worth and value are a question of *taste?*

GOD, *incredulously:* But Cain, there are eagles and sparrows, lions and mice—is every bird to be an eagle? Are there to be no mice? Let a man do well, and he shall be accepted.

CAIN: I have done well and I am humiliated!

GOD: You hated Abel before this day, so you cannot say you have done well.

EVE, *rising from the corpse:* You argue with *Him? She rushes to tear at Cain, Adam holding her back.* Kill him! He's a murderer! *Weeping, held by Adam, she calls:* Take his life!

GOD: Surely you repent this, Cain.

CAIN: When God repents His injustice, I will repent my own!

LUCIFER: Why should he repent? Who sent death down here? You did! *He points to God.* There is the murderer!

ADAM: Watch your mouth!

LUCIFER: He arranged it all from beginning to end! *Eve stops weeping, straightens, astonished, turns to God.* Do You deny Azrael was here this morning while they slept? *To Eve:* Ask him!

EVE: You sent the Angel of Death?

   Pause.

GOD: Yes.

EVE: Lord God ... did you want this?

Pause.

GOD: Eve ... soon the multitudes will spring from this first family and cover the earth. How will the thousands be shepherded as I have shepherded thee? Only if the eye of God opens in the heart of every man; only if each himself will choose the way of life, not death. For otherwise you go as beasts, locked up in the darkness of their nature. *Slight pause.* I saw that Cain was pious, yet in him I saw envy too. And so I thought—if Cain was so enraged that he lift his hand against his brother, but then, remembering his love for Abel and for me, even in his fury lay down his arms? *To Cain:* Man!—you would have risen like a planet before the generations, the victory of God, first brother and the first to reject a murder. Oh, Cain, how I hoped for thee!

ADAM, *to Eve:* Do you understand? He was trying to help us. *She stands rigid, wide-eyed.* Eve, you must beg his pardon.

EVE, *turning to God:* But why must my child have died? You could have tested me, or Adam or Abel—we could *never* have killed.

GOD: Woman, a moment ago you commanded me to take Cain's life.

EVE: But I ... I was *angry.*

GOD: Cain was also angry. *She turns away, rejecting.* Do you understand me? *Beginning to anger.* Then am I a wanton murderer? Speak! What am I to you?

ADAM: Eve! Tell him you understand!

EVE: I do not understand ... why we *can't just live*!

GOD: Because without God you'll murder each other!

EVE, *furiously:* And with God? With God?

GOD: Then do you want the Devil? Tell me now before the multitudes arrive. Who do you want!

ADAM: You, Lord, you!

GOD: Why? Your innocent son is dead; why!

ADAM: Because ... how do I know?—maybe for someone, somewhere, even this ... is good? Right?

GOD, *outraged:* You are all worthless! The mother blames God, the father blames no one, and the son knows no blame at all. *To Lu-*

cifer: Angel, you have won the world—and I hereby give it over to your ministry.

ADAM: *Him!*

GOD: This is the chaos you want, and him you shall have—the God who judges nothing, the God of infinite permission. I shall continue to do the hurricanes, the gorillas, and all that, but I see now that your hearts' desire is anarchy and I wash my hands. I do not want to be God . . . any more! *He starts away.*

LUCIFER, *dashing after Him:* Lord! You don't mean—not me all by myself!

GOD: That's what you've been after, isn't it?

LUCIFER: No, no—with You! It's out of the question for me to run the world alone.

GOD: But what do you need Me for?

LUCIFER: But I can't—I can't *make* anything!

GOD: Really! But you're such a superb critic.

LUCIFER: But they're two entirely different things!

GOD: Perhaps once you're in charge you'll become more creative. *He starts away again; Eve rushes to Him.*

EVE: Wait, Lord, please!

GOD: Oh, woman, for thy torment especially I am most deeply sorry. Good-bye, dear Eve. *He starts away.*

EVE: But what do we do about Cain?

Now He halts, turns, alert.

LUCIFER, *to God:* Very well, I take the world! *To Eve:* Tell Him to go!

EVE, *to Lucifer:* But what about Cain?

LUCIFER: There'll be no more talk about Cain. The boy simply got caught in a rotten situation, and no emotions are called for.

GOD: She seems to have a question—

LUCIFER: She is free! She has no further questions! *To Eve:* Tell Him to go back to His hurricanes.

EVE, *to Lucifer:* But He murdered my son.

GOD: But what is the question?

EVE: HE MURDERED MY SON!

GOD: And what is the *question,* woman!

LUCIFER: You've got your freedom! Stop here!

EVE, *to Lucifer:* But how—*turning to Cain's adamant face:* How do I hand him his breakfast tomorrow? How do I call him to dinner? "Come, mankiller, I have meat for thee"?

CAIN, *holding his ground, his profile to her eyes:* It was not my fault!

EVE, *crying out to God:* How can we live with him!

GOD: But what did you say to me a moment ago—"Why can't we just live?" Why can't you do it? Take your unrepentant son and start living.

LUCIFER: Why not? Will blaming Cain bring Abel back?

EVE: But shouldn't he . . . shouldn't he repent?

LUCIFER: You mean a few appropriate words will console you?

EVE: Not words, but . . . *To Cain:* Don't you feel you've done *anything*?

LUCIFER: What's the difference what he feels?

EVE, *with high anxiety:* You mean nothing has *happened*?

LUCIFER: There is no consolation, woman! Unless you want the lie of God, the false tears of a killer repenting!

EVE: But why must they be false? If he loved his brother, maybe now he feels . . . *She breaks off, backing a step from Lucifer, and turns to God:* Is this . . . why he can't be God?

GOD, *quickly:* Why can't he be God?

LUCIFER: I can and I will be—I am the truth!

EVE: But you . . . *In fear:* you don't . . .

ADAM: He doesn't love us!

EVE: Yes!

GOD: And that is why, whatever you do, it's all the same to him—it's only his power this angel loves!

ADAM AND EVE, *rushing to God:* Father, save us!

GOD: Oh, my children, I thought you'd never understand!

LUCIFER, *with a furious, bitter irony, as God approaches the beseeching people:* And here He comes again—Father Guilt is back! *Rushing to Cain:* Cain, help me! You're the one free, guiltless man. Tell God you have no need for Him! Speak out your freedom and save the world!

CAIN—*he has been staring in silence; now he turns his dead eyes to Lucifer:* Angel, none of this seems to matter, you know? One way or the other. Why don't you let it all go?

With a near-sob Lucifer claps his hands over his ears, then, straightening, he comes to a salute before God.

LUCIFER: You have my salute! You have gorgeously prearranged this *entire* dialogue, and it all comes out the way You want—but You have solved absolutely nothing!

GOD, *lifting His eyes from the kneeling Adam and Eve:* Except, angel, that you will never be God. And not because I forbid it, but because they will never—at least not for very long—believe it. For I made them not of dust alone, but dust and love; and by dust alone they will not, cannot long be governed. *Lucifer bursts into sobbing tears.* Why do you weep, angel? They love, and with love, kill brothers. Take heart, I see now that our war goes on.

ADAM AND EVE: No, Lord!

Lucifer looks at God now, clear-eyed, expectant.

GOD: It does go on. For love, I see, is not enough; though the Devil himself cry peace, you'll find your war. Now I want to know what is in your heart. Tell me, man, what do you feel?

CAIN: I am thirsty.

GOD, *after a slight pause:* So in thy thirst will I sentence thee, Cain—to live. And in this loneliness shalt thou walk forever in the populous cities, a fugitive and a vagabond all the days of thy life. And whoever looks on thee will point and say, "There is the man who murdered his brother."

CAIN, *coming alive:* Better kill me now! They will stone me wherever I go!

GOD: No. I declare to all the generations: Whoever slayeth Cain, vengeance shall be taken on him sevenfold. For I will set a mark upon thee, Cain, that will keep thee from harm.

CAIN: What mark?

GOD, *holding two index fingers pointed toward Cain's face:* Come to me, my son. *Terrified, Cain comes up to His fingers, and He comes around behind Cain, who is facing front, and presses his cheeks, forming a smile which Cain cannot relax. God lowers His fingers.*

CAIN, *smiling:* What is the mark?

GOD: That smile is.

CAIN: But they will know that I killed my brother!

GOD: Yes, they will know, and you will smile forever with agony in your eyes—the sundered mark of Cain who killed for pride and power in the name of love.

Smiling, his eyes desperate, Cain turns to Eve. She cries out and hides her face in her hands. He tears at his cheeks, but his smile remains. He lowers his hands—a smiling man with astonished, terrifying eyes.

GOD: Adam? Eve? Now the way of life is revealed before you, and the way of death. Seek Me only in your hearts, you will never see My face again.

Lucifer, who has been staring off, swerves about. The people come alert, startled. God turns and walks upstage.

ADAM, *rushing a half-step behind God:* What'd you say? Lord, I don't understand . . . *God continues, moving into light. Adam halts, calling.* Did you say *never*?

EVE: What does that mean? Almighty God! *She starts to run up toward Him, but He disappears among the stars. Adam, above her now, turns down to Lucifer.*

ADAM: Angel! *He comes down to Lucifer, his finger rising toward the angel.* Did he mean that you are . . . ?

Lucifer turns from the vanished God to Adam, his face twisted with puzzlement.

ADAM AND EVE, *with a heartbroken, lost cry:* Who is God?

LUCIFER: Does it really matter? Why don't you have a nice breakfast together—the three of you—and forget the whole thing? After all, whoever God is, we have to be sensible. *He walks away, glancing back to Eve.* And whenever you'd like to start the dancing—just call.

EVE: Don't ever come back!

LUCIFER, *pointing insinuatingly at her:* You know exactly what I mean.

Lucifer walks into darkness. Adam and Eve turn to Cain.

ADAM: He condemned you to wander the earth. You'll have to go.

CAIN: But he let me live; there was some forgiveness in that. There's too much work here for one man, Father.

EVE: How can you ask forgiveness? *Indicating Abel.* You can't even weep for him. You are still full of hate!

CAIN: And your hate, Mother? *She turns away.* How will I weep? You never loved Cain!

ADAM: Spare one another . . . !

EVE, *turning to the corpse:* I loved him more. *To Cain:* Yes, more than you. And God was *not* fair. To me, either. *Indicating Abel.* And I still don't understand why he had to die, or who or what rules this world. But this boy was innocent—that I know. And you killed him, and with him any claim to justice you ever had.

CAIN: I am not to blame!

EVE: Are you telling me that nothing *happened* here? I will not sit with you as though nothing happened!

ADAM: Ask her pardon! *Cain turns away from both.* Cain, we are surrounded by the beasts! And God's not coming any more—*Cain starts away.* Boy, we are all that's left responsible!—ask her pardon! *Cain, adamant, the smile fixed on his face, walks out.* Call to him. Pardon him. In God's name cry mercy, Eve, there is no other!

With his arm around her he has drawn her to the periphery, where she stands, her mouth open, struggling to speak. But she cannot, and she breaks into weeping. As though in her name, Adam calls toward the departed Cain: Mercy!

The roars, songs, and cries of the animals fill the air. Adam looks up and about, and to the world, a clear-eyed prayer: Mercy!

CURTAIN

PLAYING FOR TIME

A screenplay based on the book by Fania Fenelon

PLAYING FOR TIME

Fade in on Fania Fenelon singing. Her voice is unheard, we hear only the opening music.

Cut to a sidewalk café in the afternoon. German soldiers relax, accompanied by French girls. We are in German-occupied Paris, 1942.

Cut to the Nazi flag flying over the Arc de Triomphe.

Cut to Fania accompanying herself on the piano in a Parisian ballad warmed with longing and wartime sentiment. The audience, almost all German troops and French girlfriends, is well-behaved and enjoying her homey romanticism, which salts their so-far epic conquests with pathos and a bit of self-pity.

Nothing in her manner betrays her hostility to Nazism and its destruction of France in the recent battles. She hopes they are enjoying their evening, promises to do what she can to help them forget their soldierly duties; but to the knowing eye there is perhaps a little extra irony in a look she casts, a smile she pours onto the upturned face of a nearby officer that suggests her inner turmoil at having to perform for the conqueror. She is radiant here, an outgoing woman who is still young and with a certain heartiness and appetite for enjoyment.

She is roundly applauded now at the number's end, and she bows and backs into darkness.

Cut to a train of freight cars, moving through open French farmland.

Cut to the inside of one freight car. It is packed with people, many of them well-dressed bourgeois, sitting uncomfortably jammed in. The ordinariness of the types is emphasized, but above that their individuation. Moreover, while all are of course deeply uneasy and uncomfortable, there is no open alarm.

A husband is massaging his wife's cramped shoulders.

A mother is working to remove a speck from a teenage daughter's eye.

Worker types survey the mass with suspicion.

A *clocharde*—a beggar woman off a Paris street—wrapped in rags, and rather at home in this situation, surveys the company.

A second mother pulls a young boy away from a neighbor's bag of food.

Chic people try to keep apart; they are soigné, even bored.

Students try to bury themselves in novels.

Two intellectuals scrunched up on the floor are playing chess on a small board.

A boy scout of twelve is doing his knots on a short rope.

An old asthmatic man in a fur-collared coat is urged by his wife to take his pill. He holds it between his fingers, unhappily looking around for water.

Cut to Fania, dressed in a beautiful fur coat and fur hat; her elegant valise is at her feet. She is carrying a net bag, with some fruit and a sausage, bread, and a bottle of water, which she offers the old man. He gratefully accepts it, takes his pill, drinks a sip, and returns her the bottle.

Beside Fania on the straw-covered floor sits Marianne, a girl of twenty, quite well dressed and overweight. Marianne has an unmarked, naive face. She is avidly glancing down at Fania's net bag.

FANIA: Have another piece of sausage, if you like.

MARIANNE: I'm so stupid—I never thought to take anything.

FANIA, *kindly:* Well, I suppose your mother has always done that for you.

MARIANNE: Yes. Just a tiny piece . . . *She breaks off more than a tiny piece.* I still can't believe I'm sitting so close to you! I have every one of your records, I think. Really—all my friends love your style.

Marianne bites her sausage and chews sensually.

FANIA: Do you know why they arrested you?

MARIANNE—*glances about nervously for an interloper:* I think it was because of my boyfriend—he's in the Resistance.

FANIA: Oh!— Mine too.

MARIANNE—*reaches under her coat:* I adore him! Maurice is his name.

She hands a snapshot to Fania who looks at it and smiles admiringly. Then Fania opens her soft leather purse and hands a snapshot to Marianne.

FANIA: He's Robert.

MARIANNE, *looking at photo:* Oh, he's fantastic! —a blond! I love blonds. *They return photos.* In the prison they kept beating me up. . . .

FANIA: Me, too.

MARIANNE: . . . They kept asking where he is, but I don't even know!—They nearly broke this arm. *Glancing around:* But somebody said it's really because we're Jewish that they picked us up. Are you?

FANIA: Half.

MARIANNE: I'm half too. Although it never meant anything to me.

FANIA: Nor me.

They silently stare at the others. Marianne glances down at Fania's food again.

FANIA: You really shouldn't eat so much.

MARIANNE: I can't help it; I never used to until the prison. It made me hungry all the time. I just hope my boyfriend never sees me like this—you wouldn't believe how slim I was only a few months ago. And now I'm bursting out of everything. But my legs are still good. Don't you think? *She extends her leg rather childishly.* I still can't believe I'm sitting next to you! I really have all your records.

Cut to the boy scout, who is now sitting with a compass on his knee, studying the needle. Beside him, his mother is asleep.

FANIA: Can you tell our direction?
BOY SCOUT: South.

A nearby worker overhears.

WORKER: It's probably going to be Munich. They need labor on the farms around there.
SECOND WORKER: I wouldn't mind. I love the outdoors.

A nearby woman adds her wisdom.

WOMAN: They have those tiny little thatched houses down there. I've seen photographs.
FIRST CHESS PLAYER: In my opinion, we'll be machine-gunned right where we sit—and I'm especially sorry for your sake, Madame Fenelon—your music is for me the sound of Paris.
FANIA: Thank you.
MARIANNE, *quietly:* I'm not sure I could do farm work—could you?
FANIA—*shrugs:* Have you ever worked?
MARIANNE—*a little laugh:* Oh no—I never even *met* a worker till the prison. I was in school or at home all my life. *The little laugh again.* And now I don't even know where my parents are. . . . *She verges on a shivering fear with startling rapidity.* Would you mind if we sort of stuck together?

Fania puts an arm around her and Marianne nestles gratefully into Fania's body. A moment passes; Fania reaches into her net bag and gives Marianne a bonbon. Marianne avidly eats it and Fania pats her hair as though, in effect, forgiving her another dietary lapse.

Cut to the boy scout, alert to some change in the compass. He takes it off his knee, shakes it, then sets it back on his knee.

FANIA: Has it changed?
BOY SCOUT: We've turned to the east.

The first chess player turns to the scout, then leans over to read the compass himself. He then resumes his position, a stare of heightened apprehension growing on his face.

SECOND CHESS PLAYER, *reassuringly:* But a compass can't be right with so much metal around it, can it?

Cut to a sudden explosion of indignation from deep in the crowd; people leaping up to escape something under the hay on the floor; yells of disgust and anger. . . . The mother and little boy emerge from within the crowd, he buttoning his pants. . . .

MOTHER: Well, what is he supposed to do!
FIRST MAN: He can use the pail over there!
SECOND MAN: The pail is full.
FIRST MAN, *yelling up to a grill high in a wall of the car:* Hey! Let us empty the pail!

Only the sound of the clanking train returns. Defeated, the deportees rearrange themselves to find dry places on the floor. The train lurches.

Cut to the slop pail, filled with urine, overturning.

Cut to people, with higher disgust, fleeing from the contents and crowding each other even more, some even remaining on their feet.

Cut to Marianne coming out of Fania's embrace. She whispers in Fania's ear, while placing a hand on her own stomach. Fania glances down at her with distress.

FANIA: Try to hold out—they'll *have* to open the doors soon.
MARIANNE: Could I have another sip of water?
FANIA: But only wet your mouth. You've got to try to discipline yourself.

Marianne drinks from the water bottle. Fania, as she is replacing the stopper, happens to catch the thirsty stare of the old asthmatic man. She hesitates, then holds out the bottle, which is taken by the asthmatic's wife. The old man sips; he is weaker than earlier.

Cut to the nearly full water bottle. Superimposed on it is the crowd in its present postures, which are still rather normal for the circumstances—some are standing to avoid the floor, some are alert and energetic.

The water level in the bottle drops; and the superimposed crowd is losing its energy, with people unconscious, one on top of the other; lips are parched, signs of real distress. . . .

Cut to Fania, asleep sitting up. Marianne awakens, lips parched, tries to get a drop out of the bottle, but it is empty. She looks into Fania's net bag, but it too is empty. Only half alive, Marianne, expressionless, sees a fight starting near her as a man pushes a woman away—and the woman is lowering her dress. . . .

MAN: Do it over there!—this is *my* place!

The woman trips over someone, looks down. . . .

Cut to the old asthmatic man. He's dead. His wife, spiritless and silent, holds his head in her lap.

Cut to the faces of the deportees experiencing the presence of the dead man. Unable to bear it any longer, Fania climbs up to the grill.

FANIA: Halloo! Listen! We've got a dead man in here! Halloo!

Surprisingly now, there is a squeal of brakes. People are thrown against each other, and the train stops. Expectation, fear, hope . . .

Cut to the freight-car doors rolling open. A powerful search-light bathes the crowd, blinding them. The people try to get to their feet and gather their belongings.

From outside, half a dozen kapos leap into the car—these are prisoners working for the administration—and, armed with truncheons, they pull people out of the car onto the ground. ("Hurry up, everybody out, get moving" . . . etc.) They are brutal, enjoying their power.

Cut to the debarkation area. Under the spectral arc lights the cars are being emptied. Kapos are loading valises onto trolleys, but with a certain care, like porters.

Cut to the train platform. Late at night. Still wearing her fur coat and hat, Fania half unwillingly gives up her valise to a kapo.

This kapo eyes Marianne's body and gives her a toothless come-on smile.

Cut to a sudden close-up of Dr. Mengele. This monster, the so-called Angel of Death, is a small, dapper man with a not unattractive face. He is the physician in charge of the selections, and in this shot is simply standing at the edge of the milling crowd, observing the people. Now he nods slightly, an order.

Cut to SS guards pushing the people into a rough line, one behind the other. A dozen or more guard dogs and handlers keep the proceedings lively. Snarls electrify, the air is filled with the whining of eager dogs. But the violence is still controlled.

Dr. Mengele faces the head of the line. With a gesture to right or left, with hardly a second's interval between individuals, he motions people toward several waiting trucks (marked with the Red Cross), or to an area where they stand and wait. Those in the latter are generally stronger, male, and younger.

And so the line moves rapidly toward Mengele's pointing fingers, and the crowd parts to the left and the right.

Cut to Fania, right behind Marianne on line, speaking into her ear.

FANIA: It's going to be all right—you see?—the Red Cross is here.

Cut to people being loaded onto the open-backed "Red Cross" trucks. Babies are passed over the crowd to mothers, the aged are carried aboard with the stronger helping. The air still carries the whining and barking of the dogs, the sounds of hurried commands.

Once again, intermittent close shots individualize the crowd, the types, relationships. The crowd, in fact, is relieved to be aboard and moving to some destination.

Cut to the trucks pulling away. Marianne and Fania, alone on the ground, look up at the packed truck that remains. Kapos raise its tailgate and fasten it.

FANIA: Wait—we're supposed to get on, aren't we?
KAPO: How old are you?

FANIA: I'm twenty-eight, she's twenty.
MARIANNE: I wouldn't mind a walk—may we?
KAPO, *with the very faintest glimmer of humor—he too is exhausted, skinny:* You can walk.

The kapo hurries up ahead and boards the truck. The truck starts to pull away, leaving the two women behind.

Cut to the people on the truck. The camera memorializes the faces we have come to know on the train—the boy scout, the chess players, the boy scout's mother, and so on. The truck moves off into darkness.

Cut to Marianne and Fania as they look around at the darkness—shapes of dark buildings surround them. Down the track we hear the activity of the guards and those selected to live.

FANIA: I guess we follow the trucks.

The two move together into the darkness.

Cut to a strange orange glow in the night sky. Is it a massive reflection of bright lights or is it flame? It comes from some half a mile off.

Cut to Fania and Marianne walking, looking up at the glow.

FANIA: There must be some sort of factory.

Out of the darkness a gaunt kapo pops up and starts walking along with them. He puts an arm around Marianne.

KAPO: Listen . . . I'll give you coffee.
FANIA, *pulling the kapo's arm away from Marianne:* This must be some high-class place—a cup of coffee for a woman?
KAPO: That's a lot. *Points arrogantly at Marianne.* See you later, Beauty.

Fania protectively grasps the frightened Marianne's hand and they move on into the dark toward the glow.

Cut to the reception area. Fania and Marianne enter the dimly lit room, perhaps twenty by forty feet. They enter uncertainly, unsure if they're supposed to be here. Five Polish women prisoners, employed here, are lounging around a table. One cleans her nails, another reads a scrap of newspaper, another is combing her companion's long hair. They are hefty, coarse, peasant types.

FANIA, *after a moment:* Is this where we get our things back?

She asks this question because—as we see now—along one wall of this room and extending out into a corridor which leads deeper into the building are, in neat piles, hundreds and hundreds of valises, stacks of clothes, piles of shoes, bins full of eyeglasses, false teeth, underwear, sweaters, gloves, galoshes, and every other imaginable personal item.

The Polish women turn to Fania and Marianne. One of them beckons silently, and the two approach her.

From the corridor enter two SS women in uniform. One of them is Frau Schmidt, the brutal, stupid German supervisor of the operation. They halt and expressionlessly observe.

The first Polish woman stands up from the table and simply takes Fania's handbag out of her hand. The second Polish woman grabs hold of Fania's fur coat and pulls it off her. Bag and coat go into the hands of the SS women, who admiringly examine them.

FIRST POLISH WOMAN: Your shoes.

Fania and Marianne, both in fear now, remove their shoes, which are carried to Frau Schmidt by the Poles. Frau Schmidt examines the expensive shoes appreciatively.

FIRST POLISH WOMAN: Undress.

Cut to Fania and Marianne, sinking into a stunned astonishment. And now hands working scissors enter the shot. Their hair—Fania has braids which are hard to cut—is almost completely removed, leaving tufts.

Cut to a long number—346,991—being tattooed on an arm. Backing off, we see it is Marianne's arm. She is now in a ludicrously outsized dress and shoes far too large. The same for Fania, who is staring down at her own tattoo. The tattooer is a male kapo, who works with his tongue sticking out the corner of his mouth.

Cut to a hundred or so women being handed dresses, some worn to mere shreds. Others are having their hair shorn as they wait to be tattooed. SS women move about, in charge.

Cut to Frau Schmidt, who is handed the little chess set from the train; she admires it, as well as the boy scout's compass. She sets them on the counter. They are then placed by a Polish woman in a receptacle already loaded with toys, stuffed animals, soccer balls, sports things.

Cut to Fania, nearby, as she recognizes these relics; her eyes flare with terror. She turns toward a nearby window.

Cut to the window. We see the eerie glow in the sky.

Cut to one of the Polish women, all but finished pinning Fania's plaits on her own hair, imitating Fania's sophisticated walk as her sister workers laugh.

Fania, humiliated and angered, touches her bare scalp.

Cut to the work gang, from Fania's point of view. An exhausted woman collapses at the feet of Lagerführerin Maria Mandel, who gestures toward a wheelbarrow. As kapos carry off the woman, one of her arms brushes Mandel's coat. Mandel viciously hits the arm away, brushing off her coat sleeve as the woman is dumped into the wheelbarrow.

POLISH WOMAN: How do I look, Jew-Crap?
FANIA: I'm not Jew-Crap, I'm French!

An uproar of laughter, and out of nowhere a smashing slap knocks Fania reeling to the floor. Over her stands SS Frau Schmidt, a powerhouse, looking down with menace.

Dissolve to dark.

Cut to the quarantine block—this is the barracks; dimly lit by a hanging bulb or two; a corridor between shelves, in effect, where women lie with barely room to turn over. The shelves go to the ceiling.

Fania and Marianne enter the corridor, escorted by a Polish woman, the Blockawa or Block Warden. She gestures for them to take bunks above and turns to leave.

The women in the bunks are cadaverous, barely able to summon interest in these new arrivals.

FANIA: Where are the people we came with? They went off on the trucks . . . ?

The Blockawa grips her arm and leads her to a window and points out.

Cut to the orange sky-glow. But from this closer distance smoke can be seen rising from a tall stack.

Cut to Fania, Marianne, and the Blockawa. The Blockawa points upward through the window.

BLOCKAWA: Your friends. You see? —cooking. You too, pretty soon.

The Blockawa cutely blinks both eyes, grins reassuringly, and walks away.

Cut to Marianne, quietly sobbing as she lies beside Fania on their bunk.

FANIA: Marianne? Listen to me. Come, girl, stop that.
MARIANNE: Why are they doing this? What do they get from it?

Fania glances to her other side where, on the shelf beside her, lies a famished-looking woman who might well be dead.

FANIA, *turning back to Marianne:* I've always had to have an aim in life—something I wanted to do next. That's what we need now if we're ever to get out of here alive.
MARIANNE: What sort of an aim?

Fania looks down into corridor below at the Blockawa, on patrol with a truncheon in her fist.

FANIA: If I ever get out of here alive, I'm going to kill a Polish woman.

Fania lies back, shuts her eyes, hating herself a little.

MARIANNE: I'm so hungry, Fania. Hold me.

Fania, on her back, embraces Marianne; then she turns the other way to look at the woman on her other side; she is skeletal, absolutely still. Cautiously Fania touches her skin and draws her hand away at the cold touch. Then she gives her a little shake. The woman has died.

Now she leans over the edge of the bunk and calls to the Blockawa.

FANIA: There's a dead woman up here.

The Blockawa, club in hand, allows a moment to pass; she slowly looks up at Fania with the interest of a seal, then strolls away.

Cut to a close shot of Fania and Marianne in their bunk. Marianne stares in fright at the corpse, then hides her face in Fania's side.

FANIA: We must have an aim. And I think the aim is to try to re-member everything. I'll tell you a story. . . . Once upon a time there was a prince named Jean and he was terribly handsome. And he married a princess named Jeannette and she was terribly beautiful.

Marianne comes out of hiding under Fania's arm—she is childishly interested. . . .

MARIANNE: And?
FANIA: And one day the prince said, "My dear, we must have an aim in life, we must make children," and so they. . . .

As Fania talks, slowly fade to a double exposure of Fania and Marianne. Snow falls over the image of the two women in their bunk: a forest; now spring comes; flowers appear and green grass; brook ice melts—always over the image of Fania and Marianne dragging stones, carrying wood, digging drainage ditches. . . . And finally, once again, in their bunk—now without the dead woman, and they are both asleep, side by side. And both are haggard now, with the half-starved look of the other prisoners.

A voice blares out: "ATTENTION!"

Cut to the barracks. Women start to come obediently out of their bunks into the corridor. The Blockawa yells.

BLOCKAWA: Remain in place! Does anybody know how to sing *Madame Butterfly*!

Astonished silence. The Blockawa is infuriated.

BLOCKAWA: Does anyone know how to sing *Madame Butterfly*!

Cut to Fania, unsure whether to volunteer; she glances at Marianne, who urges her silently to do so. Below in the corridor the Blockawa starts to leave. Fania suddenly lunges and, half hanging out the bunk, waves to the monster woman. . . .

FANIA: I can!

Cut to Fania, entering from exterior darkness into a lighted room. She halts, looking around in total astonishment.

Cut to the musicians' barracks dayroom. Fania, as in a wild dream, sees some twenty-five women, most seated behind music stands, badly but cleanly dressed; some with shaved heads (Jewesses), others still with their hair. Unlike her former barracks, with its faint and few light bulbs, there is brightness here, although it is actually quite bare of furniture.

In the center stands a Bechstein grand, shiny, beautiful. At the sight of the piano, Fania's mouth falls open.

Compared to these women Fania is indeed woebegone—dirty, in ludicrously enormous shoes, a torn and ill-fitting dress.

Elzvieta, an older Pole with a full head of hair, approaches Fania and with a wet cloth wipes her face. Fania regards this kindness incredulously. Now Elzvieta runs her pitying fingers down Fania's cheek.

Etalina, petite, Rumanian, eighteen, brings a lump of bread and puts it in Fania's hand.

ETALINA: I'm Etalina. I saw you in Paris once, at the "Melody." *Fania bites into the bread.* My parents took me there last year for my birthday—I was seventeen.

Michou enters the group—a tiny, determined girl of twenty, a militant communist, terribly pale, with a soft poetic voice. Etalina indicates her (not without a slight air of joking superciliousness toward this wraith).

ETALINA: But she's the one who recognized you. This is Michou.
MICHOU: I saw you yesterday coming out of your barracks and I ran and told our kapo—she promised to audition you—
FANIA: What audition?
ETALINA: For the orchestra—us. *With some awe.* Our conductor is Alma Rosé. *Calls offscreen.* Charlotte, come and meet Fania Fenelon! *To Fania.* She's one of our best players, but she's shy as a deer. She can do Bach solos. . . .
CHARLOTTE—*enters shot. Almost a whisper as she curtsies:* I'm honored to meet you.
FANIA: How do you do, Charlotte. *To Etalina:* Rosé?—there was a string quartet by that name. . . .
MICHOU: Alma is the first violinist's daughter.
FANIA: Then her uncle must be Gustav Mahler—the composer. . . .
ELZVIETA: Yes; she has a fantastic talent.
ETALINA: But not a warm heart, be careful. . . .

Michou touches Etalina to shush her, looking offscreen.

Cut to Alma Rosé, as she makes her entrance—there is instant silence and respect. Now three Blockawas—Polish prisoners acting as police in effect, and all weighty types—appear and look on with belligerent curiosity. They don't approve this coddling of Jews.

Alma comes toward the group. She is thin, extremely Germanic, scrubbed clean, her shabby clothes brushed. Her face shows her determination, even fanatical perfectionism—her only defense here.

ALMA: You are Mademoiselle Fenelon?
FANIA: Yes, Madame.

ALMA: You play the piano?
FANIA: Oh yes, Madame!

The fervor of her voice causes an excited giggle among some of the onlookers.

ALMA: Let me hear something from *Madame Butterfly*.

Alma goes to a chair, sits; others arrange themselves. Fania approaches the fabulous piano; it is all like a dream—she is slogging along in these immense men's shoes, a fuzz of hair on her bald head, her face gaunt from the near-starvation diet—and she sits before the keys and can't help bending over and kissing them. She starts to play "Un bel di". . . .

Cut to Fania's hands. They are crusted with filth, the nails broken. She is stiff and strikes a double note.

Cut to Fania, at the piano. She stops, blows on her fingers. Now she plays and sings. After two bars . . .

Cut to the group. All are glancing at Alma's reaction—she is quickened, eager to claim Fania for her orchestra.

Cut to Fania. In her face and voice, confident now and warm, are the ironic longings for the music's life-giving loveliness. The mood is shattered by the sounds of the scraping of chairs and people suddenly standing. Fania turns, stops playing.

Cut to Lagerführerin Mandel, entering the dayroom; she is chief of the women's section of the entire camp. About twenty-eight, tall, blond, shining with health, beautiful in her black uniform. Musicians, Blockawas, all are standing at rigid attention before her. Fania sees this, and attempts to do likewise—although only half successfully in her state of semi-shock.

MANDEL: At ease.

She comes and examines Fania, head to foot. And to Alma . . .

MANDEL: You will take her.
ALMA: Yes, Frau Mandel, certainly—she is very good.
MANDEL, *facing Fania:* She is wonderful.

There is something competitive in Alma's face.

MANDEL: Do you know any German music?
FANIA—*hesitates, her eyes lowered in trepidation:* Yes . . .
MANDEL: I am Lagerführerin Maria Mandel, in command of all women in this camp.
FANIA—*nods in deference:* I . . . had fogotten to tell Madame Rosé . . . that I really can't join the orchestra . . . unless my friend 346,991 is admitted also—she has a beautiful voice. *Now she meets Mandel's surprised look.* She is in Barracks B. *Mandel is silent; surprised actually.* Without her, I . . . must refuse . . . I'm sorry.

Absolute astonishment strikes the expressions of the other musicians.

Cut to Mandel, who looks at Fania for an additional moment, her mind unreadable.

Cut to the kapos, furious, but more incredulous than anything else.

Cut to Fania and Tchaikowska, a kapo, hurrying down a camp "street" (a corridor between barracks buildings). Fania is urging Tchaikowska to go faster. . . . They turn the corner of a building and come upon about twenty women who are being driven by club-wielding Blockawas. Many of these women are near death, falling down, crawling.

In the background, Mala comes to a halt; with her an SS officer. She is a tall, striking Jewess, wears the Star. But—oddly enough—there is no subservience in her manner but rather a seriousness and confidence. She carries a thick notebook.

Marianne is being pulled and struck by a Blockawa whose pressure she is resisting, trying to get back into the barracks building.

FANIA, *to Tchaikowska, pointing:* That's her! Quick! Marianne. . . !

Fania drops behind the kapo Tchaikowska—who has the authority here and who walks up to the Blockawa.

TCHAIKOWSKA: Mandel wants this one.

Marianne nearly faints into Fania's arms as they start to move away from the surprised Blockawa and the deadened, staggering group of women.

Cut to Marianne, her face still smudged with dirt, deep scratches on her neck. Incredibly enough she is singing to Fania's piano accompaniment in the musicians' barracks.

Cut to Mandel, legs sheathed in silk, her cap off, letting her blond hair fall to her shoulders. She listens. Alma stands a deferential few paces behind her. And in the background, the musicians, all listening.

Fania is playing encouragingly, glancing from time to time up at Marianne to urge her on. Marianne has a fevered look in her eyes, she is singing for her life. The song ends. Silence.

MANDEL, *to Alma:* Get them dressed.

Cut to Marianne, who starts to sway but is held up by Fania.

Cut to a counter; behind it from floor to ceiling is the clothing of the dead.

Blockawas, and the Chief here—Frau Schmidt—stand rigidly at attention. Mandel is holding up a brassiere which she places over Marianne's large breasts. Then she gives it to Marianne. Now she takes a pair of fine silk panties, holds them up for Fania, who accepts them.

MANDEL, *to Frau Schmidt:* Find shoes that fit her.
FRAU SCHMIDT: Of course. *To Fania:* They look very small, what size are they?
FANIA: Four.
FRAU SCHMIDT, *to Mandel:* I doubt very much that we have . . .
MANDEL: Feet must be warm and comfortable or the voice is affected. Find them for my little singer.

Frau Schmidt is irritated but obedient.

Fania and Marianne are thankful to Mandel, but what is the meaning of this incredible insistence?

Mandel exits, leaving Frau Schmidt rummaging in the bin full of women's shoes.

A Blockawa sweeps a woolen coat off the counter and furiously throws it at Fania, who blocks it with her arm.

While Frau Schmidt continues to search, Fania's eye transforms the pile of shoes.

Dissolve to women's legs walking on a railroad station platform. In effect, the shoes come alive on the wearers' feet and move about on a sidewalk.

Cut to Alma, tapping on her podium with her baton, raising her arms to begin a number; the orchestra is ready. Suddenly eyes catch something off-camera and all spring to their feet and at attention.

Mandel enters, followed by her orderly. Mandel is carrying a box full of shoes, four or five pairs.

Cut to Mandel. Her eyes are happy, somehow softened.

MANDEL: Sit down here, Fania.

Fania comes to her from the piano bench, sits before her at her gestured command, Mandel sets the box of shoes down, takes out a pair of fur-lined boots—and kneels before Fania!

Fania is now torn; she dares not turn down these incredible gifts, but at the same time she fears what accepting them may imply for her future. She looks down at the fur boot in Mandel's hand....

Cut to a close shot of the boot. The camera either vivifies this boot, gives it the life of its deceased owner—or actually fills it with a leg, and we see the pair of boots on living legs ... perhaps walking on a city street.

Cut to Mandel, rising to her feet as Fania stands in the fur boots. She looks up from them to Mandel's pleased face and can't help resolving her conflict by saying ...

FANIA: *Danke schön,* Frau Lagerführerin.

Cut to Mandel. Her pleasure flows onto her face; there is an element of masterly dominance in her expression, and some sort of affection.

Cut to the entire orchestra, rehearsing. Fania has hands poised over the keyboard; Alma, baton raised, starts the piece—an orchestral number of von Suppé. The sound is not quite horrible, but very nearly. The forty-odd players, apart from some of them being totally inadequate, are distressed by hunger and fear and never quite keep the music together.

Cut to the orchestra. The camera introduces us to the main supporting characters:

Elzvieta, a very good violinist, a rather aristocratic Pole who, as a non-Jew, still has her hair.

Paulette, a woman in her twenties, German-Jewish, an excellent cellist, who is presently pained by the bad playing of her compatriot beside her, who is . . .

Liesle, a bony, timid, near-hysterically frightened mandolin player, trying desperately to keep up with the beat. Belgian.

Charlotte, a violinist, fine player, slim and noble-looking, Belgian, extremely intelligent, poetic face.

Etalina, a wisecracker, small, Rumanian, violinist, a tomboy.

Michou, French, plays the flute, a militant communist. Further in the background of the story are . . .

Giselle, a freckled, very young French girl who can barely play drums at all, but is too young to despair, and thus beats away as loudly as possible.

Berta, a teacher.

Varya, cymbals. A Pole who has her hair.

Katrina, Polish, a very bad guitarist, stubborn, unteachable; has her hair.

Olga, Ukrainian accordionist, a dumbbell who will later take over the orchestra.

Greta, Dutch accordionist, country girl, naive and scared at all times; very poor player.

Esther, a taut, militant Zionist who bears in her intense eyes the vision of Palestine; accordionist.

Tchaikowska, leading kapo.

From time to time, one or more of the secondary characters will emerge on the foreground of this story in order to keep alive and vivid the sense that the "background group" is made of individuals. If this film is to approach even an indication of the vastness of the human disaster involved, the minor characters will have to be kept dramatically alive even in shots where they are only seen and don't have lines.

Cut to Alma, tapping angrily on the podium. . . . the orchestra breaks off.

ALMA: Why is it so loud? This is not band music, we are not playing against the wind—why can you not obey my instructions! *A note of futile and somehow dangerous anxiety on the verge of real anger.* Music is the holiest activity of mankind, you must apply yourselves day and night, you must listen to yourselves, you must aspire to some improvement. . . ! You cannot simply repeat the same mistakes. . . .

She can't go on, and simply walks hurriedly out of the room to recover herself. For a moment, the women keep an abashed silence.

ETALINA: At ease, Philharmonic.

The women set down their instruments and stand and stretch. . . . Etalina comes to Fania at the piano.

ETALINA: I think you've upset her—your being so good; she suddenly heard what we really sound like.

Paulette enters the shot and Liesle. Then Giselle.

FANIA: Well it *was* a bit loud. . . .
PAULETTE, *of Liesle:* She can't learn that number—we've got to go loud or she's had it.
LIESLE, *defensively, a whine:* I only studied less then six months in my whole life.
ETALINA: And that's the smartest six months *you* ever spent. *To Fania:* It's not her altogether—it's the maestro herself who's brought on this trouble.
FANIA: Why?
ETALINA: We were simply a marching band when we started— we'd play the prisoners out to their work assignments. But Alma got

ambitious, and the first thing you know we're doing these orchestral numbers, giving concerts for the high brass ... playing Beethoven, for God's sake. She's a victim of her own pride and we're in trouble now.

MARIANNE, *entering the shot:* Do we ever get dinner?

LIESLE—*laughs:* Listen to her...!

ETALINA: The slops'll be here any time now, dear.

FANIA: Why trouble, Etalina?

ETALINA: Because once the big shots started coming to hear us they began getting bored hearing the same three numbers.

PAULETTE: We have no other orchestrations....

ETALINA: And no composer ever wrote for this idiotic kind of instrumentation. I mean, piccolos, guitars, flutes, violins, no bass, no horns, no ...

MICHOU, *to Fania:* You don't orchestrate, do you?

Obviously Fania doesn't, but her mouth opens and her eyes are inventing....

PAULETTE: I'm really getting worried—we've done practically the same concert at least a dozen times. The Commandant sometimes doesn't even stay to the end.

MARIANNE—*her frightened eyes turn to Fania:* But you do know how to orchestrate, Fania! *Fania looks into her scared face.* And they could play all sorts of things!

FANIA: Actually—*to the women*—I can.

ETALINA AND PAULETTE: *Orchestrate?*

FANIA: Well, yes ... not professionally, but I ...

MICHOU: I knew it!

Paulette swerves about and yells to the women.

PAULETTE: She can orchestrate!

Etalina and Paulette instantly take off down the length of the room flanked by a dozen women all cheering and talking ... and come to Alma's door where Etalina knocks.

Cut to Alma's room. Alma is sitting by a window, baton still in her grip. Etalina and Paulette step into the room.

ETALINA: We thought you'd want to know, Madame—Fania Fenelon knows how to orchestrate.

The importance of this news is evident in Alma's expression. She stands. Fania is brought forward and into the room.

ALMA, *to the others:* Leave us. Leave us, please.

She shuts the door on the women. The last face we see is Marianne's, imploring Fania to press on. Alma gestures to the bed where Fania sits as Alma sits on the chair facing her. Fania looks around at the clean, bare room.

ALMA: Tell me the truth, Fania.

FANIA: Yes, I can—I don't see why not.

ALMA: And I suppose you . . . actually studied?

FANIA, *plunging on:* At the Paris Conservatory.

ALMA: Oh, Fania—what luck! What luck to have you! There's been a terrible pressure on me for some weeks now . . . for something new. . . .

FANIA: So they tell me. . . .

ALMA: I'm so exhausted and rushed that I've simply been unable to, myself. Could you start with. . . ? *She picks up piano music from a table.* I have a piano score for *Carmen.* . . .

FANIA: Well, I suppose, yes, I could do *Carmen.* . . .

ALMA: Or something German . . . here's another von Suppé. . . .

FANIA: I can't bear von Suppé. . . .

ALMA: I know, but they adore anything by von Suppé and we must try to please them, Fania. *Their eyes meet. Alma is a mite defensive, but it comes out with strength.* Well, that is elementary, it seems to me.

FANIA: I suppose. But I prefer to think that I am saving my life rather than trying to please the SS.

ALMA: And you think you can do one without the other?

Fania shuts up; clearly it is a dilemma, but she is also not trusting Alma. Now Alma relents.

ALMA: You'll begin immediately.

FANIA: I'll need people to copy the parts . . . and music paper.

ALMA: We can't possibly get music paper. . . .
FANIA: Couldn't you request some?
ALMA: There is a war on, my dear!

Suddenly, in this exclamation is Alma's *own* German indignation.

ALMA: Come—I'll find paper, and you and the girls can draw the lines yourself. *Fania rises, goes past her to the door.* Fania? *Fania turns to her, a slight smile.* I can't help striving for perfection; I was trained that way, I can't change now.
FANIA: Madame, I'm hardly in a position to criticize you when I am also trying to please.
ALMA: Exactly—but we are artists, we can't help that; you have nothing to be ashamed of. *Alma now comes to Fania—and in a more confessing, intimate tone:* Please try to hurry the work—they're so very changeable toward us, you see? Something new and surprising would be—*her fear is outright, open*—a tremendous help. So you'll be quick, Fania?

Cut to Fania. Her eyes are fillng with terror and determination. . . .

Cut to the dayroom, that evening. A concert is in full swing, primarily for Commandant Kramer and Dr. Mengele, but other officers are here too, including Frau Schmidt and Lagerführerin Mandel, forming an audience of perhaps twenty.

Madame Alma Rosé, face aglow, is apprehensively conducting, pushing the stone uphill.

The camera detects the players' abilities—the few good ones trying to overflow onto the sounds of the shaky ones.

Kramer, Dr. Mengele, and Mandel are naturally seated in the front "row." Mandel is interested; Dr. Mengele, who knows music, is very attentive, also amused; Kramer, a bull-necked killer, is struggling to keep his eyes open.

The number is ending with a flashy run on the piano by Fania. There is applause, more or less perfunctory.

Alma turns and bows as though before a gigantic audience.

ALMA: And now, with your permission, *meine Damen und Herren*—a bit of popular music by our new member, Fania Fenelon.

Mandel alone eagerly applauds.

Fania accompanies herself, singing a smoky, very Parisian ballad. And as she sings . . .

Dissolve to Dr. Mengele, his face superimposed on Fania. Then we see him with finger raised, directing deportees emerging from a freight car to right and left, death or life. *Flames reflect orange light on his face.*

This gives way to . . .

A close up of Mengele. He seems actually attracted to Fania's voice and music.

Cut to Fania, finishing her number—her face is tortured, but she is singing, fully, beautifully, to the finish.

Cut to the audience. Now there is a more heartfelt applause. Fania takes bows, her eyes trying to evade the monsters applauding her.

Cut to Fania, dousing her face with water as though trying to wash herself clean.

Cut to the dormitory. Marianne is drawing out a box from under her bed—she opens it, takes out a package of margarine, starts to dig some out with a finger—and looks up guiltily, her finger nearly in her mouth.

Fania is standing nearby, having discovered her. Fania is still drying herself from the shower.

FANIA: Why do you steal when you know I can't stand margarine?

Marianne starts to put the margarine back in the box, Fania comes and forces it back into her hand. Fania's voice is losing its control.

Other women look up from their beds, still others are entering the dormitory—and gradually all are drawn to this.

FANIA: Anything you want of mine I wish you would simply take, Marianne! *Turning to the other women:* And that goes for everyone—I don't want to keep anything from anyone who wants it. . . . And I hope you'll do the same for me if I'm desperate.

ETALINA: But Fania, we can't very well share everything.

FANIA: I refuse to turn into an animal for a gram of margarine or a potato peel!

PAULETTE: You don't mean share with the Poles too, though.

Fania hesitates . . . glances down the dormitory where half a dozen Polish women stand about—heavy, tough, their contempt evident despite their curiosity of the moment. (Katrina: Beefy, appalling guitarist. Varya: Athlete, shrewd, cymbals.)

ETALINA: Count me out, dear—those are monsters; even here in the same hell as we are, they're just praying every one of us goes to the gas. You share with those bitches, not me.

ELZVIETA—*a delicate, gentle Pole, beautiful head of hair:* We're not all like that.

Slight pause.

PAULETTE: You just have a pet Jew—you like Fania, but you're an anti-Semite, Elzvieta.

ELZVIETA, *timidly:* But I really am not. My father was an actor; we had a lot of Jewish friends in the theater.—I'm really not, Fania. *Glancing at the satiric Etalina.* In my opinion, Etalina—*with a glance toward the Poles*—they think that you people are probably going to be . . . you know . . .

ETALINA: Gassed. —You can say it, dear.

ELZVIETA: Well, the point is that they want to feel superior because they'll probably live to go home, when the war ends . . . being Gentiles. *To Fania.* They're more stupid than evil.

FANIA: Then we should try to teach them.

After the first shock, Etalina laughs. Then another and another until, with glances toward the stolid, suspicious, and bovine Poles, the whole gang are laughing their heads off; and finally the Poles too join in.

GISELLE—*a freckle-faced, red-haired Parisian tomboy:* To hell with this—tell us about Paris—when were you there last? What are they wearing?

Women gather around.

FANIA: I was in Drancy prison almost a year.

PAULETTE: Well, it can't have changed much—where are the skirts now?

FANIA, *indicating:* Oh, to here (*the knee*) but very full—the girls look like flowers.

MARIANNE: The heels are very high—the legs look terrific. You can't buy stockings so they paint their legs. My mother wouldn't let me, though.

PAULETTE: And the hair?—there were some women in a convoy the other day—I think from Holland—curls on top of their heads. . . .

FANIA: In Paris too—piled up top-curls. —Where are those women?

ETALINA: They're burned up by now, I guess. What about songs? —You know any new ones?

FANIA, *to Etalina:* The way you say that, Etalina . . .

ETALINA: That they're burned up?—why not say it? We'll be better prepared for it when our time comes.

GISELLE, *insistently:* Talk about Paris, Fania. . . .

LIESLE: Are they still playing swing?

FANIA: Are you Parisian?

LIESLE: No. But we went there for a vacation just before the war— play us some of the new songs, will you?

OTHERS: That's a great idea. . . . Come on, Fania. . . . Do you know "Stormy Weather"? . . . What was the name of your nightclub? . . . Did you make many records? . . . She's really famous, you know. . . .

The group moves out into the dayroom.

MICHOU: Can you play by ear? . . . Come, sit down. . . .

Fania sits at the piano, Marianne beside her, when . . .

Cut to Shmuel, in prisoner's stripes. He is an electrician, now taping a wire along a wall of the dayroom. He is forty-five, perhaps deranged, perhaps extraordinarily wise, it's hard to say. He's like a little toy animal, large eyes, curly hair, desperately shy. He makes little peeking glances at the assembling women, but there's some air of persistence about him, too.

Cut to Fania, who senses some indecipherable communication from him and lets her gaze linger on him for an instant. Then she breaks away and begins to play the intro for "Stormy Weather."

After the first couple of lines, Marianne interrupts, unable to restrain herself even though she is breaking up Fania's number.

MARIANNE: Could I, Fania? Please?

Fania is quite astonished, looks at her with an embarrassed smile to cover her own resentment.

MARIANNE: I just have such a yen for it suddenly! Do you mind?

Fania, embarrassed, shrugs and obliges, accompanying Marianne, who sings the number—but "appealingly," sentimentally, where Fania sang intelligently, suavely.

Cut to the Polish women. They are identifiable, in part, by the fact they all have hair. They have come out of the dormitory and gather a little apart, and are pleasurably listening.

And before the music has a chance to die on Marianne's number, Fania picks up another, singing herself.

Camera pans the women's faces . . . maybe two dozen clustered around the piano . . . shorn, gaunt captives, yet this music brings up their lust to live and a certain joy. . . .

A chorus of players pick up a lyric and join Fania, singing all together.

Cut to Alma Rosé. Her door opens onto the dayroom, and she is about to protest the noise . . . but her gesture aborts and she stiffly concedes the moment, turns and goes back into her room, shutting the door.

Cut to the next morning, outside in the camp "street." About twenty players form up outside the musicians' barracks. Each wears a bandanna, a uniformlike element, and of course the Jewesses have the yellow Star on their clothing. The Gentiles are indiscriminately mixed in, perhaps four or five of them, identifiable mainly by their hair.

It is gray, just before day, very cold. Fania is in place at one corner of the formation; Alma Rosé appears from the barracks, sees her, and halts.

ALMA: You don't have to do this, you're not in the band.
FANIA: I would like to see it . . . if it's not forbidden.

Alma is surprised, then shrugs, goes around to the head of the formation, raises her baton, and this crazy band, with no horns but with fiddles, flutes, accordion, guitars, and cymbals, goes marching off behind Alma, who marches like a Prussian.

Cut to the camp "square." The band is playing "stirring" march music on a low bandstand. Before them in blocks of five square stand the women prisoners about to go off to work.

Some of them are ill, supported by a neighbor's hand; some are fiercely erect, some old, some teenagers—their shoes don't match, some feet are wrapped in rags, and their clothes are ripped rags.

Cut to a close shot of Fania. Her gaze has moved to a point . . . which is . . .

An angry prisoner.

This woman has caught Fania's eye and mimes spitting at her in contempt.

Cut to Fania, quickly lowering her eyes.

Cut to SS men, some handling attack dogs, ordering the prisoners to march. The whole mass moves across the mud.

SS OFFICER, *a whip against his boot, beating time: Eins, zwei, drei . . .* hup, hup, hup!

Cut to Fania, lifting her eyes, forcing herself to watch. Suddenly up to her ear comes Shmuel. Frightened, surprised, she turns to him swiftly.

SHMUEL, *wild-eyed:* Live!

He quickly limps away, his toolbox on his shoulder.

Cut to the dayroom. Women, lining paper with pencils and straightedges, are spread out around Fania near a window. Outside the gray light of winter afternoon.

Charlotte, a good violinist, is practicing some distance away—a Bach chaconne.

Marianne is staring out a window nearby, thinking of food.

Fania is seated, studying a piano score, pencil poised over a lined sheet on which a few notes have been set down. She is intense—worried?

Liesle is repeating the same three bars on her accordion, with the same mistakes.

GISELLE, *musing to no one in particular:* Imagine!—painting their legs! I'd love *that*. . . .

Etalina passes behind Fania and, glancing down at the few notes she has written, halts, surprised.

ETALINA: Is that all you've done? *Fania glances up defensively.* Christ, at this rate we'll need another Hundred Years' War to get a score out of you.

Charlotte enters the shot, carrying her violin.

CHARLOTTE: Will you stop bothering her? Orchestrating is tough work even for experts.

Alma comes out of her room, comes over to Fania, and looks down at the sheet. Then she looks at Fania with real surprise.

ALMA: I have to speak to you.

Alma goes out into her room. Fania stands, as she follows her out, sees . . .

The Polish women, triumphantly laughing (softly, though) and pointing at her and miming her decapitation.

Cut to Alma's room.

ALMA: Then you lied?—you can't orchestrate at all, can you?
FANIA: I'm quite able to do it; I'm sure I can.

ALMA: What is it, then?

FANIA: One of the women this morning—spat at me.

ALMA, *not understanding:* Yes?

FANIA: I hadn't realized . . . how they must hate us.

ALMA: Oh. Yes, of course; what did you expect?

FANIA: Well I . . . I just hadn't thought about it.

ALMA, *now sensing some remote criticism of her own character, is angry:* Perhaps you are too conscientious a person for the orchestra . . .

FANIA: No, no, I didn't mean . . .

ALMA: If you'd be happier back in "B" Barracks . . .

FANIA: Madame, please—I wasn't criticizing you. *Unstrung.* I'm just not used to being hated like that.

ALMA, *decisively:* Fania—there is life or death in this place, there is no room for anything else whatever.—I intend to rehearse that piece tomorrow; I want the parts by morning. If you are able, that is. Are you?

FANIA, *defeated, yet determined:* Yes, Madame.

She walks angrily past Alma out the door.

Cut to the dayroom. Through the window nearby we see darkness of night. Reflection of a big searchlight, which revolves somehere beyond our line of sight, a rhythm of this flashing light.

Fania at the piano is alone, working out the orchestration. She tries a chord. There is the jarring sound of three rifle shots. She looks up, waits; then silence. Someone probably got killed. She plays the chord again; writes notes.

From outside we hear the hair-raising screeching of someone being destroyed—and the shouts of men killing. Then silence. Fania is in sharp conflict with herself; she knows she is walling herself up against all this. Steels herself again. Plays the chord. Can't continue. Gets up, walks past dormitory doorway. She looks in.

Cut to the dormitory, at night. The whole orchestra, some forty, asleep in beds.

Cut to Fania, in the dayroom, passing the dormitory door, goes into a dark narrow corridor at the end of which is a door. She opens this door. . . .

Cut to the toilet. On the toilet bowl Marianne is straddling a man, a kapo still wearing his striped prisoner's hat. In his hand is gripped two sausages. Marianne turns and sees Fania, but turns back and continues with the man, who is looking straight up at Fania.

Cut to the dayroom. Through the window the first light of dawn. Backing, we find Fania with several pages of completed score under her hand . . . exhausted, but finishing it. She is fighting self-disgust; at the same time is glad at her accomplishment. A hand enters the shot, with a piece of sausage held between forefinger and thumb. Fania looks at it.

Pull back to Marianne, standing beside Fania, offering the piece of sausage. Fania stares at it, then up at Marianne.

MARIANNE: Take it—for saving my life. You must be starved, working all night.

Fania is not looking at her judgmentally but with sorrow and fear. Marianne sets the piece of sausage on the keyboard.

MARIANNE: I'm not going to live to get out of here anyway.
FANIA: But if you do? Marianne? What if you live?

Marianne is silent, then with a certain stubborn air, walks away. Fania looks at the sausage. Tries not to eat it. A desperate struggle to refuse this seeming compromise with her own disgust. Finally she does eat it—and gives way to a look of almost sensual enjoyment as she carefully lengthens out the chewing. Then she swallows, stands in intense conflict, her hands clasped to her mouth as she walks about with no escape.

The sudden sound of ear-piercing whistles.

Fania looks out a window, frightened, bewildered.

Three Blockawas, led by their chief, Tchaikowska, come running into the dayroom, buttoning up their coats as they rush past Fania into the dormitory.

Cut to the dormitory. The Blockawas, yelling, " *'Raus, 'raus, schnell* . . ." rip off blankets, push and slap the women out of bed. The women at first are in shock, but quickly obey, start dressing.

Cut to the train platform. Dawn. The band is rushed into a formation before a line of freight cars whose doors are shut. SS men stand waiting, along with kapos preparing to pounce on the luggage.

Commandant Kramer is standing in an open area, beside him Frau Lagerführerin Mandel, in a cape and cap. Kramer signals Alma, who starts the orchestra in a bright march.

Car doors are rolled open; inside a mass of people who are pulled and driven out onto the platform by kapos, their luggage taken.

Cut to a mother, being torn from her child, who is tossed onto a waiting truck. Mother rushes to Frau Mandel to plead with her; Mandel strikes her across the face with a riding crop.

Cut to Fania, by the dayroom window. She sees this, starts to turn away in horror, then forces herself to turn back to the window.

Shmuel suddenly appears outside the window and sees her, glances around, then hurries out of sight.

He enters the dayroom. With a glance of caution behind him he hurriedly limps over to Fania.

SHMUEL: Don't do that.
FANIA: What?
SHMUEL: Turn away. You have to look and see everything, so you can tell him when it is over.
FANIA: Who?

His eyes roll upward, and he dares point upward just a bit with one finger.

FANIA: I don't believe.

A grin breaks onto his face—as though she has decided to play a game with him.

FANIA: Why do you pick me?
SHMUEL: Oh, I always know who to pick!

A crazy kind of joy suffuses his face as he backs out the door.

SHMUEL: Live!

Cut to the smokestack. Dawn. For an instant the stack is in the clear—then it belches a column of smoke.

Cut to the dayroom. Evening. Mengele, Kramer, and Mandel listen to the orchestra, along with their retinues. Fania, accompanying herself, is singing "Un bel di" in an agonized and therefore extraordinarily moving way. She is just finishing. When she does, Mandel stands, applauding—she is excited as a patron, a discoverer of talent, and turns to Kramer, who is also clapping his hands.

MANDEL: Did you ever hear anything more touching, Herr Commandant?
KRAMER: Fantastic. *To Mengele:* But Dr. Mengele's musical opinions are more expert, of course.

Cut to Fania, staring at the ultimate horror—their love for her music.

Cut to the entire dayroom.

MENGELE: I have rarely felt so totally—moved.

And he appears, in fact, to have been deeply stirred.

ALMA: You might thank the Commandant, Fania.

Fania tries to speak, can't and nods instead—gratefully.

FANIA—*finally a whisper: Danke schön,* Herr Commandant.
KRAMER: I must tell you, Mademoiselle Fenelon . . .
FANIA: Excuse me, but my name is really not Fenelon. Fenelon was my mother's name.
MANDEL: What is your name, then?
FANIA: My father's name was Goldstein. I am Fania Goldstein. Excuse me, I didn't mean to interrupt, Herr Commandant.
KRAMER: You must learn to sing German songs.
ALMA: I will see that she learns immediately, Herr Commandant.
KRAMER, *continuing to Fania:* Originally, Mademoiselle, I opposed this idea of an orchestra, but I must say now that with singing of your quality, it is a consolation that feeds the spirit. It strengthens us for this difficult work of ours. *Very* good.

He turns and goes out, followed by his retinue and Mengele. The orchestra is aware that Fania has helped them remain in favor and thus alive.

Mandel turns back at the door and beckons to Fania, who comes to her.

MANDEL: Is there anything you especially need?
FANIA, *out of her conflict, after a struggle:* A . . . toothbrush?
MANDEL—*gestures to Tchaikowska, who approaches:* You will send to Canada for some parcels. *To Fania:* With my compliments.

Mandel exits.

FANIA, *to Tchaikowska:* To *Canada*?!

Cut to a long shot of the smoking chimney.

Cut to a counter set in open air beside anther barracks. Behind it are the black-market girls—sleek, fed, laughing, busy trading with a few desperate-looking women who hand over a slice of bread for a comb or piece of soap. On the counter are perfumes, lotions, soap, and a pile of used toothbrushes. These "Canadians" all have hair—Czechs, Poles, Dutch . . .

FIRST BLACK MARKETEER: Welcome to Canada. So you're the Frenchy singer—what would you like? *Fania picks up a toothbrush. Charlotte accompanies her.* That just came off the last transport—it's practically new and very clean—they were mostly Norwegians. That'll be a good slice of bread.

The black marketeer holds out her hand. Fania takes out a chunk of bread. Charlotte intercepts, returning it to Fania.

CHARLOTTE: I said this is on the Chief!
BLACK MARKETEER, *cheerfully:* What's wrong with trying? *To Fania:* Here's your junk, stupid.

Set aside at one end of the counter are forty tiny packets in soiled and much-used paper. Charlotte and Fania load their arms.

Cut to the high excitement in the dayroom as the girls open their gift packages, which contain, in one case, a bit of butter and a pat of jam which a girl ever so carefully smears on a cracker-sized piece of bread, or an inch of sausage and a chip of chocolate to be savored for a full five minutes, and so forth.

Marianne, suffering, gobbles up her bread and jam in one gulp. Fania nearby is swallowing. She takes out her toothbrush.

MARIANNE: You got a toothbrush!—can I see? *She takes it, examines it, reads words on the handle.* From Norway. Looks almost new. *Offering it back:* Nothing like having important friends, right?

Fania's hand stops in air. But then she takes the toothbrush and forces herself to look directly into Marianne's eyes.

MARIANNE: Whoever that belonged to is probably up the chimney now. *Fania is silent.* So why are you superior?
FANIA: If I ever thought I was, I sure don't any more.

Etalina enters the shot . . . addressing all.

ETALINA: I'll say one thing, Fania—I feel a lot safer now that the Chief is so hot for you.

Some of the women laugh, titillated . . . the Poles loudest of all.

ETALINA: Although I wouldn't want to wake up in the morning next to that Nazi bitch's mug.
FANIA: I don't expect to. But it's not her face that disgusts me.

Esther speaks—a shaven Polish Jewess, angular, tight-faced.

ESTHER: Her face doesn't disgust you?
FANIA: No—I'm afraid she's a very beautiful woman, Esther.
ESTHER: That murderer you dare call beautiful?

Others react against Fania—"Shame!" "You toady!" "Just because she favors you!"

FANIA, *overriding:* What disgusts me is that a woman so beautiful can do what she is doing. Don't try to make her ugly, Esther . . . she's beautiful and human. We are the same species. And that is what's so hopeless about this whole thing.
MICHOU: What's the difference that she's human? There's still

hope—because when this war is over Europe will be communist—and for that I want to live.

ESTHER: No. To see Palestine—*that's* why you have to live. You're Jewish women—*that's* your hope: to bring forth Jewish children in Palestine. You have no identity, Fania—and that's why you can call such a monster human and beautiful.

FANIA: I envy you both—you don't feel you have to solve the problem.

ESTHER, *anxiously, aggressively: What* problem! I don't see a problem!

FANIA: She is human, Esther. *Slight pause; she is looking directly into Esther's eyes.* Like you. Like me. You don't think that's a problem?

Fania's eye is caught by Marianne slipping out the dayroom door.

Cut to outside the barracks. While two kapos expectantly watch, Marianne opens a bar of chocolate they have given her and bites into it. They lead her around the corner of the barracks and out of sight. One of them has a bottle half filled with wine.

Cut to Fania, asleep in her bunk. Marianne appears, starts to climb in—she is tipsy—slips and lands on her behind on the floor with a scream. Women awaken.

ETALINA: At least let *us* get some rest, Busy-Ass.

MARIANNE, *to Etalina:* What's it to you? *To Fania:* Say!—your hair's coming back white!

FANIA: Come to bed, Marianne. . . .

MARIANNE: Oh, screw these idiots. . . .

VOICES: Shut up! Whore! I'm exhausted! She's disgusting! Somebody throw her out! Shut up!

MARIANNE, *to the whole lot:* Well, it so happens one of them was a doctor from Vienna. . . .

ETALINA: She just went for a checkup!

MARIANNE: And he thinks we are never going to menstruate again! *Silence now.* Because of this . . . this fear every day and night . . . and the food . . . can sterilize . . .

She looks around at their stricken faces. She climbs up, helped into her bunk by Fania.

Cut to a series of close-ups:
ESTHER, *praying quietly:* Shma Israel, adonai elohaynu . . .
    Elzvieta crosses herself and prays quietly.
    Other women are praying.
    Fania is silent, staring, while beside her Marianne lies on her back asleep and snoring.

Cut to two kapos, carrying Paulette on a stretcher across the dayroom to the exit door. Paulette, the young cellist, is in high fever. Alma attempts to explain to the kapos in pidgin . . .

ALMA: Do you understand me? —she is musician, cellist, not to be gassed. To hospital, you understand? Typhus, you see? We need her. Well, do you understand or not! *At the door:* Wait!

Cut to Alma rushing over to Tauber, an SS officer, and Mala. Mala is the tall, striking Jewess, wearing the Star, but who appears to show no obsequiousness toward Tauber, the SS officer beside her. Kapos approach carrying Paulette on a stretcher.

ALMA: Excuse me, Herr Commandant Tauber—with your permission, would Mala instruct these men to be sure this girl is not . . . harmed? She is our cellist and must go to the hospital—she has high fever, typhus perhaps. I don't know what language they speak. . . .

Without waiting for Tauber's permission, Mala stops the kapos.

MALA: Parl' Italiano? *They shake their heads negatively.* Espagnol? *They shake their heads again.* Russky? *Again.*
KAPO: Romany.
MALA: Ah! *In Rumanian:* Be sure to take her to hospital, not death—she is a musician, they need her.
KAPO: *In Rumanian:* We understand.

They walk off with Paulette. Tauber and staff move off with Mala.

Cut to the dayroom. The orchestra members are clustered at the windows watching this.

MICHOU: Isn't she fantastic?
FANIA, *amazed:* But she's wearing the Star!
MICHOU: Sure—that's Mala, she's their chief interpreter. She's Jewish but she's got them bulldozed.
FANIA: How's it possible?

Alma re-enters the dayroom, goes to her podium, leafs through a score.

MICHOU: She's been here for years—since the camp was built—she escaped once; she and five others were supposed to be gassed, so they'd been stripped, and she got out through an air vent. Ended up stark naked going down a road past the Commandant's house. She's afraid of absolutely nothing, so when he stopped her she demanded some clothes; they got to talking, and he found out she speaks practically every language and made her an interpreter.
LIESLE, *proudly:* She's Belgian, you know—like me.
CHARLOTTE: She was in the Resistance. She even has a lover.
ETALINA: And handsome!
FANIA: Now you're kidding me.
ETALINA: It's true—Edek's his name—a Polish Resistance guy. He's got a job in the Administration.
MICHOU, *starry-eyed:* They're both unbelievable— they've saved people— a few anyway, and helped some. They're afraid of nothing!
ALMA: Fania! *From Alma's viewpoint we see the group turning to her.* Come here now and let us go through your Schubert song. *Fania comes to the piano, sits.* You must try the *ch* sound again—Dr. Mengele has a sensitive ear for the language, and it's his request, you know. Begin . . .

Fania sings a Schubert song with *"lachen"* in the verse, pronouncing it "lacken."

ALMA: No, no, not "lacken"—"la*ch*en . . ."
FANIA, *trying, but . . . :* Lacken.
ALMA: *Lachen! Lachen! Lachen!* Say it!

Alma's face is close to Fania's; Fania looks into Alma's eyes and with a sigh of angry defeat . . .

FANIA: *Lachen.*

ALMA: That's much better. I hope you won't ever be stupid enough to hate a *language*! Now the song once more . . . I want you perfect by Sunday. . . .

Fania, her jaw clenched, forces herself into the song.

Cut to the train platform. It is barely light. Freight-car doors roll open, and the deportees are hustled out. From within the dormitory we hear women yelling and screaming.

Cut to the dormitory. Tchaikowska, burly chief of the barracks, and other Blockawas are pulling Etalina out of her bunk by the ankles, and she lands with a bang on the floor. The other inmates are yelling. . . .

VOICES: Why can't you wake up like everybody else! Why are you always making trouble! and so on . . .

Alma appears on the scene with Fania nearby. Tchaikowska bangs a fist on Etalina's back.

ETALINA: I said I didn't hear you call me!
ALMA—*now she smashes Etalina across the face:* You're a spoiled brat! You will obey, d'you hear?

Alma's face, infuriated.

Cut to Alma's face. She is conducting. Great anxiety about the sounds coming forth. Suddenly she strides from the podium to Etalina. She is near hysteria as she bends over Etalina, who looks up at her in terror.

ALMA: Are you trying to destroy us? That is a B flat; do you know a B flat or don't you? *Etalina is cowering in terror.* I asked if you know B flat or if you do not!

With a blow she knocks Etalina off her chair.

ETALINA, *screaming—she is a teenager, a child:* I want my mother! Mama! Mama!

She collapses in tears. Fania goes to her, holds her.

MICHOU: You'd better get some discipline, Etalina. You're not going to make it on wisecracks.

Alma looks at Fania, a bit guiltily now that her anger has exploded, then goes out into her own room. Fania waits a second, then obediently follows her in and shuts the door.

Cut to Alma's room. Fania is massaging Alma's shoulders and neck as she sits in a chair by the window. Alma moves Fania's fingers to her temples, which she lightly massages. After a moment she has Fania massage her hands, and Fania sits before her doing this.

ALMA: Talk to me, Fania. *Fania keeps silent, wary of expressing herself.* There must be strict discipline. As it is, Dr. Mengele can just bear to listen to us. If we fall below a certain level anything is possible. . . . He's a violently changeable man. *Fania does not respond, only massages.* The truth is, if it weren't for my name they'd have burned them up long ago; my father was first violin with the Berlin Opera, his string quartet played all over the world. . . .

FANIA: I know, Madame.

ALMA: That I, a Rosé, am conducting here is a . . .

FANIA: I realize that, Madame.

ALMA: Why do you resent me? You are a professional, you know what discipline is required; a conductor must be respected.

FANIA: But I think she can be loved, too.

ALMA: You cannot love what you do not respect. In Germany it is a perfectly traditional thing, when a musician is repeatedly wrong . . .

FANIA: To slap?

ALMA: Yes, of course! Furtwängler did so frequently, and his orchestra idolized him. *Fania keeping her silence, simply nods very slightly.* I need your support, Fania. I see that they look up to you. You must back up my demands on them. We will have to constantly raise the level of our playing or I . . . I really don't know how long they will tolerate us. Will you? Will you help me?

FANIA: I . . . I will tell you the truth, Madame—I really don't know how long I can bear this. *She sees resentment in Alma's eyes.* . . . I am trying my best, Madame, and I'll go on trying. But I feel sometimes that pieces of myself are falling away. And believe me, I recognize that your strength is probably what our lives depend on. . . .

ALMA: Then why do you resent me?

FANIA: I don't know! I suppose . . . maybe it's simply that . . . one wants to keep *something* in reserve; we can't . . . we can't really and truly wish to please them. I realize how silly it is to say that, but . . .

ALMA: But you *must* wish to please them, and with all your heart. You are an artist, Fania—you can't purposely do less than your best.

FANIA: But when one looks out the window . . .

ALMA: That is why I have told you *not* to! You have me wrong, Fania—you seem to think that I fail to see. But I *refuse* to see. Yes. And *you* must refuse!

FANIA—*nearly an outcry:* But what . . . *She fears it will sound accusatory* . . . what will be left of me, Madame!

ALMA: Why . . . yourself, the artist will be left. And this is not new, is it? —what did it ever matter, the opinions of your audience? —or whether you approved of their characters? You sang because it was in you to do! And more so now, when your life depends on it! Have you ever married?

FANIA: No, Madame.

ALMA: I was sure you hadn't—you married your art. I did marry . . . *Alma breaks off. She moves, finds herself glancing out the window, but quickly turns away.* . . . Twice. The first time to that . . . *She gestures ironically toward her violin case lying on her cot.* The second time to a man, a violinist, who only wanted my father's name to open the doors for him. But it was my fault—I married him because I pitied myself; I had never had a lover, not even a close friend. There is more than a violin locked in that case, there is a life.

FANIA: I couldn't do that, Madame, I need the friendship of a man.

ALMA—*slight pause:* I understand that, Fania. *She is moved by an impulse to open up.* Once I very nearly loved a man. We met in Amsterdam. The three good months of my life. He warmed me . . . like a coat. I think . . . I could have loved him.

FANIA: Why didn't you?
ALMA: They arrested me . . . as a Jew. It still astonishes me.
FANIA: Because you are so German?
ALMA: Yes. I am. *Slight pause.* In this place, Fania, you will have to
be an artist and only an artist. You will have to concentrate on one
thing only—to create all the beauty you are capable of. . . .
FANIA, *unable to listen further:* Excuse me, Madame . . .

She quickly pulls open the door and escapes into the dayroom;
Alma is left with her conflict and her anger. She goes to her violin
case on the bed, takes out the instrument. Some emotion has lifted
her out of the moment; she walks out of the room.

Cut to the dayroom. Alma enters; the women come quickly out
of their torpor, reach for their instruments. Alma halts before them
and looks out over them. And with an expression of intense pride
which also reprimands and attempts to lead them higher, she
plays—and extraordinarily beautifully—the "Meditation" from
Thaïs, perhaps.

Jew, Gentile, Pole, kapo—Etalina herself and Fania—everyone is captivated, subdued, filled with awe.

As the final crescendo begins, Frau Schmidt and two kapos
armed with clubs enter. Everyone leaps up to attention.

FRAU SCHMIDT: Jews to the left, Aryans to the right!
KAPOS: Quick! Hop, hop! Move; quick; five by five!

In the milling around to form two groups, Marianne pushes
through and just as the groups make an empty space between them,
she pulls an uncomprehending Fania into that space, where they
stand alone facing Frau Schmidt.

MARIANNE: She and I are only half.
FRAU SCHMIDT: Half! Half what?
MARIANNE: Half Jewish. Both our mothers were Aryan.

Frau Schmidt's face shows her perplexity as to the regulations
in such cases. Alma steps out of the Jewish group and goes to her.

ALMA, *sotto voce, in order not to embarrass her:* Mixed race—are
not to be gassed, I'm quite sure, Frau Schmidt. *But Fania overhears*

and is moved by gratitude and surprise. But what is this selection for
. . . if I may ask?

FRAU SCHMIDT—*her hostility to Alma is quite open:* You belong
with the Jews, Madame. *Alma steps back into her group, humiliated
but stoic.* Jews! Your hair is getting too long! Haircuts immediately!
To Fania and Marianne: You two, follow me!

She makes a military about-face and goes out. The two women
follow.

Cut to a tiny office in the administration building. The overstuffed noncom is poring over a book of regulations open on a table
as Fania and Marianne stand looking on. He lip-reads, his finger
moving along the lines.

Now he finds something, nods his head appreciatively as his
comprehension gains, then he looks at the women.

SERGEANT: In this case you are allowed to cut off the upper half of
the Star of David.

Marianne reacts instantly, ripping a triangle off her coat. (The
Star is actually two separate triangles superimposed.) Fania is uncertain, does nothing.

Cut to the dayroom. Much agitation: an impromptu sort of trial
is taking place. Sides are taken with Marianne and Fania alone in
the middle.

Fania and Marianne both have half-stars on their dresses. As
they are attacked, Marianne reacts with far more anguish than
Fania, who, although disturbed, is strong enough to remain apart
from any group.

ESTHER: You've behaved like dirty goyim, you've dishonored the
Jews in your families.

MARIANNE: But if it's the truth why should I hide it? I *am* only
half. . . .

ETALINA: Maybe they'll only be half-gassed.

Laughter. Varya, who is standing with other Poles, steps out of
the group.

VARYA: You ashamed to be Jews. You, filth. But you never be Aryan. God always spit on you. We Aryan, never you! *Spits.* Paa!

Her sister Poles guffaw and heavily nod agreement.

ESTHER: For once the Poles are right!
ETALINA: It's disgusting!—cutting the Star of David in half?
MARIANNE: Why not?—if we can avoid the gas?
FANIA: Since when have you all become such Jewish nationalists? Suddenly you're all such highly principled ladies?
ELZVIETA: Bravo! You get up on your high horse with them because you don't dare open your traps with anybody else!
FANIA: I'm sorry; your contempt doesn't impress me. Not when you've accepted every humiliation without one peep. We're just a convenience.
ESTHER: The blood of innocent Jews cries out against your treason!
FANIA: Oh, Esther, why don't you just shut up? I am sick of the Zionists-and-the-Marxists; the Jews-and-the-Gentiles; the Easterners-and-the-Westerners; the Germans-and-the-non-Germans; the French-and-the-non-French. I am sick of it, sick of it, sick of it! I am a woman, not a tribe! And I am humiliated! That is all I know.

She sits on a chair by the window, her face turned from them. After a silence . . .

MARIANNE: You're all just jealous. And anyway, we're just as much betraying the Catholics—our mothers were Catholic, after all.

Fania suddenly gets up and escapes through the door into the dormitory.

Cut to Fania, seated on a lower bunk, is sewing the upper half of her Star back on. Marianne enters and behind her some of the other arguers are approaching in curiosity.

MARIANNE: What are you doing that for? *Fania is silent.* Fania?
FANIA—*glances up at the group with resentment, then continues sewing:* I don't know. I'm doing it. So I'm doing it.

She sews angrily—angry at herself too.

Cut to the barracks "street" outside the dayroom; through windows we see the orchestra and Alma conducting a practice session—phrases are played, then repeated.

The rhythm of a passing beam of the arc light ceaselessly surveys the camp, but here it is only an indirect brightening and darkening.

Coming to the corner of the building, Fania turns into the adjacent street just as a hanging bulb overhead goes out. Shmuel is standing on a short ladder, then descends, leading a wire down with him which he busies himself peeling back to make a fresh connection. Fania hardly looks at him or he at her, this conversation being forbidden.

The music continues in the background from within the dayroom.

SHMUEL: Behind you, in the wall.

Fania leans against the barracks wall; stuck in a joint between boards is a tiny folded piece of paper which she palms.

FANIA—*a whisper:* Thank you.

SHMUEL: Don't try to send an answer—it's too dangerous; just wants you to know he's here . . . your Robert. *She nods once, starts to leave.* Fania? They are gassing twelve thousand a day now. *Her face drains. He goes up the ladder with wire.* Twelve thousand angels fly up every day.

FANIA: Why do you keep telling me these things? What do you want from me!

Shmuel makes the bulb go on, the light flaring on the wild and sweet look in his face. He looks up.

SHMUEL: Look with your eyes—the air is full of angels! You mustn't stop looking, Fania!

He perplexes and unnerves her; she claps hands over her ears and hurries along the barracks wall. As she turns the corner she nearly collides with Tchaikowska, who is enjoying a cigarette. She is standing next to the door to her own room. Fania gives her a nod, starts to pass, when the door opens; a kapo comes out buttoning his shirt.

TCHAIKOWSKA: Two more cigarettes—you took longer this time.
KAPO: I'm broke—give you two more next time.

Marianne comes through this door. She is eating meat off a bone. She sees Fania, is slightly surprised, but goes on eating. The kapo gives her ass a squeeze and walks away.

Tchaikowska goes into the room.

Fania sees into the room—Tchaikowska is straightening the rumpled bed in what is obviously her room.

Cut to a barracks street. Fania catches up with Marianne, who is stashing the bone with some slivers of meat still on it in her pocket.

FANIA: At least share some of it with the others—for your own sake, so you don't turn into an animal altogether!
MARIANNE: Jealous?

She walks away, flaunting her swinging backside and enters the dormitory.

Cut to Fania playing the piano with the orchestra. (A light piece—airy, popular music.) The keyboard starts tilting. The orchestra stops, breaking off the music.

Four kapos are turning the piano on its side, onto a dolly.

Fania rescues her music and skitters out of the way, astonished and frightened. Alma and the orchestra look on in silent terror as the piano is simply rolled out of the building and through the door to the street. Does it mean the end of the orchestra? All eyes go to Alma, who is clearly shocked and frightened. After a moment, as though nothing had happened:

ALMA: Let us turn now to . . . to ah—*she leafs through music on podium*—the Beethoven . . .
GISELLE: Madame?—if I could make a suggestion . . .
ALMA: I'm sure this will soon be explained . . .
GISELLE, *desperately:* But why wait till they "explain" it, Madame! I used to play a lot in movie houses . . . on Rue du Four and Boulevard Raspail . . . And I could teach you all kinds of Bal Musette numbers . . . you know, real live stuff that won't bore them. I mean, listen just for a minute!

She plays on her violin—her face perspiring with anxiety—a Bal Musette, lively, dance music. . . .

Enter Frau Lagerführerin Mandel, and Commandant Kramer, with two SS aides.

All but Giselle spring to attention.

TCHAIKOWSKA: Attention!

Giselle looks up from her violin, nearly falls back in a faint at the threatening sight of the big brass, and stands at rigid attention.

MANDEL: At ease. The officers have decided to keep the piano in their club for the use of the members.

KRAMER, *to Alma:* I thought you could manage without it, Madame.

ALMA: Of course, Herr Commandant . . . it was only a little extra sound to fill out, but not imperative at all. We hope the officers will enjoy it.

KRAMER: Which one is Greta, the Dutch girl?

An accordion squeaks . . . it is in Greta's hands.

ALMA: Come!

Greta comes out of the orchestra, accordion in hand. Kramer moves forward, inspecting her fat, square body. She hardly dares glance at him, her eyes lowered.

KRAMER: Open your mouth. *In terror she does so. He peers in at her teeth.* Do you have any disease?

GRETA—*a scared whisper:* No, Herr Commandant.

KRAMER, *to Alma:* Dr. Mengele tells me she's not a very good player.

ALMA: Not very good, no, although not too bad—but she . . . she works quite hard . . .

KRAMER: But you could manage without her.

ALMA, *unwillingly:* Why . . . yes, of course, Herr Commandant.

Cut to Fania, flaring with anger at Alma.

Cut to Kramer, signaling one of the SS aides, who steps forward to Greta, preparing to take her off. Greta stiffens.

KRAMER, *to Greta:* My wife needs someone to look after our little daughters. You look like a nice clean girl.

General relief; Greta is simply rigid. Mandel takes a coat from the second SS aide and hands it to Greta, who quickly and gratefully puts it on. The first aide leads her to exit, and she nearly stumbles in her eagerness to keep up with him, her accordion left behind.

KRAMER, *turning to Alma:* This Sunday you will play in the hospital for the sick and the mental patients. You will have the Beethoven ready.

ALMA: Yes, Herr Commandant. I must ask your . . . toleration, if I may—our cellist has typhus and now without the accordion we may sound a little wanting in the lower . . .

KRAMER: I will send one of the cellists from the men's orchestra— they have several from the Berlin Philharmonic—he can teach one of your violinists by Sunday.

ALMA—*the idea knocks the breath out of her, but . . . :* Why . . . yes, of course, I'm sure we can teach one of our girls by Sunday, yes.

Kramer turns and strolls out.

MANDEL, *as though the orchestra should feel honored:* It will be very interesting, Madame—Dr. Mengele wants to observe the effects of music on the insane.

ALMA: Ah, so!—well, we will do our very best indeed.

Mandel walks over to Fania.

MANDEL, *pleasantly:* And how are you, these days?

FANIA, *swallowing her feelings:* I am quite well . . . of course, we are all very hungry most of the time—that makes it difficult.

MANDEL: I offered to send an extra ration this week before the concert on Sunday, but Madame Alma feels it ought to be earned, as a reward afterwards. You disagree?

Fania glances past Mandel to Alma, who is near enough to have overheard as she turns pages in a score. Alma shoots her a fierce warning glance.

FANIA, *lowering her gaze in defeat:* It's . . . not for me to agree or not . . . with our conductor.

Cut to Alma's room. Alma is pacing up and down, absolutely livid, while Fania stands with lowered gaze—this could be her end.

ALMA: How do you dare make such a comment to her!

FANIA: I don't understand, Madame—I simply told her that we were hungry. . . .

ALMA: When they have managed to play a single piece without mistakes, I will recommend an extra ration—but *I* will decide that, do you understand? *Fania is silent.* There cannot be two leaders. Do you agree or don't you?

FANIA: Why are you doing this?

Alma doesn't understand.

FANIA: We are hungry, Madame! And I saw a chance to tell her! Am I to destroy every last human feeling? She asked and I told her!

ALMA, *a bit cowed, but not quite:* I think we understand each other—that will be all now. *Fania doesn't move.* Yes?—what is it?

FANIA: Nothing. *Makes a move to go.* I am merely trying to decide whether I wish to live.

ALMA: Oh come, Fania—no one dies if they can help it. You must try to be more honest with yourself. Now hurry and finish the Beethoven orchestration—we must give them a superb concert on Sunday.

Alma walks to a table where her scores are, and sits to study them. Fania has been reached, and turns and goes out, a certain inner turmoil showing on her face.

Cut to Etalina, being coached by a young cellist, a thin young man with thick glasses and shaven head. Most of the orchestra is watching them avidly—watching *him,* the women standing around in groups at a respectful distance, the Poles also.

His hands, in close shots, are sensuous and alive and male. The camera bounces such shots off the women's expressions of fascination and desire and deprivation.

Fania tears her gaze from him, and tries to work on her orchestrations—on a table.

Cut to the cellist's hands. He is demonstrating a tremolo. Etalina tries, but she is awkward. He adjusts her arm position.

Cut to Paulette, just entering the dayroom from outside. She is barely strong enough to stand. Michou rushes to her with a cry of joy. Fania sees her, and leaps up to go to her; and Elzvieta also and Etalina.

ETALINA: Paulette! Thank God, I don't have to learn this damned instrument!

Cut to the group helping Paulette to a chair; Paulette is an ascetic-looking, aristocratic young lady.

FANIA: Are you sure you should be out?
ELZVIETA: Was it typhus or what?
ETALINA: She still looks terrible.
FANIA: Sssh! Paulette? What is it?

Paulette is trying to speak but has hardly the strength to. Everyone goes silent, awaiting her words.

PAULETTE: You're to play on Sunday . . .
ETALINA: In the hospital, yes, we know.
FANIA: You don't look to me like you should be walking around, Paulette. . . .
PAULETTE, *stubborn, gallant; she grips Fania's hand to silence her:* They plan . . . to gas . . . all the patients . . . after . . . the concert.

A stunned silence.

FANIA: How do you know this?
PAULETTE: One of the SS women . . . warned me. . . . I knew her once. . . . She used to be . . . one of the . . . chambermaids in our house. So I got out.

Alma enters from her room, sees the gathering, then sees Paulette.

ALMA: Paulette! How wonderful! Are you all better now? We're desperate for you! We're doing the Beethoven Fifth on Sunday!

Paulette gets to her feet, wobbling like a mast being raised.

FANIA: She's had to walk from the hospital, Madame—could she lie down for a bit?
PAULETTE: No! I . . . I can.

She gets to the cello, sits, as though the room is whirling around for her. Etalina rushes and hands her the bow. The orchestra members quickly sit in their places.

ALMA, *at podium:* From the beginning, please.

The Beethoven Fifth begins. Paulette, on the verge of pitching forward, plays the cello. The pall of fear is upon them all now. Fania has resumed her place at the table with her orchestrations. She bends over them, shielding her eyes, a pencil in hand.
She is moved to glance at the window. There, just outside it, she sees . . .
Shmuel, at the window. He is pointing at his eyes, which he opens extra wide.

Cut to Fania, startled. Then, lowering her hands from her eyes, forces herself to see, to look—first at Paulette, and the orchestra, and finally at . . .
Alma, conducting. She is full of joyful tension, pride, waving her arms, snapping her head in the rhythm and humming the tune loudly, oblivious to everything else.

Cut to Paulette feverishly trying to stay with the music; her desperation—which those around her understand—is the dilemma of rehearsing to play for the doomed.

Cut to Fania, at one end of the dormitory corridor between bunks, wringing out a bra and heavy stockings over a pail. Her expression is tired, deadened; she has been changing, much life is gone from her eyes. Nearby, in dimness, Tchaikowska and another Blockawa are lying in an embrace, kissing; Tchaikowska glances over, and with a sneer . . .

TCHAIKOWSKA: Now you do her laundry? —the contessa?

Fania takes the bra and stockings down the corridor to Paulette's bunk, hangs them to dry there. Paulette is lying awake, but weak.

PAULETTE: Thank you. I'm troubled . . . whether I should have told the other patients—about what's going to happen. What do you think? *Fania shakes her head and shrugs.* Except, what good would it do them to know?
FANIA: I have no answers any more, Paulette.
VOICES: Shut up, will you! Trying to sleep! Sssh!
FANIA: Better go to sleep. . . .

Across the corridor, Charlotte is staring at Michou with something like surprise in her expression, self-wonder. Michou turns her head and sees Charlotte staring at her, and shyly turns away.

Fania now climbs into her own bunk, lies there open-eyed. Other women are likewise not asleep, but some are.

Fania lies there in her depression.

She shuts her eyes against the sounds from outside—the coupling of freight cars, a surge of fierce dogs barking, shouts—her face depleted. Now Charlotte's head appears at the edge of the bunk. Fania turns to her.

Charlotte timorously asks if she may slide in beside her.

CHARLOTTE: May I?

Fania slides over to make room. Charlotte lies down beside her.

CHARLOTTE, *with a certain urgency:* I just wanted to ask you . . . about Michou.

Now their eyes meet. Fania is surprised, curious.

Charlotte is innocently fascinated, openly in love but totally unaware of it.

CHARLOTTE: What do you know about her? I see you talking sometimes together.
FANIA: Well . . . she's a militant; sort of engaged to be married; the kind that has everything planned in life. Why?

CHARLOTTE: I don't know! She just seems so different from the others—so full of courage. I love how she always stands up for herself to the SS.

FANIA—*slight pause; she knows now that she is cementing an affair:* That's what she says about you.

CHARLOTTE, *surprised, excited:* She's spoken about me?

FANIA: Quite often. She especially admired your guts. *Slight pause.* And your beauty.

Charlotte looks across the aisle and sees Michou, who is asleep.

Cut to Michou, emphasizing her hungered look in sleep, her smallness and fragility.

Cut to Fania and Charlotte.

CHARLOTTE: She's so beautiful, don't you think? I love her looks.

FANIA: It would be quicker if you told me what you don't like about her.

CHARLOTTE, *shyly laughing:* I don't understand what is happening to me, Fania. Just knowing she's sleeping nearby, that she'll be there tomorrow when I wake—I think of her all day. I could see her face all through my fever ... I just adore her, Fania.

FANIA: No. You love her, Charlotte.

CHARLOTTE: You mean ... ?

FANIA: You're seventeen, why not? At seventeen what else is there but love?

CHARLOTTE: But it's impossible.

Fania softly laughs.

CHARLOTTE: Are you laughing at me?

FANIA: After all you've seen and been through here, is that such a disaster?

CHARLOTTE: How stupid I am—I never thought of it as ...

FANIA: In this place to feel at all may be a blessing.

CHARLOTTE: Do you ever have such ... feelings?

FANIA, *shaking her head:* I have nothing. Nothing at all any more. Go now, you're still not well, you should sleep.

Charlotte starts to slide out, then turns back and suddenly kisses Fania's hand gratefully.

FANIA—*she smiles, moved:* What a proper young lady you must have been!

Charlotte shyly grins, confessing this, and moves away down the aisle. She pauses as she starts to pass Michou. The latter opens her eyes. Both girls stare in silence at one another—really looking inward, astonished at themselves. Now Michou tenuously reaches out her hand, which Charlotte touches with her own.

Cut to Fania, observing them. A deep, desperate concern for herself is on her face. She closes her eyes and turns over to sleep.

At the distant drone of bombers, Fania slowly opens her eyes. Turns on her back, listening.

Cut to a series of close-ups: Michou, Paulette, Liesle, Etalina, and others; they are opening their eyes, listening, trying to figure out the nationality of the planes.

Now the Polish Blockawas, some in bed with each other, do the same.

Cut to Fania. She has gone to a window and is looking out onto the "street." The sound of the bombers continues.

Cut to the barracks "street," SS guards in uniform carrying rifles—five or six of them converging and looking upward worriedly.

Cut to Fania, turning from the window and momentarily facing the apprehensive, questioning stares of the Blockawas. She starts to pass them; Tchaikowska reaches out and grasps her wrist.

TCHAIKOWSKA, *pointing upward:* American? English? *Fania shrugs, doesn't know. Tchaikowska releases her.* Too late for you anyway.

Fania's face is totally expressionless—yet in this impacted look is torment that another human could do this.

FANIA: Maybe it is too late for the whole human race, Tchaikowska.

She walks past, heading for the dayroom, not her bunk.

Cut to Fania, under a single bulb, alone in the dayroom. She has pencil in hand, orchestrating—but she looks off now, unable to concentrate. Elzvieta appears beside her, sits.

ELZVIETA: So it's going to end after all. *Fania gives her an uncomprehending glance.* Everyone tries to tell you their troubles, don't they.

FANIA: I don't know why, I can't help anyone.

ELZVIETA: You are someone to trust, Fania—maybe it's that you have no ideology, you're satisfied just to be a person.

FANIA: I don't know what I am anymore, Elzvieta. I could drive a nail through my hand, it would hardly matter. I am dying by inches, I know it very well—I've seen too much. *Tiredly wipes her eyes.* Too much and too much and too much . . .

ELZVIETA: I'm one of the most successful actresses in Poland. *Fania looks at her, waiting for the question; Elzvieta, in contrast to Fania, has long hair.* My father was a count; I was brought up in a castle; I have a husband and Marok, my son, who is nine years old. *Slight pause.* I don't know what will happen to us, Fania—you and I, before the end. . . .

FANIA, *with a touch of irony:* Are you saying good-bye to me?

ELZVIETA, *with difficulty:* I only want one Jewish woman to understand. . . . I lie here wondering if it will be worse to survive than not to. For me, I mean. When I first came here I was sure that the Pope, the Christian leaders did not know; but when they found out they would send planes to bomb out the fires here, the rail tracks that bring them every day. But the trains keep coming and fires continue burning. Do you understand it?

FANIA: Maybe other things are more important to bomb. What are we anyway but a lot of women who can't even menstruate anymore—and some scarecrow men?

ELZVIETA, *suddenly kissing Fania's hand:* Oh, Fania—try to forgive me!

FANIA: You! Why? What did you ever do to me? You were in the Resistance, you tried to fight against this, why should you feel such guilt? It's the other ones who are destroying us—and they only feel innocent! It's all a joke, don't you see? It's all meaningless, and I'm afraid you'll never change that, Elzvieta! *Elzvieta gets up, rejected, full of tears.* I almost pity a person like you more than us. You will survive, and everyone around you will be innocent, from one end of Europe to the other.

Offscreen, we hear the sounds of a train halting, shouts, debarkation noises. Elzvieta turns her eyes toward a window.

Cut to a convoy debarking in the first dawn light. SS and kapos and dogs.

Cut to Elzvieta, riven by the sight now, sinking to her knees at a chair, and crossing herself, praying. Fania studies her for a moment ... then she goes back to work on her orchestration, forcing herself to refuse this consolation, this false hope and sentiment. She inscribes notes. Something fails in her; she puts down pencil.

FANIA: My memory is falling apart; I'm quite aware of it, a little every day ... I can't even remember if we got our ration last night ... did we?

Tchaikowska appears from the dormitory door—she is drinking from a bowl. Now she walks to the exit door of the dayroom, opens it, and throws out the remainder of milk in the bowl, wiping the bowl with a rag.

Elzvieta, still on her knees, watches Tchaikowska returning to the dormitory; she tries to speak calmly. . . .

ELZVIETA: You throw away milk, Tchaikowska?
TCHAIKOWSKA: It was mine.
ELZVIETA: Even so ...
TCHAIKOWSKA: Our farm is two kilometers from here—they bring it to me, my sisters.
ELZVIETA: But even so ... to throw it away, when ...

She breaks off. Tchaikowska looks slightly perplexed.

TCHAIKOWSKA: You saying it's not my milk?
ELZVIETA: Never mind.

TCHAIKOWSKA, *tapping her head:* You read too many books, makes you crazy.

She exits into the dormitory. Elzvieta swallows in her hunger, and, as Fania watches her, she bends her head and more fervently, silently prays.

Cut to the barracks "street," silent and empty for a moment; suddenly the blasts of sirens, whistles, and the howling of pursuit dogs. From all corners SS guards and dog handlers explode onto the street. They are in a chaotic hunt for someone.

Prisoners are being turned out of barracks onto the "street," lined up to be counted, hit, kicked. . . .

Cut to the hunters, crashing into the dayroom with dogs howling. Blockawas are coming out of the dormitory, throwing on clothes. SS women accompany the guards. Alma comes out of her room questioningly.

Cut to the orchestra, fleeing from bunks in the dormitory as hunters rip off blankets, overturn mattresses—screaming in fear of dogs, shouting.

Cut to the players, being driven outside into the "street."

Cut to the "street." Scurrying to form ranks and trying to dress at the same time, the players are calling out their names and coming to attention. Before them stand an SS officer and a dog handler, beside Tchaikowska who is checking names off a roster she holds.

Alma stands at attention before the officer.

TCHAIKOWSKA: All accounted for, Mein Herr.
SS OFFICER, *to Madame Alma:* Do you know Mala?
ALMA: Mala? No, but I have seen her accompanying the Commandant, of course—as an interpreter.
SS OFFICER: She has had no contact at all with your players?
ALMA: No, no, she has never been inside our barracks, Herr Kapitän.

The SS officer now walks off, followed by the handler and dog. Michou is the first to realize.

MICHOU: Mala's escaped! I bet she's gotten out!

The orchestra is electrified. . . .

CHARLOTTE, *to another:* Mala's out!

Blockawas are pushing them back into barracks.

PAULETTE: Fania!—did you hear!

Cut to the "Canada" girls. Deals are going on at their tables, and a girl prisoner comes hurrying up. A quick whisper to one of the dealers.

GIRL: Mala got out . . . and Edek too!
DEALER: With Edek? How!?
GIRL: They got SS uniforms somehow, and took off!

Business stops as three or four dealers cross themselves and bow their heads in prayer.

Cut to Alma, at the podium, going through a score, with Fania alongside her pointing out something on it.

The following lines of dialogue are all in close intimate shots—since they dare not too openly discuss the escape. (All are in their chairs, instruments ready for rehearsal.)

CHARLOTTE: What a romance! Imagine, the two of them together—God!
MICHOU: I saw him once, he's gorgeous—blond, and beautiful teeth. . . .
LIESLE: She's a Belgian, like me. . . .
ESTHER: What Belgian? She's Jewish, like all of us. . . .
LIESLE: Well, I mean . . .
ELZVIETA: Edek is a Pole, though—and they're going to tell the world what's happening here.
ETALINA: Imagine—if they could put a bomb down that chimney!
ELZVIETA: Now the world will know! Let's play for them The Wedding March! . . .

She raises her violin.

CHARLOTTE, *readying her bow on the violin—devoutly:* For Mala and Edek!

MICHOU: Mala and Edek!

Etalina, on time for once, readies her instrument.

Cut to Shmuel, bowing to Alma, his toolbox on his shoulder.

SHMUEL: I'm supposed to diagram the wiring, Madame. I won't disturb you.

Alma nods, lifts her baton, and starts the number.

Shmuel, as the number proceeds, has a piece of paper on which he is tracing the wiring. He follows along one wall to the table in a corner of the room, where Fania is seated with a score she is following, pencil in hand.

Fania senses Shmuel is lingering at a point near her; and as he approaches her, his eyes on the wiring, he exposes the paper in his hand for her to read. She glances at Alma at the end of the room, then leans a little . . .

Cut to the note, reading: ALLIES LANDED IN FRANCE.
Shmuel's hand crumples the paper.

Cut to Shmuel, swallowing the note. Then taking his toolbox and slinging it onto his shoulder, he hurriedly limps away and goes out the exit without turning back.

Fania turns and looks out the window, and sees . . .

The by-now familiar arrival of new prisoners as seen from the dayroom window. Shmuel walks out of the shot, his place taken by . . .

Mandel—who is leading Ladislaus, a four-year-old boy, away from his mother, who is at the edge of a crowd of new arrivals, watching, not knowing what to make of it. The mother now calls to him; we can't hear her through the window. Ladislaus is beautiful, and Mandel seems delighted as she gives him a finger to hold on to.

Note: The character of this particular crowd of prisoners is somewhat different—they are Polish peasant families, not Jews. They are innocently "camping" between barracks buildings, far less tensely than the Jews on arrival, and the kids are running about playing, even throwing a ball. Infants are suckling; improvised little cooking fires, etc. . . . So that Ladislaus's mother is only apprehensive as she calls to him, not hysterical at his going off with Mandel.

Cut to the orchestra, continuing to play. Etalina is turning with a look of open fear from the window; she leans to Elzvieta beside her and unable to contain herself, whispers into her ear.

Alma sees this breach of discipline.

ALMA, *furiously:* Etalina!

The music breaks off.

ETALINA, *pointing outside:* Those are Poles, not Jews. . . . They're Aryans, Madame!
MICHOU: Why not? Hitler always said they would kill off the Poles to make room for Germans out there.
ETALINA: But look at them, there must be thousands. . . . They'd never gas that many Aryans! *To Alma:* I think they're going to give them this barracks, Madame!

Mandel and Ladislaus enter.
Silence. Mandel now picks up Ladislaus to show him off to the orchestra.

MANDEL: Isn't he beautiful?

Only Tchaikowska and the other Blockawas purr and smile. The orchestra sits in silence, not knowing what to make of this or Etalina's theory.

MANDEL, *to Alma:* What's the matter with them?
ALMA: It's nothing, Frau Mandel—there seems to be a rumor that these Aryan Poles will be given our barracks. . . .
MANDEL: Oh, not at all, Madame—in fact, I can tell you that there will be no further selections from within our camp. Of course we have no room for new arrivals—so for them . . . there will be other arrangements.

Cut to Fania, turning out toward the window; she sees a line of trucks loading the peasants for gassing.

Cut to the child's mother being pushed aboard—but now she is fighting to stay off the truck and looking desperately about for her child.

Cut to Mandel, now fairly surrounded with players who, in their relief, can now express feeling for the beautiful child. Featured here is Marianne, who is chanting a nursery rhyme and tickling his cheek. . . .

MARIANNE: Hoppa, hoppa, Ladislaus
Softly as a little mouse . . .

Mandel, with an almost girlishly innocent laugh, presses the child's face against her own. Then putting him down, and bending to him, holding his hand.

MANDEL: And now we are going to get you a nice new little suit, and shoes, and a sweet little shirt. *She gives a perfectly happy, proud glance at the orchestra.* Work hard now—we are all expecting an especially fine concert for the hospital on Sunday! *To child:* Come along.

She exits with Ladislaus hanging on to her finger.

Cut to the "street," teeming with life a few moments before, now totally cleansed of people. Mandel leads the boy so as to avoid the dying embers of cooking fires, other debris left by the crowd, bundles, cookpots. . . .

Kapos are policing the area, throwing debris into hand-drawn wagons. A kapo picks up a ball, and as Mandel approaches he bows a little and offers it to her. She accepts it and hands it to Ladislaus and walks on, tenderly holding his hand.

Cut to the players, clustered at the door and windows, watching Mandel going away. They are all confused, yet attracted by this show of humanity.

GISELLE: So she's a human being after all!
ESTHER: She is? Where's the mother?
ETALINA: Still—in a way, Esther . . . I mean at least she adores the child.

ESTHER, *with a wide look of alarm to all:* What's happening here. . . ?
PAULETTE: All she said was that . . .
ESTHER, *shutting her ears with her hands:* One Polack kid she saves and suddenly she's human? What is happening here!

From the podium, Alma calmly, sternly summons them with the tapping of her baton.

ALMA: From the beginning, please! We have a great deal to do before Sunday.

Silently they seat themselves. And Beethoven's Fifth begins.

Cut to the searchlight from a tower, sweeping the street. Sirens sound and the searchlight is extinguished.

Cut to Marianne, singing; she breaks off as the sirens sound. And all lights go out.
As the sirens die out, bombers take over.
The players sit waiting in the dark, eyes turned upward toward the sound. As the sound rises to crescendo, Alma exits into her room; and as she is closing the door she catches Fania's eye. Fania rises, approaches the door.

Cut to Alma's room. Still in darkness, Alma sits. The bombers are fading.

ALMA: I will be leaving you after the Sunday concert, Fania. *Fania is surprised.* They are sending me on a tour to play for the troops. I wanted you to be first to hear the news. *A different camera angle reveals the excitement and pride in her expression.* I am going to be released, Fania! Can you imagine it? I'll play what I like and as I like. They said . . . *Elated now, filling herself:* they said a musician of my caliber ought not be wasted here! . . . What's the matter? I thought you'd be happy for me.
FANIA: Well, I am, of course. But you'll be entertaining men who are fighting to keep us enslaved, won't you.
ALMA: But that is not the point! I . . . *Only an instant's difficulty.* I am German, Fania; I can't help that, and I will play for German soldiers.

FANIA, *changing the hopeless subject:* And what about us? We're going to continue, aren't we?

ALMA: I have suggested you to replace me.

FANIA—*nods, consenting:* Well ... *A move to leave.* I hope ... it ends soon for all of us.

She turns to grasp the doorknob.

ALMA: Why are you trying to spoil my happiness?

Fania turns to her, trying to plumb her.

ALMA: I will be playing for honorable men, not these murderers here! Soldiers risk their lives...!

FANIA: Why do you need my approval? If it makes you happy then enjoy your happiness.

ALMA: Not all Germans are Nazis, Fania! You are nothing but a racialist if you think so!

FANIA: Alma—you are German, you are free—what more do you want! I agree, it is an extraordinary honor—the only Jew to play a violin for the German Army! My head will explode...!

She pulls the door open just as SS Frau Schmidt walks up to it. Shock. Schmidt is the powerhouse who runs the clothing depot and knocked Fania down earlier on for speaking out of line.

ALMA: Why ... Frau Schmidt ... come in ... please!

The lights suddenly go on. All glance up, noting this wordlessly.

SCHMIDT: I wanted to extend my congratulations, Madame Rosé—I have just heard the great news.

ALMA, *ravished:* Oh, thank you, thank you, Frau Schmidt. This is very moving to me, especially coming from you.

SCHMIDT: Yes, but I always express my feelings. I would like you to join me for dinner tonight—a farewell in your honor?

ALMA: I ... I am overwhelmed, Frau Schmidt. Of course.

SCHMIDT: At eight, then?—in my quarters.

ALMA: Oh, I'll be there.... Thank you, thank you.

Schmidt exits. Now, eyes glistening with joy, Alma turns to Fania.

ALMA: Now ... now you see! That woman, I can tell you, has tried everything to be transferred ... she is desperate to get out of here, and yet she has the goodness to come and wish me well on my departure.

FANIA, *stunned:* Well I certainly never expected that of her. . . . But who knows what's in the human heart?

ALMA: You judge people, Fania, you are terribly harsh.

Alma is now sprucing herself up for dinner, brushing her skirt, straightening her blouse. . . .

FANIA: And Mandel saved that child. Maybe they figure they're losing the war, so . . .

ALMA, *at the height of her hopes for herself:* Why must everything have a worm in it? Why can't you accept the little hope there is in life?

She is now putting on her coat.

FANIA: I'm all mixed up. Schmidt wanting to get out is really unbelievable, Alma—she's gotten rich running the black market; she's robbed every woman who's landed here ... every deal in the place has her hand in it. . . .

ALMA, *extending her hand:* I am leaving in the morning, Fania—if we don't see each other ... Thank you for your help.

FANIA, *taking her hand:* You are totally wrong about practically everything, Alma—but I must say you probably saved us all. And I thank you from my heart.

ALMA: You can thank my refusal to despair, Fania.

FANIA: Yes, I suppose that's true.

Cut to an honor guard, and SS at attention.

The whole orchestra is filing into this room through a doorway. They are in their finest; atmosphere is hushed, eyes widened with curiosity, incredulity at this whole affair.

For at center stands a coffin, flowers on it, the top open. But the orchestra is ranged some yards from it.

When they have all assembled, enter Commandant Kramer, Dr. Mengele, other brass—

And finally Mandel, her finger in the hand of little Ladislaus, who is now dressed in a lovely blue suit, and linen shirt, and tie, and good shined shoes, and holding a teddy bear.

First Kramer, Mengele, Mandel, and the other brass step up and look mournfully into the coffin. Now the orchestra is ordered to pay its respects by a glance from Mandel to Fania.

Cut to Mandel, her eyes filling with tears.

Cut to the orchestra. A feeling of communion; they are starting to weep, without quite knowing why.

Cut to Alma—in the coffin. Fania looks down at Alma dead—she is bewildered, horrified. Then she moves off, her place taken by Paulette, then others. . . . The sound of keening is beginning as they realize it is Alma who has died.

Cut to the black market. Fania is pretending to trade a thick slice of bread for some soap with the chief black marketeer, a brazen girl who is smelling the bread offered.

FANIA: What happened?
BLACK MARKETEER: Schmidt poisoned her at dinner.
FANIA: How do you know!
BLACK MARKETEER: They shot her this morning.
FANIA: Schmidt!?
BLACK MARKETEER—*nods:* Nobody was getting out if she couldn't. 'Specially a Jew.
FANIA: Then she really wanted out!
BLACK MARKETEER: Well, she'd made her pile, why not?

Both their heads suddenly turn to the same direction at a booming sound in the distance.

BLACK MARKETEER, *looking questioningly at Fania:* That thunder or artillery?

They both turn again, listening in the midst of the market.

Cut to Olga, the Ukrainian accordionist, who has apparently inherited the conductorship; she is robot-like in her arm-waving as she leads them in the Fifth Symphony—but it all falls to pieces, and Fania hurries up to the podium.

OLGA, *before Fania can get a word out:* No! I have been appointed and I am going to conduct!
FANIA: Now listen to me!
OLGA: No! I am kapo now and I order you to stop interfering!
FANIA: Olga, dear—you can barely read the notes, you have no idea how to bring in the instruments!
OLGA: Go back to your seat!
FANIA: You'll send us to the gas! Mengele will be there on Sunday—he won't stand for this racket—it's nonsensical! Now let me rehearse, and on Sunday you can stand up in front and wave your arms, but at least we'll be rehearsed!
ETALINA: Hey!—sssh!

All turn to listen . . . once again there is the sound of a distant booming.

ETALINA: God . . . you suppose Mala and Edek found the Russians and are leading them here?
GISELLE: I bet! That was artillery. The Russians are famous for their artillery . . . !
OLGA: All right, listen! *She is desperately trying to fill out an image of authority.* I know a number. It's very famous with us in the Ukraine. We are going to play it. First I.

Olga takes up her accordion and launches into a "Laughing Song," a foot-stomper polka, full of "Ha-ha-ha, hee-hee-hee," etc.
Orchestra looks at her, appalled, some of them starting to giggle.
Blockawas led by Tchaikowska appear and, loving it, begin doing a polka with one another, hands clapping. . . .
There is sharp whistling outside.
Tchaikowska hurries out into the street as players go to the windows. . . .

Cut to a gallows. The hanging of Mala and Edek. They have both been horribly beaten, can barely stand. Mala stumbles to her knees but flings away the hand of the executioner and stands by herself under the noose.

The camera now turns out . . . picking up part of the immense crowd of prisoners forced to watch the executions.

Cut to prisoners, en masse—in fact, the whole camp, tens of thousands, a veritable city of the starved and humiliated, ordered to watch the execution. This is a moment of such immense human import—for one after another, in defiance, they dare to bare their heads before the two doomed lovers and create a sea of shaven heads across a great space, while SS men and kapos club at them to cover themselves.

Cut to the gallows—and the drop. Both Mala and Edek are hanging.

Cut to the sky.

Dissolve from sky to rain.

Cut to the dayroom at night. Rain is falling on the windows. Girls are practicing in a desultory way, breaking off in mid-note to talk quietly together. Fania is at her table; she is playing with a pencil, staring at nothing, her face deeply depressed, deadened.

Now Michou, who is at another window a few yards away, calls in a loud whisper . . .

MICHOU, *pointing outside:* Fania!

Fania looks out the window.

Cut to Marianne, on the "street," just parting from the executioner, a monstrous large man, who grimly pats her ass as she rushes into the barracks.

Cut to Marianne, entering the dayroom from outside, shaking out her coat, and as she passes Michou . . .

MICHOU: With the executioner?

Marianne halts. All around the room the expressions are angrily contemptuous, disgusted.

MICHOU: He killed Mala and Edek, did you know?
MARIANNE: Well, if he didn't, somebody else would've, you can be sure of that.

She starts toward the door to the dormitory, then halts, turns to them all.

MARIANNE: I mean to say, dearies, whose side do you think *you're* on? Because if anybody's not sure you're on the side of the executioners, you ought to go out and ask any prisoner in this camp, and they'll be happy to tell you! *To Michou:* So you can stick your comments you know exactly where, Michou. Any further questions?

She looks about defiantly, smiling, exits into the dormitory, removing her coat.

The truth of her remarks is in the players' eyes. They avoid one another as the women resume practicing. Esther comes to Fania.

ESTHER: You shouldn't let her get away with that.—I'd answer but nobody listens to what *I* say. . . .
FANIA: But she's right, Esther, what answer is there?
ESTHER: I am *not* on their side—I am only keeping myself for Jerusalem.
FANIA: Good.
ESTHER—*Fania's uninflected, sterilized comment has left her unsatisfied:* What do you mean by that, Fania?
FANIA: That it's good, if you can keep yourself so apart from all this. So clean.
ESTHER, *asking, in a sense:* But we're not responsible for this.
FANIA: Of course not, nothing here is our fault. *Finally agreeing, as it were, to go into it:* All I mean is that we may be innocent, but we have changed. I mean we know a little something about the human race that we didn't know before. And it's not good news.
ESTHER, *anxiously, even angry:* How can you still call them human?
FANIA: Then what are they, Esther?
ESTHER: I don't like the way you . . . you seem to connect such monsters with . . .

Suddenly, Giselle calls out sotto voce—she is sitting with Charlotte.

GISELLE: Mengele!

Dr. Mengele's importance is evident in the way they leap to their feet as he enters. His handsome face is sombre, his uniform dapper under the raincoat which he now opens to take out a baton and Alma's armband, which has some musical insignia on it.

OLGA, *at rigid attention:* Would the Herr Doktor Mengele like to hear some particular music?

Mengele walks past her to the door of Alma's room.

Cut to Mengele, entering Alma's room. He looks about at the empty bed and chair, as though in a sacred place. Then he takes the baton and hangs it up from a nail in the wall above a shelf, and on the shelf he carefully places her armband. Now he steps back and, facing these relics, stands at military attention for a long moment.

The camera turns past him to discover, through the doorway to the dayroom, Fania looking in, and others jammed in beside her, watching in tense astonishment.

MENGELE: Kapo!
OLGA, *rushing into room:* Herr Doktor Mengele!

She goes to attention.

MENGELE: That is Madame Rosé's baton and armband. They are never to be disturbed. *He faces the relics again.* In Memoriam.

Fania greats this emotional display with incredulity, as do others nearby.

Now the dread doctor turns and walks into the dayroom, the players quickly and obsequiously making way for him, and standing with attentive respect as he goes by.

As he passes into the center of the dayroom, his heels clacking on the wooden floor in a slow, pensive measure, the tension rises—no one is sure why. And he halts instead of leaving them, his back to them. Why has he halted, what is the monster thinking?

Cut to the players. They have risen to a dread tension, their faces rigid.

Cut to Mengele. He turns to them; he has an out-of-this-world look now, an inspired air, as though he had forgotten where he was and only now takes these faces into consciousness. He seems less angry than alarmed, surprised.

Fania, unable to wait for what may come out of him, takes a tenuous step forward and bows a little, propelled by her terror of death, now, at this moment.

FANIA: If the Herr Doktor will permit me—the orchestra is re-solved to perform at our absolute best, in memory of our beloved Madame Rosé.

Only now does Mengele turn that gaze on her, as though he heard her from afar. Fania's voice is near trembling.

FANIA: I can assure the Herr Doktor that we are ready to spend every waking moment perfecting our playing.... We believe our fallen leader would wish us to continue ... *Beginning to falter:* to ... to carry on as she ... inspired us....

The sound of bombers overhead. Mengele reacts, but in the most outwardly discreet way, with an aborted lift of the head. But the girls understand that he knows the end is near, and this heightens their fear.

He changes under this sound from the sky, and strolls out as though to show unconcern. As soon as he is out of sight several girls break into weeping. Fania feels humiliated, and goes alone to her table....

ETALINA, *weeping:* It's the end! You felt it, didn't you, Fania! He's going to send us to the gas!
PAULETTE, *asking Fania's reaction:* The way he stared at us!
CHARLOTTE: The thing to do is rehearse and rehearse and rehearse! *To Liesle:* To this day you've never gotten the Beethoven right! Now here, damn you! *She thrusts an accordion at her.* Work on that ar-peggio! *She notices Fania looking upward.* What's the matter?

The whole group turns to Fania questioningly—they are scared, panicked. She is listening to the sky.

FANIA: I can't understand why they don't bomb here. They could stop the convoys in one attack on the rails.

ELZVIETA: They're probably afraid they'll hit *us*.

MICHOU: It's political—it always is—but I can't figure out the angles.

ESTHER: They don't want it to seem like it's a war to save the Jews. *They turn to Esther.* They won't risk planes for our sake, and pilots—their people wouldn't like it. *To Fania:* Fania . . . if they do come for us and it's the end . . . I ask you not to do that again and beg for your life. . . .

FANIA, *guiltily:* I was only . . .

ESTHER, *crying out—a kind of love for Fania is in it:* You shouldn't ever beg, Fania!

Cut to Lagerführerin Mandel entering from the rain. She wears a great black cape. She looks ravaged, desolate. She goes to a chair and sits, unhooks her cape. In one hand now is seen . . .

The child's sailor hat. It is held tenderly on her lap.

Cut to Mandel, in a state of near shock; yet an air of self-willed determination too, despite her staring eyes.

Olga, now the kapo, looks to Fania for what to do. Others likewise glance at her. Fania now comes forward and stands before Mandel.

Mandel comes out of her remoteness, looks at Fania.

MANDEL: The duet from *Madame Butterfly.* You and the other one.

Fania turns to the girls—Giselle hurries into the dormitory.

GISELLE, *running off:* Marianne? Come out here . . . !

Mandel now stands and walks to a window looking out at the rain. Meanwhile Charlotte and Etalina have taken up their violins to accompany.

Marianne, half asleep, enters from the dormitory and comes to Fania. And now they wait for Mandel to turn from the window and order them to begin. But she doesn't. So Fania walks across the room to her.

Cut to Fania, arriving beside Mandel, who is staring out at the rain-washed window. Fania's eyes travel down to the hat in the other woman's hand.

FANIA: We are ready to begin, Frau Mandel.

Mandel seems hardly to have heard, keeps on staring. After a moment . . .

FANIA: Is something the matter with the little boy?

Mandel now glances at Fania—there is an air of dissociation coming over the Nazi's face.

MANDEL: It has always been the same—the greatness of a people depends on the sacrifices they are willing to make.

Fania's expression of curiosity collapses—she knows now.

MANDEL: I gave him . . . back.

Now Mandel is straightening with an invoked pride before Fania, stiffening. But she is still struggling with an ancient instinct within her.

MANDEL: Come now, play for me.

She goes to her seat. Fania, nearly insensible, joins Marianne—who greets her with a raised eyebrow to keep their hostility intact. Charlotte's violin starts it off, the duet from Act II.

MARIANNE (*as Suzuki*): *It's daylight! Cio-Cio-San.*
FANIA (*as Butterfly*)—*mimes picking up an infant, cradling it in her arms: He'll come, he'll come, I know he'll come.*
MARIANNE (*as Suzuki*): *I pray you go and rest, for you are weary. And I will call you when he arrives.*
FANIA (*as Butterfly*)—*to her "baby": Sweet thou art sleeping, cradled in my heart . . .*

Cut to Mandel, stunned by the lyric and music; but through her sentimental tears her fanatic stupidity is emerging.

FANIA (*as Butterfly*) (*voice-over*): *Safe in God's keeping, while I must weep apart. Around thy head the moonbeams dart. . . .*

Cut to the group.

FANIA (*as Butterfly*), *rocking the "baby": Sleep my beloved.*
MARIANNE (*as Suzuki*): *Poor Madame Butterfly!*

Cut to Mandel, fighting for control, staring up at Fania. And Fania now takes on a challenging, protesting tone.

FANIA (*as Butterfly*): *Sweet, thou art sleeping, cradled on my heart. Safe in God's keeping, while I must weep apart.*

The sound of bombers . . . coming in fast, tremendous.
Sirens.
Mandel comes out of her fog, stands . . . girls are rushing to windows to look up. The lights go out.
The sound of bombers overhead and nearby explosions.
There is screaming; in the darkness, total confusion; but Mandel can be seen rushing out into the night, a determined look on her face.

Cut to the railroad platform. Bombs explode.
Despite everything, deportees are being rushed onto waiting trucks, which roar away.

Cut to a series of close shots: Kramer kicking a deportee. . . . Mandel commanding a woman to board a truck. . . . And Mengele, face streaming, his eyes crazed as he looks skyward; he goes to an SS officer.

MENGELE: Hurry!—faster!

Cut to the warehouse hospital. "The Blue Danube" is in full swing as the shot opens. At one end of the vast shadowy space is the orchestra, "conducted" by Olga.
The few good violinists like Elzvieta and Charlotte saw away as loud as possible.
The Bechstein piano has been brought in and Fania is playing.
The sick, what appear to be hundreds of them, are ranged in beds; the insane, some of them clinging to walls or to each other like

monkeys; about a hundred so-called well prisoners in their uniforms ranged at one end; dozens of SS officers, male and female, in one unified audience sit directly before the players.

Cut to a dancing woman emerging from among the insane; heads turn as she does a long, sweeping waltz by herself; shaven head, cadaverous, a far-out expression.

SS glance at her, amused.

Cut to the prisoners. A humming has started among them to "The Blue Danube."

Cut to Mengele, Kramer, and SS officers. These high brass notice the humming—they take it with uncertainty—is it some kind of demonstration of their humanity?

Cut to the prisoners. They have dared to hum louder—and the fact that it is done in unison and without command or authorization enlivens them more and more.

Cut to Commandant Kramer, starting to get to his feet, when Mengele touches his arm and gestures for him to permit the humming as harmless. Kramer half-willingly concedes, and sits.

Cut to the orchestra. "Blue Danube" ends. With no announcement, in the bleak silence, Olga picks up her accordion. Fania and Paulette immediately come to her and have a quick whispered conversation while trying to appear calm.

FANIA, *sotto voce:* Not the "Laughing Song"!
OLGA: But they want another number!
PAULETTE: But they're all going to the gas, you can't play that!
OLGA: But I don't know any other! What's the difference?

Olga steps from them and begins to play and sing the "Laughing Song," which requires all to join in.

And as it proceeds, some of the insane join in, out of tempo to be sure, and . . .

Kramer is laughing, along with other SS.

Patients in beds are laughing. . . .

Cut to Fania, in her eyes the ultimate agony.

Cut to Mengele, signaling Kramer, who is beside him, and the latter speaks to an aide at his side. The aide gets up and moves out of the shot. . . .

Cut to the orchestra. The "Laughing Song" is continuing.

Cut to a door to the outside, which is opening. Kapos are leading half a dozen patients through it.

Cut to the orchestra. The "Laughing Song" continues; now Paulette sees the kapos leading people out. Her cello slides out of her grasp as she faints. "Laughing Song" is climaxing. Michou is propping up Paulette while attempting to play and laugh.

Cut to the hospital warehouse. Patients, orchestra, and SS are rocking along in the finale, as more patients are being led out through the door.

Cut to the dayroom. Later that night. The players are sitting in darkness while some are at the windows watching a not very distant artillery bombardment—the sky flashes explosions.

Fania, seated at her table, is staring out the window. She is spiritless now.

Players' faces, in the flashes of light from outside, are somber, expectant.

Cut to a fire in the dayroom stove, visible through its cracks. Michou is grating a potato into a pan. Charlotte is hungrily looking on. This is very intense business.

Cut to Olga, the new conductor, emerging from Alma's room: She is very officious lately.

OLGA: All right—players? We will begin rehearsal. *Heads turn to her but no one moves.* I order you to rehearse!
ETALINA, *indicating outside:* That's the Russian artillery, Olga.
OLGA: I'm in charge here and I gave no permission to suspend rehearsals!
ETALINA: Stupid, it's all over, don't you understand? The Russians are out there and we will probably be gassed before they can reach us.

GISELLE: Relax, Olga—we can't rehearse in the dark.

ETALINA: She can—she can't read music anyway.

OLGA—*defeated, she notices Michou:* Where'd you get those potatoes?

MICHOU: I stole them, where else?

OLGA, *pulling her to her feet:* You're coming to Mandel! —I'm reporting you!

From behind her, suddenly, Fania has her by her hair.

FANIA, *quietly:* Stop this, Olga, or we'll stuff a rag in your mouth and strangle you tonight. Let her go.

Olga releases Michou.

CHARLOTTE: She was only making me a pancake, that's all.

FANIA: Sit down, Olga—we may all go tonight.

OLGA: I don't see why.

ETALINA: We've seen it all, dummy, we're the evidence. *Olga unhappily stares out a window.* I feel for her—she finally gets an orchestra to conduct and the war has to end.

Cut to a series of close shots: the players' faces—the exhaustion now, the anxiety, the waiting.

Cut to Etalina, just sitting close to Fania.

ETALINA: I think I saw my mother yesterday. And my two sisters and my father.

FANIA, *coming alert to her from her own preoccupations:* What? Where? What are you talking about?

ETALINA: Yesterday afternoon; that convoy from France; when we were playing outside the freight car; I looked up and . . . I wasn't . . . I wasn't sure, but . . .

Their eyes meet; Fania realizes that she is quite sure, and she reaches around and embraces Etalina, who buries her face in Fania's breast and shakes with weeping.

FANIA: Oh, but what could you have done?

Cut to Lagerführerin Mandel, entering the dayroom. All rise to stand at attention, faces flaring with anxiety. Mandel is wide-eyed, totally distracted, undone. Etalina is weeping as she stands at attention.

MANDEL: Has anyone come across that little hat? *Silence. No one responds. Amazement in faces now.* The little sailor hat. I seem to have dropped it. No?

Heads shake negatively, rather stunned. Mandel, expressionless, exits.
The players sit again.
Etalina has an explosion of weeping.

FANIA, *comforting her:* Sssh . . .

Marianne now comes over to Fania, who is stroking Etalina's face.

MARIANNE: I just want you to know, Fania, that . . . you turned your back on me when I needed you, and . . . I don't want you to think I'm too stupid to know it.
FANIA: What are you talking about? *Marianne bitterly turns away, as* . . . Are you a little child that I should have locked in the closet?

Marianne walks away to a window, adamantly bitter.

Cut to Michou, feeding Charlotte pieces of pancake from a pan, as she would a child.

Cut to Fania, looking with a certain calculation at . . .
Elzvieta, who blanches and turns from an explosion in the sky, and crosses herself.
Fania comes up to her.

FANIA: Elzvieta? *She takes out a small but thick notebook:* I would like you to keep this. It's my diary—everything is in there from the first day.
ELZVIETA: No, no. You keep it. You will be all right, Fania. . . .
FANIA: Take it. Take it, maybe you can publish it in Poland. . . .
ELZVIETA—*starts to take it, then doesn't:* It's impossible, Fania—I feel like I'm condemning you! You keep it, you will live, I know you will!

FANIA: I am not sure . . . that I wish to, Elzvieta.
ELZVIETA, *realizing, she looks deeply into Fania's dying eyes:* Oh no
. . . no, Fania! No!

She suddenly sweeps Fania into her arms, as . . .
Two troopers enter. These are not SS men; they carry rifles and
combat gear.

TROOPER: Jews left! Aryans right! Hurry up!

The players scurry to form up. . . .
Fania and Elzvieta slowly disengage—it's good-bye.

Cut to an open freight car. Dawn is breaking; rain drenches
some twenty-five players in this freight car ordinarily used for coal.
Fania now is lying on her back with her eyes shut, the players extending their coats to shield her. The train slows.

Nearby two Wehrmacht troopers are huddled over a wood-
stove; women also cluster around for warmth.

These men are themselves worn out with war, dead-eyed.

Marianne makes her way over to one of the troopers and gives
him a flirty look.

MARIANNE: How's it going, soldier?

The trooper's interest is not very great.

MARIANNE: Could a girl ask where you're taking us?

She comes closer—and with mud-streaked face, she smiles. . . .
Now he seems to show some interest in her.

MARIANNE: 'Cause wherever it is, I know how to make a fellow
forget his troubles. Where are we heading?
TROOPER, *shrugging:* Who knows? I guess it's to keep you away
from the Russians, maybe . . . so you won't be telling them what
went on there. Or the Allies either.
MARIANNE: Going to finish us off?
TROOPER: Don't ask me.

The train stops.

Cut to a flat, barren, endless landscape covered with mud.

Cut to an SS officer mounting onto the car; below him on the ground are several other SS plus dogs and handlers.

The officer looks the players over, then points at Marianne. She steps forward. He hands her a club.

SS OFFICER: You are the kapo. Get them out and form up.

Officer hops down and moves off to next car.

Cut to Marianne, who hefts the club in her hand and turns to the players, who all seem to receive the message her spirit emits— they fear her.

MARIANNE: Out, and form up five by five.

She prods Charlotte in the back as she is starting to climb down.

CHARLOTTE: Stop pushing me!

Marianne viciously prods Paulette, who falls to the ground as Michou and Giselle seek to intercede; and Marianne swings and hits Giselle, then goes after Michou, and both escape only by jumping down and falling to their hands and knees. Now Marianne turns to the *pièce de résistance*—

Fania is practically hanging from the supporting hands of Charlotte and Etalina, who are moving her past Marianne.

MARIANNE: She can walk like anybody else.
ETALINA: She's got typhus, Marianne!

She beats their hands away from Fania, who faces her, swaying with a fever. Marianne swings and cracks Fania to the floor of the car.

Cut to a vast barn or warehouse, its floor covered with hundreds of deportees in the final stages of their physical resistance. They are practically on top of one another; and over all a deep, undecipherable groaning of sound, many languages of every European nation.

Now a shaft of daylight flashes across the mass as a door to the outside is opened and through it a straggling column of deportees moves out of this building.

The door closes behind them, followed by . . .

The sound of machine guns.

Cut to the little group of players around Fania, who are wide-eyed, powerless. She is propped up in Paulette's lap now, panting for breath.

Fania opens her eyes . . .

ETALINA, *slapping Fania's hands:* That's better . . . keep your eyes open . . . you've got to live, Fania. . . .

Now Fania, half-unconscious, sees past Etalina . . . to . . .

A woman and man making love against a wall.

A man barely able to crawl, peering into women's faces.

MAN: Rose? Rose Gershowitz?

Cut to a Polish woman, surrounded by the ill and dying, giving birth, with help from another woman.

Machine guns fire in near distance. Along with the baby's first cries.

Cut to Fania, receiving these insanely absurd sounds with a struggle to apprehend. And now she sees . . .

The Polish woman who just gave birth, standing up, swaying a little, wrapping her rags about her as she takes her baby from a woman and holds it naked against herself.

Cut to Fania, ripping the lining out of her coat—which was lying on top of her as a blanket—and gestures for Paulette to hand it on to the Polish woman, which is done. And the baby is wrapped in it.

Light again pours in from the opening door, and another column of deportees is moving to exit and death. And as this column stumbles toward the door, urged on by SS men and kapos . . .

Shmuel appears in the barn door. The light behind him contrasts with the murk within the building, and he seems to blaze in an unearthly luminescence.

He is staring in a sublime silence, as now he lifts his arms in a wordless gesture of deliverance, his eyes filled with miracle, and turning, he starts to gesture behind him. . . .

A British soldier appears beside him and looks into the barn.

Cut to the British soldier. His incredulous, alarmed, half-disgusted, half-furious face fills the screen.

Cut to a panoramic shot: a shouting mass of just-liberated deportees throwing stones. Some of these people are barely able to stand, some fall to their knees and still throw stones at . . .

A truck filled with SS men and women, their arms raised in surrender, trying to dodge the stones. Several trucks are pulling away, filled with SS.

Fania is being half-carried by Michou and Etalina, and others near them.

ETALINA: Please, Fania, you've got to live, you've got to live. . . !

Michou suddenly sees something offscreen, picks up stones and starts throwing. . . .

MICHOU: There she is! Hey rat! Rat!

Paulette and Esther turn to look at . . .
Marianne.
In the midst of the mob, Marianne is being hit by stones thrown by Michou. Other deportees are trying to hold on to Marianne to keep her from escaping. . . .

FANIA'S VOICE: Michou!

Michou turns to . . .
Fania, steadied on her feet by the others, staring at . . .
Marianne, frightened, but still full of defiant hatred.

Cut to a British communications soldier, with a radio unit, coming up to Fania.

SOLDIER: Would it be at all possible to say something for the troops?

Fania registers the absurdity of the request.

SOLDIER: It would mean so much, I think ... unless you feel ...

She stops him by touching his arm; all her remaining strength is needed as she weakly sings the "Marseillaise."

FANIA:

> *Allons enfants de la Patrie*
> *Le jour de gloire est arrivé*
> *Contre nous de la tyrannie ...*

Fania's eyes lift to ...
The sky. The clouds are in motion.

Cut to a busy, prosperous avenue in Brussels—1978 autos, latest fashions on women, etc. . . .

Cut to a restaurant dining room. The camera discovers Fania at a table, alone. It is a fashionable restaurant, good silver, formal waiters, sophisticated lunch crowd. Fania is smoking, sipping an aperitif, her eye on the entrance door.

Of course she is now thirty years older, but still vital and attractively done up and dressed. And she sees ...

First, Liesle, the miserable mandolin player, who enters and is looking around for her. Fania half-stands, raising her hand. As Liesle starts across the restaurant toward her, Charlotte enters behind her. And she recognizes Liesle.

Keeping Fania's viewpoint—Charlotte quickly catches up with Liesle, touches her arm; turns, a pause; they shake hands, then Liesle gestures toward Fania's direction and they start off together.

Cut to Liesle and Charlotte arriving at the table; Fania is standing; a pause. It is impossible to speak. Finally, Fania extends both her hands, and the other two grasp them.

FANIA: Liesle! —Charlotte!

They sit, their hands clasped. After a moment ...

LIESLE: We could hardly believe you were still singing—and here in Brussels!

CHARLOTTE: I'm only here on a visit, imagine? And I saw your interview in the paper!

Words die in them for a moment as they look at one another trying to absorb the fact of their survival, of the absurdity of their lives. Finally . . .

FANIA: What about the others? Did you ever hear anything about Marianne?
LIESLE: Marianne died.
FANIA—*it is still a shock:* Ah!
LIESLE: A few years after the war—I can't recall who told me. She was starting to produce concerts. She had cancer.
CHARLOTTE: I have two children, Fania . . .
FANIA: Charlotte with children! Imagine!

A waiter appears. He knows Fania.

WAITER: Is Madame ready to order or shall we . . . ?
FANIA: In a few minutes, Paul. *With a glance at the other two:* We haven't seen each other in thirty years, so . . . you must ask the chef to give us something extraordinary; something . . . absolutely marvelous!

And she reaches across the table to them and they clasp hands.

Cut to their hands on the white tablecloth, and their numbers tattooed on their wrists.
The camera draws away, and following the waiter as he crosses the restaurant, we resume the normality of life and the irony of it; and now we are outside on the avenue, the bustle of contemporary traffic; and quick close shots of passersby, the life that continues and continues. . . .

FINAL FADE-OUT